A CENTURY OF
POLITICS IN THE
KINGDOM

Owen O'Shea, from Milltown, Co. Kerry, is Communications Officer with Kerry County Council. A former Labour Party press officer and election candidate, he was a journalist with *Kerry's Eye* and Radio Kerry. He is the author of *Heirs to the Kingdom: Kerry's Political Dynasties* (2011).

Gordon Revington is a journalist with *Kerry's Eye*, who writes on Irish political history, rural affairs and sport. He contributed to *Kerry 1916: Histories and Legacies of the Easter Rising – A Centenary Record* (2016).

A CENTURY OF
POLITICS IN THE
KINGDOM

A COUNTY KERRY COMPENDIUM

OWEN O'SHEA AND GORDON REVINGTON

MERRION
PRESS

First published in 2018 by
Merrion Press
An imprint of Irish Academic Press
10 George's Street
Newbridge
Co. Kildare
Ireland
www.merrionpress.ie

9781785372018 (Paper)
9781785372025 (Kindle)
9781785372032 (Epub)
9781785372049 (PDF)

British Library Cataloguing in Publication Data
An entry can be found on request

Library of Congress Cataloging in Publication Data
An entry can be found on request

Interior design by www.jminfotechindia.com
Typeset in Minion Pro 11/14 pt

Cover design by www.phoenix-graphicdesign.com

Front cover, top left: Leader of the Labour Party Dick Spring and deputy leader Barry Desmond at the party's press conference, 10 Nov. 1982 (photograph: Paddy Whelan/*The Irish Times*). Top right: Kerry South TDs John O'Donoghue and Jackie Healy-Rae share a joke at the counting of votes at the 2007 general election (*Kerry's Eye*). Bottom: Fianna Fáil leader Charles Haughey enjoys a cup of tea while campaigning in Killarney in 1982, pictured with, l–r: Senator Tom Fitzgerald, John O'Leary TD, John O'Donoghue, John Buckley (Killarney Bakery), and Cllr Jackie Healy-Rae (behind Haughey) (Michelle Cooper-Galvin).

Back cover, clockwise from top left: Clann na Poblachta TD Kathleen O'Connor (right) following her election in Feb. 1956, with her mother, Catherine O'Connor, and Clann na Poblachta leader Seán Mac Bride TD (Brian Fitzgerald). Austin Stack TD. Catherine (Kit) Ahern TD. Checking the ballots at the counting of votes in Kerry North at the 1969 general election, including Anna Spring, Tom McEllistrim TD (FF) and Gerard Lynch TD (FG) (*The Kerryman*). Fine Gael leader Garret FitzGerald with supporters during the February 1982 election campaign (*The Kerryman*/Kevin Coleman).

Contents

Foreword by Mícheál Lehane   vii

Introduction   1

1. 'Ireland must be governed by Irishmen for Ireland's benefit'   5
   Kerry's First Teachtaí Dála

2. Thorny Wires   19
   Murphy and O'Sullivan: The Bitterest of Political Rivals

From Buckingham Palace to Caherdaniel: The aristocrat nurse
who became the first woman councillor in Kerry   33

3. 'Castleisland swam in porter ... and drunkenness prevailed'   37
   The Councillor Unseated for Plying Voters with Drink

4. 'Struck him violently in the mouth'   51
   The Kerry TD Who Punched a Colleague in the Dáil Dining Room

'The Queen of Balochistan': The Tarbert woman elected to the
Pakistani Parliament   62

5. 'Mr and Mrs Fred'   65
   Kerry's Original Political Power Couple

6. 'If there are women candidates, we hope they will be
   of the right kind'   78
   The Fate of Kerry's Women Politicians

'Why are all the people talking about Dick Spring, Mammy?':
The Tánaiste and the night of the four votes   90

7. 'We must not expect great things of Miss O'Connor
   in the Dáil'   94
   The Kerry North TD Who Was Too Young To Vote for Herself

8. 'The man who sits in the chair is not a proper or
   suitable man'   107
   The Highs and Lows of Local Authority Politics in Kerry since 1899

'Single-minded pursuit of his objectives': Kerry's pioneering education minister   121

9.   'Three weeks' turmoil, agitation and disturbance'   125
     Kerry's By-Election Battles and their National Significance

10. 'For a paper to be valid it must have recorded on it
     a first preference'   139
     How a Kerry Candidate Rewrote the Irish Electoral Rulebook

'Pack your bags and get out': The councillor who took his
own council to court   154

11. 'Politics in my blood'   158
     Kerry: Where Political Dynasties Reign Supreme

12. 'Blood streamed down his shirt'   173
     Threats, Thefts, Splits, Assaults and Other Electioneering Shenanigans

'You are very badly in need of a rest': The Kenmare spin-doctor
at Seán MacBride's side   187

13. The Kingdom's political diaspora   191
     Kerry's Political Representatives Outside the County and Overseas

14. 'They forget that we exist and that there are
     such places as Kerry'   202
     A Selection of Quotes about Kerry Politics over the Last Century

An apology from the BBC: Senator Ross Kinloch, 'The McGillycuddy
of the Reeks'   219

     Appendices

          1. Kerry TDs since 1919   223

          2. Kerry Senators since 1922   255

          3. General Election Results since 1918   268

     Glossary and Abbreviations   273

     Endnotes   274

     Index   288

Foreword

Viewed from the outside Kerry politics is often entertaining, at times unruly and on occasion just a little difficult to fathom. That, unsurprisingly, provides fertile ground for myths, legends and half-truths. This book offers a view that looks far beyond such narrow confines. The result is that most precious of things, a history recalled with both unsparing detail and a light touch.

Owen O'Shea and Gordon Revington have managed to pare back the caricature version of this most engaging of subjects. The facts and the true stories, replete with glistening colour, are recorded and recalled here with no little aplomb.

It's a history that on the face of it has some clearly identifiable foundations underpinning it. There are the families whose names have been printed on ballot papers in Kerry for several decades. Names like Spring, O'Donoghue, Healy-Rae, McEllistrim and Moynihan. There are other notable cornerstones, too, such as the six TDs from the county who have sat at the cabinet table over the course of the last century. The names Austin Stack, Fionán Lynch, John Marcus O'Sullivan, Dick Spring, John O'Donoghue and Jimmy Deenihan are stitched deep into the fabric of Kerry politics.

However, that much is, of course, obvious to those well versed on this particular topic. This book mines further and deeper to reveal something more than mere straightforward accounts of these ministers' time in government, such as John Marcus O'Sullivan's clash with the Catholic bishops in 1926 when he amalgamated a large number of the State's primary schools. The bishops were fearful that it could lead to more co-education, which was 'very undesirable'. Before that there is the work done by Austin Stack in establishing the country's new legal system.

Scroll further on through the decades and you find there are fifty years when there is no Kerry TD at the Cabinet table. That changed in 1982 when Dick Spring was appointed Tánaiste. But it is the prospect of electoral defeat rather than political elevation that can sometimes offer the greatest insight into politics in Kerry. After surviving by a very slender margin in 1987, the then Tánaiste would speak at length about that harrowing experience and conclude that while much of his focus in the preceding years had been on national issues 'others were down on the ground taking my votes'.

There have been some other stinging rebukes from defeated politicians. The irony that the judgement of voters was counted and weighed in sports halls, which they helped build, was also pointed out.

Those words are illustrative of the raw components that fuel Kerry politics; that need to serve the constituency, to deliver things there from 'up in Dublin' and, above all, to convince the electorate that you can do it better than your rivals. Ideally, too, and in a manner akin to the county's best footballers, there should be national recognition of the perfect Kerry politician's skills.

This book reminds us that just getting the chance to even attempt to do all that can prove arduous. There are stories of blood streaming down shirts, fingers breaking during a brawl at an after-Mass political meeting, and tales of vast quantities of alcohol being used to influence voters.

Through it all though the work of Owen O'Shea and Gordon Revington peels back the layers of a political environment that was rarely calm but one that functioned effectively. It's something that remains noteworthy given the deep-seated bitterness sown during the Civil War. The scale of that conflict in the county was pithily described by Breandán Ó hEithir in *The Begrudger's Guide to Irish Politics* when he wrote about it reaching 'new heights of viciousness by the spring of 1923'.

When Kerry County Council returned to handling everyday business three years later, it was a forum almost exclusively dominated by men. While four women were elected to the Dáil in Kerry since the foundation of the State, it would take until 1977 before Kit Ahern became the first woman to chair the council, that same year she also won a Dáil seat in Kerry North. The difficulties facing women are summed up by the son of the late Mary O'Donoghue, who severed on the council for over twenty years up to 1985. 'My mother often said that when she went into the council first, there were a lot of male conservatives there who found it difficult to see a woman coming in,' Paul O'Donoghue said.

Despite this attitude, there had been some success for women candidates in the council elections in the 1920s, most notably the election of Sinn Féin's Gobnait Ní Bhruadair in 1920. Councillor Ní Bhruadair, or Lady Albinia Lucy Brodrick, was born into a British aristocratic family but would spend most of her life in Caherdaniel and even got shot in the leg by police along the way.

If Ní Bhruadair was one of the most exotic political imports to Kerry, then there's a multitude of people who left the county and attained high office elsewhere. The most striking adventure is unquestionably the election of Bridie Wren from Tarbert to Pakistan's first parliament in 1973. It all gives a lie to the charge made by some that Kerry politics is perpetually inward-looking.

Read on through these pages and a complex, colourful and always captivating political world will be revealed with a refreshing authenticity.

Mícheál Lehane is Political Correspondent
with RTÉ and a native of Cahersiveen.

Introduction

It wasn't just the world of sport that the renowned Kerry journalist and wordsmith, Con Houlihan, was inclined to comment on from time to time. 'Most of our songs are merry and most of our elections are sad,' he wrote of Kerry politics in 1973.[1] Houlihan, who had made his own contribution to political debate in the county through the short-lived and locally circulated newspaper *Taxpayer's News* in the late 1950s, must have been in a melancholic mood at the time of writing because elections in Kerry over the last century or so have been anything but sad. Nor have they been dreary, dull or boring. And that notion has been part of the reason this book came about – to cast light on some of the fascinating, exhilarating, sensational and often riveting electoral ups and downs of the political rollercoaster in the Kingdom over the course of the last hundred years or so.

Another well-known Kerry journalist, Katie Hannon, of RTÉ's *Prime Time*, wrote that politicians are 'a breed apart'.[2] This seems to be especially true of Kerry politicians. One of the reasons for this is that they have had to shout a little louder than many of their counterparts in other counties due to the perceived belief that Dublin and the east coast are where national political priorities lie. 'As far as I can see,' declared the Fianna Fáil TD for Kerry South, Jack Flynn, in 1948, 'Government ministers resident in Dublin consider Dublin as Ireland. They forget that we exist and that there are such places as Kerry.'[3] Flynn gave voice to what has been a fairly persistent theme throughout Kerry politics since Dáil Éireann first came into being in 1919: a sense of peripherality, a belief that the county hasn't had its fair share of the national pie, and the conviction that those 'above in Dublin', as Jackie Healy-Rae used to put it, don't give Kerry adequate political attention and largesse. If this has been the case, it hasn't been for want of trying on the part of Kerry deputies and senators who have represented the county over the past century with enthusiasm, vociferousness and style.

Kerry's earliest representatives in the Oireachtas, emerging from and politicised during the revolutionary period, were ambitious for their county and their country: 'I hope to see a Gaelic Ireland, the home of strong and happy men and women in which a thousand splendid things could be done,' declared the first TD for East Kerry, Piaras Béaslaí during the Dáil debate on the Anglo-Irish Treaty in 1922.[4] Béaslaí was one of dozens who made the transition from the IRA 'Flying Columns' to the new parliamentary assembly. Another such TD was Stephen Fuller, who survived the infamous Ballyseedy Massacre during the Civil War. Other determined and far-seeing Kerry members of early cabinets included Fionán Lynch, who was Minister for Fisheries and Lands, and John Marcus O'Sullivan, who, as Minister for Education, established the system of vocational education in Ireland.

Coincidentally, the six Kerry deputies who have served in cabinet are connected by their involvement in political relations with our nearest neighbour. Austin Stack – the first minister from Kerry – was responsible for Home Affairs and the Dáil courts from 1919 to 1922. He accompanied Éamon de Valera to the talks with David Lloyd George which led to the Anglo-Irish Treaty negotiations, the Irish delegation to which included Fionán Lynch. Their successors in cabinet, Dick Spring and John O'Donoghue, would both play their own roles in further sensitive Anglo-Irish agreements in 1985 and 1998. From 2011, Kerry had a seat in cabinet again: former Kerry football captain, Jimmy Deenihan, who set in train the commemorations of the 1916 rebellion and the subsequent revolutionary period.

The story of the century from a political-party perspective is very much the dominance of the two main parties after the foundation of Fianna Fáil in 1926 and Fine Gael in 1933. Over the course of the century, these two parties dominated and it wasn't until the Fianna Fáil meltdown of 2011 that the party was without a seat in Kerry. Fine Gael's record varied, with major decreases in support and the depletion of its organisation on the ground in the middle part of the century, but the party continued to retain a foothold. Labour's strength owed as much to the dominance of the Moynihan and Spring dynasties as it did to party allegiances, while Sinn Féin has only been a resilient feature of the political landscape in recent years, especially in Kerry North. While Clann na Poblachta and Clann na Talmhan gained council and Oireachtas representation in the 1940s and 1950s, none of the other smaller parties has ever made a breakthrough. With some notable exceptions, Independents have only succeeded in recent years, but many of those who have succeeded had previously split from Fianna Fáil. Independents have found it hard to break the dominance of the major parties; one-term Independent county councillor and former Kerry GAA great, Mick O'Connell, observed in a damning critique that if he'd known how wedded voters were to the main parties, 'I wouldn't have chanced it … Clinics and clientelism and bending the rules is not for me.'[5]

Serious matters of state aside, politics in Kerry has often been a source of good old-fashioned entertainment for voters and the press. The history of Kerry politics over the past century is full of fascinating stories of bitterness, rivalries, campaign shenanigans and personal and political rows which have fuelled pub talk and the column inches far more than the minutiae of policies and legislation. The century is also replete with remarkable electoral battles, results of national significance, several national political firsts and a steady supply of parliamentarians who have made a significant impression on the national political stage. Apart from ministers who have impacted on their various government departments, many other TDs and senators have made an impression on Irish political history – among them Dan Kiely, whose Supreme Court challenge of 2015 changed the way votes are counted in Ireland. John O'Donoghue's fall from grace in 2009 was a seminal moment in Irish politics, as was the night in 1987 when Tánaiste Dick Spring held his Dáil seat by just four votes. Two of the four Kerry women who have sat in the Dáil won history-making by-elections – one of them, Kathleen O'Connor, was so young when elected that she wasn't on the electoral register.

And there are plenty of similar stories which we have enjoyed bringing to light – many of them for the first time. Remarkable tales, like the councillor who was unseated for plying voters with drink, the north Kerry woman who became a politician in Pakistan, the aristocrat who was invited to Buckingham Palace as a child and went on to become the first woman elected to Kerry County Council, the 'hanging judge' who represented Tralee in parliament, the Kerry senator who received an apology from the BBC, the councillor who took his own council to court, the night the gardaí were called to a meeting of a Fianna Fáil cumann in north Kerry, and the Dáil candidate deselected because he wasn't popular enough, all feature in these pages.

We hope that we have captured the excitement and tension, the rivalries and resentments, the seminal debates and discussions, and the good old-fashioned fun and games that have characterised the political cauldron in the county over the last century.

Owen O'Shea and Gordon Revington

1

'Ireland must be governed by Irishmen for Ireland's benefit'

Kerry's First Teachtaí Dála

At 3.30pm on the afternoon of 21 January 1919, a group of twenty-seven men gathered in the Round Room of the Mansion House in Dublin. Just a month previously, each of them had been elected to the British parliament at Westminster. As candidates of the Sinn Féin party, however, they had pledged not to take their seats if elected, in protest at a delay in introducing Home Rule in Ireland and amid demands for an independent republic. The new MPs were meeting to establish their own independent parliament, Dáil Éireann, in complete defiance of British rule in Ireland. Sinn Féin had won seventy-three of the 105 Westminster parliament seats available across the island of Ireland. The result represented an overwhelming rout of the Irish Parliamentary Party, which, for a generation or more, had – under the leadership of Isaac Butt, Charles Stewart Parnell and later John Redmond – commanded majority support among the Irish nationalist electorate. In about a quarter of constituencies, including all four constituencies in Kerry, Sinn Féin candidates were returned unopposed as Irish Parliamentary Party MPs stood aside in the face of anticipated defeat and a hugely successful campaign by Sinn Féin against the conscription of Irishmen to Britain's world war effort and a clear and vociferous demand for Irish sovereignty. Most of those elected were in prison at the time for offences against the realm and just twenty-seven members – each calling themselves a Teachta Dála (TD) – of the new parliament assembled at the appointed time.

As those present were called to order, Cathal Brugha, following his appointment as Ceann Comhairle, read the roll of those returned at the 1918 election who now sat in a self-declared independent parliament. Brugha's list included those representing the four parliamentary constituencies of Kerry:

Co. Chiarraidhe (thoir)	Piaras Béaslaí	I láthair
Co. Chiarraidhe (thuaidh)	An Dr S. Ó Cruadhlaoich	Fé ghlas ag Gallaibh
Co. Chiarraidhe (theas)	Fionán Ó Loingsigh	Fé ghlas ag Gallaibh
Co. Chiarraidhe (thiar)	Aibhistín de Staic	Fé ghlas ag Gallaibh[1]

The only Kerry representative *i láthair* or present was the new TD for East Kerry, Piaras Béaslaí.[2] His colleagues Dr James Crowley (North Kerry), Fionán Lynch (South Kerry) and Austin Stack (West Kerry) were each *fé ghlas ag Gallaibh* or 'imprisoned by the foreigners'. The Dáil asserted the exclusive right of the elected representatives of the Irish people to legislate for the country and adopted a Provisional Constitution and approved a Declaration of Independence. It also approved a Democratic Programme, based on the 1916 Proclamation of the Irish Republic, and read and adopted a Message to the Free Nations of the World. Following the reading of the Declaration of Independence, the Ceann Comhairle called on the East Kerry representative to speak the first words ever spoken by a Kerry deputy in Dáil Éireann:

PIARAS BÉASLAOI (ó Oirthear Chiarraighe): Is mór an onóir damhsa gur iarradh orm cur leis an ndearbhú ar Fhaisnéis Shaorstáit Éireann. Bhí sé d'amhantar agamsa is ag cuid agaibhse a bheith láithreach nuair do bunuigheadh an Saorstát Seachtmhain na Cásca, 1916, agus bhí laochraidhe cródha ann an uair sin – na daoine do rinn gníomh do réir a dtuairme. Ní mhairid na tréinfhir sin indiu: an namhaid do mhairbh iad. Acht na tréinfhir úd b'iad Fé ndear sgéal an lae indiu. Acht bíodh gur mór an truagh ná fuilid na laochraidhe sin in ár measc anseo is deimhin dúinn go bhfuil spioraid gach n-aon aca annso in ár dteannta ar an nDáil seo, agus le congnamh Dé leanfaimíd an sompla d'fhágadar san in ar gcomhair. Deireann an Fhaisnéis go gcuirfam chum cinn an Saorstát ar gach slighe atá in ár gcumas. Cialluigheann san gníomh, agus ní bhfaighmíd staonadh ó éingníomhra, is cuma cad is deire dhóibh, príosún nó dortadh fola. Agus tá muinighin ag muinntir na hÉireann asainn-na, agus againn-na asta san. Déanfaidh

Dáil Éireann gach éinnídh chum saoirse do bhaint amach agus chum an Fhaisnéis seo do chur chum críche.[3]

The East Kerry deputy had been tasked with translating the Democratic Programme of the First Dáil – which had been drafted by the Labour Party leader, Thomas Johnson – into Irish, and read it into the record. Its opening words were:

> We declare in the words of the Irish Republican Proclamation the right of the people of Ireland to the ownership of Ireland, and to the unfettered control of Irish destinies to be indefeasible, and in the language of our first President, Pádraig Mac Phiarais, we declare that the Nation's sovereignty extends not only to all men and women of the Nation, but to all its material possessions, the Nation's soil and all its resources, all the wealth and all the wealth-producing processes within the Nation, and with him we reaffirm that all right to private property must be subordinated to the public right and welfare.[4]

Béaslaí, having recited the Democratic Programme in Irish sat down and his colleague, Seán T. Ó Ceallaigh, representing Dublin College Green – and later President of Ireland – read the document in English. A short time later, after less than two hours in session, the Dáil adjourned until the following day.

So how did Piaras Béaslaí, a journalist who was born in Liverpool, end up reciting such a significant statement of intent at the first sitting of Dáil Éireann? Along with a Listowel veterinary surgeon who had graduated from Trinity College, a south Kerry national school teacher who would go on to have an illustrious career in the judiciary, and an income tax inspector from Tralee who had captained his county to win the All-Ireland senior football final of 1904, Béaslaí was one of four men who were Kerry's first ever representatives in the Dáil. Who were Kerry's first TDs and what role did they play in a parliament and polity in its infancy 100 years ago?

Piaras Béaslaí – TD for East Kerry

Liverpool was the birthplace of East Kerry's first representative in an independent Irish parliament. Percy Frederick Beasley, or Piaras Béaslaí as he was more widely known, was born in Liverpool on 15 February 1881 to an Irish Catholic family. His father, Patrick Langford Beasley (or Beazley), was a journalist and a native of Curragh, Aghadoe, near Killarney. Patrick was the editor of the *Catholic Times* newspaper in England. In his youth, Piaras holidayed with his uncle, Fr James Beazley, in south Kerry. He was educated at St Xavier's College in Liverpool and followed his father into journalism. The family moved to Dublin in 1906 and Piaras wrote for several publications, including the *Irish Independent* and the *Freeman's Journal*. A fluent Irish speaker, he had become active in the Gaelic League in Liverpool and joined the influential Keating Branch of the organisation in Dublin. He was involved in setting up the Irish-language group *An Fáinne* in 1916 and became involved in staging Irish-language amateur drama at the annual Oireachtas, an Irish language festival, which, in 1914, was held in Killarney. Béaslaí began to write both original works and adaptations from foreign languages. One of these works, *Eachtra Pheadair Schlemiel* (1909), was translated from German into Irish.

Béaslaí soon became politically radicalised, joining the Irish Volunteers on their foundation in Dublin in November 1913 and he is credited with suggesting the name 'Óglaigh na h-Éireann' for the organisation. Invited into the militant Irish Republican Brotherhood by Cathal Brugha, he became acquainted with Michael Collins as a member of its provisional committee. Prior to the Easter Rising, he took messages from Seán Mac Diarmada to Liverpool. These messages were then transmitted to the leader of Clan na Gael in the United States, John Devoy. During Easter Week 1916, Béaslaí was involved in the fighting in the north inner city, including heavy engagements at Reilly's Fort at the intersection of Church Street and North King Street under the command of Edward Daly. He was jailed for his involvement in the rebellion in Portland and Lewes prisons in England. In June 1917, he was released on amnesty along with hundreds of other prisoners. Returning to journalism, he became editor of *An tÓglach*, the Irish Volunteers magazine, and began to write for the influential Volunteer publication *An Claidheamh Soluis*.

Béaslaí was chosen to contest the December 1918 general election for Sinn Féin in East Kerry, where the Irish Parliamentary Party MP, Timothy O'Sullivan, was stepping down, like all of his party colleagues in Kerry. When the Returning Officer for South Kerry, David Roche, closed nominations on 4 December, Béaslaí was the only candidate put forward and Roche deemed him to be elected. His nomination papers were submitted by Killarney curate Fr D.J. Finucane, who led a celebratory procession headed by two marching bands from the courthouse to the Market Cross in Killarney.[5] The new MP was not present for his nomination. He was reported to be 'on the run', though he later wrote that illness prevented him from being present.[6] He did not appear in public until the first week of January at a 'very large assemblage in the Killarney Sinn Féin Hall'.[7] Just days before the Dáil assembled in Dublin, Béaslaí spoke about the three other Kerry MPs – James Crowley, Austin Stack and Fionán Lynch – who were in jail, telling a meeting in Castleisland: 'We are going to render it not alone impossible for England to keep these men in prison but to keep any kind of control over this country.'[8]

Béaslaí read the Democratic Programme to those gathered at the Mansion House in Dublin on 21 January 1919. He was jailed in March and May 1919 for his associations with the republican newspaper *An Claidheamh Soluis*, but was involved in the dramatic escape of six prisoners, including fellow TD Austin Stack, from Strangeways Prison in Manchester in October. Scotland Yard described escapee Béaslaí as '36, height 5ft 6ins., fresh complexioned, dark brown hair, proportionate build, oval face'.[9] Re-elected at the general election of 1921 for the newly formed seven-seat constituency of Kerry–Limerick West, he strongly supported the Anglo-Irish Treaty and delivered a lengthy speech in support of the agreement in the Dáil. He accepted the assertions of the Irish plenipotentiaries that the agreement, despite its flaws, offered a path to full independence. During the Dáil debate at the beginning of January 1922, he accused opponents of the Treaty of having no principles, but rather political formulas, and of offering no realistic alternative:

What we are asked is, to choose between this Treaty on the one hand, and, on the other hand, bloodshed, political and social chaos and the frustration of all our hopes of national regeneration. The plain blunt man in the street, fighting man or civilian, sees that point more clearly than the formulists of Dáil Éireann. He sees in this Treaty the solid fact – our country cleared of the English armed forces, and the land in complete control of our own people to do what we like with. We can make our own Constitution, control our own finances, have our own schools and colleges, our own courts, our own flag, our own coinage and stamps, our own police, aye, and last but not least, our own army, not in flying columns, but in possession of the strong places of Ireland and the fortresses of Ireland, with artillery, aeroplanes and all the resources of modern warfare. Why, for what else have we been fighting but that? For what else has been the national struggle in all generations but for that?[10]

Béaslaí is credited with having coined the phrase 'Irregulars' to describe those opposed to the Treaty. At the beginning of 1922, he travelled to the United States to garner support for the Treaty and the provisional government. Though again returned to the Dáil in 1922 as a pro-Treaty candidate, he did not contest the 1923 election. He decided to leave politics to become a major general in the Free State Army and was Head of Press Censorship; however, he left the army in 1924 to focus on writing and journalism.

Outside of politics, Béaslaí was a prolific poet, playwright, novelist and author. Among his publications was the two-volume *Michael Collins and the Making of a New Ireland*, which he began writing soon after Collins' death in 1922. According to the *Irish Independent*, Béaslaí 'loved Mick Collins as few men have loved another'.[11] He had introduced his cousin, Lily Mernin, to Collins and she became one of Collins' top informants. Béaslaí's plays included *Fear an Milliún Púnt*, *An Danar* and *Bealtaine 1916*. Béaslaí contributed columns to many national newspapers, as well as *The Kerryman*, throughout the 1950s. His political activity in later years was confined to lobbying for pensions for his former IRA comrades and serving as president of the Association of the Old Dublin Brigade. National Archives files on Beaslaí suggest that he was mooted as a candidate for the presidency in 1945. The archives acquired his papers after his death and total some 17,000 different documents. He never married. He died on 21 June 1965 and is buried in Glasnevin Cemetery in the same plot as fellow Kerry man Thomas Ashe and Peadar Kearney, who wrote 'The Soldier's Song'. The graveside oration was delivered by General Richard Mulcahy.

James Crowley – TD for North Kerry

James Crowley was one of many TDs in jail when Dáil deputies met for the first time in 1919. He was born in 1880 in Listowel. He studied at Trinity College Dublin and became a veterinary surgeon based in Listowel, covering north Kerry and west Limerick. He married Clementine Burson and they lived on Upper Church Street. Crowley joined the Irish Volunteers in 1914.

He became immersed in Sinn Féin through his work-related travels and ultimately became an intelligence officer for the organisation. In August 1918, he was taken into custody by the RIC 'without naming the charge' for reading a message from the Sinn Féin executive to a crowd from the balcony of the Temperance Hall in Listowel.[12] On 11 September 1918, he received a two-year sentence for taking part in a meeting on William Street on 15 August and 'making statements thereat in contravention of the Defence of the Realm Act'; Crowley had read the proclamation of 1916.[13] Along with fellow Kerry prisoners – and future fellow Kerry TDs – Austin Stack, Piaras Béaslaí and Fionán Lynch, Crowley took part in the Belfast Prison riot of December 1918.

During the December 1918 general election, Crowley was chosen by Sinn Féin to contest the North Kerry constituency. Like many candidates who were serving time, he placed advertisements in local newspapers to promote his candidacy and advise of his appointment of solicitor Daniel J. Browne as his election agent.[14] Over the course of the campaign, more than £450 was collected in parishes across north Kerry to cover campaign expenses, which included £29 spent on printing, £2 on car hire and £1 on stationery.[15] Rallies were held in support of his candidacy. In Ballylongford, a message from the parish priest, Canon Hayes, was read out to the crowd; he urged people to vote for Crowley and declared 'Sinn Féin is not only politically sound but it would be treason to Ireland to question its teachings at present ... Ireland must be governed by Irishmen for Ireland's benefit.'[16] Crowley was declared elected at the close of nominations on 4 December and was returned as MP for North Kerry on 14 December. From his prison cell in Belfast, he wrote to his new constituents via *The Kerryman*:

> my sincerest thanks for their unanimous expression of confidence in me and in the policy of Sinn Féin which I represent and which stands for the complete national independence of Ireland. The numerous unopposed returns ... will leave no doubt in the mind of the watching world on the question of Ireland's demand in common with other small nationalities for self-determination and complete independence – a claim which it shall be my pleasure and duty to support and forward as far as in me lies.[17]

Crowley was still in prison when the First Dáil sat in January 1919, but was released in April, prompting an 'occasion of much rejoicing in [Listowel] town and throughout his extensive constituency'.[18] He became a prominent IRA leader during the War of Independence and was involved in instigating the Listowel Mutiny of 1920, in which RIC officers refused to obey orders to shoot IRA prisoners. Crowley was interned again during the War of Independence; he was arrested in February 1921 on Grafton Street and taken to Dublin Castle.[19]

He supported the Anglo-Irish Treaty, but was the only Kerry TD not to speak during the Dáil debate on it. In later years, he joined Cumann na nGaedheal and became active in the Blueshirts in the 1930s; he was vice-president of the organisation in north Kerry in 1933. His wife, Clementine (Clem), was a member and president of the so-called Blueblouses, the women's wing of the organisation, in the area. Crowley held his seat in the Dáil for Cumann na nGaedheal until 1932, when he lost it due to a surge of support for Fianna Fáil. His interventions in Dáil debates were rare and he only occasionally tabled parliamentary questions. He died aged sixty-six on 21 January 1946, the thirty-fifth anniversary of the first meeting of the Dáil.

Fionán Lynch – TD for South Kerry

Fionán (also Finian) Lynch TD was born in Kilmackerin, Waterville, on St Patrick's Day of 1889. His parents Finian and Helen (née McCarthy) were teachers at the local national school and Fionán was one of a family of seven. He was educated at St Brendan's College, Killarney, and later Rockwell College, Blackrock College and St Patrick's Teacher Training College, qualifying as a school teacher in 1911. He taught briefly in Swansea in Wales – where he formed a branch of the Gaelic League – before taking up a position at St Michan's national school on Halston Street in Dublin between 1912 and 1916. While in Dublin, Lynch stayed at the hotel run by his aunt, Myra McCarthy, at 44 Mountjoy Street. Known as 'Grianán na nGaedheal', it later became a meeting point for Volunteers and the IRB, as well as a safe house for Michael Collins and others during the War of Independence. Lynch joined the influential Keating Branch of the Gaelic League and became acquainted with figures like Piaras Béaslaí and Cathal Brugha. Following his induction into the IRB, Lynch joined the Irish Volunteers and became captain of the F Company of the 1st Battalion in Dublin in 1914. On Easter Sunday, he collected Patrick Pearse from St Enda's and took him to a meeting of rebel leaders. Upon the outbreak of rebellion on Easter Monday, Lynch mobilised with his battalion at Blackhall Place and was engaged in intense fighting in the North King Street area. He retreated to the Four Courts ahead of the surrender and was jailed in Portland Prison on the Isle of Wight and later in Frongoch.

Following his release in the general amnesty of 1917, Lynch returned to south Kerry to much adulation; Patrick Pearse's mother delivered an address at his homecoming event.[20] He campaigned for Éamon de Valera during the East Clare by-election. He was a powerful public speaker. He was jailed shortly after a speech at Casement's Fort in Ardfert in August 1917 marking the first anniversary of the execution of Roger Casement. Lynch went on hunger strike in Mountjoy on 20 September with fellow Kerry men Thomas Ashe and Austin Stack and was present when Ashe took ill after being force-fed: 'Fionán spoke to him through the cell door as Ashe was taken to be force-fed and said "Stick it Tom boy." Ashe replied: "I'll stick it Fin."'[21] Ashe died hours later on the night of 25 September at the Mater Hospital.

Lynch was in jail in Belfast when he was elected MP for South Kerry on 14 December 1918. In his absence, rallies were held across the constituency, not only advocating his candidacy, but also 'in opposition to Mr JP Boland, who represented South Kerry in Parliament for the past 18 years'[22] and who was standing aside – Boland had been the Irish Parliamentary Party MP for the constituency since 1900. On his release from prison in Manchester in August 1919, Lynch took part in the operation which saw fellow Kerry TDs Piaras Béaslaí and Austin Stack escape from Strangeways Prison on 25 October. Clearly valued for his administrative and political abilities, he travelled to London as joint secretary of the Irish delegation during the Anglo-Irish Treaty negotiations in 1921. While the Irish cabinet was on the run during the War of Independence, Lynch and his wife, Bridget, hosted some of its meetings in their home at 98 Pembroke Road. Lynch was appointed to the GHQ Staff of the IRA as Assistant Director of Organisation in early 1920. A supporter of the Treaty, he told his fellow TDs that he would vote for it for four main reasons:

> because it gives us an army, because it gives us evacuation, because it gives us control over the finances of the country, and lastly, and greatest of all to me, because it gives us control over our education … I know what the people want, I know that I can speak for my own people – for the people of South Kerry, where I was bred and born …

I will have none of the compromise that drives this country again into a welter of blood.[23]

As Minister for Education from April to August 1922, one of his first tasks was to abolish the Board of Education which had sacked him from his teaching position following the Easter Rising. During his short ministry, he was responsible for primary education. During the Civil War, he was a member of the Free State Army and rose to the rank of Brigadier-General. He was one of three Cumann na nGaedheal TDs elected for Kerry in 1923. After the Civil War, he was appointed Minister for Fisheries in the first Free State government under W.T. Cosgrave, president of the Executive Council.

Lynch was never defeated at a general election and continued to serve Kerry, and Kerry South from 1937, as a Fine Gael TD. He was Leas Ceann Comhairle of the Dáil from 5 July 1938 to 12 May 1939, the second occupant of the post from Kerry.[24] Lynch studied law and was called to the Bar in 1931. He was deputy leader of Fine Gael for a short period in February 1944. He resigned as a TD on 10 October 1944, following his appointment by the Fianna Fáil government as a Circuit Court judge to the Sligo/Donegal circuit. This resulted in the first ever Dáil by-election in Kerry South, which saw Donal O'Donoghue win a seat for Fianna Fáil. Lynch retired from the judiciary in 1959. He died suddenly at his home in Dartry, County Dublin, on 3 June 1966, aged seventy-seven, shortly after celebrating the fiftieth anniversary of the Easter Rising. He was survived by his wife Brigid (née Slattery from Tralee, daughter of Thomas Slattery, chairman of Tralee Rural District Council), whom he had married in 1919, and by their five sons and one daughter. One of his seven children, Judge Kevin Lynch, presided over the Kerry Babies Tribunal in 1985.

Austin Stack – TD for West Kerry

The oldest of the four men to represent Kerry in the Dáil in 1919, Austin Stack was once described by Éamon de Valera as 'the honestest, the bravest, and the purest Republican in Ireland'.[25] Stack's entered politics after high-profile activism in his native county in the period after the foundation of the Irish Volunteers and during the Easter Rising. He was born Augustine Mary Moore Stack on 7 December 1879 in Ballymullen, Tralee, to William Moore Stack and his wife, Nanette O'Neill. His first employment was as a clerk in the office of solicitor John O'Connell and he later worked as an income tax collector in south and west Kerry. In his youth, he was a member of the Young Ireland Society and the Irish National Foresters, due to the influence of his father, who had been a Fenian leader and a member of the Land League. His mother had been jailed for her involvement in the Land League. Stack came to prominence on the playing field when he captained Kerry to the All-Ireland senior football title of 1904 (which was played in 1906). He had founded the John Mitchels club in Tralee with Maurice McCarthy and was its first club captain and secretary. His father William Moore Stack had been a founder member of the GAA in Kerry.[26] The young Stack's administrative skills saw him serve as Kerry GAA county board secretary from 1904 to 1908 and chairman from 1914 to 1917.

One of the most high-profile figures of the revolutionary period in Kerry, Stack was active in the Irish Republican Brotherhood from 1908 and became its linchpin in the county in the years before the Rising. He joined the Irish Volunteers upon the inception of the group in 1913. He attended the meeting in Tralee at which the local company was formed on 10 December. By the middle of 1914, he was the leader of the Volunteers in Tralee. They met at the old roller-skating rink at the Basin in the town. Following the split in the organisation in the autumn of 1914, Stack supported Eoin MacNeill and he was elected to the central executive of the Irish Volunteers. As preparations were made for the Easter Rising in April 1916, Stack became the key organiser in Kerry. During a visit to Tralee on 27 February 1916, Pádraig Pearse briefed Stack on plans to land arms from Germany for the Rising at Fenit. Stack remained secretive in his preparations, involving only Paddy Cahill, a future Kerry TD. They mobilised the Tralee Volunteers at the Rink on Easter Sunday. On hearing that Roger Casement had been arrested and that the arms landing had failed, he went, unarmed, to the RIC Barracks where Casement was being held and was immediately arrested. He was sentenced to death (later commuted to a prison term) and led prisoners on a number of hunger strikes.

While in jail in Belfast, Stack was elected Sinn Féin MP for West Kerry in December 1918. In a letter to his brother, which was read to a large rally on Denny Street in Tralee weeks before the election, Stack stated that the anticipated Sinn Féin victory in the poll had to be 'of a decisive character in order to show that the constituency is solid for complete independence

Piaras Béaslaí, the first TD for East Kerry (National Library of Ireland).

North Kerry's first TD, James Crowley and his wife, Clementine Burson.

as against sham Home Rule legislatures which England may be offering us in settlement'.[27] The sitting Irish Parliamentary Party MP, Thomas O'Donnell, stood aside, leaving Stack as the only contender. Upon handing in the nomination papers on his behalf, Stack's solicitor, J.D. O'Connell, told those gathered that Stack 'would not sit in the Imperial Parliament; he is to sit in your own Parliament – in your Irish Parliament in Dublin'.[28] The new MP was in jail in Manchester when the First Dáil met. Nine months later, he escaped from jail, along with Piaras Béaslaí and others, and returned to Ireland.

Austin Stack made history by becoming the first Kerry man to hold a cabinet position in an Irish government. From

West Kerry TD, Austin Stack, the first Kerry native to serve in an Irish government.

Fionán Lynch who was the first TD to represent South Kerry (Lynch family).

November 1919 to January 1922, he was Minister for Home Affairs, his primary duty being the establishment of a new legal administrative system. He oversaw the administration of the 'Republican Courts' or Dáil courts. During this period, Stack's secretary solicitor was Daniel J. Browne from Listowel, later secretary to the Minister for Justice and Local Appointments Commissioner. Stack accompanied Éamon de Valera to post-Truce talks with British prime minister David Lloyd George in London. He was the only Kerry TD to oppose the Anglo-Irish Treaty and campaigned vehemently against it. As his biographer, Fr Anthony Gaughan, noted, for Stack, 'the Anglo-Irish treaty was a disaster. Between its signing (6 December 1921) and the outbreak of the Civil War (28 June 1922) he was one of its principal opponents, doing all in his power to prevent it from being ratified, and later campaigning against it not only in Ireland but among Irish-American supporters of Sinn Féin in the USA.[29] Historian Diarmaid Ferriter states that Stack 'came to epitomise republican opposition' to the agreement.[30] He told the Dáil debate that the accord was a 'rotten document'.[31] He invoked the memory of his father, William, who had fought in the 1867 Fenian rebellion:

I was nurtured in the traditions of Fenianism. My father wore England's uniform as a comrade of Charles Kickham and O'Donovan Rossa when as a '67 man he was sentenced to ten years for being a rebel, but he wore it minus the oath of allegiance. If I, as I hope I will, try to continue to fight for Ireland's liberty, even if this rotten document be accepted, I will fight minus the oath of allegiance and to wipe out the oath of allegiance if I can do it. Now I ask you has any man here the idea in his head, has any man here the hardihood to stand up and say that it was for this our fathers have suffered, that it was for this our comrades have died on the field and in the barrack yard.[32]

Stack remained an unequivocal supporter of Éamon de Valera. When de Valera resigned as president of the Dáil following the vote on the Treaty, Stack told the Dáil that he was 'ready to commit suicide the moment Mr de Valera let us down – and I am.'[33] He travelled to the US with Valentia native and Louth TD J.J. O'Kelly ('Sceilg') in March 1922 to lobby against the Treaty. In June 1922, he was returned to the Third Dáil as one of seven TDs for Kerry–Limerick West. Stack, along with other anti-Treaty deputies, formed a 'republican cabinet' in which he was Minister for Finance. He was arrested by the Free State Army in County Tipperary in April 1923 and a hunger strike during this term of imprisonment caused lasting damage to his health. In 1923, Kerry refused to play the All-Ireland final against Dublin in protest against his imprisonment.[34]

Following his release from prison in 1924, he continued to campaign for Sinn Féin at home and abroad and was elected joint secretary at the party Ard Fheis in November 1924. He declined to join Fianna Fáil in 1926 and was the only Sinn Féin TD elected in Kerry at the June 1927 general election. He was not a candidate at the second election of 1927 (September), which marked the end of his political career. He died on 27 April 1929 at the Mater Hospital in Dublin. He had married Una 'Winnie' Gordon in 1925 and had begun to take legal studies, with the aim of becoming a barrister. A GAA club in his native Tralee is named after him. A stand in Austin Stack Park was named after him on 1 May 1932 and the entire grounds were named after him on 4 June 1944. A bust of Stack is located in the Dáil chamber in Leinster House.

2

Thorny Wires

Murphy and O'Sullivan:
The Bitterest of Political Rivals

'Murphy and O'Sullivan' – it sounds a bit like a firm of Irish builders or an old-style public house in an Irish town back in the early twentieth century. In this case, though, it refers to two men from the Killarney area who were the bitterest of political rivals and whose clashes occurred not only on the hustings at both national and local elections, but also in the courts on a number of occasions. With its origins just a few years before the establishment of Dáil Éireann, theirs was a mutual antagonism almost without parallel in that parliament. It reached its peak when a petition was launched to unseat the successful candidate in the Westminster election for the constituency of East Kerry in 1910, despite John Murphy and Eugene O'Sullivan being members of the same party. They did, however, represent different approaches and attitudes to politics and their careers contribute to the body of evidence that contradicts the commonly held view that there had been no significant ideological differences between Fianna Fáil and Cumann na nGaedheal (later Fine Gael) and that the Civil War alone was the point of fracture at which their paths diverged.

After the foundation of the state, Murphy became active in Fianna Fáil, whereas O'Sullivan, despite maintaining his position as an Independent, was embedded in the Cumann na nGaedheal community. O'Sullivan was a cousin of Professor John Marcus O'Sullivan (the son of Michael, a brother of Tim O'Sullivan, who was elected to parliament for the East Kerry constituency in the general election of August 1910) and Dr Billy 'Gogo' O'Sullivan, who won his seat in Seanad Éireann and became the leader of Fine Gael in the chamber. Professor O'Sullivan served as Minister of

Education from 1926 to 1932. There was another man named John Marcus O'Sullivan involved in politics in this period – Eugene's brother – who was elected to Kerry Council in 1926 and 1928. The Cumann na nGaedheal party did not contest local elections as a party, but members stood as Independents, ratepayers or farmers.

John Murphy was the elder by five or six years and he was the first into the political field. He stood unopposed for the East Kerry seat in parliament in 1900, as a representative of the Irish Parliamentary Party. A member of the Transport Union for many years, the bulk of Murphy's contributions to debates in Westminster were devoted to instances of Kerry people being evicted from their lands. In 1907, he was instrumental in the re-instatement of Dan O'Shea to his farm at Cleeney, Killarney, from which he had been evicted in 1887 by Lord Kenmare. Murphy was co-opted to both Kerry County and Killarney Urban councils in the opening years of the twentieth century. He replaced Thomas Kearney (deceased) for the Scartaglin Electoral Division to the county council early in 1901 and was then selected to replace Michael O'Sullivan, the Emporium owner – and Eugene O'Sullivan's employer – on Killarney Urban District Council, following the businessman's death on Christmas Eve of 1902. So it seems that Murphy had the support of the O'Sullivan family at this time. He did not contest the Urban Council election in 1905 and he had no further involvement in politics for some time. Murphy was returned from the Killarney Electoral Division to Kerry County Council in the election of 1902, beating Maurice Leonard, who would, ironically, be declared disqualified from holding his seat on Killarney Urban Council in 1909. He was re-elected to the county council for Killarney in 1905 and again in 1908, unopposed in his candidacy on both occasions, but he did not contest the division in June 1911 when J.T. O'Connor (of whom more follows) took the seat, defeating James Maher-Loughnan and another candidate.

In the meantime, Eugene O'Sullivan had left his home in Firies to work in the drapery owned by a family cousin, Michael O'Sullivan of the Emporium on Main Street. Eugene was a talented footballer too, captaining Dr Croke's to the Kerry County Championship in 1901 and winning a Munster Championship title with Kerry in 1902. From an early stage, he demonstrated a gift for leadership. He would later become part of the Kerry County Board, the Munster Council and Central Council, take the chair of his GAA club and the Fitzgerald Memorial Committee, which was responsible for the development of the football ground in Killarney. He was also a skilful snooker player and a tough rowing competitor, as well as a strong orator, a particularly beneficial talent in that age, when mass rallies and marching bands were essential ingredients of election campaigns.

* * *

Paddy MacMonagle, the local historian, believed that while Eugene O'Sullivan did support John Murphy initially in politics, the pair fell out somewhat abruptly. This became apparent in 1905 when Murphy, then an MP, instituted a libel action against Quinnell & Sons, the publishers of the *Kerry News*, in relation to a letter signed by Eugene O'Sullivan alleging that funds collected on behalf of the United Irish Party (the constituency organisation of the Irish Parliamentary Party) had not been promptly transferred to the treasurer. While the piece did not name Murphy, the jury at the Four Courts in Dublin agreed that it was clear that he was the person referred to and entered a decision that a libel had been committed. However, it also held that there had been no malice on the part of the publishers and damages of one farthing, the very minimum figure, were awarded to Murphy.[1] During the proceedings, the plaintiff stated that O'Sullivan had turned against him because he had used his casting vote in favour of another candidate, over O'Sullivan, when the position of clerk at the Killarney Asylum was being filled. This was just the opening skirmish in a series of many.

The next general election was set for 27 March 1906. The convention to nominate the candidate to represent the Irish Parliamentary Party in East Kerry took place on 8 January at Killarney Town Hall. It was a fractious meeting, with Murphy and O'Sullivan claiming that branches and individuals had not been accredited; it broke up in confusion after Murphy and his supporters marched out. A second convention also ended without any decision being arrived at. At the end of January, the party leader John Redmond sent a telegram declaring that, as the two conventions had 'failed through irregularities and disorder' to select a candidate, the party 'must decline to further interfere in the present election', demonstrating a certain amount of frustration with the two warring factions.[2] The row must have been a considerable embarrassment for John Redmond as John Murphy served as Redmond's secretary for a period. However, whichever candidate was elected would presumably support the Irish Party in parliament in any event. Both men contested the election and commenced extensive canvasses of the constituency. When the result of the election was declared, Murphy had polled 2,185 and O'Sullivan 2,131, giving the incumbent the seat by the close margin of fifty-four votes. The scene was already set for the dramatic rematch.

* * *

Five years later, in 1911, Eugene O'Sullivan won his seat on Killarney Urban District Council after the outgoing member, Tim O'Sullivan – Michael's son – decided not to put his name forward. At the first meeting the following week, O'Sullivan was nominated to take the position of chairman by Councillor Charlie Foley, the New Street publican, and seconded by James O'Shea. John Hilliard was also nominated. O'Sullivan won by 6–5, but Hilliard declared that O'Sullivan was a disqualified individual, for reasons that will be explained later. O'Sullivan certainly had a way of locating political enemies. John Hilliard was the head of a family that owned substantial businesses in Killarney and Tralee. A member of the Church of Ireland community, he also bred Kerry cattle on the extensive Hilliard lands, but despite the pre-eminence of the family name in Killarney, he never succeeded in being elected (legitimately) as chairman of the town council.

John Maher-Loughnan, the proprietor of the Royal Victoria Hotel, whom O'Sullivan replaced as chairman after a three-year spell, was another firm and constant opponent. He had also declined the opportunity to run for re-election in 1911, but he and O'Sullivan would have several encounters in courtrooms over property issues in the coming years. The Loughnan family had developed the hotel on the Kenmare Estate in the nineteenth century and the first telephone exchange in Killarney was located at the hotel in 1907, before transferring to New Street. However, the Maher-Loughnans were regarded as being fond of the good things in life and in October 1915, John was obliged to seek the protection of the Court of Bankruptcy. He obtained his discharges in July 1916, but he had to put the three farms up for auction in order to re-establish the hotel business. By October 1918, Lord Kenmare was seeking possession of the hotel premises over non-payment of rent.

In April 1920, the Master of the Rolls granted Eugene O'Sullivan the authority to sell land at Gortroe and other lands, having become the owner of the mortgage of the properties. John Maher-Loughnan's case was that he had fought in the war and been badly wounded and this had damaged his finances. But the tide was already turning on the family. There are pitiful accounts of the remaining members of the family departing from their home at Gortroe House in January 1931. In 1960, Beatrice Grosvenor built the Castlerosse Hotel on the site where the Royal Victoria had stood.

At the meeting in 1911, O'Sullivan duly accepted the position of chairman, a position he held until 1918, when the Sinn Féin surge resulted in Sinn Féin representatives gaining control of all the local authorities for a period. O'Sullivan was re-elected to the chair in 1926 and remained in the post until his death in 1942. He won the bulk of his legal battles with the Maher-Loughnan family and fared better than Murphy in the eventual analysis.

∗∗∗

But this is all running ahead of events as they happened, for, fresh from their battles during the 1906 general election, Murphy and O'Sullivan again fought for the parliamentary seat in East Kerry at the general election of 1910. Before this could occur, however, there was another contest to win the party nomination. The party convention was scheduled for 5 January and the two protagonists held a series of political meetings around the constituency in preparation. The *Kerry People*, operated by the Ryle family, was one of the newspapers circulating in the county and it covered the events of the time in great detail. In December 1909, Eugene O'Sullivan sought to address the ordinary meeting of the Tralee Board of Guardians and Rural District Council and was afforded the opportunity to make what was an extraordinary contribution. It was an unusual forum and an unlikely vehicle for his comments.[3] He had developed his nationalism, he said, 'not in the bye-ways in Killarney', although in the following edition of the *Kerry People* he insisted that he had actually said was 'the byways of a Solicitor's office in Killarney'. Either way, two of the members of the board asked him to withdraw, but O'Sullivan continued: 'I have stated a bold fact. I got my patriotism among the moonlighters of Firies (hear, hear). I am proud of the fact. I have the blood, the bone and the sinew of moonlighters, and if any individual man here wishes to test the material of that blood, and bone and sinew, I am here (hear, hear).'

This clearly referred to one of the most controversial incidents of the Land War in Kerry, which occurred in Molahiffe, Firies, in November 1885. The practice of paying late-night visits to individuals regarded as having taken possession of land from which others had been evicted had developed in the nineteenth century, initially through organisations such as the Whiteboys, but by this time, the use of the term 'moonlighter' had become more prevalent. On the night in question, twenty-five years earlier, a group of moonlighters entered the home of a vice-president of the local Land League, John O'Connell Curtin, in search of guns. Castle Farm was a substantial holding of around 250 acres and Curtin was a man in his sixties. Two of his daughters were also in the house. The entire family responded with fury to this invasion of their home. In the dark, shots were discharged and the elderly farmer and one of the raiders were shot dead. Two men convicted of taking part in the attack on the house were sentenced to penal servitude for life and the matter caused a huge division in the mid-Kerry area, which lingered for a considerable time. The two young Curtin women were boycotted – when they arrived to attend Mass, people got up and left – and the farm was eventually sold in February 1887. The 1909 report in the *Kerry People* demonstrates O'Sullivan's dramatic attempts to outdo Murphy's record of supporting tenants.

On a more humorous note, O'Sullivan's capacity to declare the breadth and extent of his kin in Kerry (the Emporium O'Sullivans, Dr Billy O'Sullivan from Batterfield and the nationalist figure and first Leas Cheann Comhairle of the Dáil, J.J. O'Kelly (Sceilg) were definitely relatives) afforded Murphy a chance to create mirth at his opponent's expense. At some point O'Sullivan claimed that the poet Eoghan Rua Ó Suilleabháin was among his forebears. John Murphy's riposte was that it was well known that the eighteenth-century Sliabh Luachra man had never married. But O'Sullivan's claim regarding his connection to the Firies incident that had occurred a quarter of a century earlier certainly contributed to raising the stakes in the electoral contest.

* * *

It was clear that the 1910 general election convention was going to be a fraught affair and so 150 policemen were rostered for duty in the environs of the town hall. Despite this, several 'little skirmishes' broke out. At midday, a prominent member of the United Irish Party (the parliamentary wing of the organisation), James Timothy O'Connor, approached O'Sullivan and asked him if he was prepared to abide by the decision of the convention. Not if Mr O'Connor was involved, O'Sullivan replied, since he was a

Murphy supporter. O'Connor then convened the election in the yard at the back of the town hall and J.K. O'Connor, the Castleisland businessman and county councillor, proposed John Murphy. James J. O'Shea, also a county councillor, seconded and Murphy was ratified unanimously and commenced his speech of acceptance. J.K. O'Connor also suffered the ignominy of being disqualified from his seat in the Castleisland Electoral Division. Following the county council elections in 1908, he was found guilty of providing drink and other inducements to voters, a matter that earned him mention in debates in Westminster (see Chapter 3).

In the meantime, another meeting had commenced in front of the town hall, where Jeremiah Crowley, a rural district councillor from Scartaglin, proposed Florence O'Sullivan from Ballyfinane to chair the meeting; he had chaired Killarney Rural Council for many years. This also afforded Crowley a seat on the county council to supervise proceedings and another county councillor, Cornelius Kelliher from Headford, proposed Eugene O'Sullivan as the candidate. At the national level, the party appears to have decided again to simply let the two men fight it out in their own theatre, so both men went on the ballot paper again for the right to represent East Kerry. At the conclusion of the count, O'Sullivan was declared the victor by 489 votes, 2,643 to 2,154. Murphy, whose wife had been unwell during the campaign, now submitted his petition to unseat the winning candidate because of alleged vote rigging and intimidation. This was not an unusual step for defeated candidates, but it cost £1,000 to lodge a petition, a substantial sum of money at the time. Murphy alleged thirty-nine instances of voter personation, including one in which O'Sullivan had persuaded a young man named O'Shea to vote in place of his late father and one in which O'Sullivan had actually personated another man. All of these charges were dismissed.

However, Judges Madden and Kenny both referred to the expression 'the blood, bone and sinew of the moonlighters' in the respondent's address to the Tralee Board of Guardians in determining that Patrick Daly, one of O'Sullivan's supporters, had subjected people to intimidation. Evidence of stone-throwing, kicking voters and the discharge of a revolver were not considered to have been proven and the judges found against any corrupt practice by either O'Sullivan or his supporters on the majority of the charges.. They did, however, hold that O'Sullivan and his agents had engaged in the corrupt practice of intimidation and undue influence in one instance. The election was thus declared void and the result was set aside.

Seven men were named along with O'Sullivan as having been involved in the affair and all of them were disqualified from holding public office for seven years. This obviously meant that Eugene O'Sullivan was barred from public office (although he was subsequently able to defeat this sanction and was elected to Killarney Urban Council and became chairman in 1911).

At the Killarney Petty Sessions in August 1910, Eugene O'Sullivan, John Ulick O'Sullivan and Patrick Daly were charged with using excessive influence upon eleven men in the election. The magistrates directed that they were unable to agree on the case against O'Sullivan and they refused to send any of the cases forward for trial. However, Headford farmer Cornelius Kelliher was convicted of corrupt practice in September and disqualified from holding the seat he had won on the county council. Murphy subsequently took the matter further and attempted to have O'Sullivan's name removed from the register of electors. In October 1910, at Killarney courthouse, Judge Browne held against the appellant and allowed O'Sullivan to remain on the list of voters.

With O'Sullivan disqualified, the East Kerry seat at Westminster remained empty and the writ to conduct the poll again had not been moved by the time a second election of the year was called for 8 December 1910. Eugene's cousin, Tim M. O'Sullivan, standing as an Independent nationalist, won the seat, defeating Patrick Guiney from Kanturk, who represented the All-For-Ireland League. Tim and his brother Professor John Marcus (later a government minister) married two Crotty sisters, Luisa and Agnes respectively, from Lismore in Waterford. Tim was a director of R. Hilliard & Sons and played a part in the first Irish full-length film, *The Dawn*, made in Killarney by Tom Cooper in 1936.

But the sparring between Murphy and O'Sullivan continued. *The Killarney Echo and South Kerry Chronicle*, owned by the Quinnell family, gave John Murphy a column on the front page of the paper in September 1913 and continued to run it until 1919. In January 1914, following the Urban Council election, the opinion piece entitled 'Murphy on Places, Persons and Public Affairs' stated:

> People in Killarney are surprised how Messrs James T. O'Connor, Eugene O'Sullivan, Cornelius Collins and Cornelius Counihan got at the head of the list. Of course, these elections, it is to be regretted, are never a test of anything, as there is practically no opposition, and certainly in Killarney there never was less public interest manifested

in them. The strange thing, however, is that four gentlemen who in all matters were supposed to be as far apart as North, South, East and West, came out on top.[4]

Later in the piece, there is a more direct reference to O'Sullivan: 'There are already rumours about the qualifications of Urban Councillors being tested in Killarney. I think I will test Mr Eugene O'Sullivan's right to remain in the Urban Council myself.' He goes on to suggest that his erstwhile opponent should have been disqualified as he had been a paid officer of the county council and as recently as early January 1914 had acted as a member of the County Kerry Technical Committee, 'which of course he was disqualified from doing'. Whether he did test this or not, O'Sullivan remained *in situ*. The *Cork Constitution* newspaper made a mischevious comment on the outcome of the petition: 'The two unseated English Ministerialists have been raised in the peerage, and we shall probably hear Mr Craig one of these days asking the Prime Minister whether he intends to follow this precedent in the case of Mr Eugene O'Sullivan, who is also a pledged Ministerial supporter.' Charles Craig was a unionist MP and father of the first Prime Minister of Northern Ireland, Viscount Craigavon.

＊＊＊

There was a setback for Eugene O'Sullivan, however, when the Irish Volunteers in Killarney decided to hold a fresh election of officers following an upsurge of membership in September 1914. O'Sullivan was identified as being more closely aligned with the authorities than the segment that was drilling with the intention of fighting for Irish freedom and was regarded with suspicion by many of the newer Volunteers. He did seem to misjudge the situation and Killarney Volunteers leaders Michael O'Sullivan and Michael Spillane give a colourful account of his bid to become the chairman in their joint contribution to the Military Archives. One needs to take a jaundiced view of the recollections of those speaking thirty-four years after the events described and, besides, Eugene was not, at this point, in a position to respond to their version of events, having died eighteen years previously, but it does at least paint an outline of what occurred. It is stated that O'Sullivan had canvassed the existing officers to ask them to withdraw in favour of his nomination for the chair beforehand. He arrived at the meeting 'at the head of from 30 to 40 men, and more or less took the hall by storm'. But things did not transpire as he had hoped:

> Michael Spillane was then proposed and seconded and he then took the chair. Eugene O'Sullivan protested and claimed it as his right, as Chairman of the Urban Council, to be appointed Captain of the Volunteers. Spillane replied, 'I do not want the job but if the men want me, I will act.' O'Sullivan replied, 'I know that, and you would be surprised how much I know' ... Spillane then asked all who wanted him as Captain to go to the right of the hall. There were very few left for O'Sullivan and he left the hall, after pouring abuse at An Seabhac, with a good deal less followers than came with him.[5]

'An Seabhac' was Pádraig Ó Siochfradha from Dingle, a teacher who was giving classes in Irish in Killarney and who was elected chairman of the county council in 1920 after Sinn Féin won the election. He wrote under the name 'An Seabhac' (The Hawk), *Jimín Máire Thaidhg* and *An Baile Seo Gainne* being his best-known works, and he later served in the Seanad from 1944 to 1948. John Murphy clearly identified with the republican element and in early 1918 Spillane and O'Sullivan refer to him chairing an anti-conscription meeting in Killarney.

✳ ✳ ✳

Tensions between the principal protagonists eased for a substantial period in the second decade of the twentieth century. Eugene O'Sullivan was settling into a spell of being routinely re-elected chairman of Killarney UDC, although he confronted a challenge of a rather unusual nature on 23 January 1917.[6] At 11am, Councillor O'Sullivan and his supporters arrived at the chamber for the election. Denis J. Courtney proposed and David Hurley seconded O'Sullivan for the chair and he was duly re-elected. William Ahern proposed and Mr Courtney seconded Con Counihan for the vice-chair and he was also deemed elected. However, at midday, John Hilliard and the other councillors arrived. Another meeting was begun and Thaddeus T. O'Connor proposed Mr Hilliard as chairman, a motion seconded by Peter Huggard, ironically the man who had been co-opted to fill the seat when Maurice Leonard had been disqualified in 1909. T.T. O'Connor was then elected (also unopposed) to the position of vice-chairman.

Eugene O'Sullivan MP.   John Murphy MP and his wife, Anne
                                     (née McCarthy) (Seán Murphy).

Hilliard then handed the acting clerk – none other than John Murphy – a message requiring a letter be sent to the Lord Chancellor, requesting that he, Hilliard, be appointed a magistrate, having been elected chairman. Murphy endeavoured to contact the council solicitor, Maurice McCartie, but he was in court in Cahersiveen. McCartie had been Eugene O'Sullivan's solicitor in the petition to unseat proceedings following the general election in 1910. The Lord Chancellor, though, declined to intervene, referring the matter to the Local Government Board for adjudication. In the meantime, O'Sullivan convened a meeting at which Michael Murray was appointed town clerk. Hilliard, however, wished to have John Murphy appointed to the position, but the situation was ultimately resolved, again, in favour of Eugene O'Sullivan.

There had also been an associated, tense battle involving rival supporters of the two men for the chairmanship of the county council two years earlier. The protagonists in this instance were another two Killarney members, James O'Shea and James T. O'Connor, one of those elected to the very first council in 1899 who had confronted O'Sullivan about respecting the decision of the meeting at the selection convention in 1906. O'Shea, a dairy farmer from Gortahoonig, Muckross had contested the position with M.J. Nolan the previous year and had been none too gracious about the matter following his defeat. However, when confronted by a well-known supporter of Murphy's, good grace did not enter the matter for one moment. O'Shea had been elected for the Aghadoe ED in 1914 (having narrowly lost in 1911). As chairman of Killarney Rural District Council, he was already entitled to sit as a member, but he was also elected in the poll. He challenged the incumbent George O'Gorman in 1908 and won, but in 1911, the Ballyhar man came back to win by a single vote following a recount.

As one would almost anticipate in this tale of vexatious rivalry, O'Gorman had been the man who had attempted to propose Eugene O'Sullivan at the uncompleted Irish Party convention in 1906. At the 1915 county council meeting, chairman Nolan called the meeting to order with a full schedule of members present. Fireworks had been expected and the chairman indicated that he was not putting his name forward on this occasion. John J. Sheehan (Sneem Electoral Union) proposed J.T. O'Connor for the chair and P.J. Moynihan (Headford) seconded. James O'Shea was nominated by Michael J. O'Donnell (Castlegregory, later also a member of Fianna Fáil) and John Healy (Ardfert) seconded. For a moment, it seemed as if war could be averted when the 'father of the house', Edward Fitzgerald from Cahersiveen, was asked to allow his name to go forward, but he declined after a quick discussion with O'Connor.

The vote was called and O'Connor was declared the winner by 18–8. He addressed the members and thanked those who had voted for him, including Fitzgerald, who had withdrawn in his favour. James O'Shea rose 'on a point of order'. He began by explaining his reasons for contesting the position and then referred to the 1914 election: 'I went forward then, with the same belief as I have now – and time has proved – that the man I opposed was not a suitable man for the chair of this council.' Uproar ensued. When he resumed, he said that he could contest again in 1916 and then stated 'that the man who sits in the chair is not a proper or suitable man; he is not a just man.'[7]

In the shouting that ensued, the chairman was heard to say, 'yerra, let him at it'. And O'Shea obliged, suggesting that his opponent was not an honourable man. O'Connor responded, 'Now Jamesy, take it as well as you gave it,' and drew attention to a number of other matters. O'Shea tried to get in a response, but the chairman moved to the election of the vice-chairman, which went to Jack McKenna, who was elected unopposed. As the Listowel man rose to accept the position, Healy and O'Donnell asked that O'Shea be allowed to speak and O'Connor asked O'Shea if he would withdraw and allow McKenna to be heard. He declined and, in the hubbub that followed, was heard to say, 'your vote in this room was never a vote for fair play. You were always an advocate for the poor man's son, but when it came to a question of the poor man's son, you voted against him'. Eventually order was restored and the meeting continued.

* * *

We move to the 1920s and the formative years of the Irish Free State. Eugene O'Sullivan reclaimed his position as chairman of Killarney Urban District Council in 1926 and continued to be re-elected until his death at the Imperial Hotel in Killarney on 29 May 1942. The month before he passed away, it emerged that six of the ten members of Killarney Urban District Council were disqualified from holding their seats because they had not paid their rates and the chairman had also made himself ineligible to sit in the chamber as he had not attended a meeting for over six months. He was, however, not in good health and attendance at meetings of the council was very low at this point in any event. The month after O'Sullivan died, the urban council was suspended and a commissioner was appointed and remained in place for three years.

O'Sullivan became the chairman of the Board of Killarney Mineral Waters and a member of Killarney Race Company. He also headed the first united farming association in Kerry in 1929 (Kerry Farmers' Union and Marketing Association) and chaired the committee that organised the National Ploughing Championships in Killarney in 1939. But he also made one further attempt to advance his political career, standing as an Independent candidate in the first general election of 1927 (June). His cousin John Marcus O'Sullivan was a candidate too, but Eugene came in ninth in the poll, with 2,405 votes and was only eliminated on the ninth count. Perhaps he should have pursued this ambition by formally joining the government party, for when the electors were summoned to vote again the following September, Cumann na nGaedheal had one of its most successful elections in Kerry: Fionán Lynch and John Marcus were at the head of the poll and the party took 39.9 per cent of the vote, which would never happen again.

John Murphy did adopt a political alliance, joining Fianna Fáil shortly after the party came into being. There was a particularly troubled Fianna

Fáil meeting in Knocknagoshel on 12 September 1927, which resulted in him being charged with 'falsely accusing a person of a crime punishable by law', along with Patrick J. Tuohy of Dublin, the Fianna Fáil organiser for Kerry. Also charged was Eamon Horan, the former Brigadier-General of the National Army and Clann Éireann candidate in the general election, who was charged under the Treason Clause of the Public Safety Act. He was present as Clann Éireann had entered into an agreement to support Fianna Fáil in the Dáil. All three were remanded to Limerick Prison, but when the case came before the District Court in Tralee later that month, the state entered a *nolle prosequi* against the two Fianna Fáil men.[8] John Murphy died at his home in High Street – the Park Place Hotel – on 17 April 1930, in relatively reduced circumstances, his grandnephew, Seán, said.

* * *

There was an expression years ago used to describe a person given to fractious behaviour: 'a thorny wire'. The story of the antagonism between Murphy and O'Sullivan, not to mention a number of the other people mentioned here, makes it clear that there were quite a number of thorny wires engaged in politics in Killarney during this period. Whatever provoked their intense dislike for one another, Murphy and O'Sullivan were both responsible for exacerbating the tension, seemingly rarely missing the opportunity to seek to put each other down. They were both able to generate considerable loyalty among their supporters and they certainly made the Kerry political scene a colourful one for many years. The rivalry even persists to this day, to some degree, in that hallowed arena of Gaelic football. While Eugene O'Sullivan joined Dr Croke's when he came to town and certainly contributed much to the club's early triumphs, the Murphys are a committed Legion family and Seán's bar on College Street celebrates this in vivid green and white. Other political rivalries have developed in Kerry over the years, some stretching over generations, some between members of the same parties, but none of them has ever reached the extremes that Murphy and O'Sullivan achieved, either on their own or through their followers.

From Buckingham Palace to Caherdaniel

The aristocrat nurse who became the first woman councillor in Kerry

Albinia Brodrick, the first woman elected to Kerry County Council, in 1920.

The first woman to become a member of Kerry County Council came from a prominent British aristocratic family, was the sister of the Secretary of State for War and wined and dined in her youth at Buckingham Palace. Born at 23 Chester Square, Belgrave, London, on 17 December 1861, the Honourable Lady Albinia Lucy Brodrick was the fifth daughter of William Brodrick, 8th Viscount Midleton, and his wife, Augusta Freemantle. She spent her early years in London and at the family estate in Surrey. Privately educated, she travelled widely in Europe and was fluent in several languages. She regularly visited the House of Lords with her father. Her brother, St John, the 1st Earl of Midleton, was MP for Surrey and later a cabinet minister at the War Office and Foreign Affairs (1900–3). Like his father, he was a staunch unionist and was leader of the Irish Unionist Alliance from 1910 to 1918. He was involved in negotiations on Home Rule with John Redmond. Brodrick and her family were regulars at concert and balls in Buckingham Palace. Up until 1904, she was listed on the *The Times* Court Circular and attended events hosted by the Archbishop of Canterbury.[1]

In 1904, Brodrick qualified as a certified nurse, training at the district infirmary in Ashton-under-Lyne and qualifying as a midwife in 1909. Her father had a large estate in County Cork, which she visited in her youth. She became familiar with the country and its quest for independence. She became interested in the Gaelic revival and grew increasingly sympathetic towards Irish nationalism. Visits to the Gaeltacht prompted her to learn the Irish language and she developed a revulsion towards the poverty and social conditions in rural Ireland. Writing in the *St James Gazette* in 1902, she spoke of the need to promote indigenous Irish industry. Increasingly politicised, in 1903, she wrote of Ireland as 'not the Ireland of Westminster … not the English Ireland in Ireland, which is not Ireland at all, but the bastard product of a conquest miscalled civilising'.[2] To the chagrin of her family, she began to use an Irish version of her name, Gobnait Ní Bhruadair.

The death of her father in 1907 gave her financial independence. Brodrick invested in a site at West Cove, Caherdaniel, in south Kerry, which would become her home until her death. She set up the Kilcrohane agricultural co-operative, through which members could share resources and profits with the aim of stymieing emigration and rural deprivation. She hosted classes for locals and she encouraged vegetarianism and new farming practices. The area was one of those blighted by endemic poverty and fell under the remit of the Congested Districts Board, which oversaw overpopulated areas where hunger and poverty were rife. Moved by the inadequate health services, Brodrick set about developing a hospital using her own resources. She wrote to the *British Journal of Nursing*, appealing for financial support:

> A Hospital for Kerry, for one corner of Kerry, because of the children haunted by tuberculosis, the women tortured in childbirth, the men struck low before their time ... Did you ever need to be driven eighteen miles with a fractured thigh? Has your wife bled to death in childbirth for want of help? Is it your child that goes lame for life for want of treatment?[3]

Brodrick named the site Ballincoona, or *Baile an Chúnaimh* (the home of the help). The complex of buildings required the reclamation of four acres of bog, the planting of 5,000 trees and the construction of a new road and a twenty-foot well, as well as the development of a storehouse, workshop, piggery, cattle house and other ancillary buildings.[4] With an expenditure of £2,620 in its first year, the project quickly ran into financial difficulties and only the foundations of the hospital were built. Brodrick sold her furniture, jewellery and personal belongings and continued to appeal to friends for donations to the project. Visiting the United States in 1912, she raised further revenue for the hospital and work resumed on its construction, but it never became fully operational. Brodrick offered to take in British soldiers injured in the First World War, but the offer was declined. A 'lack of money fetters us continually', she wrote.[5]

The Easter Rising in 1916 and the execution of the rebel leaders had a profound effect on Brodrick. She joined Sinn Féin and Cumann na mBan. She visited many of those interned in Frongoch in Wales after the Rising and wrote to newspapers offering advice to those planning to visit the prisoners.[6] Brodrick's new-found republicanism put her at odds with her family's unionism and she became increasingly detached from her family. Her brother, the Earl of Midleton, was particularly embarrassed. In a letter to *The Spectator* in 1916, apologising for his sister's support of the Rising, he wrote: 'She separated herself from my family thirteen years ago and I have not seen her since; she has always been very unbalanced in her views.'[7] During the 1918 general election, she campaigned for Sinn Féin candidates and in 1920 she was nominated for election to Kerry County Council in the Killorglin Electoral Division. Commenting on her candidacy, *The Kerryman* observed:

> Miss Brodrick, since her advent to Kerry, has accomplished an immense amount of great work in social improvement projects, and in carrying out philanthropic schemes generally. Always intensely Irish, she had devoted much time and patient labor [*sic*] to furthering the cause of the Gaelic League, and she has earned a reputation of being a fluent Irish speaker.[8]

Brodrick was one of five candidates returned, unopposed, and made history by being the first woman ever elected to Kerry County Council. She was a member of the County Infirmary Committee and became chair of the Kerry County Committee of Agriculture. When the Dáil tried to reduce the number of workhouses operating around the country, she resigned from the council in protest, but resumed her role soon after.[9] During the War of Independence, she sheltered IRA members and she campaigned during the Dáil election of 1921, formally nominating candidates Austin Stack, Edmond Roche, Tomás Ó Donnchú and Piaras Béaslaí.[10] She took the Anti-Treaty side in the Civil War and was present when the Dáil debated the Treaty and heckled the South Kerry TD, Fionán Lynch, from the public gallery when he spoke in its favour:

> *LYNCH:* I know what the people want, I know that I can speak for my own people – for the people of South Kerry, where I was bred and born.
>
> *A VOICE FROM THE BODY OF THE HALL:* 'No.'
>
> *LYNCH:* With one exception. Yes, a minority of one against, an Englishwoman. Well, if I am interrupted from the body of the Hall, I will reply, I say that that person should be removed from the Hall, a person who interferes with a speaker in this assembly, and I ask the chair to protect me.[11]

In April 1923, Brodrick was shot in the leg by police when she refused to stop while running errands on her bicycle for the IRA near Sneem. Arrested and jailed in the North Dublin Union, she went on hunger strike for fourteen days before being released. When Fianna Fáil was founded in 1926, she opted to remain in Sinn Féin and she ran the party's newspaper, *Irish Freedom*, for ten years, acting as editor for a time. With others like Mary MacSwiney, she left Cumann na mBan to set up the short-lived Mná na Poblachta.

In parallel with her republican activism, Brodrick employed her political nous in nursing. She was a vocal advocate of adequate training and registration for nurses; she had been a member of the Society for the State Registration of Trained Nurses from 1907. Her other area of interest was venereal disease. She wrote a paper called 'Morality in Relation to the Public Health' in which she 'broke down the silence' around sexually transmitted diseases and she chaired a National Council of Nurses Committee on the subject.[12] In April 1921, she chaired a nursing conference in Tralee which debated the need for a new hospital in the town. She lectured on the need for the professional organisation of nurses and nurses' rights, supporting calls for trade union representation for the profession.

Despite her political views, Brodrick remained a member of the Church of Ireland and played the harmonium in the church in Sneem. She continued to operate a co-operative shop in Caherdaniel. She lived a very frugal life, reputedly wearing the same pair of boots for seventeen years.[13] Albinia Brodrick died at the age of ninety-three at her south Kerry home on 16 January 1955. In her will, she left most of her wealth (£17,000) to republicans 'as they were in the years 1919 to 1921'. The vagueness of her bequest led to legal wrangles for decades. In February 1979, Mr Justice Seán Gannon ruled that the bequest was 'void for remoteness' as it was impossible to determine which republican faction met her criteria.[14]

3

'Castleisland swam in porter ... and drunkenness prevailed'

*The Councillor Unseated for
Plying Voters with Drink*

When proceedings began at the courthouse in Castleisland at one o'clock on a warm summer afternoon in 1908, the room was described as being 'packed to suffocating point and the windows had to be thrown open'.[1] A large crowd, including several journalists, had gathered to hear a series of dramatic and sensational charges against the recently re-elected county councillor, John Kerry O'Connor, who was being accused by his election opponent, Denis J. Reidy, of winning his seat in the Castleisland Electoral Division by illegal and corrupt means. Among the charges brought against Councillor O'Connor were 'bribery, corruption and intimidation of the greatest character, general treating, public houses kept open in every part of the constituency, and free drinks supplied' to voters during the election campaign. The presiding magistrate, Commissioner Maxwell, was told that, because of the way O'Connor had procured many of the votes he received, Reidy was seeking his unseating by order of the court. Reidy also wanted the result of the recent election to Kerry County Council held in the Castleisland Electoral Division to be declared void. John Kerry – better known as J.K. – O'Connor was a prominent Castleisland businessman and a Justice of the Peace who presided over the Petty Sessions court hearings in the district. Ironically, given what was to follow, O'Connor had presided over a court hearing in which fourteen men were charged in connection with a brawl in Ranalough near Currow during the 1906 parliamentary election campaign which resulted in an electioneer and a local constable sustaining injuries.[2]

O'Connor was no political novice. He had been a member of the Tralee Board of Guardians and was elected a member of the first Kerry County Council in April 1899, representing the single-seat electoral division of Castleisland. In that poll, there had been a contest for the only seat available. Redmond Roche of Maglass, also a Justice of the Peace, had been declared elected by a margin of just three votes. An immediate recount sought by O'Connor produced the same result: 469 for Roche and 466 for O'Connor. On the day after the count, however, a ballot paper was found on the floor of the Grand Jury Room in Tralee where voting had occurred. A recount was sought again and all the ballots were examined by the local Under Sheriff T.C. Goodman and legal representatives. The newly discovered paper was found to be valid, as it bore the official stamp. O'Connor was duly elected with one vote to spare over Roche.[3] O'Connor was a high-profile supporter of John Murphy, MP for East Kerry, in his political battles with his nemesis, Eugene O'Sullivan. The court hearing was told that O'Connor was a man of influence: a draper, a meal and flour merchant, a creamery proprietor and auctioneer who 'had business dealings with the great bulk of the electorate, a great many of whom were deep in his books.'[4]

O'Connor retained his seat in the council elections of 1902 and 1905. He served on several local authority committees, including the Asylum Committee, and was a member of the Tralee and Fenit Pier and Harbour Commissioners. At the 1908 poll which has held on 3 June, O'Connor was challenged, however, for the single seat on offer by another local businessman, Denis J. Reidy. Reidy was active in the Irish Land and Labour Association and had strong political support in the division. O'Connor prevailed by 555 votes to Reidy's 525 and he was declared elected by the returning officer, Maurice Moynihan. Reidy moved immediately to have the result declared void. The losing candidate believed that he had sufficient evidence to prove that the victor had achieved the result by illegal means. The court petition led to a sensational ten-day court hearing in which Castleisland was portrayed as being drowned in alcohol on a bacchanalian scale and rife with bribery, intimidation and political corruption. It was little wonder that the courthouse was packed to capacity as the court case began.

* * *

Petitioning the courts to have the result of an election declared void was nothing new in Kerry or elsewhere – though none of the previous cases involved such a catalogue of porter-induced skulduggery at the polling stations. At the 1910 general election, for example, John Murphy, who was strongly supported by J.K. O'Connor, petitioned to unseat the winning candidate, Eugene O'Sullivan, the East Kerry MP, alleging vote rigging, personation and intimidation and the election was declared void. The 1911 local elections saw a former chairman of Kerry County Council, St John Donovan, petition for the unseating of Tralee publican, Thomas Healy, who had beaten him to the seat in the Ardfert division. The court heard charges of 'an orgie [sic] of perjury' as allegations of treating voters on the roadside and supplying drink to voters at a dance were made against Healy. Healy's barrister was the Irish Parliamentary Party MP Timothy Healy, who said that there had been a 'collusion of perjury between Mr Donovan's relatives' and remarked that 'in this instance, it was not Satan reproving sin but Bacchus reproving booze'.[5] The court declared Thomas Healy's election, however, to be null and void.

✷ ✷ ✷

'Intimidation of the greatest character'

The Castleisland case opened on Tuesday, 25 August 1908, at Castleisland courthouse before Commissioner Maxwell. Denis J. Reidy, the petitioner, was represented by his solicitor, David Roche, instructing Serjeant John Francis (J.F.) Moriarty, King's Counsel – from Mallow and well known in political circles – and junior counsel Bernard Roche. J.K. O'Connor, the respondent, was represented by solicitor R.C. Meredith, who instructed A.M. Sullivan, King's Counsel (later a member of Sir Roger Casement's defence team when he was tried for treason in 1916) and E.J. (Ned) McElligott, his junior (later a Circuit Court judge; his family owned the Listowel Arms Hotel). The returning officer for the poll was Maurice Moynihan, who was represented in court by Joseph Mangan, solicitor. The court heard allegations that J.K. O'Connor had won his seat on the county council by bribing voters, supplying them with drink and intimidating them into supporting him. Barrels of porter had been placed at polling stations and Reidy's election rallies were disrupted by personation and 'gross rowdyism'. O'Connor's wife, Hanoria, was one of his principal and 'most active' agents. She had distributed whiskey to voters on the canvass and had driven many voters to the polls on polling day. One voter alleged that she had received a shilling from Mrs O'Connor in return for a promise to vote for her husband. A few days before polling, witness Jeremiah McMahon described being canvassed by the O'Connors:

> J.K. and his wife went into the house. He asked for a vote, and witness said he would give it to him. 'He asked me on the road would I take a drink of whiskey … and I said I would. Mrs J.K. was there. I drank out of a tumbler with a handle on it. Mr O'Connor filled out the whiskey and I drank it.' (Laughter). That was about the 26 May.

'Terrorism' of O'Connor's supporters

The second day of the case opened with the sensational claim, made by Denis Reidy's counsel Serjeant Moriarty, that on leaving the courthouse the previous evening, 'three witnesses for the petitioner were beaten' and subjected to 'terrorism' by O'Connor's supporters. A man had been arrested and the commissioner warned that there could be no repetition of such behaviour. The long line of witnesses continued. Before voting at Knocknagoshel, witness Timothy Warren claimed to have been offered a 'quarter of ground free for the year' by an associate of O'Connor's. Another man, Thomas Leane, claimed to have been offered a free return ticket to America. Several witnesses reported receiving but not paying for drink on the day of the election:

> Michael Culloty deposed, in reply to Sergt [sic] Moriarty, that he lived about a mile from Castleisland. He voted at that election. He remembered the Sunday Mr Reidy was holding his meeting. On that day witness was in Mr J.K. O'Connor's yard in the evening. Before he went into the yard, he was in the kitchen. He got whiskey from the servant girl. The kitchen was full and they were all getting whiskey … He had two pints of porter in the yard … It was taken from a barrel … Witness did not pay for the porter or whiskey nor did he see anybody paying for it. They all got porter.[6]

Culloty claimed he was told by Mrs O'Connor that she 'would leave a pint for me every day for six months', whereas Denis Reidy had only ordered one pint for him at some point before the election. Michael Brosnan told the court that he voted at Curranes and that prior to polling day, Mrs O'Connor came to his house to ask for his vote. There was drink available at the polling station:

> Did you get drunk there? – There was drink all over the place [laughter]. I got drunk there anyway [more laughter].

> In further examination, he said he got drink from Thomas Griffin, a son of Patrick Griffin's, Mr O'Connor's personating agent. He didn't see Maurice O'Connor, high nor dry, at the barrel of porter [laughter].

> Mr Serjeant Moriarty – Nobody was dry that day [laughter].

> Witness – The day was dry, sir. [loud laughter].[7]

'A gallon of whiskey'

A Mrs Murphy was working in the O'Connor's kitchen on the Sunday evening prior to the election. She said Dan Murphy, a local publican, was there and was in charge of a barrel of porter which had come from Hartnett's bar nearby. 'She could not tell what time it [the barrel]was brought. She was in and out of the house during the day. How did it come in, "it didn't walk in"', questioned counsel.

> Witness said she did not know.

> Did you see whiskey given out in the kitchen? – Yes.

> You had a bottle of whiskey? – Yes.

> Did you know everyone you gave whiskey to? – I knew them at the time.

> How many did you give whiskey to, thirty or forty? – Yes, the people that came from Brosna.

> The porter came from Hartnett's; did Hartnett come with it? – I could not tell you.

> Who told you to order it? – I ordered it myself (sensation in court)

Who authorised you? – I know the men were coming in on Sunday and I went to Mr O'Connor and asked him what would I get. He told me to get whatever I wanted.

What did you order? – A half tierce[8] of porter and a gallon of whiskey … I knew Mr O'Connor was holding a meeting in Brosna. There were a number of supporters with him. It was for the purpose of giving refreshments to the people that went to Brosna that I ordered the porter and whiskey in.[9]

* * *

'Seventy-three gallons of porter'

It wasn't just in Castleisland establishments that alcohol was allegedly used to influence voters. Knocknagoshel, in which there were ten public houses in 1908, was targeted not only by O'Connor, but also by Reidy, the court heard. Daniel O'Connor, a publican in Knocknagoshel, supplied drink worth £7 17s to voters on Reidy's orders, while his neighbour Simon Keane had a bill for £7 16s in the name of J.K. O'Connor and £2 9s in the name of Denis Reidy. Among the recipients of free porter on Keane's books was 'Dan the Bird', who was described in court as a 'local character'. Two other local men, Edward Devane and Cornelius McAuliffe, went to vote at Curranes and got drink at the polling station, they said. One of O'Connor's agents, Bryan O'Connor, had taken porter, whiskey and port wine to the polling station – he tapped one of the porter barrels and 'let them drink and be damned to it'. A bottle of special whiskey was reserved for the polling clerks on duty. As Justice of the Peace, J.K. O'Connor was in the advantageous position of being able to swear in the polling clerks in his own electoral division, which had five polling stations. One of those clerks was John Fitzgerald, who told the court that when he made his declaration of secrecy before O'Connor, he was told, 'You'll see me alright below.'[10]

One of J.K. O'Connor's most prominent supporters, Daniel 'Dan Spud' Murphy, took the stand on the sixth day of evidence. He denied that the candidate had instructed him to give drink to voters. Murphy accepted that he took friends of his to Maurice Hogan's public house on polling day and 'at all events' was responsible for the price of seventy-three gallons of porter. 'Are you in the habit,' the witness was asked, 'of bringing people into other public houses and treating them there?' 'Well, once in a while,' he said, to which the commissioner responded 'Only at triennial elections,' to further raucous laughter. Murphy admitted he was fully willing to lose £30 or £40 to the election because 'Mr O'Connor is a gentleman I highly appreciate.' At times, the level of farce reached new heights: 'The name of (witness) Margaret Callaghan was called. She's dead, came a voice from the body of the court, and sad to say the announcement was received with a titter,' reported the *Kerry People*.[11] The chief prosecutor, Serjeant Moriarty, took ill halfway through the proceedings and was indisposed for several days. On the sixth day of the trial, the commissioner was forced to temporarily vacate the bench and allow the defendant into his chair – it was the day on which Petty Sessions would normally be heard and only the local magistrate, one J.K. O'Connor, could formally open and immediately adjourn the proceedings to allow the current business to continue.

* * *

'Unlimited drink in every village'

A.M. Sullivan rose to present the defence case on behalf of the sitting councillor. J.K. O'Connor, he said, was not defending himself against about eighty charges of bribery, undue influence and procuring personation for the sake of his county council seat; rather, he was defending his own person against such charges. Denis Reidy was indulging in unlimited personal accusations against his client, forty of which had been absolutely disproved by the evidence produced by the petitioner himself. It was a catalogue of crime of which J.K. O'Connor was 'absolutely innocent'. O'Connor never ordered free drinks for his supporters in public houses, he never went into a public house during the election and where he learned of treating, he did all he could to prevent it:

> The candidate was not the leader. He was used by every faction and party and his name was used as a weapon to best their own opponents. In this constituency at the time the election took place there were innumerable factions, political and personal, each of whom took up one of the candidates and used him in conducting his campaign against his enemy.

As soon as O'Connor heard of what was going on, he went to publican Richard Shanahan and said there was no justification for it: 'I can beat that fellow (Reidy), three to one, and if the election is to be won by porter, I would prefer not to win it at all.' The barrister continued, according to the *Kerry People*, in 'convincing tones':

> Mr O'Connor could not stop it. In view of the provocation of Reidy himself it was impossible to stop it, and with the example before them of open houses it was impossible to expect that his friends would stand aside, and consequently this campaign of competitive treating commenced by Reidy, waxed hotter and hotter, culminating on polling day with unlimited drink in every village and where there was no village an unlimited supply of drink was served to all-comers. Competitive appeals to corruption.

'A very ordinary episode in this country'

O'Connor, his defence counsel insisted, had never gone about 'ladling out drink' when canvassing votes. No evidence had been produced to place the successful candidate in a public house with any voter. One publican, Mrs Nolan, had admitted to charging drinks at election time to whatever candidates were contesting, with or without their approval. Nobody had done so with J.K. O'Connor's sanction, O'Sullivan contended. As for the large crowd enjoying refreshments at O'Connor's on the evening of the Brosna meeting, there was nothing in the law that said a man couldn't treat friends and supporters in this way after a day of electioneering. And what was wrong with offering somebody a drink? 'Will you have a drink?' was as common as saying 'Good morning'. His client, Sullivan continued:

> met many people, and they spoke … about the crops and weather, and eventually the election came down. After a friendly conversation with a man, when one had his luncheon basket besides him, what was more natural than that he should ask the man to take a little sup of whiskey. That was a very ordinary episode in this country.

Rejecting all charges of bribery, Sullivan dismissed some of the sworn statements of witnesses, which incidentally hadn't been produced in evidence, but had been procured in that 'great, grogging, affidavit factory, Hussey's public house'. 'You might imagine,' Sullivan continued, 'the inducements there held out for people to sign their names to affidavits.' As for Mrs Hanoria O'Connor, who admittedly 'talks a little much', she had been accused of bribery despite simply offering a friend clothes in an act of Christianity a full twelve months before the election.

* * *

'Without the slightest foundation'

When John Kerry O'Connor was finally called to the stand on the eighth day of the hearing, he strenuously denied all charges. He had no knowledge of drink being supplied to voters at polling stations. On the canvass, yes, he treated friends who travelled with him to 'a nip of whiskey', but he never entered a public house in order to influence his constituents and never engaged in bribery at election time. He also rejected that he had anything to do with damage caused to Denis Reidy's home on 3 May by a group who had been plied with drink. He had ordered some refreshments for his supporters on the evening of the Brosna meeting, but denied knowing anything of Dan 'Spud' Murphy's acquisition of another tierce of porter for those present. He was upstairs with friends on the evening in question. When the respondent concluded his evidence, it was left to E.J. McElligott, O'Connor's junior counsel, to summarise his client's denial of all charges:

> Mr J.K. O'Connor came into this court not for the purpose of retaining his seat but for the purpose of vindicating his character, and vindicating the character of his wife, who was dear to him, from the shocking, gross and malignant charges heaped and piled up against him without the slightest foundation, and he has succeeded, in vindicating his wife's character, his own character, and in doing so he had achieved everything he had to achieve.

There followed much applause in court.

* * *

'Holding the crowded court spellbound'

'The "judgement day" in the now famous Castleisland election petition,' wrote the *Kerry People* correspondent, 'brought an immense crowd to and around the precincts of the Courthouse, and the decision was awaited with the keenest interest. The language in which the decision was given was worthy of the best traditions of the Irish bar, Mr Commissioner Maxwell holding the crowded court spellbound.'[12] Maxwell noted that over the course of nine days, J.K. O'Connor had faced over 100 distinct charges in a case of 'magnitude' and 'gravity': forty-five charges of treating, eleven of public houses alleged to be open for the free distribution of drink to voters, two cases of undue influence and duress, seven of illegal hiring and five of personation. The hiring of transport for taking voters to the polls, with the knowledge of the respondent, had not been proved. The charges of personation at the polling stations had not been proved. Two charges of undue influence had failed. In relation to the bribery charges, it was the view of the court that 'personal bribery' had not been proved. Charges of bribery against Mrs Hanoria O'Connor were 'groundless'. However, the allegations that J.K. O'Connor had treated voters by 'keeping an open house' had been amply proved against the respondent and several others too. The commissioner recalled a reference by the successful candidate to his belief that he would prevail by a margin of three to one, but the closeness of the result, a margin of just thirty votes, 'showed it was a nearer matter than he thought'.

'Shameful and shameless corruption'

Commissioner Maxwell did not find the evidence in relation to treating in public houses to be credible. While O'Connor claimed he had cautioned publicans like Richard Shanahan and Dan Murphy not to supply drink to voters in his name, at least £100 worth of drink had been given out in the councillor's interest. Maxwell 'did not think the amount Mr O'Connor would have to pay (had he had to pay for it), would influence him in warning publicans not to give drink in his name … He did not want to be plainly and conclusively identified with the treating'. He concluded:

> If Mr O'Connor then wanted to prevent this, the wise and proper course for him would have been to publicly denounce the practice;

and, if by doing so he lost the election, he would have gained the respect of all honourable men in the place. The excuse offered by some of the respondent's agents was that he was not to be drowned in a flood of porter, that there was open treating by the other side – in fact, it was aptly described by counsel as 'competitive treating.' There was, undoubtedly, competitive and indiscriminate treating.[13]

'It is no part of my duty,' Maxwell concluded:

> to deal with this case from the point of view of enforcing sobriety, or preaching a sermon to the voters, nor to persons who are present here in court. I think Father Matthew himself might be daunted by the task in Castleisland [laughter]. But I will say this. The law is very jealous of electoral purity. An election is not an election unless it is the free uninfluencing choice of the voters, and the serious question to my mind from a moral point of view about this case is the state of public opinion in this question of treating ... There has been, so far as treating, both specific and general is concerned, shameful and shameless corruption in this constituency, and it is a matter for tears rather than laughter that such a thing would occur. And I would appeal to the people of Castleisland, for their own sake, for the sake of this beautiful county of Kerry, where every prospect pleases, to recollect that the purity of election is essential to the success of Local Government ... it makes any man who loves his country sick and sorry to hear the evidence that has been given in this court.

The commissioner hoped that the people of Castleisland, and of Kerry generally, would 'exercise self-control' and would learn how to use local government for their own good and for the good of their county and country. Finally and most importantly, he found that J.K. O'Connor was guilty of 'corruptly supplying drink to voters for the purpose of corruptly influencing such voters'. He said he would report O'Connor's agents and those publicans who supplied drink to voters to the High Court. He added that Denis J. Reidy was himself guilty of a similar charge. The election was declared void and he ruled that the respondent and petitioner should incur their own costs in the matter. He listed the names of the many individuals who would be reported to the High

Court and, as the *Kerry People* correspondent concluded, 'the protracted proceedings terminated'.

* * *

Despite all his efforts to unseat his opponent, Denis Reidy did not take up the seat now left vacant by J.K. O'Connor. John Laurence Quinlan of Bridge Street, Tralee, previously a member of Tralee Urban District Council, who had lost his seat on that body, was co-opted to the seat. Quinlan was a member of a Castleisland family and a cousin of Patrick and William Quinlan, who were both secretaries of Kerry County Council. In November 1908, J.K. O'Connor appeared before magistrates in Tralee for the offences alleged to have been committed in and around Castleisland in the weeks before the county council election. However, by a majority of eleven to two, informations were refused and the matter would not be heard. The result 'was received with a loud cheer'.[14]

* * *

'A wave of porter'

There is only one known occasion on which a local authority election result in County Kerry ever troubled the members of the House of Lords at Westminster. The bacchanalian behaviour during the election campaign in the Castleisland Electoral Division in 1908 made it to the floor of the chamber a few years after the controversy. On 14 March 1912, the 7th Earl of Mayo, Dermot Robert Wyndham Bourke, rose to call the attention of the government to the position of certain magistrates in Ireland, including J.K. O'Connor of Castleisland, who, along with magistrates in other parts of the country, had been convicted in court of various charges and who, he argued, should be removed from their roles as a result. The earl described O'Connor's misdeeds to his fellow peers:

> Mr O'Connor is a justice of the peace for the county of Kerry and stood as a candidate for the county council for the division of Castleisland. That election will long be remembered, because Castleisland swam in porter, and treating and drunkenness prevailed. So bad was it that the Roman Catholic Bishop of Kerry, in the Lenten Pastoral,

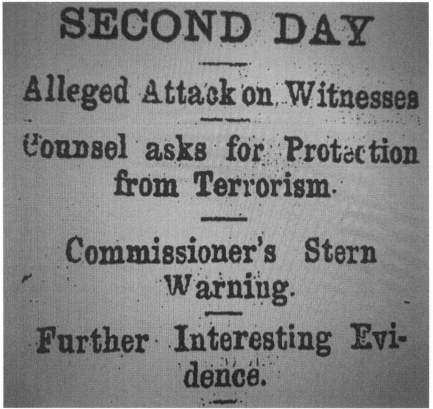

SECOND DAY

Alleged Attack on Witnesses

Counsel asks for Protection from Terrorism.

Commissioner's Stern Warning.

Further Interesting Evidence.

Coverage of the case in *The Kerry People*, 29 August 1908.

referred to it. He said: 'Another matter which a sense of duty compels me to mention is the manner in which some of our local elections are conducted. The language used, instead of being informing and elevating, is grossly personal, lowering, and demoralising.' And he concluded: 'Worse still, some of these elections are conducted without even an appearance of public decency. They become the occasion of wholesale drunkenness, and sometimes even of violence.' Mr O'Connor, at the Castleisland election, headed the poll. He is a most successful merchant in that town, and a wave of porter – you can describe it as nothing else – landed him safely on the county council bench. He headed the poll with a majority of thirty votes. But, alas! there was an election petition. Mr O'Connor appeared as respondent, and this was the result of the Commissioner's finding –

he found that the respondent had been guilty of corruptly supplying drink to voters for the purpose of corruptly influencing such voters, and that the respondent was also guilty of corrupt practices, and he declared the election void.[15]

The earl wondered why, in keeping with the law, the Lord Chancellor of Ireland had not been informed that O'Connor, as a magistrate, had not been removed from the post when he was found guilty of 'corrupt practices at an election'. Another peer, the Earl of Desart, claimed that O'Connor had only been removed from the bench in 1911 and that he had exercised judicial functions between 1908 and 1911. Responding, the Paymaster-General, Lord Ashby St Ledgers, said that for some reason the fact was not brought to the Lord Chancellor's attention. Subsequently, 'in view of a decision given by Mr Justice Kenny in another case to the effect that the office of a magistrate was *ipso facto* vacated from the date of the making of the report, the name of Mr O'Connor was removed from the Commission'.

4

'Struck him violently in the mouth'

The Kerry TD Who Punched a Colleague in the Dáil Dining Room

Seán Lemass rose to his feet in Dáil Éireann to present TDs with details of the Order of Business. It was 31 January 1952. The then Tánaiste outlined the various pieces of legislation to be debated that day, as well as a proposal that the House would not sit the following week. A number of deputies rose to oppose the Order of Business, among them the Fine Gael leader, General Richard Mulcahy, and the leader of Clann na Poblachta, Seán MacBride. Several others asked about various bills which were before the House. The Independent TD for Dublin South East, Dr Noël Browne – who less than a year earlier had resigned as Minister for Health over the controversial Mother and Child Scheme – was called to speak by the Leas Ceann Comhairle, Cormac Breslin: '*Dr. Browne:* I do not want to spend an unduly long time on the list mentioned by Deputy [Liam] Cosgrave but I should like to draw attention to the reference to an Adoption of Children Bill.'[1]

Liam Cosgrave TD, who had already spoken, interjected to say that he had not made any reference to the Adoption of Children Bill. Across the chamber from Cosgrave, on the Independent benches, the conservative firebrand TD for Laois–Offaly, Oliver J. Flanagan – then an Independent, but later a Fine Gael deputy – made an obscure comment suggesting that another member of the House would be in a better position than Dr Browne to comment on the adoption legislation: '*Mr. O. Flanagan:* Deputy Flynn would be more qualified to do that.'

Deputy Flanagan was referring to the Independent TD for Kerry
South, John (Jack) Flynn, who was not in the chamber at the time. The
Dáil transcripts do not record any reaction from other TDs to Flanagan's
off-the-cuff remark and they continued with the Order of Business. Within
a few short hours, however, Flynn was to give his response to Flanagan – in
a most unparliamentary manner.

As Flanagan dined in the busy Dáil restaurant later that evening, he
was approached by Flynn and challenged about his remarks earlier that
day in the chamber. The Fine Gael parliamentary leader, John A. Costello,
later told the Dáil in vivid detail about what followed:

> *Mr. J.A. Costello:* It is my duty to interrupt the business for the
> purpose of drawing the attention of the House and particularly your
> attention, a Cheann Comhairle, to a gross breach of the privileges of
> this House and of a particular Deputy and possibly of other Deputies
> of the House which occurred in the precincts to-night. The incident
> is one which is of very grave and particular importance and is even
> more serious from the point of view of the order and dignity of
> Parliament. Tonight, after the discussion which took place on the
> motion to adjourn this House on the conclusion of its proceedings
> to-day until next Wednesday week … Deputy O. Flanagan was in the
> restaurant talking to another Deputy, Deputy Dillon, when … Deputy
> Flynn, came behind him, caught hold of him, turned him round, used
> a very offensive and obnoxious expression and struck him violently in
> the mouth, alleging that he had during the debate spoken about him,
> Deputy Flynn. He also assaulted an usher, one of the servants of the
> House, and was guilty of extremely offensive conduct. He also made
> offensive references to another Deputy, Deputy Collins … As leader
> of the Opposition it then became my duty to inform you, so that you,
> a Cheann Comhairle, would take the necessary action and direct the
> proper steps to be taken.

The Ceann Comhairle, Patrick Hogan, insisted that the matter would
be fully investigated, suggesting it would be best dealt with by the Dáil's
Committee on Procedure and Privileges. Another deputy, Major Vivion
de Valera, asked that the Ceann Comhairle take into the account 'the
provocative personal remarks' made by Deputy Flanagan about Deputy

Flynn, which had been 'deleted from the record' of the House. The exchanges continued:

> *Mr. Seán MacBride (CnaP):* Is the Deputy [De Valera] trying to justify an assault on a member of this House?
>
> *Mr. Patrick Burke (FF):* There is only one answer to a common perjurer [Flanagan] who abuses everybody here day after day.
>
> *Major de Valera (FF):* Will the Ceann Comhairle take these remarks into account is all I ask? They were remarks which were expunged from the records.
>
> Mr. Burke: He [Flanagan] does nothing but blackguard everybody here.

Fianna Fáil's Robert Briscoe suggested that John A. Costello's account was 'not in accordance with the facts', saying that he was present in the dining room when the incident occurred and that Costello was not. Jack Flynn, who had re-entered the House, fresh from his encounter in the restaurant, concurred: 'I wish to say that Deputy Costello's statement is not a true picture of the incident.'

Within days, Flanagan and Flynn were hauled before the Dáil's Committee on Procedure and Privileges, a committee which still oversees the conduct of deputies in the Dáil. The committee's report into the matter some weeks later set out the position of both TDs, but still did not cast any light on the precise nature or import of Flanagan's comment or why Flynn found it so particularly offensive:

> Deputy J. Flynn stated to the Committee that he committed the assault above described because he had learnt that, in the course of a debate in the Dáil earlier on the same day while he was absent from the Chamber, Deputy O. Flanagan had passed a remark relating to him which would be generally understood as a gross reflection on his personal character … He felt that there was no adequate remedy, under existing Standing Orders, available to him in respect of such a remark when made under the immunity of parliamentary privilege. The remark to which Deputy J. Flynn took exception was made by Deputy O. Flanagan by way of interjection and, as explained by Deputy J. Flynn, conveyed offence to

him of a gross personal nature by innuendo. Deputy O. Flanagan was not called to order at the time because – the Committee understands – the Leas Cheann Comhairle did not grasp all the implications of the remark owing to its ambiguity and, further, he would in any case hesitate to censure it since to do so would be to draw public attention to its possible scandalous connotation. Deputy O. Flanagan denied to the Committee that any such hidden meaning was intended by him and asserted that the reference related solely to Deputy J. Flynn's political activities.[2]

The committee ruled that the use of violence in the precincts of Leinster House in this manner was 'reprehensible in the extreme', adding that 'Deputy J. Flynn was guilty of contempt in taking, as it were, the law into his own hands in redress of a grievance properly a matter for the House itself.' Flanagan's remarks were found to be in breach of the order and decorum of the House. On 5 March 1952, six weeks after the incident, the Dáil accepted and adopted the committee's report and Flynn was formally censured by the Ceann Comhairle from the chair: 'In accordance with the provisions of this report, it becomes my duty to reprimand you, Deputy John Flynn, for the assault committed by you in the precincts of the Dáil on January 31, as such assault was in contempt of the privilege of this House.'[3]

So, what had prompted Oliver J Flanagan to make an obscure personal reference to Jack Flynn during a Dáil discussion? And why had the Kerry South TD taken such umbrage and become so infuriated that he punched Flanagan in the Dáil restaurant? The answer can be found by going back a few years to when, in controversial circumstances following an alleged scandal, Flynn – who had been a Fianna Fáil TD since 1932 – was unceremoniously removed from the party general election ticket by Éamon de Valera.

* * *

John (Jack) Flynn was born at Brackhill, Castlemaine, in 1894, one of five children of Edward and Johanna Flynn. A veteran of the War of Independence, he fought with his local IRA company, the 6th Battalion of the Kerry Brigade. He was involved in numerous engagements with the Crown forces, including an ambush just a stone's throw from his home at Ballymacandy, between Milltown and Castlemaine, on 1 June 1921, in which several Black and Tans were killed. During the Civil War, he took the anti-Treaty position and became politically involved. He won a seat on Kerry County Council as a republican candidate in the Killorglin Electoral Area in 1926 and joined Fianna Fáil that same year. He became a resilient figure on the local authority. In 1932, he was the chairman of the County Board of Health, which secured funding of £55,000 from the Irish Hospital Sweeps for the construction of St Catherine's Hospital in Tralee (now the headquarters of Kerry County Council). By the time St Catherine's and a hospital at Edenburn in Ballymacelligott were opened, Flynn had been replaced by Councillor Kate Breen at the head of the Health Board because it became Fianna Fáil policy that TDs could not chair local authority sub-committees following the 1934 local elections. In 1929, Flynn was charged with membership of an illegal organisation and possession of unlicensed firearms and ammunition in the Circuit Court in Tralee. The jury returned verdicts of not guilty.

John (Jack) Flynn TD (*The Kerryman*).

Flynn was a well-known long-distance runner and a keen weight-lifter and shot-putter and his sporting profile no doubt enhanced his electoral prospects. Widely considered a hard-working and diligent public representative, he was elected to the Dáil in 1932, when Fianna Fáil swept to power under Éamon de Valera. Flynn headed the poll with nearly 13 per cent of the vote. In the then seven-seater Kerry constituency, Fianna Fáil won five of the seats. Joining the Castlemaine man in the Dáil were Eamonn Kissane, Fred Hugh Crowley, Thomas McEllistrim and Thomas O'Reilly. One of his Fianna Fáil successors in the Dáil, John O'Leary, a TD from 1966 to 1997, recalls Flynn being one of the dominant political figures in his youth and when he joined the party. Flynn, he says, was incredibly popular across the constituency of Kerry and later Kerry South, which he represented from 1937 onwards. O'Leary also recalls Flynn's somewhat nomadic lifestyle:

He was a great character and was renowned, apparently, in his younger days for going to house parties and Biddy balls; he'd be invited, picked up and taken there – there was great kudos in having a TD at a party you might be organising ... Flynn was a single man and someone of no fixed abode for much of his life as a politician. It was common for him to spend weekends in different houses around the constituency. People used often say that when the train was pulling into Killarney station on his return from Leinster House that he'd stick his head out the window to see who was there on the platform and where he could get lodgings for the weekend. Some one of his supporters from some part of the constituency would pick him up and take him to their area. His hosts would put on a party for him, but he would also use the opportunity to do some political work in the locality where he was staying. In that way, people in even the more remote parts of the constituency became familiar with him and were able to meet with him regularly to air their problems and grievances.[4]

Throughout his years in the Dáil, Flynn proved a diligent and regular contributor to debates and tabled questions to ministers with regularity. His focus was invariably rural matters such as fishing, agriculture and infrastructure, as well as social conditions and housing. Despite having retained a seat for Fianna Fáil from 1932, ahead of the 1943 general election, the frequent poll-topper was denied a nomination by the party leadership: the *Irish Press* noted that he had 'withdrawn his candidature'.[5] Contemporary newspaper accounts do not record why, but it was alleged that Flynn had been conducting a relationship with a young woman. John O'Leary recalls that the allegation doing the rounds was even more serious than that:

> Though it was never proven, as far as I know, the rumour was that a girl had become pregnant by Flynn out of wedlock and that she had gone to England. It was never discussed publicly that I can recall but the story goes that when de Valera got wind of it, he threw Flynn out of the party in order to avoid scandal.[6]

It is assumed that this is what prompted Oliver J. Flanagan's jibe linking Jack Flynn to the Adoption of Children Bill in the Dáil in January 1952. The implication was certainly sufficient to prompt fisticuffs in the Members' Restaurants hours later.

* * *

With Flynn expelled from the party, at the 1943 general election, Fianna Fáil opted for a Cahersiveen solicitor, John B. Healy, to run with Fred Crowley or, as *The Kerryman* noted, Healy 'comes on in room of Mr John Flynn'.[7] Flynn didn't contest the poll or the 1944 general election either, but he attempted to recover his political career pretty quickly and decided to run as an Independent candidate at the 1948 general election. Going into that election, there was an extraordinary situation in Kerry South in that Fianna Fáil held all three seats in the constituency. Fred Crowley from Killarney and John B. Healy from Cahersiveen had won two seats at the previous general election in May 1944, but when their constituency colleague and sitting Fine Gael TD, Fionán Lynch – a minister in some of the first cabinets – was appointed a Circuit Court judge soon after, the resulting by-election was won by Fianna Fáil's Donal O'Donoghue from Glenflesk. Just a year later, in 1945, Fred Crowley's death led to another by-election, which was won by his wife, Honor Mary Crowley. Crowley, O'Donoghue and Healy were nominated as the three Fianna Fáil candidates for the 1948 general election and faced the unlikely prospect of holding all of the three seats available.

Flynn declared himself an Independent republican candidate and he held several high-profile rallies around the constituency.[8] He played up his War of Independence credentials and he claimed that Fianna Fáil no longer represented the republican tradition. John O'Leary notes that he achieved the support of many in sporting circles, including figures like Gerald Teahan from Keel, who came on as a substitute for Kerry in the Polo Grounds in the 1947 All-Ireland, and Dee O'Connor from Lawlor's Cross near Killarney, a four-time All-Ireland winner.[9] His nomination was proposed by an old IRA comrade and neighbour from Castlemaine, Dan Mulvihill, a fellow veteran of the Ballymacandy Ambush.

The February 1948 election saw Fianna Fáil lose two of their three seats. Flynn returned to the Dáil as an Independent, taking the second seat on almost 16 per cent of the vote. Patrick W. Palmer from Sneem won a seat for Fine Gael, with only Honor Crowley retaining a seat for Fianna Fáil. On his return to the Dáil, Flynn declined to support the nomination of his former party leader, Éamon de Valera, as Taoiseach. His Dáil statement on the nomination revealed something of the enmity between the pair, as he derided the record of his former party colleagues in government:

I personally do not approve of and do not intend to support Deputy Éamon de Valera as Taoiseach, as in supporting him I feel that I would have supported the Leader of a Government which had neglected my constituency for the past four years ... nothing has been done, and there has been a wholesale flight from the land and from the countryside ... As far as I can see, Government Ministers resident in Dublin consider Dublin as Ireland. They forget that we exist and that there are such places as Kerry ... Remembering what has happened in the past four years, I could not personally support Deputy Éamon de Valera as representing that regime and the Government.[10]

Nine months later, following a short absence from Kerry County Council, Flynn headed the poll in the Killorglin Electoral Area, a seat he would hold until 1960. Whatever allegations had bedevilled him in the 1940s – whether based on fact or rumour and innuendo – had a limited impact on the Castlemaine farmer's popularity.

* * *

No documentary evidence has ever been produced to suggest why Flynn was not a candidate for Fianna Fáil in 1943 and 1944, nor do the party's archives spell out the reasons explicitly. But correspondence between party headquarters and the constituency organisation just weeks after the 1948 poll refer to the difficulties caused by the Jack Flynn 'situation' and his return to the Dáil as an Independent. Writing to the then general secretary of Fianna Fáil, Tom Mullins, the chairman of the Comhairle Dáil Cheantair in Kerry South, Fr Myles Allman – a brother of the well-known War of Independence veteran Dan Allman – described the party's predicament:

13 February 1948

Dear Tom,
The situation in which our friend Jack Flynn has left us is not an enviable one. We have but one FF deputy left and she is a woman. The constituency is 70 old miles from East to West – Mrs Crowley in Killarney is over from 50 miles from the far western end.

I would like you to impress on the National Executive that while we are prepared to face up to any situation for the party's sake our position is one that almost demands the appt [sic] of a Senator at the Caherciveen end.

This is no plea for giving us back Mr J. B. Healy. Personally, I don't think that that would mend matters at all. If the organisation was let go bang [*sic*] by him as a T.D. we can't expect it to be saved by him as a Senator.... There's no flogging a dead horse.

The Fianna Fáil general secretary responded:

27 February 1948
Rev. Myles Allman P.P.
Glenflesk
Killarney
Co. Kerry

Dear Fr. Myles,
My apologies for delay in replying to yours of February 13th. To be quite honest, I found it impossible to concentrate on letter writing during the past couple of weeks. I know you will understand.

I discussed your suggestion for a senator with Mr. Kissane [outgoing Kerry North TD Eamonn Kissane] and others and they agree to do everything possible to put it into effect if you can name a suitable man who could be relied on to stand for the Dáil on the next occasion.

As the National Executive will consider Seanad nominations on Monday night, I shall be glad if you will ring or wire me on receipt of this.[11]

Flynn's exile from Fianna Fáil was to be relatively short-lived, however. He managed to retain his Dáil seat at the 1951 general election as an Independent, again denying Fianna Fáil two seats in the Kerry South three-seater. *The Kerryman* records Flynn's nominees for the 1951 poll: 'His paper was signed by Thomas O'Connor, Farrantoureen, Lower Bridge St, Killorglin (proposer); Tod Mulvihill, Main Street, Killorglin (seconder); Michael O'Neill, Dromavelly, Killorglin; Michael Johnson, Main Street, Killorglin, Thomas McGillycuddy, do [ditto]; Micheal O'Callaghan, do; Patrick Sheehy, Reen, Killorglin; James Harmon, Farrantoureen; Michael McCarthy, Main Street, Killorglin; Daniel Griffin, Main Street, Killorglin.'[12]

By this time, Flynn's animosity towards de Valera had softened considerably. Following the election, as an Independent deputy, he supported the nomination of his former party leader as Taoiseach. This was in stark contrast to the stance he had taken just three years previously. During the debate on the nomination of the Taoiseach in June 1951, he was challenged in the Dáil by Oliver J. Flanagan, who, months later, would be on the receiving end of Flynn's fist:

> I would like to hear Deputy John Flynn, in whose constituency one of the candidates was almost torn to bits. I would like to know if Deputy John Flynn told the people of South Kerry, who pulled the headlights off Deputy de Valera's car, that Deputy Éamon de Valera was going to be his choice of Taoiseach in this country … I hope and trust that, within the next ten minutes, Deputy John Flynn will tell this House, and tell the people of South Kerry and of Ireland, who watched the reception which one of the candidates got in the Deputy's constituency, whether he got a mandate from the people of South Kerry to put Deputy de Valera back as Taoiseach.[13]

Flynn declined to rise to Flanagan's bait and was gushing in his praise for his former party leader:

> I place my trust in him [De Valera] and I feel that good will come from it. In conclusion, I wish to say that I am voting for Deputy de Valera for two reasons, (1) that in my opinion he is the embodiment of the national ideal for which our people have fought and died and that he will pursue his policy to the end, and (2) that as the leader of a large Party he is in a position to govern this country and, as such, is in a better position to carry out a policy that will be acceptable to the people than Deputy [John A.] Costello [the Fine Gael leader] who would have to negotiate with a number of smaller Parties.[14]

Locally as well as nationally, by the summer of 1951, Flynn's rapprochement with Fianna Fáil was well underway. Within months of voting for de Valera as Taoiseach, Flynn was re-admitted to his former party. At a meeting of the Comhairle Dáil Ceantair in Kerry South on 10 November 1951, 'it was unanimously decided to admit Mr J. Flynn T.D. to membership of the Organisation'.[15]

✷✷✷

One of Jack Flynn's strongest allies in the Kerry South constituency was Cahersiveen party activist, Daniel (Dan) O'Donoghue, father of Ceann Comhairle John O'Donoghue. The former minister recalls that in his youth, the family had a spare room which was known as 'Jack Flynn's room' in which the TD would spend the night if he was travelling in the Cahersiveen area.[16] Dan O'Donoghue, also a veteran of the War of Independence, remained a close friend and supporter of Flynn's, even when the latter was thrown out of the party and despite the fact that Fianna Fáil TD John B. Healy was O'Donoghue's uncle and was a neighbour of the O'Donoghue family in Cahersiveen. O'Donoghue sought the Fianna Fáil nomination for the local elections of 1955 in the Killorglin Electoral Area, but failed to win the party's backing. He decided to contest the election as an Independent. Jack Flynn, by then back in the fold, appealed to O'Donoghue to stay with the organisation and said that 'he himself on one occasion had been disowned by Fianna Fáil but that he had stood by them and was now back in the ranks.'[17] Flynn's pleas fell on deaf ears and though Dan O'Donoghue didn't succeed in 1955, he was elected to Kerry County Council as an Independent in 1960. His wife, Mary, was co-opted to his seat on his death in 1964 and re-joined Fianna Fáil.

* * *

Jack Flynn retained his seat for Fianna Fáil at the general election of 1954, but he was dramatically unseated in 1957 when Sinn Féin won its first and only Dáil seat in Kerry South courtesy of John Joe Rice from Kenmare. The defeat heralded the beginning of the end of Flynn's political career and in 1960 he stood down as a member of Kerry County Council. In October 1957, Jack Flynn and his wife, Mary (née Ryle), sold their forty-acre farm and home at Brackhill, Castlemaine,[18] and moved to Killarney, where the couple ran the East Avenue House guesthouse on a site which had been owned by Mary's first husband, Denis O'Connor, a Tralee garage owner and member of the army who had died in 1946. Following the sale of that business in the 1960s, the couple retired to Tralee and lived in Caherslee. Jack Flynn died in Dublin on 22 August 1968.

'The Queen of Balochistan'

The Tarbert woman elected to the Pakistani parliament

'The Queen of Balochistan', Bridie Wren (Jehan Zeba), pictured in Pakistan in 1993 (Catherine Kelter).

Quite a number of Kerry's sons and daughters have left Ireland and made significant marks on their adopted countries, but few have had as transformative an experience as that of a young nurse from Tarbert who met and became smitten by the son of a chieftain from India. Jennifer Wren, later Jehan Zeba, went on to represent her adopted people in government, ran successful companies and earned the love and respect of her adopted people. Born Bridget (Bridie) Wren in Ballinoe, Tarmons, Tarbert, during the First World War, Bridie went to England to study to become a nurse and adopted the name Jennifer in what may have been an expression of her independence. But it was not long before she left Britain and adopted a lifestyle, a culture and a religion that were far removed from what she had been used to as the child of a family of small farmers, with four sisters and two brothers.

In 1939 she met Qazi Mohammad Musa, the son of the Khan (leader) of the Qalat District in Balochistan in what would later become Pakistan when the country won its independence. Qazi Musa was studying philosophy in Oxford at the time. His brother, Qazi Mohammad Essa was a prominent member of the Pakistani Movement and the All-India Muslims. The man regarded as the founder of Pakistan, Mohammad Ali Jinnah stayed with the family from time to time. 'We met at his college, at a party – you know what students are like,' she recalled later, 'I was a Catholic, he was a Muslim. I think I became Islamic at the time. There is no difference in any of these religions except some people believe in one god, some in another and some in lots of gods.'[1]

Qazi Musa had been matched with a wife in Pakistan when he was fourteen and his family was anxious about the new woman in his life, but they married in 1940 and Jennifer became Jehan Zeba. There were five children in the earlier marriage, but relations between the new union and Qazi Musa's previous wife remained cordial and she continued to live nearby. There had been worries that those opposed to the new marriage – and the unconventional nature of it – might lead to someone poisoning one or both of them. This concern passed in time, however. Jennifer was respectful of the ways of life and the religion of the people and they responded with admiration for her.

Qazi and Jennifer settled in Balochistan in 1947, the year after Pakistan had achieved its independence. They had one son, Ashraf Jehangir Qazi. Despite being the country's largest province, Balochistan had the highest poverty rate and the lowest literacy rate of the four provinces up until the 1970s. Its arid conditions were described by the *Daily Telegraph*: 'The area, which is hemmed in by russet mountains and tormented by dust devils and temperatures in excess of 50 degrees Celsius, was retained within the borders of British India after the Second Afghan War in 1881.'[2] Having been brought up near the banks of the Shannon, Balochistan's hot conditions must have been an enormous change for Jennifer. The couple's home was described as a 'thick, mud-walled, colonial-era home that was festooned with daggers, tigers' heads and photographs of her extravagantly whiskered in-laws'.[3]

Tragically, Qazi Musa lost his life in a road traffic accident in 1956. Jennifer remained in her husband's home town, Pishin. Having initially considered returning to Ireland with her son, aged fourteen when Qazi Musa died, she decided to remain in Pakistan. She paid a visit home to Ireland in the 1960s, but found no reason to leave the country in which she had made her home and which had warmly embraced her as a citizen. She had also been away for a considerable period of time. However, people who spoke English with her were still able to detect the remnants of her Irish accent.

She joined the National Awami (Freedom) Party and won a seat in Pakistan's first parliament (National Assembly) in 1970. She proudly signed the new Pakistan Constitution in 1973, but she continued to agitate for 'her' people and contended that there were insufficient safeguards for the community of Balochistan. She also clashed with the government due to her refusal to cover her head with a veil or wear the burqa. It was a defiant position to take in a time of political turmoil. She also aggravated sections of the country by espousing education, particularly for women. She demonstrated her courage when she acted as a go-between for the groups that had taken up arms in resurrection and the government. She was never afraid of taking risks if she thought that they were the best course of action. The imposition of martial law ended her seven-year term in the National Assembly, but she remained the tribal head in her region and continued to irritate the government through her promotion of education and her setting-up of both the first women's association and the first family-planning clinic in the region. 'You can't liberate women until you liberate men,' she remarked.[4] For the tribesmen, she always remained 'Mummy Jennifer', and was christened the 'Queen of Balochistan'.

Jennifer ran an ice plant for a time and also provided assistance to Afghan refugees who had fled the Soviet invasion. In her later years, 'visiting foreign journalists mused about how the wild, tribal frontier, where women are in purdah and even goatherds carry Kalashnikovs, was an unlikely place to find an elderly Irish widow serving afternoon tea'.[5] The area later became a stronghold for the Taliban and since then has been generally out of bounds to foreigners. Jennifer (Jehan) Zeba died at the age of ninety on 12 January 2008. Her funeral through Pishin was attended by thousands and the doors and windows of the town were shuttered up. She was laid to rest in the traditional Qazi burial ground and President Pervez Musharraf telephoned her and Qasi Musa's son, Ashraf, to convey his condolences. Ashraf became a senior diplomat and served as ambassador to the United States for a period.

5

'Mr and Mrs Fred'

Kerry's Original Political Power Couple

Their social, class, family and political backgrounds could hardly have been more different. One was an IRA gun-runner who was born on a farm in rural north Cork and who fought British forces at some of the seminal engagements of the War of Independence in Kerry. The other was the daughter of a Westminster parliamentarian and a member of one of Dublin's best-known and wealthiest merchant families who grew up in one of London's most affluent suburbs. They came from opposite ends of the social and political divide. But between them the couple represented the constituency of Kerry South in Dáil Éireann for just shy of forty years without a breach. Frederick Hugh Crowley and Honor Mary Boland also set a political record when, on his death in 1945, Honor Mary became the first woman in Irish political history to succeed her husband at a by-election to the Dáil. Honor also holds the distinction of being the first female TD ever elected in Kerry.

Honor Mary Boland was born on 19 October 1903 in Dublin, the eldest of six children of John Mary Pius Boland and his wife, Eileen (Eily) Quirk Moloney, a native of Melbourne, Australia, and of Irish ancestry. Moloney was from a wealthy family who lived in various hotels around Europe, having left Australia after a lengthy drought in Victoria in 1892. John Pius Boland was a member of the famous – and equally wealthy – baking and flour-milling family which owned Boland's Mills in Dublin, the largest bakery in Ireland, coincidentally one of the buildings occupied by rebels during the 1916 Rising. Boland's own life story is of interest. He was born on Capel Street in Dublin on 16 September 1870 and both his parents died when he was a child. He was raised, along with six siblings, by his mother's half-brother, the auxiliary bishop of Dublin, Dr Nicholas Donnelly.

As a child, he and his siblings often holidayed on Rossdohan Island near Sneem, where he is said to have first developed his love of Kerry.[1] He was educated in Dublin, Birmingham and Bonn before graduating with a BA from London University in 1892 and a MA from Oxford. He was called to the Bar in 1897.

A keen sportsman who played rugby and tennis at college, Boland excelled at tennis and was invited to attend the first Olympic Games in Athens in 1896. He won the singles and doubles finals – with Friedrich Traun of Germany in the latter competition. He ranks as both Britain's and Ireland's first Olympic champion. At the Games, Boland objected when the Union Jack was hoisted alongside the German flag in Athens when he won the doubles, demanding a green flag with a harp; it was still not available when he won the singles. The presentations were of silver rather than gold, silver and bronze at this time. During holidays in the south-west of Ireland as he grew older, Boland was moved by the high levels of illiteracy and poverty in the area and also developed a love for the Irish language.[2] Though he had been called to the Bar, instead of a legal career, he chose politics. His daughter, Bridget, later explained part of his motivation:

> My father discovered to his horror that practically no-one [in the south-west of Ireland] could read and write. In such schools as there were, only English was allowed to be taught, and, particularly in mountain country where they might be six or eight miles from a school and with no transport of course, if the children attended at all the lessons were in a language they didn't speak, and the teachers were even forbidden to answer questions in Irish ... So largely from a desire to secure better education, particularly in the South and West, my father became actively nationalist.[3]

Aged just thirty, Boland was elected the Irish Parliamentary Party MP for South Kerry in 1900 – he was the only candidate – and became party whip in Westminster in 1906. In parliament, he championed issues like trade, education and the Irish language and was instrumental in the patenting of the Irish Trade Mark and the setting-up of the National University of Ireland. Among his constituency initiatives were the development of a carpet factory in Glenbeigh, as well as an Irish summer school in the area and the introduction of New Zealand flax as a crop in south Kerry. In 1918, Boland became acting Chief Whip of the Irish Parliamentary Party at Westminster, but he stood down at the December 1918 general election in which Sinn Féin's Fionán Lynch won the South Kerry seat as that party surged to win seats across the country. So embittered was he at the loss of his seat and the rise of a party which he abhorred that Boland did not return to Kerry for over thirty years – and then only returned to visit his daughter, Honor, who resided in Killarney. Boland later published a memoir, *Irishman's Day: A Day in the Life of an Irish MP* (1944), which drew on his experiences of parliamentary life and describes his constituency. He received an honorary doctorate in law from the National University and he died in London on St Patrick's Day, 1958.

Honor Boland had something of an idyllic childhood. While her father was an MP, the family lived at 40 St George's Square, a five-storey terraced house in Pimlico in London a short distance from Westminster, which was replete with gardeners, a cook and numerous other servants. When parliament wasn't sitting, the Boland family lived in Dublin. Honor holidayed in south Kerry with her family as a child; they rented the home of the Liberator, Daniel O'Connell, in Derrynane. Honor, her brother and four sisters 'lived barefoot and ran wild, seals basked on the foreshore, everyone caught enormous fish, and the bats were chased out of the bedrooms every night with tennis racquets'.[4] Honor attended school at the Convent of the Sacred Heart in Roehampton in Surrey, where her mother was Head of School. Mrs Boland was a prominent Catholic during her time in London, serving as general secretary of the Catholic Truth Society of England for many years. The college was also attended by Honor's sister, Bridget Boland, who became a well-known playwright, novelist and screen-writer; she later documented her childhood and that of her siblings in an autobiographical work, *At My Mother's Knee* (1978). Honor began her career as a social worker in London. Her work 'was among the blind in the cathedral parish of Westminster bringing them to Mass on Sundays and looking after their needs generally. She also belonged to the committee which provides holidays for children from the slums'.[5]

* * *

Frederick (Fred) Hugh Crowley was born in Gurteen, near Banteer, County Cork, to Michael and Honor Crowley (née Cronin) on New

Year's Eve 1880. His father operated the Rathmore Mills and was one of the founder members of the Land and Labour Association, with Michael Davitt. Fred attended the North Monastery School in Cork City and received a diploma in textile manufacturing from the University of Leeds in 1912. Shortly after his return to Ireland, his family moved to Rathmore, close to the Cork–Kerry border, where they farmed. Fred joined the Irish Volunteers in Rathmore and was a member of the local company at the time of the Easter Rising. He was also an enthusiastic member of the Gaelic League. A veteran of the War of Independence, he was a key figure in the IRA in Kerry in the early 1920s and was involved in many important incidents, such as the Headford Junction Ambush in 1921 alongside fellow future Kerry TDs like Johnny Connor and Thomas McEllistrim.

Fred Crowley and Honor Mary Boland met in the late 1930s. He had been the Fianna Fáil TD for Kerry South since 1927. When Honor introduced her prospective husband – now a member of the independent national parliament representing the constituency her father once had at Westminster – to her father, John Pius, the encounter was fraught with the usual awkwardness between a man and his future son-in-law at their first introduction. However, they soon found something of common interest to discuss, as Honor's sister, Bridget, recalls:

Honor told Maureen [their sister] and me that Fred Crowley had asked her to marry him. What on earth would this do to my father? Fred at the age of sixteen had run away from home to join the IRA in the Easter Rising, and had now for years been a member of the Dáil, for part of my father's old constituency in South Kerry. We decided to introduce him initially just as a friend. We sat on the edge of our chairs to watch how they would get on. Fred was paralysed at first, but after a while he mentioned a part of the constituency where he was trying to get a road built. My father, who had been politely struggling to keep some sort of conversation with this poor dear shy young man, sat up, 'Do you mean to tell me they haven't built that road yet?'

'They have not! Would you believe it?!'
'And the bridge to Valencia [sic] Island?'
'Nor that!'

They were off, roads and bridges and schools and local industries – it was the well-being of the Kerryman that was really all either of them cared about.[6]

The bridge from the mainland to Valentia Island off the south Kerry coast wasn't built for many years thereafter; it would continue to be a controversial political issue locally and ironically it dominated the by-election campaign which followed Honor's death in 1966. Fred and Honor married in 1939. At the time, Fred – as an ex-IRA man – was being followed while in England by Special Branch officers. During the wedding reception in London, he noticed two detectives hanging around 'unobtrusively' outside. With his brother-in-law, Brendan, he approached the pair and they invited them to join the celebrations, which they did.[7] The couple resided at Danesfort on the outskirts of Killarney and John Pius Boland often stayed with them at their home in his constituency of old. He had been pre-deceased by his wife in 1937.

* * *

Fred Crowley's political career was well established by the time he met the daughter of his constituency predecessor. He was first elected to Kerry County Council in 1917 for the Killarney Electoral Division and for the Killarney Electoral Area from 1926 – he frequently topped the poll in that district in the 1930s and 1940s. Like so many TDs, the council seat gave Crowley a profile and platform for national politics and he was first elected to the Dáil at the September 1927 general election; he had stood as a candidate at the June 1927 general election, polling 3,370 votes, but failed to win a seat. From 1937, when Kerry became two constituencies, Crowley – once dubbed by the *Cork Examiner* as 'one of Kerry's live wire representatives in An Dáil'[8] – represented Kerry South. Reflecting his interest in rural and agricultural affairs, he was president of the Irish National Ploughing Championships, which took place on Lord Kenmare's estate in Killarney in February 1939. He was also a director of the Irish Tourist Association, president of the Killarney Trout Anglers' Association and a member of the Governing Body of University College Cork.

In the Dáil, Crowley's contributions were frequent and dealt with the usual bread-and-butter topics for any rural deputy – forestry, turbary rights for tenants (in places like Tooreencahill and Tureenamult, for example), roads, land drainage schemes, employment and farming issues. Textiles and new industries were regularly discussed, as was the need for the establishment of technical schools to teach textiles. This was a familiar topic for Crowley, who was drawing on his own educational experience, and his speeches were usually laden with contemporaneous statistics and research findings. In a debate in 1942, he advocated that pubs in rural areas be allowed to open on Sundays and in the mornings:

> it would mean a great hardship on the farming community if the public houses did not open till 10 o'clock in the morning. Anybody who knows the conditions under which farmers have to travel to a fair on a cold, frosty day, or on a wet and blustery day, arriving at 6 o'clock in the morning, will realise that there is no sense in expecting these farmers to wait for a drink until the public houses open at ten o'clock.[9]

He took a slightly different approach to the consumption of liquor at dances however, arguing 'that all drinks at dances should be abolished. When I say that, you can call me a pussyfoot, if you like, but I am very emphatic about the abuses that have taken place at dances'.[10] The effects of the dancehall phenomenon were also outlined in a letter to the *Irish Press*:

> The waves of restless feeling, of anxiety to get away from home, and of being in state of perpetual motion, which have spread throughout the world, seems now to have touched the shores of this country. The serious side is that the rush for indoor amusement has hit hard the manly outdoor sport so prevalent in this country twenty years ago.[11]

For a brief period in the mid-1940s, Fred Crowley was one of three Fianna Fáil TDs who held all available seats in Kerry South. At the May 1944 general election, Crowley had headed the poll and was elected alongside party colleague John B. Healy from Cahersiveen and Fine Gael's former minister Fionán Lynch of Waterville. Just a few months later, however, Lynch was appointed a Circuit Court judge and had to step down from the Dáil. In the resultant by-election, the Fianna Fáil candidate, Glenflesk teacher Donal O'Donoghue, was elected, giving that party an unprecedented and unparalleled three seats in the constituency.

* * *

Fred Crowley died while still a TD on 5 May 1945 after a period of ill health. He and Honor had no children and the attention of party headquarters quickly turned to his widow, then aged just forty-one, to fill the political void. She was seen as the obvious candidate for the by-election. Asking the wife of a recently deceased deputy to stand for the Dáil was dubbed by Fianna Fáil's John O'Leary as the 'put up the widow' phenomenon and this was by no means the only example of the phenomenon in Irish politics.[12] Polling day for the by-election was set for 4 December 1945. The Fianna Fáil selection convention was held on 10 November and was presided over by the Minister for Lands, Seán Moylan. Crowley's sole opponent in the poll was Senator Edmund Horan of Clann na Talmhan. A farmer from Rathmore, Firies, he had come very close to being elected in the May 1944 general election when he stood as an Independent and won 23 per cent of the poll. He was subsequently elected on the Agricultural Panel of the Fifth Seanad. He joined the agrarian party, Clann na Talmhan, which had yet to gain any major foothold in Kerry, but would later secure several county council seats through Bill Dennehy, Patrick Woulfe and Francis Chute. Fine Gael, meanwhile, had initially chosen Patrick Palmer, a teacher from Sneem, to contest the by-election, but he was quickly withdrawn – four other by-elections were being held on the same date and the party chose to focus its resources on just one, in Clare, where it was defending a seat it already held.

The Taoiseach, Éamon de Valera, spoke in support of Honor Crowley at rallies in Cahersiveen, Killorglin and Killarney. When the votes were counted, Crowley outpolled Horan by 10,483 votes to 8,018. On her election, Crowley said she was 'more than a little proud of the fact that she was the first woman ever to represent a Kerry constituency'.[13] Apart from succeeding Fred Crowley in Leinster House, she also took over her late husband's county council seat, retaining it at each local authority election until her death and topping the poll in the Killarney Electoral Area at each election. Her successor in the Dáil, John O'Leary, recalled that Honor was widely known as 'Mrs Fred', such was the esteem in which her husband was held. He described her popularity:

> Mrs Crowley was a very popular TD and this was reflected in the fact that she never lost a general election or a county council election as long as she was in politics. During elections, I never heard anything

bad said about her. She had a particular appeal among women voters which was a great advantage to her.[14]

One of just five women in the Dáil when she took up her seat in 1945, Honor Crowley immersed herself in constituency work, receiving an average of forty letters per day as a TD.[15] She tabled many parliamentary questions during her Dáil career and was also a regular contributor to debates on a range of issues, such as widow's pensions, psychiatric services, children's health, industrial development, road conditions and housing, frequently citing her experience as a county councillor. She showed the same interest in tourism as her late husband, who had been a director of the Irish Tourist Association. The impact on tourism of the rain in Killarney was the focus of one Dáil contribution:

> Quite often the weather is so wet that people just cannot leave the hotel or guest house. Many of them take hotel or guest house accommodation on the basis of bed and breakfast and after breakfast have to go out and amuse themselves. Quite often the rain is pouring down and they have nowhere to go. The Tourist Board should make provision for indoor amusements … On a week day they can go into the shops but on a Sunday they are just wandering about in mackintoshes looking very miserable and deciding never to come back again. If the Tourist Board are helped by way of grant or something else they could encourage tourists to stay here even when the weather is bad.[16]

She also appeared to have had difficulty convincing colleagues of the merits of investing in tourism at a time when the industry was in its infancy:

> A lot of people do not realise that the tourist industry benefits everybody. When trying to put through a grant for the Tourist Association through the county council, I know that quite often the farmers on the council will say: 'What good is it to us: it is only good for the hotels in Killarney and elsewhere?' They do not realise that, after all, the tourists eat the produce of the farms.[17]

Many of her contributions had women's issues at their heart, such as a discussion on the uniforms of the first female members of An Garda Síochána in 1958:

I hope the girls will be well turned out. I hope they will be smartly dressed, that their uniform will be smart and will look good. I hope it will not be frumpish but, instead, well-designed and attractive. The girls will have that extra feeling of smartness if they know they look smart and they will be better Guards for that reason.[18]

She also advocated for welfare centres where mothers could share their child-rearing experiences and learn skills as basic as how to read a clinical thermometer. She also called for greater availability and choice of medical services for women.[19]

Not afraid to challenge a male-dominated Dáil, Crowley disagreed with speakers who suggested women should not be employed in particular factories: 'Most women are neat with their fingers and their talents could be used in the factories to great advantage.'[20] The post-war price of household commodities also occupied her mind and she gave an insight into the demands on the housewife of the time:

Though the housewife may read in the paper that the cost of living is stationary, if she goes into shops to do her weekly shopping and finds the prices have gone up, you would not blame her for thinking that, though the cost of living had officially remained stationary, the cost of housekeeping has definitely gone up … I will take two or three articles used in every household in rural Ireland. One of them is oatmeal. Oatmeal, to my mind, should be one of the cheap commodities, but recently it went up very much in price. If every child going to school in the winter and every man going to work could have a hot meal of porridge for his breakfast, it would stand him in good stead during the day, especially when you realise that many men depend on bread and tea only for their midday meal. Another thing that has gone up is sausages. The cost of bacon and meat is so high that the housewife has often to rely on sausages to fill the gap.[21]

Honor Crowley became the first woman to represent Ireland on the Council of Europe when she was appointed to become part of the Irish delegation to its meetings by Éamon de Valera in 1954. The *Irish Independent* reporter who covered the first council meeting she attended in Strasbourg in October 1954 noted that 'it was in an atmosphere of unusual tenseness that Mrs Honor Crowley TD made her debut at Strasbourg … feminine representation altogether numbered about six, she told me, including energetic Miss Klompe from Holland who appears to be a veteran of Council meetings ... "Anything", she adds, "that brings politicians from various countries together for international discussion is good." Mrs Crowley, the writer observed, was most impressed by the evening's entertainment for delegates, in which 'the male dancer, lightly clinging to the hand of his almost immobile partner, tumbled, leaped, and pirouetted around her [Crowley] with frenzied enthusiasm'.[22]

* * *

In her first general election proper in 1948 and throughout the 1950s, Honor Crowley's Dáil seat was rarely in jeopardy. In his memoirs, John O'Leary described the electioneering techniques of the time, which added to the theatricality of politics and also secured the party seat:

> A marching band would be hired to drum up a bit of atmosphere and it would do a couple of rounds of the town before the main event. We would have a platform up in College Square ready to go. Mackey Shea, or occasionally Batt O'Connor, would supply the lorry. Key to the success of any rally was a good public address system – I came to be a great believer in a decent loudspeaker, a good microphone and, most importantly, good, strong batteries to drive the amplification. Apart from allowing Mrs Crowley to be heard over the noise from the thousands gathered, it also meant that hecklers could be drowned out. Con O'Leary, the electrician in Plunkett Street, used to supply the sound system, as did Jack Scully now and again; he had an electrical shop under the Town Hall clock.[23]

Despite the electoral successes, during Crowley's career, the strength of the party organisation she had inherited from her husband, particularly in Killarney and east Kerry, waned and the cumann structure for which Fianna Fáil was renowned went into decline. In May 1956, the then party leader, Seán Lemass, wrote to Honor Crowley and her then constituency colleague, Jack Flynn, saying he was 'somewhat perturbed to notice the considerable falling off in the number of Cumainn registered in Kerry South for this year'.[24] John O'Leary, who had become a key constituency organiser for Crowley, noted a fall-off in the number of cumanns registered with party headquarters, but laid the blame at the door of Éamon de Valera – who he believed was disinterested in the party network – as much as the local TDs. From 1961, Crowley was joined in the Dáil by party colleague Timothy 'Chub' O'Connor from Killorglin and they divided the constituency to great effect to maximise the party vote. She came close, however, to losing her Dáil seat at the 1965 general election when she had only forty-five votes to spare over Labour's Michael Moynihan, a senior trade union activist from Killarney. It was also the first election outing for Dingle's Michael Begley of Fine Gael – later a TD and junior minister – who polled well. But the status quo in Kerry South was not disturbed and Timothy 'Chub' O'Connor (FF) and Patrick Connor (FG) retained their seats.

Following her husband's death, Honor Crowley had moved from her home at Danesfort to live with friends, Tim and Frances O'Sullivan, on Woodlawn Road, Killarney. In the summer of 1966, she took ill and received medical treatment in London. She died on 18 October 1966, a day before her sixty-third birthday. Her death led to a by-election in

Frederick (Fred) Hugh Crowley, Fianna Fáil TD for Kerry South, 1927–45 (Michael Hand).

Honor Mary Crowley, Fianna Fáil TD for Kerry South, 1945–66.

President Éamon de Valera lays a wreath on Honor Crowley's grave following her funeral at Muckross Abbey in October 1966 (*The Kerryman*).

Kerry South in which her seat was won by party colleague John O'Leary in a campaign which became part of the political folklore of Kerry. The late TD's remains were removed from O'Sullivan's house in Dromhall to St Mary's Cathedral for Mass the following morning. Present were the Taoiseach, Seán Lemass, and the president, Éamon de Valera. De Valera had paid a private visit to her at her home in the days before her death. Her sisters, Maureen Boland, Ann Shaw and Bridget Boland, joined the rank and file of the local party organisation in mourning the loss. Bridget described how:

> the whole town of Killarney went into mourning with flags at half-mast on all the public buildings, and the President and the entire Cabinet and most of the Opposition front bench came down to join the 'mountainy men' who came from all over Kerry for the funeral. Several of the latter said to me: 'Yours is a wonderful family, Miss Boland, you'd never know any of them were politicians at all.'[25]

The remains were removed from the cathedral to Muckross Abbey, where Crowley had asked to be buried; her husband Fred had been interred in his native Dromtariffe, near Banteer in north-west Cork, but his remains were brought to Muckross Abbey for burial alongside his wife a few years later. Their modest headstone a short distance from the walls of the Franciscan abbey bears the inscription 'Crowley' and states that it was 'Erected by their friends'. In a tribute paid to her in the Dáil on the day she died, Seán Lemass said that 'her devoted and dedicated public service was in the highest and best traditions of Irish public life, and fully in keeping, also, with the best traditions of the family from which she came'.[26]

6

'If there are women candidates, we hope they will be of the right kind'

The Fate of Kerry's Women Politicians

With the establishment of the new county and urban district councils in 1899, women could become members of the new local authorities, but it took a while before any woman succeeded in filling such a position in Kerry. Women were eligible to contest positions on the Boards of Guardians (BGs) and Rural District Councils (RDCs) and some women were elected to the county and urban authorities in 1899, but none won a seat in Kerry. Anne Margaret Rowan of 13 Princes Quay was a member of the Tralee Poor Law Guardians, having been elected along with Francis Mary Philipa Donovan in March 1897, and she did put herself forward for the Urban Council poll, but finished well down the field. Miss Donovan had her brother St John as a colleague, while Annie Rowan's brother, Lieutenant-Colonel Rowan, was also a member of the Guardians. St John was elected chairman of the inaugural county council in April 1899, shortly after Miss Donovan herself was elected in the Ballynahaglish Division to the Tralee RDC/BG. Their lives were to remain very close.

The Killarney Poor Law Guardians also acquired a female member at the 1899 election, Theresa Leonard of New Street, who headed the poll, which included six male candidates in the Killarney Union. Her husband, Maurice, was already well established in the Board of Guardians and he was also a member of, and indeed chaired, the old Killarney Town Commission, as well as being a member of the Grand Jury. He was the agent for Lord Kenmare, having taken over that role from Sam Hussey on his retirement in 1886. When he married Theresa in December 1893, he became her second husband. She had previously been married to a solicitor, the late Eugene Downing. She was elected to the Killarney Board of Guardians in the Killarney Rural Division in 1899 and this time around she was joined by Elizabeth, Viscountess Castlerosse, a daughter of the 1st Baron Revelstoke, Edward Charles Baring. Lady Castlerosse was the wife of Valentine Browne, the 5th Earl of Kenmare, who was one of the first members of Kerry County Council. Although the Brownes were Roman Catholic, the earl held unionist views and, as a peer of the realm, sat in the House of Lords. The family first arrived in Killarney in the sixteenth century when an earlier Valentine Browne had been appointed Surveyor General of Ireland. Lady Castlerosse, of Killarney House, devoted much of her energy to improving housing for the poor in Killarney.

Getting votes was not easy for women, as illustrated by the profile of the electorate that gave Mrs Leonard her seat on the Board of Guardians in 1899: 340 male voters and 120 female voters. Tralee also introduced two women members in its Rural District Council election in 1899, Mary E. Harrington (née Cremin) of Nelson Street (now Ashe Street), wife of the proprietor and editor of the *Kerry Sentinel* Ned Harrington, and Francis Donovan, whose parents, Sir Henry and Lady Donovan, had decided to give her the male rather than the female version of her name. This pair, and Miss Rowan, differed somewhat from the two women elected in Killarney as they were associated with the suffragette movement, whereas Lady Castlerosse and Theresa Leonard were very much supporters of the establishment. Mrs Leonard was, however, a member of the Women's Poor Law Guardian Committee along with Annie Rowan and Francis Donovan, who was the president of the organisation. Unfortunately, Mrs Harrington's term of service proved a short one, for she died on 11 June 1900. Another Mary Harrington, of the Monster House, 35 The Mall, a widow running a bar/grocery shop and bakery, was co-opted to replace her, but she lost her seat in the June 1902 election. Miss Donovan, on the other hand, won a succession of district and Guardians elections and had a lengthy term of service. She had been planning to become a nun with the Bon Secours order, but left when her sister-in-law Susan died to work as a governess for her brother St John's four young children.

A formidable lady, Donovan delighted in swimming across Tralee Bay from her brother's home at Seafield, The Spa, and she taught her charges how to swim. She certainly caused consternation among some of her colleagues when she proposed that drink be banned from meetings and that any member found to be under the influence should suffer sanctions. It is a little ironic that the other candidate elected in some of these elections was Thomas Healy, of the Mall, Tralee, who was also (for a time) a member of both Kerry County Council and Tralee Urban Council. He outpolled Miss Donovan's brother St John Donovan for the seat on Kerry County Council in the Ardfert Electoral Division in 1908. The former chairman complained that some ballot boxes had been interfered with, but a recount only reduced the margin of Healy's win. When Healy again won the contest for the division in 1911, Donovan felt obliged to seek a petition to unseat him for supplying drink to voters and two months after the election, he succeeded in the court. However, he did not take up the seat.

*　*　*

The first successful female candidate to be elected to one of the principal four councils in the county was Bibiana 'O'S' Foran, who won her seat on Listowel UDC in 1908, but this did not lead to a rush of other women putting themselves before the electorate. Foran had already earned herself a place on Listowel Urban Guardians in 1905 and also sat on the Tralee Union of Guardians and Rural Councils. She and her husband Jeremiah had bought the Northern Star pub on Lower William Street in Listowel in 1901 and re-opened it under the name The Horseshoe Bar. She was particularly active in organisations endeavouring to improve health and welfare in the community. She was elected Cathaoirleach of the Listowel Board of Guardians (although not the RDC), but she went on to take her commitment to a national level, becoming a member of the Women's National Health Association after attending the launch of the organisation in Dublin in 1907. She later organised the local branch of the body's Sláinte Insurance Society. She was also an inaugural member of the Peamount Sanatorium and showed great commitment to the fight against tuberculosis.

In 1908, Foran presented a silver watch to the Listowel Feis committee for the winner of the competition for the best Irish essay on 'Tuberculosis and How to Prevent It'. She was listed among the candidates for the 1914 UDC election, but was not elected. Bibiana Foran retired to 1 Seaview Park, Ballybunion, in later life and died at the age of eighty-four on St Patrick's Day, 1946, after some years of suffering from indifferent health. Female public representatives continued to be rare enough to be the subject of curiosity for some time.

A Cahersiveen couple, Maurice and Teresa Fitzgerald, both won seats on their local Emlagh Division of the Rural District Council in 1911, Maurice having been an outgoing member. Teresa and Maurice ran the Kenneigh Hotel between Cahersiveen and Waterville. Teresa did not seek re-election to the RDC in 1914 and Maurice lost his county council seat. He was defeated by 109 votes, but a total of 280 votes had been declared invalid. However, 192 of these – constituting the entire poll at the booth – had been incorrectly declared 'spoiled' by the returning officer at the Ballinskelligs polling station because the voter registration forms were on the ballot papers. *The Kerry Evening Post* noted that, 'The irony of the matter is that the presiding officer at Ballinskelligs [O'Connell] who made the blunder of spoiling 192 votes is a cousin to the defeated candidate, and had been recommended by him to the Returning Officers as a competent presiding officer.' Maurice lodged a petition on the result, but the outcome remained unchanged. He stood unsuccessfully for the council in 1926.

Mary O'Shea, of Valentia Road, Cahersiveen, was the wife of James J. O'Shea, a publican. She was elected to the Cahersiveen Rural District Council in 1911 and headed the poll in the Killorglin Electoral Area to win her county seat in 1926. The couple ran the Central Bar and James was also a shoemaker. They had three children, both John and Joan becoming doctors and Mary Etta who married Thomas Comerford, an accountant in the Provincial Bank. Joan married Dr Niall O'Higgins, a brother of Kevin O'Higgins who was assassinated in 1927. Mary's grandson Dr Jim Comerford recalls that she told him she ran for the local authority following 'a dare' from republicans. James died relatively young and Mary was a widow for almost fifty years. She passed away on 6 March 1952 aged 85. The next woman to sit on an urban council did so with a flourish: Maud Walsh outpolled all but one candidate to win her seat on Tralee UDC in 1914. She took an impressive 849 first preferences, with the next candidate on the schedule getting 785. Mrs Walsh was originally from Wexford, the sister of Lord Justice James O'Connor. She was married to solicitor Harry Walsh, a son of one of the members of the inaugural Tralee UDC John Walsh, a director of John Donovan & Sons, the milling company, and also a member of the Harbour Board. John chaired the council from 1905 to 1909 and died in February 1915. Maud and Harry lived at Derrybeg, Oakpark, and Harry was the vice-chairman of the Tralee

Board of Guardians and Rural Council when he died in November 1916. Following his death, Maud moved to Dublin and in 1927, she was elected to Pembroke Urban District Council as vice-chairperson. When Pembroke Union District Council was abolished in 1930 and merged into Dublin City Council, she remained a member. She died in May 1940.

∗ ∗ ∗

However, women were not universally welcomed on these government bodies. When Maud Walsh was proposed for the vice-chair of the Tralee Board of Guardians, one of the members stated that he had no problem with the lady as a member, but would not abide her being in the chair and left the meeting. The *Kerry Weekly Reporter* of 3 January 1920 did not consider more women councillors as necessarily worthwhile either. Under the heading 'Notes on News', it read:

> Women as public representatives would, it is said, not allow men all their own way, and would in fact check the sterner sex, if they were inclined to be extravagant. That is generally true of the home which unprogressive persons say is the proper sphere for woman. The man is tamed in the home, and it would be a good thing from the public point of view, if the man in his representative capacity was restricted somewhat in his efforts – whenever these efforts run in the wrong direction. But women too can be extravagant, and such types we do want to represent us … If there are women candidates, we hope they will be of the right kind.[1]

∗ ∗ ∗

The writer in the *Kerry Weekly Reporter*, a paper owned by the Raymond family which adhered to broadly unionist convictions, would certainly have been thoroughly dismayed by the next woman to break into politics, for this was a lady of some significance, not least because she was the first woman elected to Kerry County Council. The former Honourable Albinia Lucy Brodrick was the fifth daughter of William Brodrick, 8th Viscount Midleton. Her brother St John, 1st Earl of Midleton, was the nominal leader of the Irish Unionist Alliance and later Secretary of State for War and Secretary of State for India. Albinia was privately educated and even wrote a song for Irish unionists ('Irishmen Stand'). She trained as a nurse. But a couple of spells spent learning Irish around Cork and the Gaeltacht revealed to her the deep poverty in which many people were living in rural Ireland and in 1908 she bought a house and over thirteen acres near Westcove, Caherdaniel, and set up an agricultural co-operative. She visited the US to raise funds to establish a hospital and named the property Ballincoona ('the Home of Help'). The executions following the Rising seemed to convince her to adopt a different approach and she joined Cumann na mBan and Sinn Féin.

Elected to Kerry County Council in 1920 under an Irish reconfiguration of her name, Gobnait Ní Bhruadair, she sheltered IRA men at the hospital. She took the anti-Treaty side in the Civil War. She was shot and wounded in April 1923 and was subsequently arrested. She went on hunger strike before being released. Gobnait became the proprietor of the Sinn Féin paper *Irish Freedom* from 1926 to 1937, acting as editor in later years, and she also founded the right-wing republican Mná na Poblachta in 1930s. Brodrick remained a Church of Ireland member, however, and played the harmonium in Sneem Church. She died in 1955 and was buried in Sneem before a large gathering that included a representative of Taoiseach Éamon de Valera and a number of other prominent people. The pall-bearers included John Joe Rice, who would be elected Sinn Féin TD for Kerry South two years later. As for the writer in the *Kerry Weekly Reporter*, that paper had ceased to be published in the year she was elected to the council.

The 1920 elections also provided a seat on Killarney UDC for Kate M. Breen of High Street, who was standing on behalf of Sinn Féin. Among her ten brothers were Canon John Breen, who would become president of St Brendan's College, and Fr Joseph Breen, who is commemorated in the title of the grounds of Kenmare Shamrocks GAA club. Another brother, Fr Francis, was a curate in Killorglin, but he died at a relatively young age. Perhaps the force of this female councillor is best illustrated by an early motion to the UDC to remove the names of anyone associated with the British administration from signage on the streets of her native town and have the streets rededicated to either patriots or saints. Breen won her seat on the county council in 1926 as a republican, rather than as part of Sinn Féin, but when she was re-elected in 1928, she had aligned herself with Fianna Fáil. She was elected vice-chairman of the council and became the chairman of the Board of Health; it is significant that it was during the 1930s that both the tuberculosis treatment hospital at Edenburn and St Catherine's County Hospital at Rathass, Tralee, were opened. She was nominated to the General Council of County Councils (of which she was also the vice-chairman), was a member of the Governing Body of University College Dublin and, in 1933, she was appointed to the inaugural Food Prices Commission. In that year, she moved to Castlegregory, where her brother John was the parish priest, and did not put her name forward for the 1934 Killarney town election. However, the move to the Tralee Electoral Area did not prevent her from retaining her seat at county level. She was a candidate to represent Fianna Fáil for the 1937 general election, but lost out to Tom McEllistrim and Eamonn Kissane. She died shortly after the national poll, on Christmas Day, 1937.

Breen was directly succeeded as chair of the Board of Health by another female member, Sheila O'Neill of Henry Street, Kenmare, where Sheila and her husband Arthur operated a public house. Arthur had also chaired the Board of Health for a spell, but he passed away in August 1935 aged just forty-two and Sheila was co-opted to take his seat. Sheila was elected vice-chair of the General Council of County Councils and was the first woman in the country to be elected to a Conservatory Board when she was appointed to the Kenmare Board from 1936 to 1942, even chairing that body for a period. In her later life, she was the branch manager in the Department of Social Welfare in Kenmare and acted as a National Health Agent. She died in Dublin in July 1964.

* * *

It took some time for a woman to attain the chair of any of the four local authorities in Kerry, despite these early breakthroughs. But, in fact, even women members became relatively rare: after Sheila O'Neill was defeated in 1942, Kerry County Council did not have a women member among their twenty-six members for some years. This deficit was rectified when Honor Crowley (FF), herself the daughter of a former MP and the widow of Deputy Fred Crowley, was co-opted onto the council in May 1945. Crowley proved politically resilient, never failing to get re-elected until her death in October 1966. Fianna Fáil's Kit Ahern, later a senator, was elected in the June 1967 election and ten years later she became the first woman to chair Kerry County Council. Ahern, once described by *The Kerryman* as 'a small, neat woman',[2] would win a Dáil seat in Kerry North in 1977 and enjoy a healthy political rivalry with her colleague, Thomas McEllistrim. Apart from Ahern, Mary O'Donoghue (FF, 1982–3), Toiréasa Ferris (SF, 2005–6) and Norma Foley (FF, 2018–19) have also been chairpersons. One of the principal obstacles to the election of women to chair the bodies was that there were no – or at least very few – female members of the authorities. There was an interval of over eleven years between Mrs Crowley's arrival and Kathleen O'Connor's co-option in tragic circumstances in March 1956 to fill the seat of her late father Johnny Connor. O'Connor was returned to the Dáil in the by-election to replace him in February 1956 and Caoimhín Ó Cinnéide from Dingle was co-opted to her seat on the council a year later.

Mary O'Donoghue from Cahersiveen was another formidable vote-getter and was co-opted to replace her late husband Dan in 1964. Though pregnant at the time, she promised her husband on his deathbed that she would take his place in the Killorglin Electoral Area and she retained the seat until 1985, when her son, John O'Donoghue, later a cabinet minister and Ceann Comhairle, replaced her. John later recalled that as a widow, his mother handled her political career with aplomb: 'She was a draper, a publican, drove a hackney car, had a small farm, was an insurance agent, an auctioneer, a councillor, and she sold loose tea and sugar.'[3] Another son, Paul, also a county councillor until 2014, described the male-dominated political world in which their mother found herself:

> My mother often said that when she went into the council first, there were a lot of male conservatives there at the time who found it difficult to see a woman coming in and some who found it extremely unusual to find a very heavily pregnant young woman from south Kerry coming in to take a seat. She often said there were a lot of raised eyebrows at that time.[4]

Republican in her outlook, she flew a black flag outside her home on Main Street, Cahersiveen, during the H-Block hunger strikes in the early 1980s. Often mooted as a Dáil candidate, she never won a Fianna Fáil nomination, with Charlie Haughey once telling her, 'Mary, you should put up one of the lads.'[5]

It was not until 1991 that more women arrived in the council chamber: both Breeda Moynihan-Cronin, daughter of TD Michael, and Maeve Spring, sister of TD Dick, won seats for Labour. After that, representation

Francis Donovan, a member of the Tralee Poor Law Guardians from 1897, and whose brother, St John, was the first chairman of Kerry County Council in 1899 (Michael Latchford).

did improve as Toiréasa Ferris was co-opted to replace her father Martin Ferris in July 2003 and the following year she retained her seat and was joined in the chamber by the Fianna Fáil pair Anne McEllistrim and Norma Foley, both of whom were succeeding previous generations of their respective families. Breeda Moynihan-Cronin had resigned, as she was also a member of Dáil Éireann. Her former secretary, Marie Moloney, won back the seat in June 2009 and when she was elected to the Seanad, Moynihan-Cronin returned to the council by co-option, so three of the twenty-seven councillors were women by 2009. This number increased to four when Gillian Wharton-Slattery was co-opted to replace Labour's Arthur Spring upon his election to the Dáil in 2011.

Following the reforms of local government in 2014, there were thirty-three seats on the county council. Both Toiréasa Ferris and Norma Foley remained undisturbed in Tralee, while Listowel upheld an honourable record of recognising the worth of women members by returning both Aoife Thornton of Fine Gael and Dianne Nolan of Sinn Féin. South and West Kerry elected Norma Moriarty, bringing the total to five female members. However, Anne McEllistrim and Gillian Wharton-Slattery failed to retain their seats. These losses were redressed to a degree when Maura Healy-Rae was co-opted to take Danny Healy-Rae's seat, when he won election to Dáil Éireann, at the meeting of March 2016. She joined her brother Johnny on the council. Aoife Thornton (FG) became Mayor of Listowel Municipal District in 2016 and in 2018 Norma Moriarty (FF) took the chair in the South and West Kerry Municipal District.

Mary O'Shea of Valentia Road, Cahersiveen, who was elected to Kerry County Council in 1926 (Judge Kevin O'Higgins).

Mary O'Donoghue of Fianna Fáil, who succeeded her husband, Dan, on Kerry County Council in 1964, and was chairperson in 1982–3.

But the picture in the Urban Councils was even starker for women for a very long time. Following Maud Walsh's progress in Tralee in 1914, there was a gap of sixty years before Maureen Henry Fitzgerald (FF) won her seat in June 1974. There had been no female candidates in that whole period. Fitzgerald, a Boherbee shopkeeper, did inspire change, for Kay Caball, a daughter of the former Fianna Fáil TD for Kerry North, Dan Moloney, joined her on the council when both were elected in 1979 and in 1985, another shopkeeper, Mary O'Halloran (FF), won a seat, although she was now the only woman member. This Oakpark lady had the honour of becoming Tralee's first woman Cathaoirleach in 1992.

Maeve Spring and Norma Foley took their seats on Tralee Town Council in June 1994. Five years later, when Bríd McElligott-Rusk (FG) and Miriam McGillycuddy (Labour) won seats, Tralee suddenly had a 25 per cent quotient of women members. Moreover, Maeve Spring (1997) and Miriam McGillycuddy (2007) acted as cathaoirligh while Norma Foley was twice in the chair of the UDC and was also elected Mayor of the Tralee Municipal District for 2017–18. Foley's deputy in 2006 was Labour's Karen

Tobin, which resulted in a rare female double team. Tralee has continued to elect women, with Tobin and Maisie Houlihan (SF) maintaining the one-quarter representation in 2004 (Toiréasa Ferris and Norma Foley were still on the council), while the last Tralee Town Council created a new record when this pair was joined by Mairead Fernane, Gillian Wharton-Slattery and Grace O'Donnell to make it five out of twelve. Two of the newcomers, Mairead Fernane and Grace O'Donnell, were also elected to the chair in 2010 and 2011.

Back in Killarney, Kate Breen's departure to live in Castlegregory in 1933 was followed by a long interval before another woman claimed a seat on the urban authority seventy years later. This candidate was Fianna Fáil's Sheila Dickson-O'Shea, who was co-opted to serve in place of her father Mort O'Shea in 1998. She retained her seat in the election the following year, but lost out in 2004. A sister of the former Kerry football team manager Pat O'Shea, she also served as president of the Irish Nurses' Organisation in 2008. Sheila Casey was elected in 1999 for Fine Gael and held her seat in 2004. She became the first woman to chair the Killarney council in 2002 and was chair for a second time in 2006. In 2009, Killarney again had no female councillor.

Listowel, as previously mentioned, has had a stronger record of women members on its council and was the first to elect a woman at its head. Bibiana Foran was certainly a forceful figure in her time, but in Listowel, too, for a long period, getting women to put their names on ballot papers proved difficult. Indeed, for a number of years, getting anyone at all to stand for Listowel UDC was challenging. A number of the 1925 council resigned and in 1928, just three candidates – virtually what remained of the outgoing administration – were persuaded to stand and they were duly allowed to function, but only after being granted ministerial consent to act. In 1934, the twelve seats were filled, but there was no contest for them and even when the number of members was reduced to nine in 1942, and again in 1945, there were only enough candidates to fill those seats. It wasn't until 1950 that another set of contests occurred.

When her moment arrived, Maria Gorman of Fianna Fáil proved to be a thoroughly resilient candidate. She ended a long period of no female representation when she won her seat in 1979. She lost it again in 1985, but regained it in 1991 and was returned in the subsequent four elections. She served as Cathaoirleach on her triumphant return in 1985 and did so again on six further occasions. Mary Horgan, a daughter and granddaughter of former TDs for Kerry North (Jack and Gerard Lynch), was elected in 1994 and was quickly joined by Margo Kennedy-Henchy (FF) in May 1996, following the death of her father Councillor Albert Kennedy. Jacqueline Barrett (later Barrett-Madigan), also Fine Gael, who was confined to a wheelchair following a childhood illness, was elected at all three of the last Listowel UDC elections and her presence meant that the needs of the disabled were constantly in the minds of the members and officials. Following the death of Sinn Féin's Anthony Curtin, Dianne Nolan was co-opted to the chamber, bringing the final tally of women to three out of nine on the departing Listowel Urban District Council.

'Why are all the people talking about Dick Spring, Mammy?'

The Tánaiste and the night of the four votes

Scrutinising the ballot papers during the recount at the 1987 general election in Kerry North, l–r: Tom O'Halloran (Fianna Fáil legal adviser), Tom McEllistrim TD, Donal Spring (brother of Dick), Donal Browne (State Solicitor for Kerry) and returning officer and county registrar, Louise McDonough (Kevin Coleman/*The Kerryman*).

'Why are all the people talking about Dick Spring, Mammy?' a youngster asked her mother as they enjoyed lunch at a busy restaurant in the centre of Tralee.[1] The chatter all around was dominated by politics. It was Wednesday, 18 February 1987, and a short distance away, at the CYMS Hall at the end of Denny Street, the votes cast by the electors of Kerry North at the general election the previous day were being counted. 'Because they are worried he might lose his job,' the girl's mother replied. 'But,' said the child, 'can't he get the dole, like Martin?'

How prophetic it was that just four days before the 1987 general election, *The Kerryman*'s lead headline read 'Spring sounds the alarm'?[2] The report explained that Dick Spring, the Tánaiste, leader of the Labour Party and TD for Kerry North, was alleging that there was a sophisticated campaign to undermine his position and deprive him of the Dáil seat he had held since 1981 – and which his father, Dan, had held without a break since 1943. Fianna Fáil and Fine Gael were conspiring to split his vote, Spring told a press conference. Just weeks before, Spring had walked out of the coalition government which Labour had put together with Fine Gael under Garret FitzGerald at the beginning of 1983. The coalition had struggled to balance the books in the midst of an economic recession and a dispute over health service cuts. Labour was in the doldrums and had been at 5 per cent in one pre-election opinion poll. But despite the unpopularity of the government and the prevailing economic crisis, *The Kerryman* noted that anything less than Spring heading the poll in Kerry North would be 'a sharp rebuke to the Kerryman who has had such a high profile in Irish politics in the past five years'.

A week later, when the ballot boxes were opened, Spring's worst fears were almost realised. Like many candidates, he didn't go to the count immediately and instead waited at home for news from the tallymen. But when nobody had contacted him by 11am, his suspicions grew. His brother, Arthur, turned up, with 'his chin down around his knees', at noon and he knew there was a problem – a quick calculation and Spring was convinced he would lose out by about twenty-five votes.[3] Spring's first-preference return was down 10 per cent on the November 1982 poll and had fallen by almost 3,000 votes to 6,739. In a spectacular performance, Fine Gael senator and former Kerry senior football captain, Jimmy Deenihan, had polled over 10,000 votes to surge to the head of the poll, ahead of Fianna Fáil's Denis Foley on 7,611 and Fianna Fáil's Tom McEllistrim on 6,161.

With Deenihan elected comfortably on the first count and Denis Foley taking the second seat thanks in part to a healthy transfer from the third Fianna Fáil man in the field, Dan Kiely, the Labour leader and Tom McEllistrim were left to slog it out for the last seat. At the end of the sixth and final count, shortly after 10pm, McEllistrim was just five votes behind Spring and returning officer, Louise McDonagh, declared that Deenihan, Foley and Spring had been elected. McDonagh later described what followed as 'one of the most traumatic nights of my life'.[4] Tom McEllistrim, a former junior minister whose family had been represented in the Dáil since 1923, demanded a recount immediately and so began one of the most gripping electoral battles in the history of Irish politics.

In the only known case of the popular and well-known Ideal Homes Exhibition interfering with the timing of the counting of votes in an Irish general election, count staff were forced to commence the recount immediately rather than adjourn until the following day as the count centre was needed to host the interior decorating roadshow. McDonagh, whose father, Louis, from Listowel, had been a county councillor for many years, had little choice but to proceed and the ballot counting began all over again, not least because finding another secure location where the ballot boxes could be held overnight would have been difficult, as she later recalled:

With hindsight and the experience I now have, I would have postponed the recount until the next day. I would never again start a recount at twelve o'clock at night ... [but] I would have had to remove everything to a different counting centre ... I had the late Donie Browne [former state solicitor for Kerry] with me as my legal adviser ... he was brilliant and knew proportional representation better than anybody I had ever known.[5]

The Kerryman captured something of the drama, as well as the fatigue, as the clock ticked on into the wee hours and a total of 34,000 papers were rechecked and scrutinised:

> In the hall, or the streets and in the pubs, people referred to friends, brothers, mothers and sisters who could have 'swung it' had they voted. Everyone seemed to know someone who was going to vote for Mac or Spring but didn't. By midnight it became clear that the recount would go on until about 3.00am and each passing minute after that they seemed to draw more people to their beds ... As the clock struck one a hard core of around 250 dedicated followers remained – determined to stick it out till the sweet or bitter end.[6]

Throughout the recount, Tom McEllistrim's legal adviser was solicitor Tom O'Halloran and Dick Spring relied on the legal advice of his brother, Donal, and barrister, Joe Revington. Every doubtful paper was agonised over. As the recheck continued, Spring spoke live on RTÉ television to presenter Brian Farrell in a studio in Dublin in what one commentator described as an interview which represented 'the symbolic unchaining of a man who had been undergoing torture all day'.[7]

> It's been a harrowing day. I kept saying during the campaign there's no such thing as a safe Labour seat and God, my words are rather proven ... For the first time in four years, I'm very single-minded this evening. I've tended to look at national issues, probably primarily for the last four years. I've spent an awful lot of time at Cabinet meetings while the others were down on the ground taking my votes.[8]

In studio, minister Barry Desmond wished his leader well – his party colleague Liam Kavanagh TD had seen the tallies and reassured Desmond that transfers from Kiely and Foley should see Spring through.[9] The nation 'watched in fascination', said Spring's biographer, Stephen Collins. 'Spring, leaning over a crush barrier in the early hours of the morning, gave every appearance of a man about to face the gallows. It was one of those rare moments which gave the public a glimpse of just how unpredictable politics can be.'[10] In the commotion and the heat, Spring's sister, Kay, fainted, but didn't fall to the ground, such was the crowd around her.

The net change from the recount was just one vote and McEllistrim was now four votes behind Spring. Louise McDonagh noted that the 'pressure was unreal … You could have cut the atmosphere with a knife and an awful lot of people stayed until five in the morning as there was an air abroad that there would be political blood spilt on one side or the other'. Tom McEllistrim, McDonagh said, was 'amazingly gracious about the whole thing',[11] a view later echoed by Spring. At 5.14am, McDonagh approached the microphone for the final time and confirmed the three representatives returned from Kerry North – Jimmy Deenihan, Denis Foley and Dick Spring. 'At 5.27am, it was all over,' the *Kerryman* scribe concluded, 'the cars in Denny Street were frosted up and the joyous scenes of the previous afternoon were but a memory.' A legal challenge to the result initially mooted by the McEllistrim camp soon faded and the result stood. 'The biggest shock really,' Spring said afterwards, 'was that I felt I had worked my butt off. I really had worked night and day. I had done an awful lot for north Kerry. But I suppose I was the one that got the blame.'[12]

7

'We must not expect great things of Miss O'Connor in the Dáil'

*The Kerry North TD Who Was
Too Young To Vote for Herself*

The road surface was later described as having been 'most slippery' and 'treacherous'.[1] It was Sunday, 11 December 1955, and Johnny Connor, the Clann na Poblachta TD for Kerry North, was driving along a road in his constituency which was very familiar to him, the main route between Abbeyfeale and Castleisland. Connor was returning from a meeting of the party's national executive which had been held in Dublin the previous day. Clann na Poblachta was, by 1955, a smaller party than it had been at the height of its powers in the late 1940s and the Kerry North TD was a key member of its national committee. Shortly after 2pm, Connor's Ford Consul, of which he was the only occupant, swerved across the centre of the road on a bend near Headley's Bridge and collided head-on with a Ford Zephyr 6 being driven in the opposite direction by a Tralee ophthalmic doctor, Patrick O'Donnell. The bonnets of both cars were 'bashed in' and Connor's breastbone was 'smashed to pieces'.[2] Connor 'died within a short time' at the scene and the last rites were administered by a priest from south Kerry who had been travelling on the road and came upon the accident moments after it occurred.[3] It was the first and only time that a TD for Kerry North died in office.

The esteem in which Connor was held in political circles was reflected by the huge attendance at his funeral in St John's Church, Tralee, several days later. Chief among the political mourners was the Taoiseach and leader of Fine Gael, John A. Costello, whose party had led the first inter-party government with, among others, Clann na Poblachta, between 1948 and 1951. 'The late deputy represented the constituency of North Kerry and during his comparatively short term in the House he endeared himself to everybody with whom he came in contact,' Costello told the Dáil in his tribute. 'He was a big man, in every sense of the word, and was not afraid to give his views whether in this House or in private. Sincerity, integrity and a deep love of his native country were his outstanding characteristics.'[4] Also among the funeral mourners were ministers General Richard Mulcahy, Oliver J. Flanagan and leading figures from all the major political parties, as well as the Clann na Poblachta leader and former IRA Chief of Staff, Seán MacBride. At the graveside in Rath cemetery, MacBride told mourners that 'We have had many fearless fighters in the cause of Independence but we have no more fearless one than Johnny Connor ... The mountains and the fields of Kerry, and indeed the seas that surround Ireland, bear silent witness to his courage and integrity. His whole life was devoted to the struggle for Independence and unity of Ireland.'[5]

✶ ✶ ✶

Johnny Connor, or O'Connor, which was his family name, had broken the mould in the Kerry North constituency when he won a seat for Clann na Poblachta at the 1954 general election. Born at Poulawaddra, Farmer's Bridge, near Tralee, in July 1899, Connor left school at fifteen years of age to work on the family farm.[6] He joined the Farmer's Bridge Company of the Irish Volunteers in 1914 and was active in the locality in the months before the Easter Rising in 1916. He was a member of the Kerry No. 1 Brigade of the IRA during the War of Independence, later transferring to a Flying Column with the No. 2 Brigade under the legendary IRA leader Dan Allman. He became a close associate of another prominent IRA activist and future Fianna Fáil TD, Thomas McEllistrim, and was involved in numerous ambushes and engagements against the RIC in the late 1910s and early 1920s, such as the attacks on police barracks in Gortatlea, Brosna and Scartaglin and high-profile ambushes at Headford Junction and Ballymacandy. Renowned for his ability with a Lewis Gun, he earned the nickname 'Machine Gun Connor'.[7] When the Civil War broke out, Connor fought on the side of the anti-Treaty forces. In 1923,

Johnny Connor, Clann na Poblachta TD for Kerry North, 1954–5 (O'Connor family).

while on the run, he was captured in a dug-out near his home and he was jailed in Tralee, the Curragh and Mountjoy, where he went on hunger strike.

Connor emigrated to Chicago after his release from prison, returning home in 1930 to run the family farm at Farmer's Bridge, as well as an auctioneering business. He married Margaret Corkery of nearby Ashill and took up employment as a clerk of works for the Board of Health, overseeing cottage repairs. He didn't give up his republican activism, however, and was jailed with other IRA members in the Curragh during the Second World War. Connor became interested in politics and was drawn to the republican socialist party, Clann na Poblachta, which had been founded by a former leader of the IRA, Seán MacBride, and which claimed to be the true republican party alternative to Fianna Fáil. Established in 1946, the party appealed to those disillusioned with Éamon de Valera and offered a social democratic vision, attracting figures such as Dr Noël Browne, Peadar Cowan and Kenmare native, Noel Hartnett, with whom Connor would serve on the party's national ruling body. Johnny Connor joined the party not long after its foundation, impressed by MacBride's socialist and republican principles.

Drawing on his IRA profile and his advocacy of the rights of small farmers, Connor decided to enter electoral politics in the late 1940s and – not for the first or only time in Irish elections – he deliberately dropped the 'O' from his surname to ensure a higher placement on the ballot paper, which listed candidates in alphabetical order by surname. He was nominated by Clann na Poblachta to contest the general election of February 1948 in Kerry North, an election following which the party helped to form the first ever inter-party government under John A. Costello. However, Connor had less success than his ten party colleagues

CLANN NA POBLACHTA

KERRY NORTH & SOUTH

1. CLANN NA POBLACHTA, IN 1948, ENDED ONE-PARTY DICTATOR-SHIP.

2. CLANN NA POBLACHTA ENDED HUNGER STRIKES, MILITARY COURTS, AND EXECUTIONS.

   CLANN NA POBLACHTA GAVE YOU INTERNAL PEACE IN THE TWENTY-SIX COUNTIES.

3. CLANN NA POBLACHTA WON INTERNATIONAL RECOGNITION FOR THE REPUBLIC OF IRELAND.

5. CLANN NA POBLACHTA IN THIS ELECTION STANDS FOR:
   (a) RESTORATION OF FOOD SUBSIDIES AND SO A LOWER PRICE FOR ESSENTIAL FOODSTUFFS;
   (b) REPATRIATION OF EXTERNAL ASSETS SO THAT IRISH MEN CAN WORK AT HOME AT A LIVING WAGE;
   (c) THE ENDING OF EMIGRATION AND UNEMPLOYMENT.
   (d) MAKING PARTITION AN INTERNATIONAL ISSUE.
   (e) THE PRESERVATION OF THE GAELTACHT AND THE LANGUAGE.

Johnny Connor & John Joe O'Leary

the Clann na Poblachta Candidates in Kerry, stand for this programme:

JOHNNY CONNOR

Chairman of the County Committee of Agriculture.
Member and former Chairman of Kerry Co. Council.
Member of the Mental Hospital Committee.
Member of the Housing Committee.
A practical farmer who earns his livelihood solely from farming.

JOHN JOE O'LEARY

A Governor of University College, Cork.
Chairman of the Mental Hospital Committee.
Member of Kerry County Council.
Member of Committee of Agriculture.
Member of Vocational Education Committee.
Member of the Housing Committee.
Active in all phases of public life in South Kerry

JOHNNY CONNOR   JOHN JOE O'LEARY

VOTE No. 1
For JOHNNY CONNOR in North Kerry.
VOTE No. 1
For JOHN JOE O'LEARY in South Kerry.

After that, vote in the order of your choice for the candidates who are pledged to support the Inter-Party.

2k15

Advertisement from Clann na Poblachta candidates in Kerry during the 1954 campaign (*The Kerryman*, 8 May 1954).

who were elected in other parts of the country; he polled in fifth place with 4,390 votes in the four-seat constituency, but failed to usurp the incumbents: Thomas McEllistrim and Eamonn Kissane of Fianna Fáil, Independent Paddy Finucane and Labour's Dan Spring. Connor's running mate, John Walsh from Ballylongford, picked up over 1,500 votes, but his transfers weren't enough to secure a seat for the new party.

Later that same year, Connor made the breakthrough when he was elected to Kerry County Council in October 1948. He was one of four councillors[8] elected in what was the new party's first local authority election outing and which – in a county like Kerry, which was then strongly dominated by Fianna Fáil and Fine Gael – reflected the immediate popularity of the fledgling party. Connor was immediately elected council chairman for a year and also served in the chair in 1951–2, further raising his political profile. When the inter-party coalition collapsed in 1951, in part due to Noël Browne's hugely controversial Mother and Child Scheme, Connor stood in his second general election. There was a slight increase in his first-preference vote, but it was to be 1954 before he prevailed. Seán MacBride spoke at rallies in Tralee and Listowel in support of his candidate during the campaign and emphasised that the freedom of Ireland could only be achieved through economic freedom.[9] Connor stressed his farming credentials – his election literature described him as 'a practical farmer who earns his livelihood solely from farming' – and he called for the restoration of subsidies for essential foodstuffs.[10] He also asked for transfers to candidates from parties like Fine Gael and Labour.

On election day, 18 May 1954, Johnny Connor took the fourth and final seat in Kerry North, unseating Fine Gael's John Lynch from Listowel. He had secured 5,003 first preferences and almost 14 per cent of the vote. In his victory address, he decried the 'evil of partition' and expressed confidence that the four Kerry North deputies would fight partition in a unified way.[11] By the time Connor finally made it into the Dáil, Clann na Poblachta was on the wane. Its national vote had plunged from over 13 per cent in 1948 to just 3 per cent six years later. It had become a Dáil party of just three members – a significant drop from the ten seats it had won in 1948. Connor's only Dáil colleagues were MacBride and John Tully from Cavan. The party opted not to formally join the second inter-party government which John A. Costello formed after the election, instead agreeing to a confidence-and-supply arrangement whereby it would support the government in votes on budgetary matters and motions of confidence. This meant that the party held no seats in cabinet, so its influence was nowhere near as significant as in the 1948–51 period.

* * *

Johnny Connor's only daughter, Kathleen, often helped her father with his constituency work, acknowledging correspondence, writing to constituents and acting as a *de facto* secretary to the deputy at a time when TDs had no formal administrative support and no constituency offices. Kathleen was born on 30 July 1934 and grew up at the family home at Poulawaddra. She recalled it being a 'very political household'. Those on the run from the authorities for their IRA activities, including many from Northern Ireland, often stayed in the house in the 1940s.[12] 'You couldn't avoid it,' she said of the republican politics at the time. Her father gave her books on the revolutionary period and the writings of IRA man Dan Breen and the house was often raided by police. Her father, she remembered, was very impressed by Seán MacBride and his republican zeal.[13]

Kathleen received her second-level education at the Irish language-school, Coláiste Íde, in Dingle before embarking on a teacher-training degree at Carysfort College in Dublin. When her father contested his third Dáil election in 1954, Kathleen's studies in Dublin prevented her from becoming involved in the election campaign in Kerry North, nor was she present when the votes were counted. The first she heard of her father's election was when three of her fellow students ran towards her in her corridor in Carysfort with the news, shouting 'He's in, he's in.'[14] It was a melancholic moment for Kathleen and the family – just four years previously, in 1950, her older brother Brendan had died in a tragic accident. But the trainee teacher was proud of her father's achievement: 'He was popular with people in the constituency. There was an awful lot of poverty at the time especially among small farmers.'[15] As Kathleen was completing her studies in Dublin when Johnny took up his seat in the Dáil, she regularly visited his Leinster House office to assist him with his political work: 'It was great to be there seeing some of the biggest names in politics like De Valera and Cosgrave. I'm only sorry I didn't ask more of them for their autographs.'[16]

* * *

Tragedy struck when Johnny Connor died just a fortnight before Christmas in 1955. Kathleen joined her mother, Margaret, and her younger brother, Pádraig, as the chief mourners at his funeral. For Kathleen, the funeral was to be the occasion of a memorable encounter with the Clann na Poblachta leader. Seán MacBride came to the family home to sympathise. 'He was a towering figure – you knew you were in the presence of greatness with him,' Kathleen recalled.[17] MacBride broached the subject of the forthcoming by-election which would be held to replace the late TD: 'MacBride came to the house and went to my mother to try to get her to stand. She was the obvious choice. There was great pressure on her to go but she wouldn't. He approached me and said it was his opinion that I had the only chance.'[18]

MacBride's enthusiasm for a member of the family to contest the by-election belied the precariousness of the political situation at the time – the coalition government, supported from the outside by Clann na Poblachta, could not afford to cede a seat to Fianna Fáil. Not alone was the government reliant on three Clann na Poblachta votes; MacBride's parliamentary party faced the prospect of shrinking to two TDs, putting the party's very existence into greater jeopardy. He needed a strong candidate to replace Johnny Connor in Kerry North and the obvious choice was a close relative, in keeping with the time-honoured Irish political dynastic tradition – in a similar scenario in Kerry South just ten years previously, Honor Mary Crowley of Fianna Fáil had succeeded her husband, Fred, in the Dáil following his death while in office. 'You're our only chance,' MacBride told Kathleen hours after her father was buried. 'It was a very personal vote and there was nobody else to stand.'[19]

The 21-year-old Kathleen – who had just taken up a teaching position at Meen national school, in Knocknagoshel, about twenty miles from Tralee – was placed in an unenviable position:

> I didn't want to run. I had just qualified as a teacher. I was barely old enough to vote for myself [having just turned twenty-one, then the legal minimum age for voting, it would be several months before she would be included on a new electoral register]. My older brother Brendan had died and my younger brother, Pádraig, was still in school. I thought women were to be seen and not heard. But apart from MacBride, members of Clann na Poblachta were encouraging

me to run. And I had great pride in what my father had achieved – he was a hero to me.[20]

* * *

Within weeks of her father's death, Kathleen O'Connor was formally nominated as the Clann na Poblachta candidate for the by-election which was set to take place on 29 February 1956. It was to be the first and only by-election ever to take place in the constituency of Kerry North. O'Connor's formal proposer as a candidate was an Annascaul-based doctor, Dr Henry Vincent O'Donoghue. He had been active in the Volunteers with Johnny Connor prior to the Easter Rising and was in Dublin when the rebellion began. Following a period in jail, he later served as medical officer of the IRA in Kerry during the War of Independence. The seconder of O'Connor's nomination was another IRA veteran and former Fianna Fáil TD, Stephen Fuller from Kilflynn, the sole survivor of the Ballyseedy Massacre of 1923. Though there was a family connection, having her nomination papers signed by a member and former deputy – Fuller was a TD from 1937 to 1943 – of a rival party must have been a fillip for O'Connor's campaign and was a testament to the esteem in which Johnny Connor and his family were held across the political spectrum.

Fianna Fáil in Kerry North decided to contest the by-election with Listowel-based councillor and national executive member Daniel 'Danny Jim' Moloney as their candidate. But that was to be the extent of O'Connor's opposition in the poll. The decision of the other parties not to put forward candidates had as much to do with the national political dynamic and the stability of the Fine Gael–Labour–Clann na Talmhan coalition as it had to do with the inevitable strength of a family member standing in the place of a recently deceased deputy. The other government parties were acutely aware of the vulnerability of their Dáil majority and knew that diluting the pro-government and anti-Fianna Fáil vote by fielding their own individual candidates would seriously risk ceding a seat to the opposition.

Dan Moloney therefore found himself up against the might of all three government parties – Fine Gael, Labour and Clann na Talmhan, who rowed in behind O'Connor – as well as Kathleen's own party, Clann na Poblachta. All three of the coalition party leaders visited the constituency to rally support. They placed advertisements in *The Kerryman* encouraging support for the young teacher. Fine Gael's John A. Costello, Labour's

'Kerry is Loyal': Message seeking support for Kathleen O'Connor, by-election candidate in Kerry North (*The Kerryman*, 25 February 1956).

Brendan Corish and Joseph Blowick of Clann na Talmhan addressed pre-election rallies in Listowel and Tralee. Fianna Fáil brought all its heavy hitters to Kerry North too, prompting Seán MacBride to suggest at a rally in Dingle that Fianna Fáil's electioneering methods were 'most interesting' and that 'every evening imported crowds were brought by cars to Mr de Valera's meetings.'[21]

It was evident from the outset that Clann na Poblachta would seek to appeal to emotion and play up the loss of the former deputy and the candidacy of his bereaved daughter. A campaign message in *The Kerryman* on 18 February made this clear to voters:

> Is it possibly the hand of fate that has provided that Johnny O'Connor's death should result in a young person of sufficient ability and tradition entering our public life. It is, in effect, the handing over by one generation to another. Indeed Kathleen is a good deal older that her father was when he was fighting with the people of Kerry for our National Independence.[22]

Fianna Fáil hit back, however, by alluding to the importance of policy over personality at many of its public meetings and in newspaper advertisements. In a pointed message just days before polling, the party suggested that 'sentiment' – code for sympathy – shouldn't come into people's minds when voting. Under the heading 'Reality or Sentiment?' and beside a picture of Dan Moloney, a message from Fianna Fáil's Seán Lemass read: 'Politics is, or should be, a matter of principles and not personalities. Candidates should be elected to the Dáil mainly because of their views and politics. Fianna Fáil is contesting the By-Election on the basis of its declared policy and programme.'[23] At the party selection convention, Lemass had gone even further when he accused Fine Gael of making it impossible for people in Kerry North to give 'a clear-cut verdict on the Government's policy' by failing to nominate a candidate. Instead, Fine Gael was going along with Clann na Poblachta in 'playing the sympathy card':[24]

> They [Fine Gael] have carefully calculated, in terms of votes, the natural sympathy of decent folk, regardless of politics, for a young girl recently bereaved and consider if it may pay off to Fine Gael's advantage … Fine Gael's decision [not to contest the election] was based on tactics and not on any decent emotion. Their tears are bogus and are a tribute to their cleverness and not to their sympathies … Is the whole business merely a carefully hatched scheme to get another silent vote in the Dáil lobbies for whatever the Fine Gael whips may decide? … Our candidate regards membership of the Dáil as an important public duty and an opportunity of hard work on behalf of the people and not as a personal reward or anything similar.

Lemass' rhetoric and Fianna Fáil's tactics did not succeed. When the ballots were counted at the Ashe Memorial Hall on Denny Street in Tralee on 1 March 1956, Kathleen O'Connor outpolled Dan Moloney by 18,176 votes to 15,828. She had almost quadrupled the vote Johnny Connor had received two years before, albeit in a two-horse race on this occasion. O'Connor is the third youngest deputy elected since the foundation of the State.[25] In his concession speech, Dan Moloney remarked that success was always going to be difficult owing to the fact that 'there was a four-pronged attack on them [Fianna Fáil] the whole way through' from Fine Gael, Labour, Clann na Talmhan and Clann na Poblachta. 'Miss Kathleen O'Connor speaking in Irish and English,' The Kerryman recorded, 'thanked the people of North

Kerry for electing her and the other parties and all the gallant workers of Clann na Poblachta. She hoped she would be able to look after their interests as well as her father had done.'[26]

* * *

'A small, slight girl, too young to have cast a vote in her own favour, became a new TD for North Kerry yesterday,' declared the *Cork Examiner* on the morning after Kathleen O'Connor's election. 'Clad soberly in black, the brown-haired Miss O'Connor's face was lighted with gladness ... when the Returning Officer of the election, Mr TG Clarke, County Registrar, declared the result.'[27] Just a week later, on 7 March 1956, the new deputy, accompanied by her mother, was welcomed at the gates of Leinster House by Seán MacBride and took her seat in the Dáil the following day. The *Cork Examiner* captured the moment she entered the chamber:

> Twenty-one-year-old Miss Kathleen O'Connor received a friendly welcome from a fairly full Dáil to-day when she took her late father's seat in the House. Before she was introduced to the Leas Ceann Comhairle, Mr Cormac Breslin, she chatted gaily to Mr Seán MacBride, TD, in one of the lobbies while waiting for question time to end. All was quiet when she came down the stairway and crossed the soft Dun Emer carpet to the Chair. Then as she was being escorted to her seat a storm of applause burst from the benches of the Government supporters. Some gallants in the Fianna Fáil benches joined, as did people in the crowded public gallery. Miss O'Connor, who looked very chic in a black tailored costume and wore a tight-fitting black hat, smiled winningly.[28]

The newspaper also noted that Kathleen O'Connor was not the first spinster elected to the Dáil – Mary MacSwiney TD and Senator Margaret Pearse had preceded her in that regard. The *Daily Express* observed that O'Connor was 'the slip of a girl who is too young to have a vote herself'.[29] Apart from being the youngest TD in the Fifteenth Dáil, Kathleen O'Connor was one of just seven women deputies at the time – another of whom was Fianna Fáil's Honor Mary Crowley of Kerry South – and she was one of just three Clann na Poblachta TDs. Dublin's *Evening Mail* published a rather patronising and condescending editorial on the north

Kerry result and echoed Lemass' accusations about the impact of the sympathy factor:

> The shouting in North Kerry is over, and the pleasant-looking young school teacher steps into her dead father's place in Dáil Eireann … the Inter-Party forces have no cause to be wildly jubilant. In a poll as near as makes little difference to that of the 1954 election there were nearly 3,000 fewer votes cast for them. It may be suggested that these lost or missing votes are due to displeasure on the part of individuals in regard to the obvious appeal to unthinking sentimentality implicit in the very choice of a young lady of 21 altogether without political experience, merely because she happens to be her father's daughter … We must not expect great things of Miss O'Connor in the Dáil, at any rate not at once. If she is at hand with reasonable regularity to trip into the division lobby when the bell rings it will be all that will be required of her until she decides for herself whether she will be a real politician or a permanent rubber stamp …[30]

The article was generous enough to congratulate the new TD on her electoral feat, but only in the context of achieving that election while too young to vote for herself. The *Evening Mail* was prophetic, however, in its recognition of the daunting task facing the young woman from a rural constituency. The task of servicing a constituency of the size of Kerry North and the requirement to be present in Leinster House so regularly soon overwhelmed the 21-year-old deputy. Not long after her election, she realised that the political life was not for her. She decided not to contest the 1957 general election. Before leaving the Dáil, however, she played her part in collapsing the coalition with the government, signing, on 28 January 1957, with her colleagues MacBride and John Tully, a motion of no confidence in the government, which precipitated its end. Her constituency colleague, Paddy Finucane of Clann na Talmhan, had also withdrawn his support for the coalition.

At the Clann na Poblachta selection convention in Kerry North, Seán MacBride announced that when Deputy O'Connor had agreed to contest the by-election, it was on the clear understanding that she would not be expected to stand at the following general election.[31] During her short time in the Dáil, she tabled less than a dozen parliamentary questions on constituency matters, such as a new sewerage scheme for Ballyferriter and an auxiliary creamery in Ballybunion, but she never spoke in a debate. Remarkably, Deputy O'Connor was involved in a car accident not far from where her father had died in December 1955. While travelling between Abbeyfeale and Newcastle West in September 1956, her car was part of a pile-up of five vehicles, but she and all others involved escaped serious injury.[32]

Kathleen O'Connor's decision to leave politics in 1957 left Clann na Poblachta in the lurch and they decided not to field a candidate in Kerry North. By failing to nominate a successor, the party 'abandoned the north Kerry seat' which her father had battled to win.[33] O'Connor's by-election opponent, Dan Moloney, headed the poll as Fianna Fáil swept back into government. O'Connor quietly returned to her teaching role and never entered the political arena again. She later married Eamon Fitzgerald and lived at Oakpark, Tralee. At a gathering of former female TDs in Leinster House in December 2008 to mark the ninetieth anniversary of the election of the first woman to the Oireachtas, she was the oldest former female member present.[34] Kathleen O'Connor-Fitzgerald died on 13 December 2017 at the age of eighty-three.

Members of the First Dáil pictured on 22 January 1919, including East Kerry TD Piaras Béaslaí (second row, fifth from left). (National Library of Ireland)

Members of the Irish delegation to the Anglo-Irish Treaty negotiations of 1921, including Kerry TD Fionán Lynch (front right, stooping). (National Library of Ireland)

J.J. O'Kelly TD (left), a native of Valentia Island and TD for Louth, who was the first Leas Cheann Comhairle of Dáil Éireann with Austin Stack, Kerry TD and Minister for Home Affairs, 1919–22.

Kerry South TD Fionán Lynch addressing the crowd during a general election. (Lynch family)

Fianna Fáil TDs pictured in 1927 including three Kerry TDs, Thomas O'Reilly TD (second row, eighth from right), Thomas McEllistrim TD (back row, second from left), and William O'Leary (back row, third from right). (UCD Archives)

Stephen Fuller (right), Fianna Fáil TD for Kerry North, 1937–43. (Paudie Fuller)

Clann na Poblachta TD Kathleen O'Connor (right) pictured on her first day in Dáil Éireann following her election in the Kerry North by-election of 29 February 1956, pictured with her mother, Catherine O'Connor, and Clann na Poblachta leader Seán MacBride TD. (Brian Fitzgerald)

Observing the counting of votes at the 1965 general election in Kerry South, including Honor Crowley TD (centre with spectacles in her hand) and Timothy 'Chub' O'Connor TD (second from right), both of whom were re-elected. (*The Kerryman*)

Campaigning for the Fianna Fáil candidate, John O'Leary (front, centre), during the 1966 by-election in Kerry South.

Group of Fianna Fáil figures in Kerry pictured with President Patrick Hillery in the 1970s, front, l–r: Marie McEllistrim, Peggy Courtney-O'Sullivan, Annette Courtney, President Patrick Hillery, Anne O'Shea, Kitty Healy, Eileen Cahill. Back, l–r: John O'Leary TD, Tim Moriarty, Tom McEllistrim TD, Cllr Seán O'Keeffe, Mary Frances O'Connor, Cllr Tommy Cahill, Donal Courtney, John B. Healy (TD 1943–8), Timothy 'Chub' O'Connor TD. (Patrick O'Connor)

Some of those observing the counting of votes at the 1966 by-election in Kerry South, including Jackie Healy-Rae (front, centre) and Minister Neil Blaney, director of elections, to his immediate right.

Checking the ballots at the counting of votes in Kerry North at the 1969 general election, including Anna Spring, Tom McEllistrim TD (FF) and Gerard Lynch TD (FG). (*The Kerryman*)

Fianna Fáil supporters in Killorglin at the 1977 general election, including Cllr Jackie Healy-Rae, Cllr Tommy Cahill and Timothy 'Chub' O'Connor TD (third from right). (*The Kerryman*)

Michael Begley TD (right) addresses a Fine Gael rally in Dingle at the 1977 general election. Also pictured are Minister for the Gaeltacht Tom O'Donnell TD (centre), Senator Jackie Daly (left of Begley), and Paul Coghlan (back). (*The Kerryman*)

Fine Gael rally in Listowel during the 1977 general election campaign. (*The Kerryman*)

Three members of the McEllistrim family, Thomas Jnr, Thomas Snr and Thomas III, who served as TDs for Kerry North, pictured with Fianna Fáil leader Jack Lynch.

8

'The man who sits in the chair is not a proper or suitable man'

The Highs and Lows of Local Authority Politics in Kerry since 1899

Prior to the enactment of the Local Government (Ireland) Act, 1898, the administration of the towns and districts was broadly carried out by three main bodies, the Grand Juries and the Guardians of the Poor and Rural District Councils. There were also Town Commissions in Tralee and Killarney. The Grand Juries were responsible for the construction and maintenance of roads and allied structures, lunatic asylums, courthouses and pounds and had the power to levy a local tax (cess) for the purpose of undertaking these duties. The members were elected from a limited franchise up to 1872 and were afterwards appointed by assize judges. The Poor Relief Ireland Act of 1838 set up the Poor Law Authorities, made up of Justices of the Peace and another restricted franchise consisting of ratepayers. The Guardians of the Poor in Kerry established six unions in Kerry – Tralee, Killarney, Listowel, Cahersiveen, Dingle and Kenmare – and their responsibilities included operating the workhouses in their districts; this ambit was extended in 1846 to incorporate the provision and equipping of hospitals and dispensaries for the poor. Five years later, the Nuisances Removal and Prevention of Diseases Act made the Guardians responsible for the dispensary system and medical relief. In 1856, they took over the administration of burial grounds. The registration of births and deaths was appended in 1863 and three years after this, they took over the administration of public sewers under the Sanitary Act. Under the Public

Health Act 1878, the Guardians became the rural sanitary authorities. Meetings of the Boards of Guardians took place on a regular basis, while meetings of the Grand Juries were more occasional events.

The Local Government Act of 1898 set up the new county councils, including Kerry County Council, as well as the Urban District Councils (including in Tralee, Killarney and Listowel), which initially took over many of the functions of both of the earlier bodies. The Grand Juries were abolished as effective forces in local government as the powers were now invested in the county councils. The councils were in charge of hospitals (including mental), public health, courthouses and housing as well. The Boards of Guardians and Rural District Councils now just administered the relief of the poor, but the levy of the Poor Rate became the responsibility of the county councils, which also drew the 'county demand' (financial contribution) from the urban councils for infrastructure running through their administrative areas. Under the Local Government Act, 1925, Rural District Councils were abolished and the responsibilities were taken over by the county authorities. This led to the new Boards of Health and Public Assistance being set up in the counties of Ireland, but these were ultimately abolished in August 1942 and their duties were taken over, again by the county councils. In the following years, particularly after the establishment of the Irish Free State, further powers were devolved to the local authorities. But there was one other very significant change in the Local Government Act – women were permitted to vote in the elections of the members. The last Grand Jury of Kerry consisted of: Capt. James D. Crosbie JP, Ballyheigue Castle; Frederick R. Bateman JP, Bedford, Listowel; George R. Browne JP, the Kerries; James E. Butler JP, Waterville; Faulkiner Collis-Sandes, Tieraclea, Tarbert; The Hon. A. De Moleyns JP, Dingle; Major-General Sir Thomas Dennihy, Brook Lodge; St John Henry Donovan JP, Seafield, Spa; Thomas Galvin JP, Ballyard, Tralee; John E. Hussey JP, Edenburn; Richard Latchford JP, Oakvilla, Tralee; John White Leahy JP, Southill; Maurice Leonard JP, Killarney; Capt. R. Leslie JP, Tarbert House; Capt. J. McGillycuddy JP, Aghadoe; R McCyntre, JP, Kenmare; Robert McCowen JP, Barrow; Colonel Leahy Nash JP, Ballycarty; Daniel O'Connell, Derrynane; Lieutenant-Colonel R.J. Rice JP, Bushmount; Lieutenant-Colonel William Rowan, Belmont, Ballyard, Tralee; Gen. F. Trench JP, Abbeyfeale; Colonel Harrison Trent Staughton, Ballyhorgan.

The first election to the new Kerry County Council took place on 6 April 1899 and the new assembly met for the first time at the Grand Jury

Room (in the courthouse on Ashe Street) sixteen days later, on 22 April. There were thirty-three seats: twenty-two were filled by election in county electoral divisions (EDs), six were reserved for the chairmen of the Rural District Councils in the county, which remained in place, three were nominated by the Grand Jury and two further seats were available to be filled by co-option by the members themselves, if they chose to do so. Three of the electoral divisions were uncontested, but those who stood came largely from the landowning and business-owning segments of Kerry society. Captain Crosbie and St John Donovan from the Grand Jury won seats and were joined by Lords Castlerosse (elected) and Ventry (chairman of Dingle RDC), along with other notable names, Thomas McDonagh Mahony, James Baily and J.K. O'Connor. Richard Latchford was one of the co-options, with David M. Moriarty (a losing candidate), but James Butler, John E. Hussey (a son of Sam Hussey), Robert McCowen and Captain John MacGillycuddy also failed to win sufficient votes. There was to be a first recount, too, as Redmond Roche, Maglass, Ballymacelligott, was initially elected in the Castleisland ED after a result of Roche 469, J.K. O'Connor 466 was declared. O'Connor sought a recount, which yielded the same result. However, the following day, a voting paper was discovered on the floor of the Grand Jury Room (where the polling booth was located) and O'Connor sought a second recount. O'Connor was duly declared elected by a single vote.

At the first meeting of Kerry County Council, David Doran of Kenmare was chosen to chair the election of the first chairman. He presided over the election of St John Donovan to the position. Donovan, born in 1856, was the son of (later Sir) Henry Donovan, Cloghers House, the miller and chairman of the Tralee Town Commissioners for nineteen years. He remained in the chair until 1901. He also headed the poll to win a seat on the first Tralee Urban District Council. He had previously chaired the Tralee Town Commissioners, the Tralee and Fenit Harbour Commissioners, Tralee Race Company and was High Sheriff of Kerry in 1909. His first wife Susan died in 1891 and in 1909, St John married Eileen O'Connor of Ballyseedy. In 1905, he sold his controlling interest in the family businesses to R&H Hall of Cork, staying on as a director. He died in February 1916.

Other notable members of the first Council included:

- Richard Latchford (1842–1912), of Oakvilla House, Oakpark, who was from another of the big milling families. As the operator of

Derrymore Mill, he was familiar with the quality of the water in the Derrymore River and was instrumental in prevailing upon the Tralee Town Commissioners (of which he was a member for thirty-two years) to establish the waterworks upstream in order to supply fresh, piped water to the town in 1879. He was also elected to Tralee Urban District Council in its first five elections and sat on the Tralee and Fenit Harbour Commissioners.

- William O'Donnell, of the Kerries, Tralee, was a cousin of Thomas O'Donnell, MP for West Kerry from 1900 and 1918. He was an authentic Solomon Grundy: he died on 11 February 1928, his birthday and the date on which he got married. He had been president of the Irish Land League in Tralee and a friend of MPs Tim and Ned Harrington. He chaired the Rural District Council for Tralee, which gave him a seat on Kerry County Council and was also a Justice of the Peace. He died in 1928, aged eighty-two.

- Patrick O'Donnell, cousin of William, died in June 1907. The radio equipment to be seized by a group including the three Volunteers who drowned at Ballykissane Pier on Good Friday, 1916, was supposed to be brought to and set up in his house in Ballyard to communicate with *The Aud*, which was transporting guns from Germany for use in the Rising.

- John O'Donnell, a brother of Patrick's, who ran a grocery business on Bridge Street, had been a member of the Tralee Town Commission prior to its remodelling as the Urban District Council. He was a veteran political activist, having strongly supported Rowland Blennerhassett in his campaign against J.A. Dease for the Westminster seat in the 1872 Kerry by-election. Following the Parnell split, he backed Sir Thomas Esmonde to defeat Ned Harrington and also supported the political career of his relative Thomas O'Donnell against Edward Julian (later Kerry County Council). He died in October 1920.

- John P. O'Donnell was a publican on Bridge Street, Tralee. He was a son of Patrick's and was co-opted to take his seat at the meeting following his father's death in June 1907. John P. died in May 1920, aged forty-two, just a few months before his uncle John.

- Michael J. O'Donnell, of Killiney, Castlegregory, was the station master in the village. He died in 1928.

- James Baily, Tralee, died shortly after the election took place in 1899. His brother John was co-opted in his place.
- Lord Castlerosse was disqualified and the former MP Jeremiah D. Sheehan of the Inisfallen Hotel, Killarney, was co-opted to replace him at the meeting of February 1900. The peer was disqualified because he had placed his name on the register of electors when he was not entitled to, following a decision in the Revision Court in October 1899. David M. Moriarty, whom he defeated in the poll, subsequently became his law agent.
- Thomas Kearney, from Castleisland, died in February 1901 and John Murphy, MP for East Kerry from 1900 to 1910, was co-opted to take his seat.
- Florence O'Sullivan, Ballyfinnane, was the chairman of Killarney Rural District Council for the best part of a quarter of a century. He was a first cousin of Dr Charles O'Sullivan, later Bishop of Kerry, and died, aged seventy-six, in 1927.
- Denis J. O'Sullivan, son of John D. and Mary O'Sullivan, Kenmare, ran the family business and was a member of Kenmare Board of Guardians and the Rural District Council. He had been a member of the Land League and a supporter of the Irish Parliamentary Party and his father had been a friend of the Fenian James Stephens. Denis died at the residence of his brother, Rev. J.J. O'Sullivan, parish priest of Rathmore, in February 1932.
- Michael J. Nolan, Galeybridge House, Newtownsandes (now Moyvane), was an auctioneer. He sat on the Council of County Councils and the General Agriculture Committee in Dublin. He was also appointed a local government board inspector. He was in the Railway Hotel in Tralee when he suffered a stroke and died later at the Infirmary in January 1920.
- David Doran of Templenoe House, Kenmare, was chosen as temporary chair and chaired the first meeting. Doran outlived most of his colleagues. He was a Protestant and a supporter of Home Rule.

* * *

The second council was elected on 5 June 1902. There were thirty candidates for the twenty-two elected positions, with the six chairmen of Rural District Councils being *de facto* members and two further seats determined by co-options. The inclusion of three nominees of the Grand Jury had now been discontinued. There was a far less enthusiastic turnout of candidates for the second election as only four of the electoral districts were contested. The co-opted members were Timothy T. O'Connor of Cordal and John O'Donnell, of Bridge Street, Tralee. T.T. O'Connor was a member of the County Committee of Agriculture for thirty years and died in September 1934. Captain Crosbie was defeated by Edmund Harty (Causeway) for Ballyheigue, David Moriarty won Glenbeigh in his own right and Michael J. Fleming was unopposed in Kilcummin. That election of Mike Johnny Fleming, who had failed to get onto the first council, commenced one of the great family dynasties in Kerry. His brother, James (Jamsie), became part of the council in 1919, making them the second pair of brothers on the council. Mike Johnny's son, Tom Michael, retired in 1942, having succeeded his father and there was then an interregnum before his son (also Tom) was elected in 1967. He died whilst making the hay in Scartaglin in 1985 and his son (Tom III) was co-opted to the seat and remained a member until 2011, when he took his seat in Dáil Éireann and was obliged to vacate his council seat.

In 1905, there was a dearth of contests for the seats on offer, with only Dingle, Listowel, Lixnaw, Scartaglin and Valentia providing more than one candidate. The incumbent in Dingle, Thomas O'Donoghue, did not run and three men fought it out with Thomas J. Baker winning. In Listowel, William McMahon retained his seat against one opponent, but there was a change in Lixnaw, where J.E.J. Julian defeated M.S. O'Connell. Valentia also saw the sitting member defeated, as C.G. O'Connell outpolled Alexander O'Driscoll. William McMahon's final term in office was brief for he passed away on 3 September 1907 and Philip Healy of Ballygrennan was co-opted to the seat. John B. Keane was a grandnephew of Healy's. McMahon had been chairman of the Listowel Race Committee when he died.

Another councillor, Tom J. Baker, of Main Street, Dingle, died at his home in June 1934. Locally referred to as Lord Baker, he was originally from the Gallarus area. He emigrated to the US and returned in 1890 to establish a pub in Dingle (now Lord Baker's restaurant). Baker was also a poet. His work was published by Patrick Pearse in his paper *An Claidheamh Soluis*. James Edward John Julian, barrister, was the owner of a large estate, Lismore House, near Lixnaw. His father had been Samuel Julian of Crotta House, who had moved to Cheltenham in 1824 at the age of four, after the family home, Riverdale, had been burned down in an outrage of those times. He contested the 1900 general election in West Kerry as an Independent nationalist against Thomas O'Donnell, losing heavily. Called to the English Bar in 1879 and the Irish Bar ten years later, he rarely practised. He was co-opted back onto Kerry County Council in February 1910 and died in Cheltenham in 1929.

The 1908 campaign proved to be a much more vigorous one, with a number of contests and an allegation of tampering with ballot boxes in Ardfert, where Thomas Healy, a publican and grocer in the Mall, Tralee, defeated the former council chairman, St John Donovan. The recount did reveal significant alterations, but Healy still won comfortably. There was a greater sensation in Castleisland, where the defeated candidate, Denis J. Reidy sought a petition to unseat J.K. O'Connor – who had been elected by a thirty-vote margin – on allegations of bribery, intimidation and purveying drink to voters (see Chapter 3). O'Connor was indeed struck off the register of members in the court and the matter was even discussed in the House of Lords, but Reidy did not accept the seat. John Laurence Quinlan of Bridge Street, Tralee, previously a member of Tralee UDC, took up the position. Several sitting members were displaced in 1908: James O'Shea replaced George O'Gorman in Aghadoe, Michael T. Moriarty defeated Michael J. O'Donnell in Castlegregory, Con Kelliher was elected after narrowly outpolling John McSweeney in Headford, Richard Stack Cussen beat J.E.J. Julian in Lixnaw and James Sugrue won in Valentia at the expense of Alexander O'Driscoll. Sugrue did not have long to enjoy his success, though, for he died the following year. At the November meeting of 1909, O'Driscoll was co-opted back into his old seat. Julian also returned through a co-option after Cussen died, the vote being taken at the February meeting in 1910.

Councillor Con Kelliher of Headford was another who did not enjoy a long tenure in the chamber. As outlined in Chapter 2, he was found guilty of corrupt practice and disqualified, being replaced by James Egan. On the death of Timothy O'Flaherty, the vice-chairman of the Dingle RDC, T. Galvin, moved up and also took the county council seat. When John O'Donnell was co-opted back onto the council, there came to be an unusual uncle–nephew combination. John P. replaced his father (John's brother), who had died the previous year, as the representative from the Kilgobbin Electoral Division.

In January 1910, council meetings moved from the courthouse to the new County Hall in Godfrey Place, Tralee, later the location of a bowling alley and a nightclub. The following year's election featured some significant rematches and the outcomes led to recounts and another petition to unseat over supplying drink to voters. The Ardfert protagonists went at it again and Thomas Healy came out on top in the poll for the second time, but St John Donovan sought a court decision on the matter of giving alcohol to the public and Healy was declared disqualified. Donovan declined to take the seat, however, and William Barrett defeated Healy's brother, John, 12–9 in the vote to co-opt the member for Ardfert. In Aghadoe, James O'Shea and George O'Gorman were separated by just one vote out of 1,123, with O'Shea being declared the winner, but a recount overturned this and O'Gorman was declared the winner by two votes. In Ballyheigue, Thomas Lawlor upset the sitting member Edmond Harty. Things had certainly become much more fractious: *The Kerryman* remarked when the campaign was over that 'it is not exactly any great harm, as things were getting just a little trifle too lively in some divisions'.[1]

The 1914 poll, in the same electoral divisions as the previous four, came about shortly after the Home Rule Bill had been passed in the House of Commons, but the council election was a relatively tame affair, with a number of members not putting themselves before the electorate again. In Lisselton, Jack Boland took Garret Pierse's seat. James Sheehy lodged a petition over the result in Ballyheigue by alleging intimidation and other issues, but there had been almost 500 votes between the candidates. A petition was initially lodged in Ardfert, but this was withdrawn. There were no changes to the results in these instances. Once the 1914 council had settled in, things did become quite 'lively' again. The First World War commenced and Irish Volunteers groups were set up in several towns, with a number of them splitting into two distinct factions with somewhat different aims, so there was an added spice to local politics. The political 'musical chairs' continued. Jonathan Moriarty was a wool buyer, publican and shopkeeper in Dingle, but his father Michael T. Moriarty lost out in his bid to be re-elected for Castlegregory. His re-election as chairman of Dingle RDC in June 1915 (which was won upon his own casting vote over John Moore, the auctioneer from Dingle) was declared invalid by the King's Bench in Dublin in November 1915 as he claimed he did not hear a vote called in favour of Moore and maintained that the vote was a tie. Moore accordingly became a member of the county council. In another action before the King's Bench on the same day, Moore lodged an appeal against a decision made at Tralee Petty Sessions on 14 June 1915 that dismissed his claim that Michael J. O'Donnell should be disqualified as a member of the council for holding a paid office for the Dingle Light Railway Company. The Castlegregory stationmaster was paid £1 a year and had a free first-class pass on the line. The court allowed the appeal in this instance, with the result that O'Donnell was disqualified.

＊

There was radical change in 1920 when, for the first time, most of the seats were filled by a system of proportional representation in four new electoral divisions, Tralee, Killarney, Listowel and Killorglin. There were twenty-two seats determined in four electoral divisions, with the six RDC chairmen and two co-options completing the complement of thirty members. With Sinn Féin now having a firm grip on the country, the only district that was contested was Listowel and an entirely new council was elected, barring John P. O'Donnell – he had died on 3 May, less than a month before election, although his name remained on the ballot paper. At the first meeting, it was unanimously decided not to make any co-options, either to fill his seat or the two other vacancies. Each of the RDC chairs were different, too. History was made with the election of the Honourable Lady Albinia Brodrick, or Gobnait Ní Bhruadair, the first woman ever elected to Kerry County council.

Following the turbulence of the Civil War period, and owing to financial constraints, the council was suspended from 1923 to 1926 and was placed under the stewardship of Commissioner Alderman Philip Monahan. Appointed by finance minister, Ernest Blythe, who was fearful Monahan would be shot in Kerry, the commissioner set about ruthlessly collecting rates and reducing wages and pensions to restore stability. Seán O'Farrell replaced Monahan in December 1924. In the meantime, the Local Government Act, 1925, abolished Rural District Councils and transferred their powers and duties to county councils. When normal service resumed in 1926, there were thirty-four seats at issue, all by election in four electoral divisions. The result was another substantial change in membership, with just republican candidates Fred Crowley and Jeremiah O'Riordan returning. They were joined by former members Tom Baker, Michael A. O'Donnell and J.J. Sheehan, who recovered the seats they had previously held. Among the new members was John M. O'Sullivan (not the Minister for Education Professor John Marcus O'Sullivan), a brother of Eugene O'Sullivan, the chairman of Killarney UDC. A number of these councillors remained on the authority for some time. Jerh Long, Arthur Lenihan and Tom Fleming II would be replaced by sons in due course. Honor Crowley was co-opted to replace her late husband Fred when he died in 1945 and she remained in that seat until she herself died in 1966. Fred won a seat in the Dáil in 1927 and Honor won the by-election for that seat as well. The McGillycuddy of the Reeks would be elected to the Senate in 1928 and remained there (with the exception of the period when it was abolished) until 1943.

In 1926, the new chairman of the council, Jeremiah McSweeney (FF) of Castle Street, Tralee, settled in for a record-breaking fourteen years in the chair (broken only by the two-year dissolution in the early 1930s). The 1926 election also saw John (Jack) Flynn from Castlemaine commence his long career in politics, both on the local and national stage. On this occasion, he was outpolled by Mary O'Shea from Cahersiveen, one of the rare women to stand, let alone win a seat, at this time. With republican Kate Breen of Killarney also being returned, there were now two female members. Councillor Michael J. Healy's sister, Mary, married Dan O'Donoghue, elected to Kerry County Council in 1960, who was an uncle of John O'Donoghue, who would hold various government ministries (Justice, Arts, Sport and Tourism and Ceann Comhairle). Mary, co-opted in 1964 to replace her late husband, would later chair the council and both John and his brother Paul would also wear the chain of office.

∗ ∗ ∗

The council moved and sat in the new County Hall on Denny Street for the March meeting in 1928. It dedicated the new building to Thomas Ashe. That same year, just eighteen of the thirty-four sitting councillors were returned and there were several casualties, but the council was dissolved again between September 1930 and May 1932. The tenth council was elected in June 1934 – Kate Breen, having moved to Castlegregory, switched from the Killarney to the Tralee area and was returned again. There was another long interval before the next election in 1942 and the number of seats was reduced to twenty-six, each division losing two members. The Kerry Farmers' Association gained a considerable foothold, winning the highest number of seats (ten) and disturbing the dominance of Fianna Fáil in many areas. Labour made a breakthrough, with Dan Spring winning in Tralee, a seat he would hold until 1979. From its foundation in 1934 and through to the local elections of 1948, Fine Gael did not nominate candidates, despite contesting general elections in this period – their members ran variously as Farmers, Independents and United Ireland Party representatives. The year 1948 also saw Clann na Poblachta win four seats. Six years later one of these politicians, Johnny Connor, would go to the Dáil for Kerry North. Throughout the 1940s and 1950s, the council was not in the control of Fianna Fáil (or Fine Gael for much of the time) with the Farmers, Clann na Talmhan and Clann na Poblachta holding the top position at various intervals.

The year 1955 saw a third pair of brothers join the local authority: Patrick O'Connor-Scarteen for the Killarney area and Timothy, who was elected in Killorglin. They were the second of five sets of siblings to sit on the council benches at the same time following Michael J and Jamsie Fleming and were followed by Dick and Maeve Spring, Michael and Danny Healy-Rae, and Johnny and Maura Healy-Rae. In April 1956, Independent Charlie Lenihan was briefly deemed to have been disqualified for non-payment of rates, but, having paid the sum owing on the morning of the meeting, was co-opted back into the seat. The outgoing council held its last meeting at the Governor's House at the jail in Ballymullen in June 1960, moving into a new chamber at the Ashe Memorial Hall at the first meeting of the new council on 29 June. Independent James Courtney, from Castlegregory, won election here for the first time. He would remain on the council until the 1999 election, when he retired. By the 1967 poll, the two larger parties had a firmer grip on the authority, with Fianna Fáil taking twelve and Fine Gael ten of the twenty-six seats. Tom Fleming II became the third direct member of his family to enter the council, after his father (Tom Michael), his grandfather Mike Johnny and an uncle James. When Michael Doherty of Headford died, Jackie Healy-Rae of Kilgarvan was co-opted to replace him in December 1973, launching his own lengthy political career, as well as the Healy-Rae family dynasty. Tom McEllistrim II became the second member of his family to sit in the chamber and would also follow his father into the Dáil.

In 1974, Fianna Fáil experienced decisive success: the party took half the seats and Fine Gael was reduced to seven. There were five TDs in this council, four more would later enter the Dáil and one of these, along with two further members, served in the Seanad at other times. This council was historic in that Kit Ahern of Fianna Fáil became the first woman chairperson, serving in 1977–8. Fianna Fáil edged well ahead of Fine Gael

Richard Latchford, Tralee, one of the members of the first Kerry County Council, elected in 1899 (Michael Latchford).

The longest-serving chairperson of Kerry County Council, Jeremiah McSweeney (1926–30, 1932–42).

in 1979, with a majority of the seats, and Tom Fleming III became the fourth direct family member when he was co-opted to replace his late father Tom at the September meeting of 1984.

There was another procedural change for the eighteenth council, selected by voters in June 1985. The endeavour to rationalise the county in terms of moulding voting areas to fit the shape of Kerry led to a geographically bizarre electoral area that included west Kerry and eastwards to Castleisland being introduced under the title Mid-Kerry Electoral Area. An extra member was added, bringing the total to twenty-seven. Mid-Kerry had five members, Killarney, Listowel and Killorglin Electoral Areas each had six, while Tralee returned four members. Fianna Fáil remained the largest entity in the council, with thirteen seats, but took the overall majority when Independent Breandán MacGearailt joined the party in June 1986. The council moved into the new Áras an Chontae, the former St Catherine's Hospital, at Rathass, in January 1989, which is still its headquarters.

Fianna Fáil slipped back to thirteen seats in 1991, but it was Fine Gael that lost most members, the former TD Michael Begley and former senator John Blennerhassett both failing to retain their positions. While Blennerhassett had been an Independent at this point, he had remained close to the party. Michael Gleeson lost to his party colleague Breeda Moynihan-Cronin and spilt from Labour as a result, later helping to establish the South Kerry Independent Alliance and retaining a seat for many years. New legislation required cabinet and junior ministers to resign their seats on local authorities, so John Commane was co-opted to replace Dick Spring, his second cousin, in March 1993 and Paul O'Donoghue was co-opted to the seat that his brother, John, had filled in November 1997. A first cousin of the O'Donoghues, Michael D. O'Shea, was co-opted to replace the late Pat Finnegan in July 1994 and Bernie Behan was co-opted to replace Jimmy Deenihan in January 1995.

For the twentieth council, elected in June 1999, there were still twenty-seven seats, but the Mid-Kerry Electoral Area was abolished and a new Dingle Electoral Area came into being, returning three candidates. Tralee gained two, bringing its total to seven, Killarney retained its six, but both Killorglin and Listowel went back to having five each. Jackie and Michael Healy-Rae constituted a father-and-son combination in the chamber for the first time, Jackie remaining in Killarney and Michael succeeding in the Killorglin area. Labour had a good election, winning five seats as Fianna Fáil slipped back to twelve and Fine Gael took six. In 2004, however, Fine Gael did well, taking eight of the seats, although they lost P.J. Donovan. The O'Donoghue faction in Fianna Fáil put the squeeze on Brian O'Leary and he lost out to party colleague Colin Miller, but the former senator Dan Kiely was also a casualty and the party dropped a seat to eleven. This council gave Sinn Féin the chair for a year, through Toiréasa Ferris – only the third woman ever to take the chair – thanks to a voting arrangement with Fianna Fáil and the Healy-Raes. As chairperson, Ferris faced a motion of no confidence following her refusal in a *Late Late Show* interview on RTÉ to condemn the murder of Detective Garda Jerry McCabe in Adare ten years previously, but she survived the vote. The subsequent council, elected in the same manner, following the election of 2009 saw Fine Gael make a big breakthrough, taking ten seats to Fianna Fáil's seven, with Labour getting four. Both Michael and Danny Healy-Rae headed the polls in their respective electoral areas. Fine Gael's Bobby O'Connell lost a section of his support grounding in Castleisland because he switched areas from Tralee to Killarney, but he managed to retain his seat nonetheless.

There was a significant change for the twenty-third council, voted in by the public in May 2014. The new structure of local government resulted in the abolition of the Town Councils and the creation of new Municipal Districts. Thirty-three seats on the county council were filled from Municipal Districts in Tralee, Killarney, Listowel and South and West Kerry. Fianna Fáil staged something of a recovery, taking ten of the seats (rising to eleven when Michael Cahill rejoined in 2016 after five years as an Independent), but Sinn Féin was now a growing force, with five representatives being elected. Seven Independents were returned. There were also five women councillors, with Norma Foley and Toiréasa Ferris retaining their seats in Tralee, Aoife Thornton and Dianne Nolan winning for the first time in Listowel and Norma Moriarty taking a seat in South and West. This became six when Maura Healy-Rae was co-opted to replace Deputy Danny Healy-Rae following his election to the Dáil at the March meeting in 2016. Maura joined her brother Johnny in the local assembly. However, the proportion of women members fell again when the former Listowel UDC member Tom Barry was co-opted to replace Dianne Nolan of Sinn Féin in September 2017, following her resignation.

'Single-minded pursuit of his objectives'

Kerry's pioneering education minister

John Marcus O'Sullivan (left), later Professor of History at UCD, Minister for Education and TD for Kerry North, pictured with a group at UCD at the beginning of the last century, l–r: John Marcus O'Sullivan, George Clancy, Seumas Clandillon, Seumas O'Kelly, J Lennon (Helen Solterer/ UCD Special Collections).

Just six Kerry TDs have sat at the cabinet table over the course of the last century. Beginning with Kerry ministers of the 1920s, Austin Stack and Fionán Lynch, through to those of more recent times, like Dick Spring, John O'Donoghue and Jimmy Deenihan, Kerry has a proud ministerial record, despite there being a fifty-year gap between 1932 and 1982 when the county had no representation in cabinet. A key contributor to Kerry's ministerial legacy was Killarney native and Kerry North TD Professor John Marcus O'Sullivan, who not only made a profound impact in academia, but also presided over one of the biggest changes in Irish educational policy. Born in Killarney on 18 February 1881, O'Sullivan was educated at St Brendan's College, Killarney. He was a cousin of the East Kerry MP, Eugene O'Sullivan, and his uncle, Charles, was Bishop of Kerry from 1918 to 1927. Before entering politics, he pursued an illustrious career in academia, particularly at University College Dublin, where he was a student from 1898. Along with his professor at UCD, William Magennis, he founded the Academy of St Thomas Aquinas and he joined the editorial staff of *St Stephen's* magazine. In 1904, he won a scholarship to study in Germany and was awarded a doctorate in philosophy at Heidelberg University in 1906. On his return to Dublin in 1908, he was appointed Professor of History at his old *alma mater*, a position he held until his death. He became a prolific writer and published a number of works on history and philosophy, including *The Old Criticism and the New Pragmatism* (1909). He was on the Governing Body and senate of UCD for many years.

O'Sullivan first entered politics at the 1923 general election, when he won a seat in the Kerry constituency for Cumann na nGaedheal, taking the fifth of seven seats with 3,759 votes. His talents were quickly seized upon by president of the Executive Council, W.T. Cosgrave, and, in 1924, he became parliamentary secretary to the Minister for Finance, Ernest Blythe, with particular responsibility for the Office of Public Works. The Labour leader, Thomas Johnson, believed O'Sullivan, rather than Cosgrave, should have led the Executive Council.[1] In 1926, Cosgrave appointed O'Sullivan Minister for Education, a post previously held by Eoin MacNeill. A central policy position for Cumann na nGaedheal in the late 1920s had been equality of opportunity in education, but O'Sullivan inherited a system where facilities 'were often grossly inferior'.[2] A census of school buildings had revealed that over a third of schools in the county needed to be 'replaced or altered'.[3]

During his ministry, O'Sullivan lobbied for increased funding for maintenance for these schools, which were described in the Dáil as 'simply deplorable and indescribable'.[4] He oversaw the amalgamation of a large number of smaller primary schools, but met opposition from the Catholic bishops who feared that this would lead to more co-education, which was 'very undesirable'.[5] School attendance at primary level became compulsory in 1926 and O'Sullivan improved pay levels for teachers, including those in Gaeltacht schools. He also established a number of preparatory colleges to supply more Irish-speaking students to teacher training colleges. Efforts to increase and enhance the teaching of Irish were broadly considered a failure, however – O'Sullivan wasn't as enthusiastic about the language as his predecessor, MacNeill.[6]

The setting-up of the Commission on Technical Education was one of the key innovations of the period and was intended to tailor educational provision to the needs of trade and industry. Its recommendations led to what is regarded as O'Sullivan's most significant political contribution, the passage of the Vocational Education Act in 1930, which introduced vocational educational structures in Ireland for the first time. It set up thirty-eight Vocational Education Committees (VECs) around the country, a system which Professor Joe Lee noted 'did give some opportunity to poorer children to acquire a technically orientated education', rather than an exclusively academic one, but because such schools were not given the opportunity to prepare students for the Leaving Certificate examination, they were 'stamped from the outset as second rate by a public opinion weaned on the primacy of the more remunerative traditional education'.[7]

Technical schools were to be non-denominational and co-educational and this again raised the hackles of the Catholic Church. The hierarchy drew O'Sullivan's attention to a papal encyclical from Pope Pius XI which forbade co-education, so the minister asked VECs to schedule boys' classes and girls' classes at different times.[8] Transition to further education was extremely rare – in 1932, when O'Sullivan left office, just 7 per cent of children proceeded beyond primary education.[9] This was a situation that failed to improve under Fianna Fáil, as the former minister noted while speaking in Dingle in 1936:

> A matter that has aroused considerable attention in the last few weeks, especially here in Kerry, is the alarming fall in the number of children attending schools in the rural areas. But the abandonment of the countryside by almost 100,000 of our population since 1926 holds out no prospect that the position in this respect is likely to be improved within any reasonable time and that fear is further strengthened when we compare the excess of births over deaths in Kerry now and ten years ago. In 1924, the excess was 3,219 ... in 1934, it had fallen to 2,482.[10]

W.T. Cosgrave appointed O'Sullivan as a delegate to the League of Nations in 1924 and 1928–30. He continued to make voluble speeches in the Dáil and managed to retain his seat in Kerry in the face of a Fianna Fáil surge in 1932. At this time, he was national chairman of Cumann na nGaedheal. He moved to the Kerry North constituency in 1937 as a Fine Gael deputy, but lost his seat in 1943. Married to Agnes Crotty, he died in 1948 at his home at Orwell Road, Rathgar, in Dublin. One of his obituary writers described him as

> comfortably rotund, he had a dome-like head, rather dreamy yet searching eyes, and a guileless if beguiling smile ... [he was a] ceaseless student of affairs, human and otherwise, took a hand in the home: electricity and carpentry interested him, and he once made a most engaging and

electrically lit doll's house ... He grew his own vegetables, producing record tomato crops, and got perhaps more joy out of his children's mechanical toys than they did.[11]

The archives of University College Dublin hold many of O'Sullivan's personal papers and writings. A summer school in the name of John Marcus O'Sullivan is held annually in May and hosted by the Irish Vocational Education Association. One analyst of ministerial contributions to education policy, Antonia McManus, noted that O'Sullivan pursued many of the policies of his predecessor, Eoin MacNeill, 'but his single-minded pursuit of his objectives set him apart from the "wholly detached" approach of MacNeill ... John Marcus O'Sullivan's legacy to Irish education lay in his reform of the system of recruitment to training colleges and his introduction of the preparatory colleges, despite formidable opposition. His enduring legacy is the introduction of the 1930 Vocational Education Act and the vocational schools.'[12]

9

'Three weeks' turmoil, agitation and disturbance'

Kerry's By-Election Battles and their National Significance

There have been almost 140 by-elections to fill vacant seats in Dáil Éireann since 1919 and the results rarely have any major impact on the national parliamentary makeup, except, for example, where a minority government or one with a narrow majority is very dependent on the right outcome. But each of the four by-elections held in Kerry since the foundation of the Dáil has been of national significance, with political ramifications far beyond the constituencies. In two of them, history was made as national political firsts were achieved. One of those results saw the election of a woman who was so young she hadn't been registered to vote and the result of another gave one party all three seats in the one constituency. The results of these by-elections – three in Kerry South and one in Kerry North – provided for some titanic battles between the protagonists, gave the column writers plenty of drama and colour to report on and left their mark in local and, sometimes, national political folklore.

* * *

Candidate deselected for being 'so unpopular'
Kerry South by-election – 10 November 1944

The first ever by-election held in Kerry was the result of a judicial vacancy. Fionán Lynch, a former senior government minister and a prominent member of Cumann na nGaedheal (and later Fine Gael), was one of the three TDs elected for Kerry South at the general election of 1944. Lynch, of Kilmakerin, Waterville – who had been Minister for Education in the provisional government of 1922 and later served in cabinet under W.T. Cosgrave – had been in the Dáil since its establishment; he had represented Kerry and Kerry South since 1919 without a break. The snap general election of 1944 had been called by Taoiseach Éamon de Valera just a year after the previous one, which had seen Fianna Fáil retain power and secure an overall majority with over 48 per cent of the vote. At the poll held on 30 May 1944, Lynch, who was also a high-profile barrister, was again returned for Kerry South, alongside Fred Crowley and John B. Healy of Fianna Fáil.

Just a few months later, however, in October 1944, a vacancy arose in the Circuit Court on the Sligo and Donegal circuit. The Fianna Fáil government looked to the opposition benches in the Dáil to fill the judicial slot and Lynch was appointed to the bench. Notwithstanding their political differences, the Fianna Fáil leader Éamon de Valera held Lynch of the opposing Fine Gael party in high regard – they had been comrades during the Easter Rising in 1916 and remained friends. Lynch, who had been in relatively poor health since the late 1930s – he had been unable to campaign actively during the 1938 general election and had, in 1939, stood down as Leas Ceann Comhairle after just a year in the role due to poor health – accepted the appointment. He was to remain a judge until 1959.

A by-election to replace Fionán Lynch in Kerry South was set for 10 November 1944 and it immediately resulted in a serious headache for Fine Gael. The party was in poor shape in Kerry generally in the 1940s – Lynch was the only Fine Gael TD in the entire county at the time. Fine Gael and its predecessor Cumann na nGaedheal had never elected a TD other than Lynch in Kerry South. The party hadn't formally contested county council elections in Kerry in the 1930s or most of 1940s. It wasn't until 1948 that they put forward local authority candidates on the official party ticket. The party was thus denied the valuable foundations that council seats provide for Dáil candidates. Lynch's departure to the judiciary, therefore, created a huge void for his party.

The weakness of the party organisation in Kerry South was reflected in their shambolic candidate selection. A convention held on 22 October and presided over by party leader Richard Mulcahy chose Donal F. Collins from Killarney to be the party's standard bearer. Collins, formerly a member of Killarney Urban District Council – as his father, Con, had been

– was an auctioneer based on High Street. Just days into the campaign, however, Collins was unceremoniously deselected as the candidate by the Fine Gael national executive and replaced with 28-year-old farmer and general merchant Eoin O'Connell from Cahersiveen, whom Collins had defeated by just one vote at the convention.

In a dramatic letter published on the front page of the *Kerry Champion*, Collins described how just a day after the convention four or five delegates who were at the convention told headquarters that he, Collins, was 'the wrong man.'[1] The Fine Gael general secretary, Liam Burke, arrived in Killarney the following day and met party members and later told Collins he had made enquiries and had deduced that the candidate was 'so unpopular' that he would have to stand aside and allow O'Connell to contest the by-election. Collins was further warned that it would be 'detrimental to my business if I did not stand behind the chosen candidate'. Collins' signed off his letter with a stinging rebuke of the party leadership:

> I would like in view of all facts if [Fine Gael leader] Mr Mulcahy and the Fine Gael Organisation would put their 'cards' on the table and state publicly from what source my general unpopularity arose in two or three days or better still to state publicly the true reason for overthrowing the decision of the Convention. Why was my unpopularity not discussed at the Convention? That was the place to do so prior to having my name published as a candidate. Apparently, these people have not the courage of their convictions. As my livelihood covers all Kerry it would only be fair and just if Mr Mulcahy came out publicly with anything he has to say against me. Perhaps not so much Mr Mulcahy as his influential friends in Killarney. If this is Mr Mulcahy's 'Democracy' I wonder what Dictatorship is?[2]

Meanwhile, a Glenflesk native and national school teacher, Donal 'Danny Jim' O'Donoghue, was nominated by Fianna Fáil to contest the by-election. During the War of Independence, O'Donoghue had been Commandant of the 2nd Battalion of the 1st Brigade of the IRA. He taught for many years in Cork before becoming principal of Barraduff national school in east Kerry in 1933. The only other nominee for the by-election was Senator Edmund Horan. A native of Firies, Horan had contested the 1943 and 1944 elections in Kerry South on behalf of the farmers' party, Clann na Talmhan. He won a seat on the Agricultural Panel in the Seanad following the 1944 election. In 1942, ten farmers' candidates had won seats on Kerry County Council and Horan was drawing on a strong electoral base. He told voters that the government of the day 'was unable to undo in twenty years what Cromwell did in a month, that was, to restore the land to the people to whom the land belonged'.[3]

Though Fianna Fáil might have been somewhat better organised than their opponents on the ground, organising resources and money – at the height of the Second World War – presented its own challenge. John B. Healy TD was forced to write to Fianna Fáil headquarters, stating 'I find it impossible to get petrol here. I would be obliged if you could get some extra allowance for me.' The response from party general secretary, Seamus Davin, was that petrol coupons – which were rationed during the war – could only be had from the director of elections, Senator Fred Hawkins, who was based in the party office in Killarney.[4] After the by-election, the secretary of the Comhairle Dáil Cheantair, Richard Godsil from Rathmore, stated that locally the party had been left with a debt of £50 and he sought the support of head office in dealing with creditors, who were itemised by category, such as transport: 'M. O'Neill, Killorglin, 4 Traps P.D. £4'.[5] The party mobilised senior figures to address the essential after-Mass meetings. The party's archives contains a list of where ministers would be dispatched, including, for example, 'Frank Aiken – Killorglin after last Mass'.[6]

The result – after what *The Kerryman* called a 'very clean and strenuous campaign'[7] – was a comfortable win for Fianna Fáil and Donal O'Donoghue. He polled close to half the entire vote and picked up 10,986 first preferences, ahead of Horan on 6,795 and O'Connell on 4,822. The result created an extraordinary and unprecedented situation in Kerry South, if not in all of Ireland: Fianna Fáil were in possession of all three seats in the constituency, through O'Donoghue, Fred Crowley and J.B. Healy.[8] It was a historic and unique feat, which the party would never be able to repeat.

✷ ✷ ✷

'Three weeks' turmoil, agitation and disturbance'
Kerry South by-election – 4 December 1945

Within a year of the 1944 by-election, the voters of Kerry South were summoned back to the polling booths. One of the three sitting Fianna

Fáil TDs, Fred Crowley, a TD since September 1927, died in May 1945, creating another vacancy in the Dáil. His widow, Honor Mary Crowley, whose father, John Pius Boland, had been an MP for South Kerry from 1900 to 1918, was chosen to defend her husband's seat in the by-election. The couple had no children and Honor was seen by the party, locally and nationally, as his natural successor. There was no Fianna Fáil councillor other than Fred Crowley himself in his stronghold, the Killarney Electoral Area, and his widow quickly became the nominee.

However, at the time when Mrs Crowley was trying to engage with the electorate, politics and by-elections ranked low among people's priorities. The Second World War was coming to an end and the economic situation was dire. The position in Kerry South was no different and at the 1945 by-election, no more than the poll of the previous year, it was difficult to interest voters in the democratic process. A Fianna Fáil member, Jack O'Dwyer from Killorglin, wrote to party headquarters at the time, saying he 'never saw such apathy as in this district. The people were very indifferent and it is surprising that anybody went to vote'.[9] Like their counterparts, Fianna Fáil was without any meaningful resources to invest in by-election campaigns, locally and nationally, having just been through a presidential election campaign in June 1945 and the by-election in Kerry South in November 1944.[10] O'Dwyer noted 'we had no transport and very poor organisation' as the by-election loomed.

The financial strain on the party organisation locally is evident in the party archives from the time. Mrs Crowley's director of elections, Denis O'Brien, was sent 200 coupons for transport for the election campaign by the party general secretary, Tom Mullins, but was warned to hire cars for transporting the candidate and her campaigners only as a last resort.[11] Earlier in 1945, another party member, Jimmy Cronin of Main Street, Milltown, had appealed to headquarters to recompense election expenses incurred at the previous year's by-election:

> I expected to hear from you before now. As you know I was director of elections in my own area for the bye election in Kerry and should get some expenses. As you are aware, one cannot go around during election times without spending money.... As I got married recently I would be very much obliged to you if you send me on some money to cover my expenses during the election campaign.[12]

Cronin's letter was referred to the local organisation, but it is unclear if he was ever compensated. The financial plight of the party prompted a plea for money once the campaign began and advertisements were placed in *The Kerryman* seeking donations.

Polling day was set for 4 December 1945. While Honor Crowley was not opposed for the party nomination at the convention, a Dermot Horan from Inch, Castleisland, wrote to party headquarters offering his services to party leader, Éamon de Valera, explaining that:

> There has been no Fianna Fáil TD elected in South Kerry since the death of Fred Crowley RIP. As you are ... Minister of Eire and Leader of the Fianna Fail party, would you elect me as Fianna Fáil TD for South Kerry. I have only a small farm and my father has lost one of his hands.[13]

Fine Gael picked a teacher from Sneem, Patrick W. Palmer, to contest the by-election. The party was presented with an opportunity to challenge Fianna Fáil's hegemony in the constituency. Fianna Fáil held all three seats at the time. But Fine Gael seemed half-hearted about the prospect of undermining Fianna Fáil and gaining an extra seat in the Dáil. Senior parliamentary party member Dr T.F. O'Higgins told the Fine Gael selection convention in Killarney that 'the people should be spared the disturbance and upset' of by-elections in Kerry South and four others, which were scheduled for the same day in other constituencies.[14] Fine Gael, he said, believed the by-elections should be postponed, but the ruling Fianna Fáil party rejected the notion, with the result that the people of south Kerry were left to endure, as O'Higgins put it, 'three weeks' turmoil, agitation and disturbance'.[15]

Fine Gael's disarray in the previous year's by-election was replicated in December 1945. Just days after selecting Palmer to contest Kerry South, the Fine Gael leader General Richard Mulcahy told the Dáil that it had changed its mind and that it would not be contesting the by-election in Kerry South.[16] By holding five by-elections,[17] the Fianna Fáil government was forcing one sixth of the electorate to the polls for the fourth time in two years, Mulcahy argued, at a time when the country and the world faced greater issues in the immediate aftermath of the Second World War. Candidates would be 'going to the hustings to discuss matters of minor interest'. He concluded that Fine Gael would serve no national purpose by contesting any of the five by-elections, except one in Clare, where the vacancy was the party's own, a seat they would look to retain. With that, Patrick Palmer was withdrawn from the Kerry South race before he had a chance to erect a poster or knock on a door.

The Fine Gael withdrawal meant that Honor Crowley's only opponent was Senator Edmund Horan of Clann na Talmhan, who had contested the previous year's by-election. The Taoiseach, Éamon de Valera, spoke in support of Crowley at rallies in Cahersiveen, Killorglin and Killarney. When the votes were counted, Crowley outpolled Horan by 10,483 votes to 8,018. In winning a Dáil seat, Honor Crowley had set several precedents locally and nationally. She was the first woman ever elected to the Dáil from a Kerry constituency. In a national political context, Crowley had become the first woman ever to succeed her husband at a by-election. Her election ensured that Fianna Fáil continued to hold all three seats in Kerry South – with Donal O'Donoghue and J.B. Healy – but this was inevitably going to be a short-lived scenario. Facing into the 1948 general election just three years later, the Fianna Fáil trio faced a resurgent Fine Gael and a former Fianna Fáil, then Independent, Jack Flynn in the race. Former Minister of State and party activist John O'Leary recounted that, as the 1948 election loomed, party headquarters failed to force one of their sitting deputies to stand aside:

> holding three [seats] out of three was never going to be a runner – the vote simply wasn't there to elect three TDs from the one party. The problem was, however, that Fianna Fáil head office couldn't convince any of the sitting TDs to step down. Knowing full well that the party wouldn't hold three seats, the leadership wanted just two candidates, but they hadn't the courage to decide which two should be allowed to run. And when [Jack] Flynn entered the race as an ex-Fianna Fáiler and an Independent, it really threw the cat among the pigeons.[18]

When the votes were counted on 5 February 1948, only Mrs Crowley held on for Fianna Fáil and O'Donoghue and Healy were squeezed out, heralding the end of their political careers.

* * *

'It is time you woke up and did something about all this' *Kerry North by-election – 29 February 1956*

When the Clann na Poblachta TD for Kerry North, Johnny Connor (O'Connor) was killed in a road accident between Castleisland and Abbeyfeale just two weeks before Christmas 1955, it led to the only by-election ever held in that constituency. Connor, from Farmer's Bridge near Tralee, had won a seat for the party at the 1954 general election. He had a high profile in the IRA during the War of Independence and was an outspoken county councillor who was a well-known advocate for the farming community. At his funeral, Connor's widow, Catherine, was approached by the leader of Clann na Poblachta, Seán MacBride, who asked if she would contest the by-election, but attention quickly shifted to their daughter Kathleen, a recently qualified teacher, who, while she was studying in Dublin, used to help her father with his correspondence in his office in Leinster House. The 21-year-old felt compelled to defend her father's political legacy; he had been the first Clann na Poblachta TD ever elected in Kerry. Within weeks of her father's death, Kathleen O'Connor was formally nominated as the Clann na Poblachta candidate for the by-election, which was set to take place on 29 February 1956.

Again, the by-election was of significant national political importance. Following the 1954 general election, Clann na Poblachta had agreed to support an interparty government under Fine Gael Taoiseach John A. Costello, but they did so from the opposition benches, in a confidence-and-supply agreement. They had been part of the first inter-party coalition of 1948–51, but now, despite not formally being part of the coalition, they were essential to the survival of the government in an arithmetically tight situation in the Dáil. It was of considerable importance for the government to retain the Clann na Poblachta seat, so none of the coalition partners contested the poll. Kathleen O'Connor stepped up to the mark and became the first woman to seek election in the Kerry North constituency.

In an extraordinary show of strength, three party leaders and senior cabinet ministers – the Taoiseach and Fine Gael leader, John A. Costello, the Tánaiste and Labour leader, Brendan Corish, and the leader of Clann na Talmhan and Minister for Lands, Joseph Blowick – as well as the Clann

FIANNA FÁIL
NORTH KERRY BYE-ELECTION
1956

DAN
MOLONEY
THE FIANNA FÁIL CANDIDATE

POLLING DAY IS ON WED., FEB 29th 1956
From 9 a.m. to 9 p.m.
Let your slogan on that day be:
MOLONEY is the word and MOLONEY is the Man.

Vote No. 1 MOLONEY, Daniel J.

cuir fianna fáil i n-uaċtar

Published by Mariagh E. Barlin, Solicitor, Green Street, Dingle, Agent
for the Candidate, and printed by the Kerry Champion Ltd., Tralee.

Election literature of Dan Moloney, Fianna Fáil candidate at the 1956 by-election in Kerry North (Jimmy Moloney).

na Poblachta leader Seán MacBride – spoke in support of O'Connor at a rally in Listowel two days before the votes were cast and at another rally in Tralee on the eve of polling.[19] *The Kerryman* of 25 February 1956 carried a large advertisement, 'A Message from the Taoiseach to the people of North Kerry', in which the Taoiseach claimed that by electing Kathleen O'Connor, voters would 'give an example to the nation and will send a message of encouragement to the Government to go ahead with renewed vigour in their plans for the betterment of all classes and sections of the people'.[20]

Fianna Fáil decided to contest the by-election with Listowel-based councillor and national executive member Daniel 'Danny Jim' Moloney as their candidate. He was the only other runner. Whatever was felt about Labour's decision not to field a candidate – they already had a sitting TD in Dan Spring – Fine Gael's decision to stand back and not put forward a nominee was extraordinary. Fine Gael did not hold a seat in the constituency at the beginning of 1956; their former deputy, John Lynch, from Listowel had failed to retain his seat at the 1954 general election and they were now passing up an opportunity to regain it. The opt-out may have had more to do with the weakness of the constituency organisation, however. In a letter from Laois TD, Oliver J. Flanagan, to Fine Gael head office in 1954, he suggested that there was 'an urgent necessity for the awakening and reviving of the branches in North Kerry'. He noted that there was no report of the national collection in the constituency and the recent selection convention had 'lacked organisation'.[21] A memorandum from general secretary Colonel P.F. Dineen in 1955 described the organisation in the constituency as 'weak and inactive' and it was noted that there were no branches in rural areas like Causeway, Ballyheigue and Ballyduff. Dineen was forced to write to John Lynch just months after the by-election, stating, 'It is time you woke up and did something about all this.'[22]

Like the government parties, Fianna Fáil sent its heavy-hitters to the constituency to canvass for Dan Moloney. At the time, the four-seat Kerry North constituency included the Dingle Peninsula and frontbencher Donogh O'Malley – whose wife Hilda was a native of Dingle – was instructed to speak at party events in west Kerry. One of the local Fianna Fáil activists, Tom Fitzgerald from Lispole – who was later a senator and a close ally of Charles Haughey – was given responsibility for the traditional after-Mass speeches in the area. One Sunday morning during the campaign, Fitzgerald waited for his guests to arrive:

> This car pulls up and I recognised the man straight away: Donogh O'Malley, and Dermot Kinlen, who became a barrister afterwards ... They were dressed immaculately but I'd say the last drink they had was an hour before that; well-oiled the two of them were... O'Malley said to me, 'Are you Tom Fitzgerald?' ... I said we'd go on the fence there and when the boys above at the [church] door give the nod, we'll know it's the third shake of the holy water from the altar and you're on. 'Oh yeah, you'll introduce us,' said O'Malley. They started to make their way over up on the ditch and I stood up on the ditch knowing there was only a couple of minutes to go and my legs were shaking under me. The people came down and I was scared ... and I said 'Ladies and gentlemen, I am here today to introduce you to ...' and I started mentioning their names and the next thing, the crowd started laughing. Oh Jesus, this was terrible altogether. What were they laughing at and I looked at the two boys – they were after falling off the fence. The fence kind of slipped under them. O'Malley said: 'The fucking fence fell.' I said, 'You fell.'[23]

Kathleen O'Connor secured 18,176 first preferences versus Dan Moloney's 15,828 and was duly elected. Still not registered to vote at just twenty-one years of age, she became the third youngest TD ever returned to the Dáil up to that point and the first woman ever elected in Kerry North. Just as Honor Mary Crowley had set a political first in Ireland in 1945 by becoming the first ever woman to succeed her husband at a by-election, Kathleen O'Connor had also set a record: she is the first woman in Irish politics to succeed her father at a by-election. Her election represented an essential fillip to the coalition government of the day and to her party, Clann na Poblachta. But Kathleen's political career was to be one of the shortest in political history. She quickly decided that politics was not for her and she opted not to contest the 1957 general election. She returned to teaching and never again played an active role in politics in Kerry. Her decision to stand brought Clann na Poblachta's brief political success in Kerry to an abrupt halt. It would be another twenty years before a woman was elected to the Dáil to represent Kerry North.

* * *

'Mob law has returned to the country'
Kerry South by-election – 7 December 1966

Just as the death of her husband had prompted the by-election of 1945 in Kerry South, the death of Honor Mary Crowley in 1966 led to the holding of another by-election. Crowley – who had held her seat without defeat since she was first elected – had been in poor health during the summer of 1966 and she died at her Killarney home on 18 October. The by-election came at a critical time for Fianna Fáil, which was in government and transitioning to a new leader as Seán Lemass stepped aside and was succeeded by Jack Lynch. Lynch became Fianna Fáil leader on 10 November 1966. He decided to move the writs for two by-elections – the one in Kerry South and another in Waterford where the death of Fine Gael's Thaddeus Lynch had created another vacancy. The by-elections would be a critical first electoral test for the new Taoiseach and, if the result went the right way for Fianna Fáil, would be an important endorsement of the new leader. The by-elections were called for 7 December and Fianna Fáil brought its considerable manpower and resources to bear in both campaigns, but particularly in Kerry South, where they were defending their own seat. Whatever about gaining a potential seat from Fine Gael in Waterford, it would be a major blow if the party in government could not hold what it already had in Kerry South.

The electioneering supremo that was Donegal TD Neil Blaney was despatched to Killarney to manage the campaign of a young local authority official, John O'Leary, who was picked to defend Mrs Crowley's seat. Crowley had no children and no obvious familial successor. O'Leary, from Dunrine, Kilcummin, had risen through the ranks of the party organisation locally and had a high-profile footballing and athletics career. He was the favourite for the selection convention, which was hotly contested. At the 20 November selection, O'Leary saw off the challenge of Liam Cousins of Kenmare, Jack Walsh of Glencar, Diarmuid Moynihan from Rathmore and Batt O'Connor from Killarney.

Blaney ran the Fianna Fáil campaign with near military precision, mobilising local party canvassers and government ministers to great effect. Well-publicised rallies were held in the major towns and every church in the constituency was visited by speakers on behalf of the Fianna Fáil candidate. One senior minister, Charles Haughey, then Minister for Finance, felt the ire of the farming community – up in arms over low prices and campaigning under the leadership of Rickard Deasy and the National Farmers' Association – when he was jostled at an after-Mass meeting in Milltown. Blaney 'tested out a number of new ideas and tactics' during the campaign.[24] 'House to house canvassing is not enough,' he told canvassers, 'we have to do it person by person, and if someone is not in, we'll have to find out when they are in and someone will have to go back later and meet them.'[25]

With Blaney came considerable financial resources; it was to be one of the first election campaigns in which Taca money was used. Taca was a controversial and informal committee which was set up around 1965 and which raised money for Fianna Fáil by targeting wealthy businesspeople and selling access to senior ministers. It was spearheaded by ministers like Blaney, Charles Haughey and Donogh O'Malley and managed by Des Hanafin. O'Leary recalled that: 'The argument of Blaney, Haughey and Boland and the trustees of Taca, however, was that the party needed money to fight elections ... In reality, Taca was a slush fund for fighting elections and in Kerry South in 1966 the money flowed in.'[26]

Facing the might of the Fianna Fáil organisation and its resources were Fine Gael's Michael Begley and Labour's Michael Moynihan, both of whom had stood at the 1965 general election. Begley, a carpenter from Dingle, was a high-profile councillor who had been active in community organisations in west Kerry. Moynihan, a psychiatric nurse, was a senior official in the Irish Transport and General Workers' Union and had come within forty-five votes of Mrs Crowley on the final count in 1965. On that occasion, the Labour Party had been unable to afford a recount, which cost £100 at the time. At the by-election, the party's vice-chairman – and later Minister for Health and Social Welfare – Barry Desmond recognised quickly that they were 'up against the Killarney Fianna Fáil machine plus Blaney and [Minister Kevin] Boland who moved into town with their conclaves of supporters'.[27]

Neither Fianna Fáil and its Taca fund's spend, nor Labour's spend, are recorded. Fine Gael spent about £50 on ads in *The Kerryman* during the campaign, with a further £25 spent on petrol, £40 on renting 'election rooms' for the campaign headquarters and £5 on 'electrician/speakers'.[28] Speakers became an important feature of campaigns in the 1960s and there was amplification at rallies and after-Mass meetings for the first time. In 1966, those speaking were often drowned out by rivals, as the *Irish Independent* relayed: 'There was a noisy incident at Kenmare on Saturday night during electioneering in the South-Kerry by-election when the times of the Fianna Fáil and Labour meetings clashed. Fianna Fáil speakers were drowned by a pipe band which struck up to herald the start of the Labour meeting'.[29]

The advent of television gave by-election candidates a new way of communicating with voters. In 1966, RTÉ, then just five years in existence, carried a party political broadcast on behalf of Fianna Fáil which saw John O'Leary address the few of his electors who had a TV set. Owing to a poor TV reception during the broadcast and storm damage to a mast, many voters in south Kerry were unable to see it, prompting an appeal by Fianna Fáil headquarters to RTÉ, asking that it be re-broadcast, a request which fell on deaf ears.[30] The new Taoiseach, Jack Lynch, made many visits to the constituency during the campaign, as did many senior ministers like Donogh O'Malley of Limerick. As in the 1956 by-election campaign in Kerry North, O'Malley was again dispatched to west Kerry (now part of the Kerry South constituency) and was teamed up with Dingle's Tom Fitzgerald, who recalled O'Malley's very direct approach:

O'Malley was down and I was with O'Malley canvassing; he'd go nowhere without me. He used to be laughing at my way of canvassing – we'd go up to a door and he'd say 'Bang, bang, open it,' and it might be a poor woman breastfeeding her baby, it didn't make a difference, 'How're you Mary, you know this man?' he'd say.

The impact of Fianna Fáil's ground war and financial war chest ensured that John O'Leary took 12,499 votes to comfortably retain the seat for Fianna Fáil. At the packed count centre in Killarney's Town Hall, the tension was high

VOTE No. I

O'LEARY

POLLING 9am-9pm 7th Dec.

FIANNA
FÁIL

John O'Leary canvassing card for the 1966 by-election (*John O'Leary RIP*)

amid 'wild scenes of disorder.'[31] *The Kerryman* reported: 'After the announcement of the final count, barricades and politicians were swept aside as the crowd in the public area clamoured to reach O'Leary. Trestle tables on which the counting had been done were smashed and several people were thrown to the ground.'[32] Neil Blaney hailed a 'glorious day for South Kerry' on the election of a candidate 'with fire in his belly.'[33] Fine Gael's Michael Begley alleged dirty tricks, however, telling the *Cork Examiner* that a government minister had pulled down one of his posters during the campaign: 'Mob law has returned to the country,' he declared.[34]

For Jack Lynch and Fianna Fáil, there was cause for a double celebration as their candidate Patrick 'Fad' Browne won the by-election in Waterford. The successes gave Fianna Fáil their largest governing majority since 1957. John O'Leary went on to serve in the Dáil without a single defeat, until 1997, making him the longest-serving TD for Kerry South. He was Minister of State at the Department of the Environment from 1977 to 1979 and died in 2015.

10

'For a paper to be valid it must have recorded on it a first preference'

How a Kerry Candidate Rewrote the Irish Electoral Rulebook

On Wednesday, 10 February 2016, Ireland was deep in the midst of a general election campaign. The country's lampposts were covered in election posters, the party leaders' debates were in full swing and door-to-door canvassing was continuing in earnest. Despite expectations that the country would go to the polls in the autumn of 2015, the Fine Gael–Labour government led by Enda Kenny had stumbled on into the new year until Kenny finally dissolved the Dáil on the morning of 3 February. His administration had lasted its full five-year term despite inheriting a bankrupt country and having to implement one austerity budget after another. Fianna Fáil, devastated at the previous election, were plotting a comeback. The long-anticipated campaign was well underway and the ballots were due be cast on polling day, which had been set for 26 February. But two weeks before the voters went to the polls and the shape of the new Dáil was revealed, they were already counting votes in Kerry. The tallymen and tallywomen were busy scrutinising bundles of ballot papers at the John Mitchels GAA clubhouse on the outskirts of Tralee. Apart from party apparatchiks from the constituency, the count centre was teeming with barristers and legal eagles from the party's head offices. The county solicitor was present. So too were several county councillors and seasoned election observers and psephologists like Fianna Fáil's Teddy Healy, Fine Gael's Frank Quilter and Labour's Jerry Mason, party loyalists who would ordinarily have been immersed in campaigning for the general election. But it wasn't general election ballots which were being counted in the spacious sports hall a fortnight ahead of the rest of the country. Instead, those gathered were re-examining several thousand ballot papers which had been cast almost two years before and which had been the subject of a ground-breaking and protracted legal battle which went all the way to the highest court in the land, blowing a gaping hole in the way in which votes had been counted in Ireland for decades, resulting in the rewriting of the Irish electoral rulebook and changing the way elections are run in Ireland.

* * *

In June 2014, Irish voters went to the polls to elect local councillors, as well as members of the European parliament; it was customary for many years for both elections to coincide, saving electors two separate trips to the polling stations. Following the controversial abolition of town councils by the Minister for the Environment and Local Government, Phil Hogan, the local authority elections were more keenly contested than ever, with many former town council members vying for seats on the county councils. In north Kerry, one of the most experienced and battle-hardened campaigners in Kerry politics rolled the political dice for one last time. At seventy-two years of age, Dan Kiely was throwing his hat into the ring to win a council seat in the Listowel Electoral Area. Kiely was one of Kerry's most enduring, colourful, recognisable and sometimes controversial politicians. The Tarbert native had been involved in electoral politics for forty years and had been involved in Fianna Fáil for even longer. Politics was Dan Kiely's life. His father, also Dan, a native of Kiskeam in County Cork, fought in the War of Independence and was a member of Broy's Harriers in west Cork. Dan Snr was stationed in Tarbert as a garda and on retiring from the gardaí, he joined the Tarbert cumann of Fianna Fáil. One of seventeen children, Dan Jnr emigrated to New York in 1960. He worked delivering the internal mail in Goldman Sachs investment brokers on Wall Street and later worked at IBM. He was also employed part-time as a bartender in Gaelic Park in New York and was friendly with GAA stalwart, John Kerry O'Donnell. An enterprising businessman, Kiely bought the Red Mill nightclub in the city, which was on the verge of closing, for $15,000; it was turned into a dancehall which could hold 1,000 people. On returning to Ireland, Kiely invested in the Hibernian Hotel in Ballybunion and the other hotels in the south-west. He also became active in the GAA and trained the Kerry minor team in the early 1970s.

Kiely joined Fianna Fáil and had his first electoral outing at the 1974 local elections, when he stood in the Listowel Electoral Area. He wasn't elected on that occasion, but succeeded five years later and began a lengthy career on the local authority. However, Kerry County Council wasn't the extent of Kiely's political ambitions and in 1981 he won a seat in the Seanad on the Labour Panel. The following year – in both 1982 general elections – he ran for the Dáil in Kerry North alongside TDs Tom McEllistrim and Denis Foley. He did so again without success in 1987. Throughout the years in which Kiely was trying to become a TD, the Foley and McEllistrim camps had a strong grip on the party locally:

> I found it very hard to break in, in their particular set-up. They used the Listowel Electoral Area as poaching grounds; if they wanted to get delegates into cumanns and so forth, it's out there they came hunting … There's no doubt about it that the McEllistrims didn't want a second seat [for Fianna Fáil]. They didn't want it from the time of Dan Moloney in Listowel [TD from 1957 to 1961] and they didn't want it with Kit Ahern [TD from 1977 to 1981] in Ballybunion. They only wanted one TD … It caused an awful lot of tension and a lot of bitterness.[1]

Kiely managed to carve out a successful career in the Seanad, however, and he held a seat there from 1987 to 2002, when he contested his last general election as a running mate to Thomas McEllistrim III. Though losing his council seat in 2004, he was co-opted to the local authority in 2007 when Listowel's Ned O'Sullivan became a senator. He lost out again in 2009.

As the 2014 local elections approached, Kiely entered the race for the Fianna Fáil nomination for the Listowel Electoral Area. Party headquarters opted to run a candidate in the urban part of the electoral area and one from the rural area, but this wasn't announced until the night of the selection convention. This meant that Kiely, based in Ballybunion, had to contest the rural nomination and had no access to delegate votes in Listowel town. John Brassil from Ballyheigue was chosen as the rural candidate, outpolling Kiely at the selection convention by 230 votes to 182, while Jimmy Moloney was picked as the Listowel town-based candidate. Immediately Kiely asked party headquarters in Dublin to add him to the ticket, convinced that Fianna Fáil could win three seats in the seven-seater. But as the months went by, Kiely received no response, despite entreaties to TDs like Niall Collins and Michael Moynihan. Kiely claims he was assured that he would be added to the ticket, but a large meeting of his supporters convinced him that it was time to pull the plug. He resigned from Fianna Fáil to stand as an Independent. 'It's madness not to select a third candidate,' Kiely told *The Kerryman*. 'This was a hard decision after 40 years in a party I gave my whole life to. I'm very sore over it and very disappointed.'[2] Kiely's departure came amid a raft of resignations from Fianna Fáil in Kerry ahead of the local elections in 2014, including the resignations of Johnnie Wall in Tralee, Tom Doherty in Killarney and Tom Walsh in Listowel, each of them town councillors who had failed to win nominations at party conventions, but, like Kiely, were running as Independents seeking county council seats.

* * *

Kiely performed much better than many predicted. Despite being outside the fold, many Fianna Fáil members canvassed with him and he ran a strong campaign. The election on Friday, 23 May 2014, coincided with elections to the European parliament. The following morning, the ballot boxes from throughout Kerry were taken to the Killarney Sports and Leisure Centre to allow for the segregation of county council and European votes, the latter being despatched to the Ireland South constituency count centre in Cork. The local authority ballots for the Tralee and Listowel Electoral Areas were then removed to the John Mitchels GAA Clubhouse in Tralee to be counted. The returning officer for the count, Michael McMahon, a senior official with Kerry County Council and deputy returning officer for the whole county (to his colleague, John Flynn), oversaw the counts in both Tralee and Listowel electoral areas. In the normal way, papers considered by count staff to have been spoiled or where the preference of the voter was unclear were set aside. At about 8.30pm, McMahon stepped up to the microphone to announce that he was about to adjudicate on the doubtful papers and he invited each of the candidates in the Listowel area or a representative to come forward to participate in that adjudication. It had long been the practice in Irish elections that whenever a returning officer was deciding whether to include or exclude the doubtful count papers, candidates were permitted to contribute to the discussion and make a case to the returning officer if they disagreed with his rulings. But the final decision always rested with the returning officer. McMahon placed 173 doubtful papers on a table and a group of candidates and party handlers gathered round. Crucially, however, neither Dan Kiely nor a representative were present.

Kiely had decided not to go to the count centre until late on the Saturday night, opting to stay at home and receive updates by telephone from his supporters at the count. He was therefore absent for a critical part of the count. He would later argue that throughout his political career, he had never been part of the adjudication of doubtful papers. He had always been part of the Fianna Fáil organisation and the scrutiny of such ballots was always overseen by legal experts, such as Tralee solicitor Tom O'Halloran, on behalf of the candidates. When he eventually arrived at the count centre hours later for the declaration of the first count, Kiely learned from other candidates that some of the ballot papers considered doubtful – and admitted to the full count – had included papers beginning with preferences other than the number 1. Kiely was astonished and had never heard of such a practice before:

> I was told by people looking at the spoiled votes that some ballots [beginning] with a number 3 had been included as a number 1. When I heard this, it set off alarm bells for me. I didn't know this is something that had gone on for years. I was quizzed about this in the witness box later but with all the political experience I had and all the elections I ran in, I was never in there to look at spoiled votes. I felt that this was wrong and then when the margin was so narrow at the finish, I thought there might have been a chance for me to pick up votes if I had been able to see those spoiled papers.[3]

The count, which included a recount sought midway through the proceedings by Independent Michael 'Pixie' O'Gorman, ran into the Monday and Kiely asked Michael McMahon if the spoiled papers would be rechecked, but McMahon refused, saying they had already been ruled invalid and were thus excluded from any recheck. After the final count, Kiely lost out on the final seat by just two votes. He was two behind Fine Gael's Mike Kennelly and five behind Jimmy Moloney of Fianna Fáil. The seven candidates returned for the Listowel Electoral Area were declared:

Beasley, Robert (Sinn Féin)
Brassil, John (Fianna Fáil)
Kennelly, Mike (Fine Gael)
Moloney, Jimmy (Fianna Fáil)
Nolan, Dianne (Sinn Féin)
Purtill, Liam (Fine Gael)
Thornton, Aoife (Fine Gael)

Kiely's team immediately requested a recount, which was not unusual given the closeness of the result. He asked that the 173 ballots which had been excluded from the count two evenings previously also be re-examined as part of the recount, but Michael McMahon, consistent with national departmental electoral guidelines, refused. The recount proceeded and found the same margin of votes between Kiely and Kennelly. McMahon declared the result, bringing an end to proceedings.

* * *

In the days that followed, Kiely weighed up his options. He wasn't prepared to go down without a fight and give up his political career for the sake of a pair of votes. Nor was he satisfied about the ballots that had been deemed spoiled. He knew that the only course of action open to him was to petition the Circuit Court, under the provisions of the Local Elections (Petitions and Disqualifications) Act, 1974, through which the result of an election could be challenged. Knowing that he would need plenty of legal firepower to mount the challenge, he got in touch with Paul O'Donoghue. A solicitor based in Killorglin, O'Donoghue brought more than a little legal and political experience to what was about to unfold. A member of Kerry County Council from 1997 – when he was co-opted to the seat of his brother, John, who had been appointed Minister for Justice – O'Donoghue had initially been a candidate for the local elections in 2014. But the Cahersiveen native had dramatically withdrawn from the race four months before the poll, citing work commitments, and was replaced on the ticket by Norma Moriarty from Waterville. He knew a thing or two about elections, having tallied on plenty of occasions for his brother in general elections, and for his mother, Mary, a councillor from 1964 to 1985.

O'Donoghue enlisted the help of barrister Elizabeth Murphy and just days after the poll, Kiely petitioned the Circuit Court to have the result of the election in the Listowel Electoral Area declared invalid under Section 5 of the 1974 Act. There were four grounds:

- That the decision of the Returning Officer to refuse to include the re-examination of doubtful ballot papers in the recount was incorrect and unlawful,
- That the decision of the Returning Officer to adjudicate on doubtful ballots without notifying Kiely or ensuring he was present was incorrect and unlawful,
- That the result would have been different if either of those issues had been addressed at the count,
- And, most controversially, that the Returning Officer erred in including ballot papers where a sequence of preferences did not begin with the Number 1.

The last point of appeal cut to the heart of a practice which had developed in election count procedures in Ireland over many years, on occasions when more than one election took place on the same day. It had been customary in Ireland for decades for local authority elections to take place on the same day as elections to the European parliament; again, in May 2014, Irish electors had filled ballot papers for council and European elections at the same time in the polling booths. Over the years, when voters were completing two papers at the same time, it had been noticed that some voters would commence their preferences, 1, 2, 3 etc on one ballot paper and continue the same sequence of preferences 4, 5, 6 etc on the other paper. Even though electors were clearly instructed to mark preferences in order of their choice beginning with the number 1, returning officers had begun to accept that in such a scenario a sequence of numbers beginning with a number other than 1 was indicative of the voter's selection. Some voters clearly didn't distinguish between the two different ballot papers and used one continuous sequence of preferences across both papers. Returning officers – with the imprimatur of the Department of the Environment and Local Government – began to accept this practice and allowed a number other than 1 to have the same effect as a 1, provided it was a clearly arranged sequence and provided that there was an apparent logic to the behaviour of the voter. So, while a number 4 was clearly not a number 1, if the sequence on a ballot paper was sequential, the number 4 could be accepted as the voter's highest preference and thereby constitute their first preference. It was an effort to prevent the disenfranchisement of a voter where there seemed to be some logical thinking at play.

Accepting such ballots as valid was a practice that was largely unknown to the vast majority of voters, not to mention political apparatchiks. Only those most intimately involved in the adjudication of ballots with the returning officer would have seen this happen over the years, a point made repeatedly by Kiely and his legal team throughout the proceedings. During evidence given in the Circuit Court, John Fitzpatrick, who was the returning officer for the County of Dublin for over thirty-five years, noted that on the first occasion when a national and European election were held together, 7 June 1979, he discovered that there were a lot of European election papers which were marked 4, 5 and 6, etc., but which did not contain the numbers 1, 2 or 3. Having checked with colleagues he found that a similar experience was being encountered by them. Both Kiely and O'Donoghue found this practice to be perverse. 'I had been scrutinising doubtful papers from the age of eighteen,' said O'Donoghue, 'and I had never heard of 3s or 4s or 5s being admitted as first preferences in a count. I felt there was something perverse about that.'[4]

During the evidence presented to Judge Carroll Moran at the Circuit Court, O'Donoghue became alarmed when he heard reports of an informal meeting of the country's returning officers shortly before the election at which, it appeared, they discussed how they would conduct the counts and implement the departmental guidelines.[5] O'Donoghue took the view that this was an effort by the returning officers to act 'ultra vires', that is, beyond their power or authority. Kerry County Council, meanwhile, relied on the provisions contained in the Memorandum of Guidance for Local Authority Returning Officers issued before the election, which stated that they were entitled, on multiple election days, to accept as valid and admit to the count ballots containing the series of number 3, 4, 5, 6, etc., even though the ballot paper instructs voters to write the number 1 beside their first choice of candidate. The returning officer was following the guidelines – it was as simple as that.

* * *

On 14 July 2014, at Tralee Circuit Court, Judge Moran delivered his judgement to a courtroom packed with election candidates, party officials and barristers. The ruling brought little solace to the plaintiff. On whether the recount should have included a re-examination of doubtful ballots already excluded, Judge Moran was clear that under Article 81 of the Local Elections Regulations of 1995 a recount was confined only to valid papers and re-examining papers deemed invalid was not permissible. Returning officers had already made a 'quasi-judicial ruling' on spoiled votes, the judge noted, and to reconsider such matters would require the returning officer to 'appeal himself'.[6] Returning officers were not only 'not obliged', but were 'not entitled' under legislation, to include doubtful ballots in a recount.[7] He added there would be 'major practical difficulties' in re-examining doubtful ballots, some of which might have been already assimilated into the count.

In considering Kiely's demand that he should have been notified about and present at the assessment of doubtful papers, Judge Moran observed that although, at this election, Kiely did not have 'the support of a party machine' to which he would have been accustomed in Fianna Fáil, he had a 'long experience in politics' and had contested sixteen elections at a local and national level, implying that he should been well acquainted with the count process: 'All candidates have to take responsibility for what they do, or do not do, in the course of the campaign and in the course of the counting of votes and in this regard they cannot blame other persons for their own acts or omissions.' Kiely was being told in no uncertain terms that his absence from the count centre when the doubtful papers were being considered was entirely his own fault.

Finally, Judge Moran ruled on whether the admission into the count of ballot papers with a sequence of preferences beginning with a number other than 1 was correct and lawful. Kiely's argument was that those votes should have been omitted from the count, but the judge disagreed fundamentally, arguing that the 1995 regulations made clear that 'a first preference may be indicated by a mark other than one'. He accepted Michael McMahon's evidence that, in keeping with the practice of returning officers for many years, he was aiming to enfranchise voters and give effect to their voting preferences, given that there had been another election on the same day. The judge believed there was common sense in the approach set out in the guidance notes issued to returning officers ahead of the 2014 local elections, which explicitly stated what had been customary for decades: 'for the purpose of consistency, returning officers should accept as valid individual ballot papers which include a sequence of preferences (e.g. 4, 5, 6 or 6, 7) which suggest that voters followed on from preferences recorded on the ballot papers at another election held on the same day.' McMahon, the judge concluded, was therefore perfectly entitled to admit such votes and had done nothing wrong. Judge Moran dismissed the petition on all four grounds.

✳ ✳ ✳

Dan Kiely's immediate instinct was to fight on. The only remaining recourse open to him was to take the matter to the Supreme Court, which could hear a challenge to Judge Moran's ruling, but only on a point of law. Kiely's team were convinced there was enough of a public interest element to the appeal to merit a challenge at the Four Courts:

> On the way out of the Circuit Court, we had discussions. Both Paul [O'Donoghue] and Elizabeth [Murphy] believed the decision was wrong. They said there were grounds for an appeal. I came home and got loads of phone-calls from my supporters. And it began to eat me like cancer. I believed it was all wrong and I discussed it with my family. But I knew if I went to the Supreme Court, there was a big risk financially. I knew it was €10,000 at a minimum to lodge an appeal, which I didn't have. I balked for a while when I thought about what could happen to me if I lost the case. But it continued to bother me and I hopped in the car and went to Paul O'Donoghue's office in Killorglin and told him I was going to appeal it. The papers were ready. I had a week to ten days and I borrowed €500 from twenty people and I signed the appeal papers.[8]

In July 2015, Kiely was given leave to appeal the matter to the Supreme Court. Mr Justice Frank Clarke noted that there were 'net legal questions which are very clearly and succinctly set out in the document filed before this court', adding that the case should be dealt with as a matter of urgency not only for the sake of Kiely, but so that the sitting councillors who may be affected could also have certainty regarding their positions. Clarke's observations were a reminder that at least two recently elected councillors – Fine Gael's Mike Kennelly and Fianna Fáil's Jimmy Moloney (two and five votes ahead of Kiely respectively) – faced being unseated if a further recount of the ballots was undertaken. There were even suggestions that Kerry County Council as an elected body was not

validly constituted while the legal proceedings continued, but this notion
was firmly dismissed.

Kiely lodged his appeal with the Supreme Court on 2 August 2014
and Elizabeth Murphy spent much of the summer preparing the case.
Kiely and his legal team approached the former Minister for Justice and
attorney general Michael McDowell to take their argument to the Supreme
Court. Whatever about his considerable experience at the cabinet table,
McDowell, a distinguished barrister, had been through one of the longest
recounts in Irish political history – in 1997, he had lost his Dáil seat in
Dublin South East to the Green Party's John Gormley, following a week
of recounts involving some of the top legal eagles in the Law Library.
McDowell was happy to come on board, but he would not be the only
well-known figure to participate in the legal battle that lay ahead. As Paul
O'Donoghue noted: 'It was a very lopsided ship in the Supreme Court. I
felt a bit sorry for Dan, to be honest, because here we were on one side of
the court and across the way was a plethora of lawyers including barristers
Noel Whelan, Jim O'Callaghan, David Sutton and Frank Callinan. But Dan
never flinched at all of that.' Kiely, himself, was somewhat underwhelmed
by his surroundings and uncertain about his prospects: 'I was never in the
Supreme Court in my life. It was a tiny little room. I was confident that we
would win on the "3 not being a 1" issue but we weren't so sure we would
get a recount. McDowell put up a strong case.'

* * *

The eagerly awaited Supreme Court judgement was delivered just a week
before Christmas in 2015.[9] Crucially, all five Supreme Court judges ruled
that the inclusion of votes containing a sequence of numbers not including
the number 1 amounted to a mistake under Section 5 of the Local Elections
Act of 1974, which would have significant repercussions for how elections
would be conducted in Ireland in the future. Judge Donal O'Donnell cut to
the chase in his judgement:

> the sequence 3, 4, 5, or any similar sequence, does not satisfy the
> statutory requirement of *clearly* indicating a first preference. In this
> regard, it is important, firstly, that the voter has failed to comply with
> the instruction to place a 1 (whether in numeral or word) on the ballot
> paper. Secondly, it is significant that what is alleged to be a mark, in

this case indicating a first preference, is itself a numeral other than 1. The number 3 only makes sense in the context of other numerals. To that extent, the number 3 implies the existence of a number 1 and also that they are different, and that they are mutually exclusive. In the same way, 'third' implies the existence of 'first' and that they are, by definition, different things. Normally, to say that something is third means that is not, and cannot be, first.

Judge William McKechnie was even more direct:

It is beyond controversy but that for a paper to be valid it must have recorded on it a first preference. This reflects basic principles of electoral law. It can also be seen from Article 80(2) of the Regulations where it is stated that any ballot paper – '(b) on which the figure 1 standing alone, or the word "one" or any other mark which, in the opinion of the returning officer, clearly indicates a first preference, is not placed at all or is not so placed as to indicate a first preference for some candidate' – shall be invalid and not counted. Accordingly, any paper which fails to disclose such a preference must be rejected.

McKechnie said the Memorandum of Guidance for returning officers which was used in 2014 had no statutory foundation, it was 'sub-legal' and itself stated it did not purport to give a definitive statement of the law on any point. This meant its advices must yield to the primary legislation – the 1974 Act – and particularly the regulations made under that Act.

On the issue of whether Kiely was entitled to a recount, only Mr Justice Peter Charleton dissented, but the majority of judges ruled that in the circumstances 'all the votes cast at the election shall be counted afresh', under the supervision of the Circuit Court. Furthermore, they ruled that the decision of the returning officer in respect of votes containing a sequence of numbers not commencing with '1' or 'one' should be reversed and that those votes should not be allocated to any candidate during the new count. The court was essentially insisting that Kerry County Council dust down the ballot papers cast in the Listowel Electoral Area, shuffle them around or 'remix the votes' and count them afresh, the only difference being the exclusion of papers with a sequence of preferences beginning with a number other than '1'. All doubtful papers would also need to be re-examined afresh.

Kiely was 'shocked, delighted and surprised. I knew I was back into it for the long haul again. I knew I still had a chance by getting to see the spoiled votes'. Just days after the result, the Department of the Environment and Local Government issued new guidelines to its returning officers. In them, returning officers were instructed that any numerical sequence on a ballot paper that begins with a number other than '1' or 'one' is 'not to be read as clearly indicating a preference and, therefore, would be treated as an invalid ballot paper'.[10]

***

The new count was scheduled, coincidentally, to take place during the 2016 general election. Electioneering was in full swing for the Dáil election when the ballot boxes were moved from a locked safe at County Buildings in Tralee to the John Mitchels GAA Club for the second time on 10 February 2016. As the 2014 returning officer Michael McMahon had retired by this stage, a new returning officer, Charlie O'Sullivan, deputy chief executive of Kerry County Council, was appointed to oversee the count afresh. For the count afresh, Kiely was well prepared. He enlisted the support of barrister Rosemary Healy-Rae; Kiely had backed the campaign of her brother, Michael Healy-Rae, in the general election. Healy-Rae was looking to extend his political reach into the north of the county, which was, for the first time in seventy years, a single constituency. As a fellow Independent, Kiely threw his weight behind Healy-Rae and canvassed for him in north Kerry:

> I knew we needed the best team for the recount and Rosemary said she would be honoured to do it – she had done it for her father over the years. And I also had Brian O'Leary, the former councillor from Killarney who had vast experience of elections. I left the checking of the spoiled votes to Rosemary. I stayed out of it.

Because the count was taking place under the jurisdiction of the Circuit Court – on the instruction of the Supreme Court – any issues which arose during the count which could not be dealt with by agreement at the count centre would require the ruling of Circuit Court judge, Thomas E. O'Donnell. As O'Donnell happened to be sitting in Limerick at the time, this meant that Charlie O'Sullivan and County Solicitor Rosemary Cronin had to travel to Limerick Circuit Court to obtain rulings from Judge O'Donnell on a number of papers on which there was no agreement. On Thursday, 11 February, O'Sullivan and Cronin presented thirty-two doubtful ballot papers at Limerick Circuit Court for his consideration. O'Sullivan outlined his reasoning behind rejecting or allowing the papers one by one. In total he was proposing to allow twenty-seven of the ballot papers. Among the disputed papers were six to which the counterfoils were still attached with the official stamp on the counterfoil – these were rejected by Judge O'Donnell. On another ballot paper, horns, a moustache and a beard had been drawn on the photograph of one of the candidates.[11] This paper was allowed. Judge O'Donnell quipped that the voter was 'one unhappy Kerryman'. After hearing all submissions on other papers, he ordered that eighteen of the disputed ballot papers be included in the count.

The result of the count afresh was declared late on the night of 11 February. It found the same margin of votes between Kiely, Kennelly and

Pictured at Tralee Courthouse during Dan Kiely's petition to have the result of the 2014 local elections in Listowel area declared void, l–r: Elizabeth Murphy, barrister, Nuala Costello, Dan Kiely and Paul O'Donoghue, solicitor (*Kerry's Eye*).

Moloney – Kiely was still two votes adrift. Disappointed, Kiely was without regret: 'There was a weight off my shoulders and off my personal being. I had to do what I had to do. I wouldn't have lived with it if I hadn't appealed it to the Supreme Court. No regrets.'[12] Many observers declared the end of Kiely's political career, but there was almost a further rehabilitation of the doughty former senator during the protracted negotiations on government formation which went on through the spring of 2016 and Kiely was very much in the fray for a position in the Upper House:

> There was a lot of shuffling going on in government. There were a lot of phone-calls in and out. There was rumours here and rumours there. Michael Healy-Rae was offered a ministry and another position. Rosemary was rumoured to be getting that position, but it was Dan that was getting it. So, my leg was still in the pot but it just didn't work out.[13]

✷ ✷ ✷

The legacy of the Kiely case might not enthral the average voter, but it changed electoral procedures in Ireland for evermore. Never again can anything but a clearly identifiable number 1 be taken as an indication of the voter's first preference. The voter who continues a numerical sequence of preferences from one ballot paper to another on a day on which more than one election is being decided will be, in effect, spoiling one of those ballots and their vote will not be recorded. The Kiely judgement will be far-reaching and have consequences for years to come. Reflecting on the outcome, Paul O'Donoghue believes the impact on elections has been very significant:

> As someone involved in politics for many years, this case was unique, from my point of view, in every respect. Dan Kiely showed temerity and tenacity and the courage of his convictions. The legacy of the case is that it has brought clarity to counts going forward. There was ambiguity and discretion involved in the past but now there can be no further doubt. The case has done service to the electoral process.[14]

'Pack your bags and get out'

The councillor who took his own council to court

Progressive Democrats leader Des O'Malley with party candidate Michael Ahern and supporters in Killarney ahead of the 1987 general election (Michelle Cooper-Galvin).

One of the outcomes of the single transferrable vote system of proportional representation first used for the local authority elections in 1920 has been the emergence of smaller parties. On the national stage, one of the quirkier outcomes has been the doses of harsh electoral odium visited upon these smaller parties by successive electorates when they take what might be considered reasonable positions in supporting a particular government. The Progressive Democrats (PDs) is probably an unusual example as the party was an offshoot of Fianna Fáil and principally driven by the antagonism between two individuals. There were multiple Kerry threads to the PD story.

Donogh O'Malley entered the Dáil at the age of thirty-three in 1954, representing Fianna Fáil in Limerick East. As Minister for Education in Jack Lynch's administration, O'Malley introduced a measure that would provide free secondary education up to Intermediate Certificate level and an extension of free bus services for schoolchildren. He also introduced the Regional Technical Colleges, but he died suddenly on 10 March 1968 before many of these initiatives had actually been put in place. His parents had been supporters of Cumann na nGaedheal and he married Hilda Moriarty from Dingle, who is regarded as the muse that inspired Patrick Kavanagh's poem 'On Raglan Road'.

It is no accident that O'Malley was dispatched to west Kerry to canvass for candidates whenever an election or by-election was held.

After O'Malley's death, his grieving widow Hilda declined to stand in the by-election to fill her husband's seat. His nephew, Des O'Malley, accepted the challenge and won the contest by a narrow margin. However, Hilda then declared that she was seeking a nomination from Fianna Fáil to fight the 1969 general election. The members of the party backed the sitting TD and Hilda opted to stand as an Independent. She failed to win the fourth and last seat by just 200 votes. Des was appointed to the office of Minister for Industry and Commerce and supported George Colley in the leadership election against Charles Haughey when Jack Lynch resigned as party leader in 1979. The new leader – who had the backing of Kerry North TD, Tom McEllistrim – did not re-appoint his opponent. The battle lines were now well drawn. In 1982, Colley supported O'Malley in a leadership challenge to Haughey, but the leader managed to ensure that an open vote (rather than a secret ballot) was conducted and O'Malley's bid failed. He abstained on a government bill to permit the sale of contraceptives against the stated party position. He was expelled as a result and made a thoughtful speech that earned him considerable applause: 'My choice is of a kind that can only be answered by saying that I stand by the republic,' he said.

O'Malley's new party, the Progressive Democrats, emerged late in 1985. Although principally a forum for dissident Fianna Fáil supporters, it had a wide appeal. O'Malley's first Kerry rally at the Castle Heights Hotel, Killarney, in April 1986 was attended by over 700 people.[1] Among those present was the former Fine Gael TD for Kerry South, Michael Begley. One notable political figure that aligned herself with the party was former Fianna Fáil TD, senator and sitting councillor, Kit Ahern. 'I would go along with George Colley who said we have too many low standards in high places in this country,' she said in 1985.[2] Independent councillor P.J. Cronin was also briefly a member. Maureen Quill, a native of Gortloughera, Kilgarvan, who was teaching in Cork, was one of those who quit Fianna Fáil to win a Dáil seat in Cork City in two elections.

The party's most significant acquisition in Kerry was Independent councillor, Michael Ahern, a Killorglin-based solicitor. A tough advocate, he also wrote two plays and would later, sadly, be taken before his time. In January 1986, Ahern told *The Kerryman* that O'Malley was 'a man prepared to tackle real problems and issues with a no-nonsense approach. I like the man and I like his style.'[3] In February 1987, Ahern contested the general election for the PDs in Kerry South, polling a respectable 3,215 votes, but failing to win a seat.[4] Months later, he was the central figure in one of the most extraordinary actions ever taken by a public representative anywhere in Ireland, when he sought a judicial review in the High Court against the council of which he was an elected member.

On 1 May 1987, just one section (roads, transport and safety) of the Kerry County Council budget had been debated in the chamber when the Fianna Fáil majority voted to increase the commercial rate by 5 per cent to £31.1956 in the £ for the year, along with an additional £250,000 on water charges and an extra £90,000 from refuse charges. Seven of the budget programmes had not been dealt with and the chairman, Tommy Cahill, refused to allow members to open discussions on any other areas. When Senator Tom McEllistrim proposed that the rate be struck, a vote was called and the measures duly passed. A number of dissenting members left the meeting in protest, but then Councillor Ahern stunned the county by declaring that he was applying to the High Court for a judicial review of proceedings. He stated that the outcome of this challenge would have serious implications for all local authorities. As it stood, where parties had a majority on authorities, they would decide at a private meeting how they would handle the estimates. They would then go into the estimates meeting and 'guillotine all discussion', the Killorglin man said.

This motion was heard by Mr Justice Richard Johnson the following week. He granted an interim injunction restraining the county manager, Tom Collins, from applying the new rate. When the council met again in May, a motion that the county manager should mount a defence against the High Court proceedings was introduced. But four Fianna Fáil members were absent when the vote was called and the application was defeated by a single vote. The consequence of this could well be that, with the manager being constrained from defending Councillor Ahern's application, the members of the council could be named as third parties and held liable for the costs of the action, the Acting Law Agent, Mary Creally, explained. The members hastily agreed to hold a special meeting the following Friday to rescind the vote and to proceed to defend the action and voted 14–9 to permit the manager to act. Deputy Jimmy Deenihan and Councillor John Blennerhassett provided supporting affidavits to Ahern's application. The case, in which Ahern was represented by Senator Mary Robinson, came before Mr Justice John Blayney in the High Court at the end of May 1987 and he decreed that the members would have to debate the full book of estimates before a rate could be struck. The judge stated that it was clear that the City and County Management Act (1955) imposed a duty on local authorities to consider the estimate of expenses at the estimates meeting and it was clear that this had not been done. He granted an order of *certiorari* quashing the decision of the council to adopt the estimate on 1 May. The council was £3.5 million in debt at that point.

Michael Ahern's action against his own council went down like a lead balloon with some colleagues. At the reconvened meeting of the council, Councillor Ahern was welcomed by Fianna Fáil's Mick Long, who called him 'Rumpole of the Old Bailey, himself'. But the debate took a more sinister turn while Ahern was making his contribution. 'Go to the High Court. Pack your bags and get out,' Councillor Jackie Healy-Rae said, and Deputy Tom McEllistrim suggested that Ahern go to a mental home.[5] 'Go aisy,' Deputy Michael Begley added, 'that might cost us another £15,000.' The *Kerryman* editorial described the behaviour as 'an assault on Councillor Ahern that was outrageous in the languages that was used ... he had the guts to challenge the Council's decision in the High Court'. Councillors were like a 'bunch of schoolboys', it added.[6]

In January 1988, the taxing master cut the bill for the action presented by Ahern's legal practice, Ahern, Lynch and Bradley, by £6,297 to £7,903. The council's own fees had come to £1,703, so the final cost to the local authority was £9,603.[7] Michael Ahern stood down from the county council in 1991, having served just one term. He played no further role in politics and died in September 2010.

11

'Politics in my blood'

Kerry: Where Political Dynasties Reign Supreme

As in so many aspects of life, in politics, timing is critical. The phone call to the Radio Kerry newsroom came at about 11.45am. Jerry O'Sullivan, the presenter of the morning current affairs programme *Kerry Today*, answered the call in the busy office. It was 11 February 2016 and the general election campaign was in full swing. 'Jerry,' said the voice at the other end of the line. It was the unmistakable south Kerry twang of Independent TD, Michael Healy-Rae. 'Get yourself down here to Pádraig Burke's office straightaway,' he told O'Sullivan. Milltown native and solicitor Pádraig Burke was the returning officer for the new Kerry constituency and nominations were scheduled to close at noon for the general election due to take place just two weeks later. Michael was already a candidate, defending the seat he had won in 2011. Fourteen other candidates had also put their names forward for the already massively competitive new five-seat constituency. O'Sullivan grabbed a microphone and ran the short distance from the Radio Kerry studios to the office of the Courts Service on John Joe Sheehy Road in Tralee. There with Burke and Michael Healy-Rae was Michael's brother and county councillor, Danny Healy-Rae, along with Danny's son, Johnny, also a councillor, and numerous other operatives from the Healy-Rae machine. They had just got out of the lift and, as Michael later remembered, 'if the lift broke down, the whole thing was finished'.[1]

That morning had been a fairly frenetic one in Kilgarvan. Danny Healy-Rae had dressed hurriedly at home shortly after 10.30am once his mind was made up. Somebody realised that a photographic ID was required and a search for a passport ensued. But Johnny Healy-Rae reminded his father that a photograph was required 'on a disc or a stick', so he made haste to Killarney to arrange same.[2] With Danny togged out, the family made their way to Tralee. In the returning officer's office, 'somewhere between ten to and five to twelve', the brothers dallied for a few moments to make sure no other nominations were forthcoming and as the noon deadline approached, it was clear there would be nobody else in the field. Nobody else, that is, but Danny Healy-Rae. 'I'm throwing my hat in the ring, Jerry,' Danny declared to the Radio Kerry anchor as he sat down beside Burke to sign the nomination papers. O'Sullivan knew he had a scoop – one that would reverberate through the election campaign in Kerry and make national headlines the following day. The clock ticked past noon. The die was cast. The cat was thrown among the pigeons. And the latest chapter in the Healy-Rae story began.

* * *

The impact of Danny Healy-Rae's entry to the race in Kerry was seismic in its effect and it proved once again the Healy-Raes' ability to outsmart their political opponents. It was less than a week since the outgoing Independent TD, Tom Fleming, had shocked his supporters and his opponents by withdrawing from the race. Fleming – a long-serving Fianna Fáil councillor, turned Independent – had dramatically unseated the former Ceann Comhairle, John O'Donoghue, at the 2011 general election in Kerry South. But despite declaring that he was running again in 2016, he pulled out with less than three weeks to go, citing the size of the new five-seat Kerry constituency as a challenge he believed he could not surmount as an Independent with no party network or organisation, particularly in north Kerry. All the other parties seemed dazed by the void left by Fleming – his withdrawal meant that a huge swathe of the county was now bereft of either a sitting TD or any candidates; geographically, Fleming, from Scartaglin, was the only candidate at that point in the greater Castleisland and east Kerry area. On stepping aside, he was leaving an enormous part of the constituency to the mercy of the other candidates. Fianna Fáil councillors like Michael O'Shea and Niall Kelleher, as well as Senator Mark Daly, had been pleading with party headquarters to add another candidate to join councillors John Brassil and Norma Moriarty on the ticket, but HQ was resisting. None of the other parties or candidates seemed to have a strategy to deal with the new circumstances and to capitalise on Fleming's exit; none, that is, except the Healy-Raes. As Jerry O'Sullivan later recalled:

'I remember thinking afterwards that it was a risky strategy but, given their proven campaigning abilities, that if anyone could pull this off it would be them. There was a sense of the Healy-Rae machine seizing the initiative particularly given the failure of the major parties to react to Tom Fleming opting out.'[3]

If the timing of Danny Healy-Rae's nomination was a master class in political manoeuvring, so too was the subsequent campaign run by the country's best-known political brothers and the most dynamic political dynasty in Kerry. Despite having just two weeks to go to polling day, Michael and Danny carved up the county with ruthless efficiency. Voters in Danny's Killarney Electoral Area, encompassing Killarney, Castleisland and east Kerry, were asked to give him their first preference and Michael their No. 2. In the remainder of the county, it would be '1' for Michael and '2' for Danny. Instructive colour-coded maps were published in the local newspapers in order to eliminate any doubt. Danny's local election posters were dusted down and hastily erected across east Kerry. Voters were assured that this was no power grab, rather that it was an attempt to ensure the best possible political service to the people of Kerry, through not one, but two Dáil deputies. The duo claimed they had been inundated

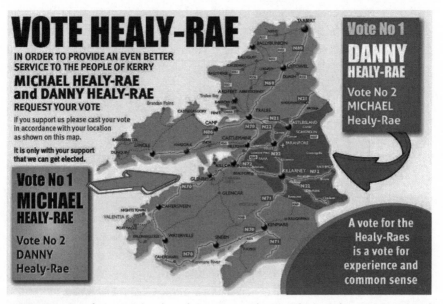

Advertisement from Michael and Danny Healy-Rae during the 2016 general election.

with calls for both to run, particularly after Fleming's withdrawal. Danny Healy-Rae wasn't slow in appealing directly to Fleming's base: 'I'm especially calling on Tom Fleming supporters, a man that I have high regard for and who sat on my right-hand side on Kerry County Council for many years, with Michael on my left, to come out and vote for me.'[4]

It was a message that resonated and a campaign that delivered. When Kerry voters went to the polls on 25 February 2016, almost four of every ten gave their first preference to a Healy-Rae. Michael Healy-Rae received 25 per cent of the first-preference votes, a whopping 20,378 votes – the highest in the country – with Danny receiving a massive transfer to bring him over the line on the second count. Standing beside his brother for the RTÉ cameras at the count centre in the Killarney Sports and Leisure Centre, Michael declared to presenter Bryan Dobson that 'some of the smart alecks above in Dublin that might have been picking on me before, well they'll have to pick through him first now before they get to me.'[5]

The success of the Healy-Raes' phenomenal achievement in 2016 owed plenty to the hard work and the renowned 24-7-365 political service provided to constituents. But it was also partly due to gradual, but effective dynasty building over the course of almost twenty years. The Healy-Rae family had been in representative politics since 1973, when Jackie Healy-Rae was co-opted to Kerry County Council as a Fianna Fáil member. Soon after his famous election to the Dáil in 1997 as an 'Independent Fianna Fáil' candidate, Jackie had been joined on the council by his son, Michael, then the most high-profile, politically, of the Healy-Rae siblings. The abolition of the dual mandate – which brought an end to Oireachtas members serving on local authorities – prior to the 2004 local elections saw Danny Healy-Rae co-opted to the council in his father's place, making Michael and Danny the fourth set of brothers ever to serve on Kerry County Council simultaneously.[6] With Michael in the Killorglin Electoral Area and Danny representing the Killarney Electoral Area, their father's foothold in the constituency was greatly enhanced. When Jackie retired from the Dáil in 2011, Michael easily filled the void left by one of the *colossi* of Kerry politics. The next generation – represented by siblings Johnny and Maura – followed their uncle and father onto the council in turn.

* * *

Though the Healy-Rae family are probably the best-known political dynasty builders in the county, they are not the only family that has succesfully engaged in dynasty building; dynastic politics has been a feature of Kerry politics for generations. Even in the earlier part of the twentieth century, many public representatives in the county were related to their immediate predecessors and successors. Fred Crowley, elected a Fianna Fáil TD in 1927, was succeeded by his wife Honor Mary when he died in 1945. In Kerry North, when Johnny Connor, the Clann na Poblachta TD, died suddenly in 1955, his daughter, Kathleen, followed him into Leinster House. The Killarney-born Minister for Education and Kerry North TD John Marcus O'Sullivan was a brother of Tim O'Sullivan, MP for East Kerry. The grip of the political dynasties tightened as the years progressed. Of the fifty-one TDs who have represented Kerry in the Dáil since 1919, thirty deputies, or almost 60 per cent of the total, have had at least one other relative in electoral politics at a national level or locally in Kerry:

John Brassil	Jackie Healy-Rae	Kathleen O'Connor
Johnny Connor	Michael Healy-Rae	Timothy O'Connor
Patrick Connor	Danny Healy-Rae	John O'Donoghue
(Scarteen)	Gerard Lynch	John O'Leary
Fred Crowley	John Lynch	John Marcus O'Sullivan
Honor Crowley	Thomas McEllistrim I	Tom Sheahan
Martin Ferris	Thomas McEllistrim II	Arthur Spring
Denis Foley	Thomas McEllistrim III	Dan Spring
Tom Fleming	Daniel Moloney	Dick Spring
Stephen Fuller	Michael Moynihan	
Brendan Griffin	Breeda Moynihan-Cronin	

Each of the five Kerry TDs elected in 2016 were related to either a former deputy or a former or sitting county councillor. Of the thirty-three members of Kerry County Council elected in 2014, thirteen or almost 40 per cent of the councillors had a close relative who was then or had been in local or national politics.

* * *

One of the county's best-known, and most enduring, political dynasties are the McEllistrims of Ballymacelligott. The father of Thomas McEllistrim

Snr, elected to the Dáil for Fianna Fáil in 1923, had been a member of the Board of Guardians and the local Rural District Council until 1914. From 1923 to 2011, with the exception of just eleven years, Kerry North was represented by one of three Thomas McEllistrims. Thomas Snr, the son of the Rural District councillor, was born in 1894 and rose to prominence during the Easter Rising and the War of Independence, when he led or was engaged in some of the most significant incidents of the conflict. T. Ryle Dwyer notes that McEllistrim 'arguably played as important a role in the War of Independence as Dan Breen or Tom Barry'.[7] He took the anti-Treaty side in the Civil War and was jailed on several occasions. His prominence as an IRA 'flying column' leader saw him elected to the Dáil in 1923, but, like many of his generation, he never spoke in the Dáil or in public about his exploits during the revolutionary period.[8] From Ahane in Ballymacelligott, Tommy Mac, as he was widely known, held the seat for forty-six years without a break, making him the longest-serving deputy in the history of Kerry politics – only three other deputies, Patrick Smith (Cavan), Neil Blaney (Donegal) and Frank Aiken (Louth), sat for longer periods.

McEllistrim Snr maintained a relatively low profile in Leinster House, with rare contributions to debates, and he never made the ministerial ranks. He was a prominent supporter of Jack Lynch in his bid for the Fianna Fáil leadership and proposed him for the role in 1966. Thirteen years later, however, Thomas McEllistrim Jnr, who replaced his father in the Dáil in 1969, was one of the instigators of the overthrow of Lynch as party leader and Taoiseach. McEllistrim Jnr took a particularly hard line in relation to Northern Ireland and believed Lynch was too soft on the national question. He told a party meeting his father had 'started guerrilla warfare in Ireland after 1916' and that he would 'turn in his grave' at the turning of a blind eye to British aircraft flying over the border and entering the Republic. McEllistrim Jnr became one of the so-called 'Gang of Five' who campaigned for Charles Haughey's leadership bid and he was rewarded with a junior ministry when Haughey became Taoiseach.

On his selection as a candidate in 1969, Thomas McEllistrim Jnr was quick to point out 'there is another generation coming up', referring to his then 9-year old son, Thomas III.[9] But when he lost his Dáil seat in 1992, it would be ten years before his son, Thomas, a Tralee area councillor, followed him into the Dáil. At the 2004 local elections, his sister, Anne, replaced him on the council, but following Thomas III's defeat at the

2011 general election, he needed a conduit back to the council to rebuild his career. When Anne was nominated to stand in the Killarney area to facilitate her brother's return to the council in Tralee, the attempt to win two seats backfired and only Thomas prevailed at the 2014 local elections. He went on to serve as mayor of Tralee and has assiduously campaigned for a nomination for the Dáil, although he was not successful at Fianna Fáil's selection convention held in January 2018. He told *Kerry's Eye* before the meeting that Fianna Fáil members 'would like to see a McEllistrim running. We've been running since the foundation of the State.'[10]

* * *

Of all the many political families in Kerry, one stands out for managing to have four generations – and five members – of the one family serve in local politics: the Flemings of Kilcummin and Scartaglin. When the Fianna Fáil members in Kerry South assembled at the Gleneagle Hotel in Killarney in January 2011 to select the candidates to represent the party at the general election on 25 February, delegates were in for a surprise. The former Minister for Justice and Ceann Comhairle, John O'Donoghue, was proposed for re-election, but the man generally recognised as, and expected to be, his running mate, Councillor Tom Fleming from Scartaglin, declared that he did not wish to be considered. Fianna Fáil headquarters had opted to put forward just one candidate and O'Donoghue's sole challenger at the convention was Glenbeigh councillor, Michael Cahill. O'Donoghue won by 160 to 138 in a close contest. Tom Fleming, meanwhile, had some harsh words for Fianna Fáil in his announcement that he was declining the opportunity to stand again: 'I cannot abide with party policy. We have been mismanaged, spending very valuable money in good times on unproductive activities. I have an independent stance and have publicly opposed aspects of the national budget on both social and economic grounds having been on record at the time stating that there should be amendments regarding draconian welfare cuts.'[11] Within hours of the convention, Fleming had decided to run as an Independent candidate. Cahill followed him out of the fold days later and would go on to campaign for Fleming in the Dáil campaign, as would Brian O'Leary, the former mayor of Killarney and son of the former Fianna Fáil deputy, John O'Leary.

Whatever about Fleming's anger at not having been offered an opportunity to contest the 2011 poll, he must have felt a sense of betrayal at not having been given another chance to make it to Leinster House – to either house of the parliament – despite being O'Donoghue's running mate on two previous occasions. In 2002, Fleming had claimed 6,912 votes and had led Jackie Healy-Rae through five counts. He was just 203 votes behind the Kilgarvan man at the conclusion. Five years later, at the 2007 general election, in the tally of first preferences Fleming finished with 6,740 votes to O'Donoghue's 9,128, assuring the Cahersiveen man his seat. Fianna Fáil took 45.8 per cent of the first-preference vote and at the finish, Fleming was just 460 votes behind Healy-Rae, who was elected without reaching the quota.

In 2011, Fleming's decision to go it alone, combined with Fianna Fáil's one-candidate strategy for Kerry South, ensured that O'Donoghue was in difficulty from an early stage. Fine Gael's Brendan Griffin was out in front with 8,808 votes and would ultimately replace his running mate, the sitting TD Tom Sheahan (5,674). Michael Healy-Rae, standing in his father's stead, had 6,670 first preferences and, vitally for Fleming, he outpolled O'Donoghue by 6,415 to 5,917. Tom Fleming had dropped a few on his previous performance, but being ahead of his former party colleague was essential for his chances. With O'Donoghue being eliminated on the third count, Fleming collected 1,389 of his second preferences and he again benefited from Independent Michael Gleeson's elimination and passed

out Healy-Rae. At the conclusion, neither Fleming nor Healy-Rae had reached the quota, but Tom Sheahan was below them and Fleming and Healy-Rae were both returned to the Dáil as Independents.

Tom Fleming III was the fourth-generation member of the political family, originally from the Inchicullane and Toormore

Thomas Fleming Snr, one of four generations of the same family to have served on Kerry County Council.

parts of Kilcummin, to sit on Kerry County Council. Although the McEllistrim and Spring families continue to have family members on the local authority and both have had deputies in Dáil Éireann for substantial portions of the hundred years that that body has been in existence, the Flemings now had a Teachta Dála in the family. And although the Springs have had three generations represented on Kerry County Council, the Flemings had gone one generation further. The Fleming association with service on elected bodies began with Tom III's great-grandfather, Michael John Fleming of Tooreenmore in Kilcummin. Mike Johnny, as he was known, had been active in the Land League and took part in a number of actions against the estate of Lord Kenmare. When the first county council election took place in January 1899, he stood in the Scartaglin Electoral Division, but was defeated by Thomas Kearney of Castleisland. However, he won a heavy vote in the next poll three years later and took the seat which he retained in 1905, 1908 and 1911 before handing over to his son Thomas Michael. He lived at Inchhicorrigane East in Kilcummin and defeated Maurice Prendiville of Castleisland for the council seat.

In 1919, Thomas Michael's brother James M. – 'Jamsie' to his family – joined him on the county council. Jamsie had also been a member of the Killarney Rural District Council and the Board of Guardians for the Coom Electoral District and he may have become a county council member through being elected to the chair of the Rural District Council (which was an entitlement of the six heads of those bodies in the county), although he may also have been co-opted to replace another member; records from this somewhat difficult period in Kerry are not always complete, but Jamsie certainly did preside at meetings of the Killarney RDC and also served as vice-chairman of the authority. The rural councils were abolished in 1925 and their functions were transferred to the county administrations.

In 1920, Sinn Féin took over the county council, when they were overwhelmingly put in place without contests. Neither of the Fleming brothers were elected, but Thomas Michael returned in 1926. He won a seat in what was now the Killarney Electoral Area, one of four such sub-constituencies under the re-organised electoral system, which included elections by proportional representation. In 1927, when the Fianna Fáil party was founded, both Thomas Michael and Jamsie were among the initial members, but another brother, John, of Toormore, remained loyal to Sinn Féin and became a close associate of John Joe Rice. Rice would win a seat for Kerry South in Dáil Éireann in 1957, although he did not take his place in the assembly due to the party's policy not to recognise it as the national parliament. John was known as 'Small Jack', since he was around 6 feet, 2 inches in height. Thomas Michael Fleming remained on Kerry County Council after the 1928 and 1934 elections, but retired in 1942. His brother, Jamsie, ran as an Independent in the election of 1942, but failed to win a seat.

There was then a significant interregnum of twenty-five years in the Fleming record before Thomas Michael's son, also Tom, put his name forward and won the seat again. He was a farmer in Scartaglin who married into a public house in the village. The Fleming name retained its substantial appeal in this generation: Tom II retained his seat in 1974, 1979 and 1984, but he collapsed and died while making the hay on his farm on 27 June 1984. At the September meeting of the council that year, Tom III was co-opted in place of his father and re-won the seat in the election of June the following year. He succeeded in retaining the Killarney area seat until he was forced to step down on his election to Dáil Éireann in 2011.

* * *

'From the earliest age that I can remember, I wanted to be a politician,' the former Ceann Comhairle, John O'Donoghue, recalled in 2010, just a year after he had been ousted from the role following a protracted expenses controversy. 'I had to have wanted to go [for election] from the earliest stage, because, to be quite frank about it, no man would have done what I did afterwards, or went through what I went through afterwards, and am going through unless his commitment was from the generic.'[12] The O'Donoghue family of Cahersiveen was deeply immersed in Fianna Fáil politics long before a young solicitor called John O'Donoghue emerged on the political scene. Theirs was a political dynasty which would last for almost five decades. John's father, Daniel (Dan), who was born in Cahersiveen in 1898, was a veteran of the War of Independence and the Civil War. He joined Fianna Fáil upon its foundation. Despite being a cousin of John B. Healy, a solicitor from Cahersiveen who represented Kerry South in the Dáil from 1943 to 1948, O'Donoghue was a loyal ally of John 'Jack' Flynn from Castlemaine. Flynn, a TD from 1932, was denied a party nomination in 1943 amid allegations of impropriety with a young woman and Healy replaced him on the party ticket for the 1943 general election. But Dan O'Donoghue stood by his friend. In the O'Donoghue house on Main Street in Cahersiveen, there was a room called 'Jack Flynn's room', where he would stay while visiting his constituents on the Iveragh Peninsula.[13]

When Jack Flynn was forced out of Fianna Fáil (see Chapter 4), Dan O'Donoghue followed him and he supported Flynn when he was returned as an Independent in Kerry South in 1948 and 1951. Flynn came back into the party fold at the end of 1951. Dan O'Donoghue sought to establish his own political career, so when the 1955 local elections came around, he threw his hat into the ring for the party nomination in the Killorglin Electoral Area. He failed to come through the convention, however, which chose Jack Flynn TD, Denis Keating, Patrick O'Shea, Patrick Moran and Timothy 'Chub' O'Connor (later a TD) as its candidates. O'Donoghue asked to be added to the party ticket and threatened to go Independent, as a report in the party archives from the Killorglin Comhairle Ceantair in May 1955 reveals. 'One way or another he would always support Fianna Fáil,' O'Donoghue told the meeting. Jack Flynn appealed to O'Donoghue to stay with the organisation and that 'he himself on one occasion had been disowned by Fianna Fáil but that he had stood by them and was now back in the ranks'.[14] O'Donoghue wrote to head office stating that he had been approached by at least 200 residents of his home town to represent them:

> the convention was canvassed to vote against me, as it was thought by Mr Flynn TD that I would take from his own vote and perhaps prevent him from heading the Pole [sic]. To my mind losing a seat is much more important than heading the Pole ... I am the third generation of my family in Cahersiveen town. I do a large business and have a large family connection. I have always been associated with the industrial development of this area ... For your information Mr Flynn TD, Mr Denis Keating and Mr Moran are all men over 65 years – I am 48. Surely young men should be given an opportunity otherwise our organisation will die.[15]

A report to head office on the matter outlined:

> One feature about the situation is that Mr O'Donoghue was one of the people who went with Jack Flynn when he left Fianna Fáil. He attributes his not being selected to the efforts of Jack Flynn and naturally is particularly sore. Our feeling about the whole thing is that the O'Donoghues going Independent will not effect [sic] the

organisation as such in the area. We were told that from the point of view of votes, he may do some damage but personally considered that this is very unlikely.[16]

This prediction proved accurate. O'Donoghue failed to win a council seat in 1955 as an Independent, albeit by a margin of just forty-one votes on the final count. But five years later, when he was again denied a Fianna Fáil nomination, he prevailed and on 29 June 1960, he was elected to the fifth of six seats in the Killorglin area as a non-party candidate.

Dan O'Donoghue's council career was to be short-lived. On 10 November 1964, four years into his first term, he died. His widow, Mary, was left to rear a family of six and was pregnant with her seventh child. She also had to run several small businesses from their home. But Mary fulfilled a deathbed wish of her husband's – Dan had asked that she take his place on the county council and that she re-join Fianna Fáil, which he had left years before. 'That is what he wanted,' John O'Donoghue recalled. 'Whether it was motivated by the fact that he feared that she might not be elected as an Independent or his love of the old party, I suspect it was a mixture of both.'[17] Mary went on to serve as a county councillor for twenty years and, despite her circumstances, carved out a successful career, as her son recalled:

The eldest of the family wouldn't have been more than 16. There were seven of us there. The youngest was born the March after he died, in November. She was an extraordinary woman because here she was, pregnant with his seventh child, her husband dead, she a widow in her 40s, living on the side of the street in Caherciveen, really facing very difficult times and she still did what she was asked.[18]

On a number of occasions she was mooted as a Dáil candidate, but she threw her weight behind Timothy 'Chub' O'Connor, who became a TD in 1961. A shrewd canvassing tactician, when she contested the council election alongside John B. Clifford in 1967, they would 'go into a house and they would ask the house to divide down the middle and they held the two seats'.[19] She was chairperson of the county council in 1982–3.

When she decided to retire from the council in 1985, John O'Donoghue took her place and two years later he was elected to the Dáil. But the O'Donoghue dynasty did not have it all their own way. In the mid-

1980s, the Fianna Fáil leader, Charles Haughey, had another candidate in mind for Kerry South – one Mick O'Dwyer, the Kerry senior football team manager, from Waterville, who had brought enormous success to Kerry on the football field. Minutes of the Fianna Fáil Constituencies Committee in 1985 and 1986 make several references to O'Dwyer: in November 1985, consultations were to take place with the Kerry senior manager, in December 1985, it was suggested that Haughey would meet with him, and by February 1986, it was a case of 'Await view of Mick O'Dwyer'.[20] John O'Donoghue refused to back down, however, despite being 'offered a District Justiceship' by the party leadership. He told Haughey 'hell would freeze over' before he stepped aside. As it happened, O'Dwyer was no longer being considered by the middle of 1986, with the Constituencies Committee noting 'it might not be possible to get him through the convention'. The same minutes note that another possible candidate could be another Kerry GAA star, 'Paudie O'Shea' [sic], but despite Ó Sé's close association with the party over many years, he never contested an election for the party. John O'Donoghue was selected and elected to the Dáil at the 1987 general election and would remain there for a quarter of a century.

* * *

Enoch Powell is usually misquoted as having said that 'all political careers end in failure'. What he actually said was: 'All political lives, unless they are cut off in midstream at a happy juncture, end in failure, because that is the nature of politics and of human affairs'.[21] Either way, the statement applies to John O'Donoghue's career, which came to an ignominious end in 2011 and heralded the end of his family's representation in politics in Kerry. During the summer of 2009, there were a series of revelations in the *Sunday Tribune* and other media about the expenses incurred by O'Donoghue during his term as Minister for Arts, Sport and Tourism from 2002 to 2007. A total of €550,000 in costs during the period included airport transfers, meals, gifts, hotel accommodation and other bills.[22] The *Sunday Tribune* described a 'six-day odyssey' of travel, including visits to the Cannes Film Festival, the Heineken Cup Final in Cardiff, the opening of new offices in Killorglin and the Ryder Cup in London, all at a cost of over €30,000. This was hugely controversial.[23]

O'Donoghue repeatedly pointed out that he had not been paid the expenses, but rather that they had been incurred on his behalf. As the controversy deepened, he attempted to defuse the situation by publishing details of his expenses since he had been elected Ceann Comhairle. A further €250,000 in expenses were claimed in his first two years in the position – to which he was elected after the 2007 general election – and these were itemised in great detail in the press, including €5,000 for VIP lounges, €633 for a night in a Paris hotel, and €500 on airport transfers from Heathrow. The new revelations fuelled calls for his resignation. In a letter to his Dáil colleagues on 11 September 2009, he insisted that it would not be proper, 'however tempting, for me, whether inside the House or outside the House, to become involved in public debate concerning my previous roles as Minister'. He had, he insisted, 'acted in good faith and with probity' at all times.[24] There was an expression of regret and an acceptance that the costs incurred 'appear high', but it was not enough. Sinn Féin insisted that he had to resign and on 6 October, in the Dáil, the Labour leader, Eamon Gilmore, told the Ceann Comhairle that he would be tabling a motion of no confidence in him. Hours later, O'Donoghue announced his resignation. He was the first Ceann Comhairle in Irish history to be forced from office.

In his resignation speech in the Dáil on 14 October, O'Donoghue offered a 'heartfelt apology to the Irish people' but insisted he was innocent of any offence:

> I never acted in secret or sought to conceal from public knowledge or accountability the expenditure on my functions. I never transgressed any procedure, guideline or regulation. I never committed any offence. I am not guilty of any corruption. I never took money or abused my office for my own enrichment. All these costs were paid to service providers. I did not receive a penny from such costs. These are the facts.[25]

Much of his speech was a defence of his behaviour and a condemnation of how he had been vilified, particularly in the fourth estate:

> In the fullness of time, it will become apparent that many matters have been distorted and exaggerated beyond the bounds of fairness. Simple techniques such as aggregating annual expenditures to produce headlines, attributing the costs of other persons' expenditures to the office-holder personally, insinuating that routine decisions in relation to expenses on car-hire or hotels were made or dictated by

me, failing to acknowledge that many expenses flowed from well established patterns of official duties such as the St Patrick's Day festival, maliciously suggesting that I attempted to reclaim charitable donations and excessive gratuities, conflation of accommodation charges, and many others were used to create an ugly, grasping, black caricature of the man I am.[26]

Within a year of his resignation, O'Donoghue came out fighting, insisting he would put his name before the people of Kerry South once again. 'I will be saying to the people of south Kerry, "You've tried the rest, bring back the best,"' he told *Kerry's Eye*.[27] He continued to insist that he had been singled out for criticism and that his expenses were not unique:

The various controversies which beset me must now be seen in the context of what ministers do and what is the norm. I read last week that [Fine Gael minister] Phil Hogan was on a trip to South Africa and it cost €30,000. If I went to South Africa and it cost €30,000, I would be across every front page in the country ... I arranged none of the hotels; I asked for no hotels; I arranged no taxis; I arranged no cars; I arranged nothing. And I tried to explain that on numerous occasions. Some people will accept it, some won't – there is very little that I can do about that.

John O'Donoghue was selected as Fianna Fáil's sole candidate in Kerry South for the 2011 general election, but the combination of the expenses controversy and an enormous slump in Fianna Fáil support across the country brought his political career to a shuddering end. When the votes were counted at the Killarney Sports and Leisure Centre on 26 February 2011, O'Donoghue observed: 'I hope that the irony will not be lost upon you that I stand here on my evening of defeat in a hall, this magnificent sports complex, which I helped to build.' O'Donoghue's brother, Paul, a long-serving county councillor, bowed out of politics at the local elections in 2014 – it was the first time in almost sixty years that the O'Donoghue name was absent from a ballot paper at an election in Kerry. Whether that name reappears on a future ballot – and whether Enoch Powell's dictum is disproved in this instance – remains to be seen.

12

'Blood streamed down his shirt'

Threats, Thefts, Splits, Assaults and
Other Electioneering Shenanigans

'Threatened with castration'

Liam Cosgrave arrived in Listowel in a last-ditch bid to secure support for Fine Gael during his national constituency tour. It was days before the general election of 1977 and the outgoing Taoiseach was facing a surge in support for Jack Lynch's Fianna Fáil, which was pushing hard for two seats in Kerry North. On the platform on Main Street, Cosgrave appealed for support for outgoing TD Gerard Lynch and his running mate, Senator John Blennerhassett. They were joined on the dais by local publican and playwright, John B. Keane, a loyal supporter. Tensions were high and some Fianna Fáil supporters had turned up on the fringes of the gathering as hecklers, a key faction in any political arena. *The Kerryman* correspondent observed the proceedings:

> The main hecklers of the evening were some women Fianna Fáil supporters. One in particular was very vociferous and despite attempts to quiet her by the old trick of boxing her in – one of Gerard Lynch's own tall sons stood in front of her at one stage – she just kept moving about and continuing her barrage. One youth who was letting everyone know he was backing Jack [Lynch] had a kick aimed at his ankle by a burly Fine Gael man and heated words ensued. There was a fair bit of shoving at one stage and, following a 'We want Jack' chant, one ardent supporter of Fine Gael got so hot under the collar as to threaten one of the hecklers (and that's putting it more politely than

he did!) with castration. However, some cooler heads nearby warned him to cool his ardour and a sort of calm returned.[1]

But the rhetoric at election hustings sometimes spilled over into actual violence. During the 1969 general election, a Kerry deputy sustained a broken finger during a brawl at an after-Mass meeting. Fianna Fáil's John O'Leary was defending the seat he had won three years previously at a by-election and he took to the platform outside the Church of the Immaculate Conception in Currow. Surrounded on the platform by his supporters, O'Leary referred to his efforts to have a local private road taken under the control of Kerry County Council so that it could be resurfaced. Such a move required the unanimous support of residents, which hadn't been secured. Two brothers from a family who weren't keen on the project were at Mass that Sunday and took umbrage to the deputy's criticism of those preventing the road improvements, as O'Leary recalled:

> I said I was trying to gets roads taken over by the county council and improved and tarred but unfortunately, I said, what can I do, I can't do every road because we still have the odd crank who won't agree with his neighbours. Next thing the people started cheering and the lads behind me were saying 'go on, go on, go on.'... There was now fierce commotion behind me and when I looked around I saw one of the brothers coming to me with the fist up. I whipped around and gave him one clip in the poll and broke my finger. He didn't connect with me. They [the brothers] were evicted off the stage, thrown out on the road. I started off again and said: 'Before I was rudely interrupted ...'[2]

∗ ∗ ∗

The curious tail of a substitute dog

An account of the drowning of a greyhound would not normally be the stuff of a front page, even in a provincial newspaper during a very quiet week. But it was not the death of the dog itself that was especially newsworthy in December 1951; it was the fact that the dog had been scheduled to feature in a rather different arena shortly afterwards. The owner was due in court on thirteen charges of obtaining money by falsely claiming that a certain greyhound was Spanish Lad. Lad's owner was Timothy 'Chub' O'Connor, merchant, of Iveragh Road, Killorglin, who would be elected to the Dáil for Fianna Fáil in 1961. Chub attached 'Spanish' as a prefix to the names of his dogs – Spanish Battleship would win the Irish Greyhound Derby three years on the trot, starting in 1953.

As was the custom at the time, the depositions were read in the District Court in Tralee and Justice R.D.F. Johnson decided that there was not sufficient evidence to proceed against the trainer of Spanish Lad, Timothy Drummond of Gallowsfield, Tralee. The trial in the Circuit Court opened in April before Judge Barra Ó Briain. Mr Vaughan Buckley SC, prosecuting, described it as 'one of the most daring frauds perpetrated in sport in this country for many years'.[3] When Chub heard the allegations from the gardaí, he commented that 'the whole thing is ridiculous'. It was alleged that the real Spanish Lad, whelped on 1 February 1947, 'disappeared'

Spanish Lad

Drowned

SPANISH LAD, Mr. Timothy O'Connor's record - breaking greyhound, was drowned on Tuesday evening when being exercised with other dogs along the banks of the Laune. When the kennel man released the dogs there was a mad rush and Spanish Lad fell into the river.

Report from the front page of *The Kerryman* of 1 December 1951.

and a dog called Brown Fergus (born 12 July 1946) ran in his place. This dog had been bought by Richard O'Brien from Charleville, but 'turned his head' in one of his trials, indicating that he was given to fighting. The owner put him up for auction, but that seemed to be the end of the matter. The greyhounds' markings were remarkably similar, but Brown Fergus had had a cyst removed by a vet and there was a residual scar, which was visible when the hair was pulled back.

At any rate, 'Spanish Lad' won a number of prizes both on the coursing fields and track, raking in a total of £774 for the owner. On 1 July 1950, he was retired to stud at a service fee of £25 per visit. At the trial, the original owner, Richard O'Brien, said that the dog he had twice inspected in the presence of gardaí in Killorglin was Brown Fergus. The vet who removed the cist agreed and so did the dog's trainer. But the crowded courthouse applauded when the decision of the jury to acquit Chub on all counts was announced.

✳ ✳ ✳

Councillor sent to jail

'A good deal of sensation was caused at Castleisland,' reported the *Kerry Sentinel* on 16 June 1907, 'when a District Councillor named John Reidy of Castleisland was arrested and conveyed to Tralee jail.' The offence? Councillor Reidy's refusal to pay a fine imposed on him at the Castleisland Petty Sessions some time previously for failing to register his dog. Reidy was described as a member of Tralee Rural District Council and a prominent member of the Castleisland Sinn Féin Society. He had been summoned before the local magistrate for failing to hold a dog licence and had refused to pay the fine of 2s 6d. He was arrested as a result and locked up in Tralee Jail for a week. Clearly a popular local representative, as he was escorted to the train station in Castleisland to be conveyed to jail, 'a crowd gathered at the railway and the fife and drum band played the accused to the station discoursing National airs'.

The release of Councillor Reidy a week later prompted similar revelry. On his arrival at Castleisland railway station the following Tuesday night,

a large crowd headed by the local fife and drum band met Mr Reidy and Mr J. Fleming who was imprisoned for a like offence at the railway station and paraded the town amidst cheers after which a vigorous speech was delivered by Mr Reidy in Gaelic on the principles and policy of the Sinn Féin movement. Mr Fleming also addressed the meeting in a few words.

* * *

'Kerry, let us be united: Give us three for Dev'

Taking down election posters is a very enjoyable pastime for party members and supporters at elections and has been part and parcel of campaigns in Kerry for a century. Even in 1932, the 'Castlemaine Notes' in the *Kerry Reporter* observed that that year's general election campaign had 'passed off here in a very orderly manner ... save the resentment shown over the tearing down of Fianna Fáil posters on election day'.[4] Over fifty years later, when Fine Gael posters were daubed with paint in the Castleisland area, director of elections Bobby O'Connell declined to point the finger, but noted that the incidents had happened in an area of strong Fianna Fáil support: 'They must be worried about something,' he opined.[5]

But it wasn't just posters which fell victim to mischievous electioneers. During the 1948 general election, Killarney had its own miniature version of Watergate when one of the party election offices was broken into, although the political consequences were nowhere near as dramatic as they were in Washington DC in 1972. The *Kerry Champion* reported on the dastardly deed, which took place in the dead of night:

Killarney Fianna Fáil Offices Broken Into

Killarney Fianna Fáil offices were broken into on Saturday night, an entry being gained by forcing the lock of the front door. The offices are situated in a vacant shop in Henn St. Apparently, the entry was effected for the purpose of removing a streamer that stretched across the street from the upper window bearing the inscription: 'Kerry, let us be united. Give us three for Dev.' The streamer was pulled down and torn.

Mr Con Courtney, Director of Elections for Fianna Fáil for South Kerry, informed our correspondent that no other damage was done and nothing was removed from the premises. Investigating the occurrence,

Detective Sergeant Whelan and Sergeant Kennealy discovered the missing streamer thrown inside the wall of Lord Kenmare's demesne a short distance away.[6]

* * *

P.J. stands with the public over St Patrick's Day 'snub'

P.J. Cronin from Rathcommane, Ballyhar, was a tough politician who was co-opted to the county council when Fianna Fáil's John O'Leary took his appointment as a Minister of State in 1977. In 1979, he won the seat for Fianna Fáil in the Killarney Electoral Area in his own right and in 1985 was elected chairman of the council for the first of three terms. On St Patrick's Day that year, he donned the chain of office and stood with other members of the public a short distance from the reviewing stand for the St Patrick's Day parade in Killarney, where deputies John O'Leary and Michael Moynihan, the vice-chairman of Killarney Urban District Council Christy Horgan and other dignitaries were observing the proceedings.

The organisation of the parade had been in the hands of the Killarney Junior Chamber and when Paul Coghlan (a member of the Junior Chamber, later a Fine Gael senator) spotted the council chairman standing among the public, he asked the farmer and meter-reader for the ESB to come up onto the stand. P.J. declined the invitation. 'Killarney people have this thing about countrymen, but if I were a Yank and I came puffing a big cigar, they'd welcome me with open arms,' the miffed P.J. said.[7] Referring to the president of the chamber, Joe Scally, he commented that 'he had politicians of all parties on the platform but he excluded me and I think it's pitiful of him'. Joe Scally said that the incident arose over an oversight as the chairman of the council had always gone to the parade in Tralee before this and indeed P.J. had stood alongside Tánaiste Dick Spring on the reviewing area in Tralee earlier on. But on this occasion, the Killarney parade took place at a later time than the one in Tralee.

Disenchanted with Fianna Fáil, P.J. joined the Progressive Democrats in March 1986, but did not remain for long. He quit in August and became an independent member of the council. He declined an offer to re-join Fianna Fáil owing to a bitter and enduring dispute with Jackie Healy-Rae that had erupted when he had joined the PDs. On 11 April 1986, a letter from the Ballyhar man appeared in The Kerryman with the title 'High

Walls'. In it, he challenged Healy-Rae to explain his statement, 'that these fellows [the newly recruited PDs] will be looking over high walls and never again heard of', which had been reported in the paper. Cronin suggested that those making such remarks 'should look seriously at what happened to Mr Marcos of the Philippines'. But Cronin's separation from Fianna Fáil did not prevent him from retaining his seat in 1991 before standing aside to pave the way for his son, Brendan, to take the seat as an Independent in 1999. Brendan has held the seat since then. The deep animosity between the Cronin and Healy-Rae families continues to this day.

* * *

'How embarrassing it would be'

That there are Fianna Fáil and Fine Gael public houses, hotels and similar establishments is a given in party politics in Kerry. There is also a scattering of Labour and Sinn Féin ones, but, for the most part, the majority of towns and villages in the county had a local hostelry which was considered 'our house' by members of the two major parties. It was always important therefore to host party functions and accommodate party luminaries in the right 'house'. In the 1950s, Fianna Fáil in Kerry South found themselves in a potentially embarrassing situation when they almost chose the wrong house for visiting ministers. A letter to head office from the constituency executive in 1952, which is contained in the party constituency archives, explains:

To: G. Boland, Hon Secretary, HQ
Date: 1 July 1952

Dear Mr Boland,
On the occasion of a recent visit by one of our Ministers to Killarney, an effort was made by the organising committee to have him accommodated at the International Hotel, Killarney which is, of course, the headquarters of Fine Gael in South Kerry. Luckily the matter was discovered in time, and alternative accommodation provided.

At a recent meeting of the Dáil Ceantair, the matter was discussed, and members are nervous that this may occur again, particularly on the occasion of Mr [Erskine] Childer's visit next week. I should be obliged, therefore, if you would ensure that he stays at some hotel other than the International, as you can appreciate how embarrassing it would be for the local Fianna Fáil supporters, if he happened to be staying at this hotel.[8]

It is assumed that Minister Childers was appropriately accommodated elsewhere.

Fine Gael faced similar embarrassment in August 1985 when there was a local political brouhaha over plans made by Taoiseach Dr Garret FitzGerald to stay in a south Kerry guesthouse during a short holiday in the area. FitzGerald and his wife, Joan, had planned to stay at the guesthouse run by Johnny Teahan and his wife at Doire East in Sneem, but changed their plans at short notice and stayed instead at the Park Hotel in Kenmare. It was alleged that the change of plan came about when Fine Gael handlers discovered that Johnny Teahan was a Fianna Fáil supporter and had canvassed with Fianna Fáil candidate Jackie Cahill in the local elections just months before (*The Kerryman* helpfully printed a picture of Teahan canvassing with Cahill). When Cahill learned of the move, he hit out at 'small-town parish-pump politics', which had deprived Sneem of the visit of a sitting Taoiseach.[9]

The alleged reasons for the cancellation of the stay with the Teahans was rubbished by Fine Gael, who insisted that Dr FitzGerald needed to stay at the hotel in Kenmare so that visiting foreign dignitaries could be received. The Taoiseach told *The Kerryman*'s John Downing: 'I had hoped to get away from everything, but that didn't prove possible. I only changed from the Teahans because of pressure of work and I had to receive people. I had to receive the Premier of Baden Wertenberg and I had other officials calling to me.' The local Fine Gael organisation had discussed the matter and party member Gerard Hussey contacted constituency secretary Tim Gleeson, asking if he was aware of 'the nature of the house politics where he [the Taoiseach] intended to stay'. Gleeson contacted party headquarters regarding the matter on two occasions. Dr FitzGerald later called to the Teahans to explain the change of reservation at such short notice.

* * *

'This man [priest] is a well known Sinn Féin supporter'

From the foundation of the State, the Roman Catholic clergy had a very strong influence in political affairs and policy-making, which has been well documented. Kerry was no exception in this regard. From their earliest days, Fianna Fáil and Cumann na nGaedheal/Fine Gael branches were often chaired by local clergy and the local cleric usually presided over party meetings and pre-election rallies. The formidable Fr Myles Allman, a brother of the legendary IRA leader Dan Allman of Rockfield, Faha, was chairman of the constituency executive of Fianna Fáil in Kerry South for many years and his influence is evident in regular correspondence with party headquarters, which is contained in the party's archives. However, the local parish priest sometimes took a dislike to the collection of monies by parties outside his church gate, an essential revenue stream for the parties. In 1952, the Fianna Fáil cumann in Ballybunion reported that it was unable to collect at the church gates as all collections had been forbidden by the parish priest.[10]

From the pulpit, the parish priest had the capacity to bend the ears of voters in favour of one party or candidate. Labour candidates and their policies were regularly the subject of sermons on the evils of communism. During the 1966 by-election in Kerry South, the parish priest on Valentia Island, Fr John Beasley, urged parishioners to boycott the polls because of repeatedly broken promises from politicians who had pledged to construct a bridge between the island and the mainland. The move prompted Fianna Fáil minister Neil Blaney to drive to Valentia two weeks before the vote with party candidate John O'Leary to promise that a bridge would be built if O'Leary received their support. Fr Beasley was convinced and appeared on a platform with Blaney and O'Leary after Mass to urge his flock to back Fianna Fáil. The tallies when the votes were counted showed that John O'Leary received the overwhelming support of the islanders.

Catholic lay organisations were very politically aware and sought to influence voters by publishing messages in newspapers setting out their views and demands during election campaigns. In 1927, *The Kerryman* carried a message from the Catholic Total Abstinence Federation condemning the 'deplorable exhibitions of surrender to intimidation in the legislature' in relation to the sale and consumption of alcohol and calling for a series of measures to curb abuse of the demon drink. They proposed the 'total abolition of all bar traffic on Sundays, elections and occasions of public excitement or danger'. Showing remarkable foresight and echoing a debate on the same subject a century later, the federation called for 'Separation, at least structurally, of places for sale of groceries, hardware and other commodities from places where intoxicants are sold'.[11]

Individual priests in Kerry also took it upon themselves to offer their guidance and advice to the political parties. In 1975, Fr Seán Cunningham of Holy Cross Priory in Tralee wrote to the then general secretary of Fianna Fáil, Séamus Brennan, offering his insights on the major moral questions facing society:

> I would like to be given an opportunity to address your party members, TDs, executive or any significant group at State level on the very important matter of public morality and the common good. I have in mind the whole area of sexual perversion and disorder, abortion, divorce, homosexuality, contraception, pornography, as well as 'integrated' education etc…[12]

Mr Brennan, later a senior government minister, passed the correspondence to Kerry North TD, Thomas McEllistrim Jnr, as it had emanated from his constituency. He was none too keen on the proposal, to say the least:

> I had several requests from this priest to address a FF gathering in Tralee and I refused on every occasion because this man is a well known Sinn Fein Supporter and in actual fact was deported out of the north for his Sinn Fein views and I would go so far as to say that he is an organiser for Sinn Fein in Tralee town. Kindly do not allow him address any FF gathering in Dublin or elsewhere and I can assure you he will not address any gathering in my constituency.

There is no further record of Fr Cunningham making contact with Fianna Fáil.

∗ ∗ ∗

'The screws should be put on Tom Mac'

'Vote number 1 Tom McEllistrim and number 2 Kit Ahern in the order of your choice' were the reported and somewhat confusing instructions to voters in Abbeydorney from one of Deputy Tom McEllistrim's agents during the 1973 general election.[13] McEllistrim, who had followed his father, also Thomas, into the Dáil in 1969, had been joined on the Fianna Fáil ticket for the second time in Kerry North by Senator Kit Ahern from Ballybunion in a bid to pick up two of the three available seats in the constituency. It had been nearly twenty years since the party had held two seats and the push was on for the double. But the campaign was bedevilled by accusations by Ahern supporters that she wasn't getting an equal billing in Fianna Fáil election literature and posters and that a joint canvass had not been conducted.

McEllistrim was the sole Fianna Fáil TD returned in 1973 and party bosses launched an inquiry into the conduct of the campaign. One of Ahern's key activists, Con O'Riordan from Moyvane, warned the people 'who have done the dirt in this campaign' that 'we know who they are and that we do not intend to tolerate them any further'.[14] He told *The Kerryman* that those who canvassed second-preference votes for candidates other than those from Fianna Fáil should be expelled from the party.[15] After the 1974 elections, O'Riordan wrote to party general secretary, Séamus Brennan, insisting that 'the screws should be put on Tom Mac to see that both are elected'.[16]

Kit Ahern was again chosen as a candidate for the 1977 general election, as one of three Fianna Fáil candidates, along with McEllistrim and Tralee's Denis Foley. But her travails were far from over. It was reported weeks before the election that 'party bosses in Dublin' were considering dropping Ahern from the ticket and replacing her with Councillor Eamy Walsh of Listowel. Political observers were rather snidely wondering 'for some time when Fianna Fáil would get around to rejecting Senator Ahern as "a loser"', given that she had failed to be elected to the Dáil on three previous occasions.[17] The reports prompted Ahern to write to head office demanding that they respond:

> I think the bosses in Dublin must refute enclosed in next issue of Kerryman. It was overheard in a Dublin pub after some Exec. Committee meeting and taken up by my enemies and Jack Lynch's in Nth Kerry – a destructive few whom I know – but it did start in Dublin. 'Ditch Jack' would have been a better heading to suit them. I don't fear for their intrigues.[18]

The Ballybunion senator's ire was to be further provoked during the 1977 campaign when McEllistrim placed an advertisement in *The Kerryman*, which made no reference to his two running mates and in which he all but discouraged his supporters to vote for Foley and Ahern.

As it turned out, Ahern went on to win a seat for Fianna Fáil in Kerry North in 1977 when she displaced Fine Gael's Gerard Lynch. But the bitterness of the 1977 campaign endured and the party constituency archives are replete with evidence of this. In a long letter to headquarters a few months after the election, Castleisland councillor, Michael Long, who was chairman of the Comhairle Dáil Cheantair, accused McEllistrim of a '*mé féin*' attitude and of attempting to 'cause friction in every Cumann and have his own organisation within the proper Fianna Fáil organisation, but he has no interest whatsoever in Fianna Fáil, only in TOM McELLISTRIM'. He continued:

6   Friday, June 17, 1977.

Statement from Tom McEllistrim, T.D.

Monday, 13th June, 1977

❛ There is a rumour going around the constituency to the effect that my seat is safe. Many of my voters might be inclined to vote for one or other of the two other Fianna Fáil candidates on that account. I think that this is a mistake. My seat could be in danger, due to the fact that we have three candidates this time. I would like to appeal to all my voters to come out and vote for me if they want me elected. ❜

The controversial appeal from Tom McEllistrim TD which was published in *The Kerryman* on 17 June 1977.

I am sure you have a copy of the famous advertisement with his photo in the *Kerryman*, the day before the election, soliciting support for 'me'. I sincerely hope that there will be a full investigation into these matters after all this is the fifth election that he has taken part in, including two County Council elections and in every case it has been his one and only concern to head the poll 'and to hell with everybody else'. The Fianna Fáil organisation is in great danger of a big break-up here in North Kerry, if something is not done about this man.[19]

The rank and file also contacted party bosses. 'If some action is not taken,' wrote Michael Murphy of the Seán Lemass Cumann in Tralee, 'Fianna Fáil in North Kerry will be controlled by one man, and we don't want to see the party here wind up like Donegal and Blaney's control.'[20] The following year, Denis Foley told general secretary Séamus Brennan that there would be a 'big blow up here in North Kerry' because of McEllistrim's attempts to dominate cumanns with his own supporters.[21] In 1978, McEllistrim succeeded in securing the top posts in the Comhairle Dáil Cheantair, with Ted Healy from Ballyheigue taking over from Michael Long as chairman and Paudie Fuller succeeding Denis Foley as secretary. At the 1981 general election, Kit Ahern lost her seat to Denis Foley. It was her last general election campaign. She remained on Kerry County Council until 1985 and joined the Progressive Democrats, but retired from politics soon after.

* * *

'Blood streamed down his shirt'

Thomas McEllistrim and Con O'Riordan were to feature regularly in publicised spats in the 1970s. 'Fisticuffs at AGM of Moyvane FF Cumann' ran the front-page splash of *The Kerryman* on Saturday, 8 January 1972. Above the headline were two pictures by photographer Xavier McAuliffe of Fianna Fáil party members during a kerfuffle 'as tempers flare'. In a dramatic opening paragraph, Tony Meade reported that:

The annual general meeting of Moyvane Fianna Fáil Cumann burst into fisticuffs on Tuesday night when Gardaí were called to restore peace between the rival factions. The melee, in which a man was kicked on the head, started after an exchange between Deputy Tom

McEllistrim, who had taken the chair for the election of officers, and Mr Con O'Riordan, a Dublin-based teacher, who is an outspoken member of the cumann.

The row began when reference was made to a party report on the inner workings of the Moyvane cumann. Following a previous annual general meeting, Cavan TD Paddy Smith had been engaged to investigate allegations that some members had been prevented from voting in the election of officers. At its 1972 gathering, all cumann officers were re-elected without challenge. A verbal exchange over the operations of the cumann and who was entitled to vote at the meeting began and quickly escalated. At one point, Deputy Tom McEllistrim interjected and stated: 'I am the boss here and I am saying who will vote.'

Con O'Riordan read a letter from party general secretary Tom Mullins, which instructed that some of those who had been denied a vote at the previous AGM should be allowed to 'participate freely' in the 1972 meeting. 'If I'm not in charge,' McEllistrim responded, 'there is not much point in my being here.' As the shouting continued, some members removed O'Riordan from the room and prevented him from re-entering. Another member, Denis Holly, 'was trying to make himself heard above the uproar, shouting that he had a democratic right to be heard by the meeting. He was then attacked by a number of others and was knocked down and kicked in the head. Blood streamed down his shirt.' Holly was taken to hospital.

Somebody had taken it upon themselves to give the local gardaí a heads-up that there might be trouble at the meeting because two officers were despatched to Moyvane prior to the meeting. Sgt Jim Groarke and Garda Maurice Twomey, who were nearby, heard the commotion and saw people being pushed out of the hall. Some sixty party members left the meeting and the election of officers continued. The day after, a garda car was sent to the home of Con O'Riordan's in-laws, with whom he was staying, such was the tension following the exchanges.

'You are very badly in need of a rest'

The Kenmare spin-doctor at Seán MacBride's side

Noel Hartnett

Noel Hartnett is one of many Kerry men and women who have made a significant contribution to Irish politics, despite not being in a high-profile elected position. Kerry people have often had a considerable behind-the-scenes impact in areas like the establishment of political parties, legislation, senior advisory roles or as political apparatchiks.

A native of Kenmare, Hartnett was a barrister, writer and broadcaster who was essential to the establishment of the political party, Clann na Poblachta, in the mid-1940s. He was born in 1909 to a strongly republican family. His father, also Noel, was a member of the Irish Republican Brotherhood. During the Civil War, the family home was burned by Free State Forces. Hartnett moved to Dublin and attended Trinity College, with the assistance of a Kerry County Council scholarship. He became known for his speaking skills, winning the Berkeley Gold Medal for oratory, and became a passionate advocate for the Irish language.

Prior to entering politics, Hartnett qualified and worked as a barrister in Dublin. He represented, along with Seán MacBride, the former Chief of Staff of the IRA, and many IRA members who were tried for paramilitary activities in the 1940s. He represented the deceased hunger-striker Seán McCaughey at the inquest into his death. Such was his closeness to MacBride that he became known as 'The Shadow of the Gunman'.[1] For many years, Hartnett lived in the lodge house at the entrance to MacBride's home in Dublin. He was a member of Fianna Fáil at the time and was on its national executive. Sources suggest that he was tipped for electoral politics and Seán Lemass is reputed to have considered him a potential cabinet minister.[2]

Hartnett's affiliation with Fianna Fáil didn't prevent him from being sacked from Raidio Éireann, where he also worked as a broadcaster, following pressure from Taoiseach Éamon de Valera, who considered him a security risk because of his role as MacBride's junior counsel. Hartnett was best known for the *Question Time* programme on the radio and was said to have been devastated when he lost his position. He had made a 'violent' speech advocating for the rights of republican prisoners, which had raised the hackles of his employers.[3] De Valera believed that such views were not appropriate for an RTÉ broadcaster. Hartnett had become extremely disillusioned with Fianna Fáil anyway and told his friend Dr Noël Browne that when he saw a cheque for the party from Killorglin native and Clery's department store owner Denis Guiney on the desk at Fianna Fáil's head office, 'he realised it was no longer the republican party he had joined'.[4] De Valera told him 'we must be practical', but Hartnett had had enough.[5]

Along with MacBride, Hartnett became a founder member of Clann na Poblachta in 1946 and was elected to its first national executive. The party was particularly concerned with social issues and aimed to move away from the Civil War divide in Irish politics, though it had a strongly republican outlook. Clann na Poblachta attracted those who had become disenchanted with Fianna Fáil, which styled itself as the republican party. Hartnett is reported to have asked Noël Browne to join.[6] One author describes Hartnett as an early example of a 'spin doctor'.[7] His excellent public relations and political advertising skills contributed to Clann na Poblachta's early electoral success, particularly in the 1948 general election. He spoke at election rallies for the party's candidates in Kerry that year; he told a rally in Listowel of 'the evils of emigration and unemployment and asked for a mandate to check these and other grievances'.[8] He was instrumental in an innovative political film, *Our Country*, which was made in London and promoted the message of Clann na Poblachta. What was described as the first political documentary ever made in Ireland opens with Hartnett asking: 'What have we done with the last twenty-five years of self-rule, independence?'[9] Narrating the eight-minute film, he continued:

> Communism will not solve these problems. State control will not solve these problems. Only you the people can solve them. Instead of flag-waving, national records and personalities, what is needed is a policy based upon realities. Instead of recriminations and self-glorification based on past events, the need is for a vision, and planning for the future.[10]

Hartnett was the party's director of elections. Having won ten seats, 'the Clann' entered the first ever coalition government with Fine Gael, Labour and Clann na Talmhan under Taoiseach John A. Costello. Hartnett had contested the Dun Laoghaire–Rathdown constituency, polling 3,281 first-preference votes, which was insufficient to win a seat, but which helped his party running mate

Dr Joseph Brennan (whose mother, Julia, was from Knocknagoshel) to win a seat in the three-member constituency. During this period, he remained on the party national executive, along with Johnny Connor from Farmer's Bridge, Tralee, who became a TD for Kerry North in 1954.

Hartnett was disappointed not to have been appointed to the Seanad by MacBride after the 1948 election and the pair grew apart during the years of the first inter-party government. He opposed Browne's Mother and Child Scheme, saying it 'interfered with the Catholic principles governing the rights of the State and of the family'.[11] In January 1951, he pressed his colleagues to leave the coalition government. A minute of a meeting MacBride held with him reveals the Kenmare man's dissatisfaction with their principal coalition partner: 'He [Hartnett] then said that he found it very hard to be associated in any way with Fine Gael because they were so corrupt and that they were making continuing corrupt appointments.'[12]

The final straw came when Hartnett resigned from Clann na Poblachta on 8 February 1951, along with Noël Browne, not just because of his concern about the direction of the party in government, but also because of the Baltinglass Affair, in which the Minister for Posts and Telegraphs, Jim Everett, controversially appointed a supporter as a postmistress in his Wicklow constituency. MacBride later wrote that Hartnett's resignation was an attempt to 'bring down the government and also to bring down the Clann'.[13] A series of angry letters between the pair can be found in the UCD Archives. In one note from MacBride to his former colleague in March 1951, he suggests to Hartnett that 'you are very badly in need of a rest'.[14] In another note to a colleague shortly after Hartnett resigned, MacBride suggested: 'There was an attempt at a Palace Revolution led by our friend N.H. It failed. He resigned. His resignation was unanimously accepted. Having left CnaP in lone glory, his sole purpose now is to do as much damage to it as he can from outside.'[15]

Hartnett was Noël Browne's director of elections for the 1951 general election, at which Browne was an Independent candidate. Hartnett won a seat on the Labour Panel of the Seanad election thereafter, a seat he held until 1954. A deeply religious man, he was described in none too flattering terms by Browne as 'a small, plump, pink-faced figure, under five feet in height … on formal occasions a quickly wetted comb was briskly produced to induce a transverse Kerry "quiff" in his hair'.[16] Browne was full of praise, however, for Hartnett's fine mind and academic ability. Hartnett played no small role in Browne's election to the Dáil as an Independent in 1957.

Noel Hartnett and Seán MacBride went on to lock political horns once more. Hartnett found a short-term political home in the National Progressive Democrats (NPD) party, which was founded in 1958 by disgruntled Clann na Poblachta members, but which lasted just five years. He stood, unsuccessfully, for the NPD in a by-election in Dublin South Central on 25 June 1958, a poll in which his former colleague, MacBride, was also a candidate.

Hartnett died suddenly in October 1960 at his home in Stillorgan, County Dublin. Tributes were paid to his legal career in the Supreme Court. He was survived by his wife and three children, including barrister Hugh Hartnett.

13

The Kingdom's political diaspora

Kerry's Political Representatives
Outside the County and Overseas

While a number of Kerry people and families have made significant contributions to society by getting elected by the people of their own county, several have succeeded in being elected in other parts of the country and several others have built strong political careers abroad. This has not just been the case over the past century. Perhaps the most significant figure from Kerry to have risen to high office abroad is William Petty-Fitzmaurice, later Lord Shelburne, who became Prime Minister of Britain (Whig Party) in 1782. Although he was born in Dublin in 1737 to John Petty and his wife Anne Fitzmaurice (a first cousin, as John had been the son of Thomas Fitzmaurice, the 2nd Earl of Kerry), he referred to having spent his childhood 'in the remotest parts of the south of Ireland', a reference to Lixnaw:

> He spent the first four years of his life unhappily at Lixnaw with his grandfather, Thomas, first earl of Kerry – described by him as a brutish, feudal tyrant. Despite pressures of high politics, he took a close interest in the administration of his Kerry estate, introducing many improvements, but displaying little in the way of indulgence towards his impoverished tenantry.[1]

Educated at Oxford, he served in the army during the Seven Years' War and entered parliament in 1760. He opted to adopt the family name Petty, after his grandfather Sir William Petty, and inherited the earldom upon his father's death in 1761. Petty was undoubtedly unfortunate in that he became prime minister during the final phases of the American War of Independence. The government was defeated the following year over what was considered to be an overgenerous settlement with the Americans in the closing stages of the conflict. Under the circumstances, his term in charge was brief.

Two other prime ministers were members of parliament for Tralee for a period, although not while serving in the highest office. Sir Arthur Wellesley, the Duke of Wellington was the man returned to Westminster by the voters of Tralee in 1807, but sat for a brief spell only, as he was also elected for Newport on the Isle of Wight shortly afterwards. Wellington was prime minister twice, from 1828 to 1830 and again for less than a month in 1834. George Canning represented Tralee from 1802 to 1806 and led Britain in 1827, when he assembled a government made up of Tories (his own party) and Whigs, but unfortunately his health deteriorated sharply and he died 119 days into his term, which remains the shortest tenure of the position.

Luke Gardiner, a builder who constructed large portions of Dublin's north side, represented Tralee from 1725 to 1727. His son Charles became an MP and the family is still commemorated in the name of the Dublin street completed in 1820 by his successors. However, it was the first Luke who laid down what was initially entitled Gardiner's Mall, later Sackville Street and now O'Connell Street, as well as Dorset Street and several others. Elsewhere, James Cuff or Cuffe (1778–1828) was the son (out of wedlock) of the 1st Baron Tyrawley and a London actress. He was elected to the Irish House in 1800 for Tulsk, but was there only until the abolition of the parliament at the end of that year. In 1819, he was elected to Westminster for Tralee and continued to sit for the constituency until his death.

Tralee had another MP who earned himself a considerable reputation, one that gained him the title of 'Lord Norbury', frequently followed by the soubriquet, 'the hanging judge'. John Toler (1745–1831) became Lord Norbury in 1800. He had sat for the town of Tralee from 1776 to 1780. He was born near Nenagh. His father was also an MP. In 1798, he was appointed attorney general for Ireland and led the prosecutions of many of those who had been engaged in the rebellion of that year. In the following year, he instigated the introduction of martial law and in 1800 was appointed Chief Justice of the Irish Common Pleas. He held this title for twenty-seven years and it was in this role that he came to be referred to as 'the hanging judge'. He presided over the trial of Robert Emmet and later Daniel O'Connell was obliged to support a petition before parliament seeking his removal, alleging that he had fallen asleep during a murder trial. Norbury survived this and it was ultimately George Canning, as prime minister, who finally got him to resign.

Thomas O'Hagan, a Belfast man who was created Baron O'Hagan of Tullahogue in 1870, was another lawyer who contested Tralee successfully in 1863 as a Liberal. Five years later, he was appointed Lord Chancellor of Ireland in Gladstone's first administration, the first Roman Catholic to hold the position in almost 200 years. His sister Mary served as abbess of the Poor Clare Convent in Kenmare for a period and was the subject of a biography by M.F. Cusack, *The Nun of Kenmare*. Also elected for Tralee was Sir Boyle Roche (1736–1807), whose principal claim to celebrity in modern times is the belief that he formed the basis for Richard Brinsley Sheridan's character Mrs Malaprop, which has provided us with the word 'malapropism' to describe misformed and confused sentences. In fact, he may have been quite an astute politician. He came from a Protestant family from County Galway. He joined the army and was knighted for his bravery during the capture of El Morro in Havana. In 1775, he was elected to the Irish parliament for Tralee, then Gowran and later Portarlington before being returned by the voters of Tralee again from 1790 to 1798. When he voted in favour of the abolition of the Irish parliament, he decided against seeking a seat in Westminster.

Another MP for Tralee, having won a by-election in 1808, was James Stephen, who represented the constituency until 1812, before becoming the MP for East Grinstead. This man would leave a very important mark on the world, although his early years included some 'alternative' incidents, including being engaged to two different women, one of whom was pregnant. He relocated to the West Indies, where he witnessed the trial of four black slaves who were charged with murder. He was convinced that there had been a miscarriage of justice after the four defendants were sentenced to death by burning. When he returned to Britain, he set about reforming what he now recognised as a flaw in society: slavery. His second wife was Sarah Clark, a widowed sister of William Wilberforce, and it was Stephen who was responsible for much of what was contained in the drafting of Wilberforce's Bills to abolish the practice. It was finally passed in 1833, the year after Stephen's death.

Outside of Tralee, John Butcher, who was born in Killarney on 15 November 1853, was called to the Bar in the UK in 1902 and represented York for the Conservatives for twenty-seven years. In 1918, the baronetcy of Danesford (Kerry) was created and he became Baron of Danesford in 1924. His titles became extinct following his death in 1935.

In December 1984, *The Mail on Sunday* published a story claiming that Margaret Thatcher, the former prime minister, was the great-granddaughter of a lady called Catherine Selewin who worked as a washerwoman and had been born in Kenmare in 1811. However, considerable doubt has been cast upon the veracity of this account of the 'Iron Lady's' family history.

Kerry has supplied plenty of Dublin Lord Mayors over the years. Going all the way back to 1674, Francis Brewster, the MP for Dingle from 1703 to 1713, had been the holder of the title. Timothy Harrington, who owned both the *Kerry Sentinel*, published in Nelson Street, Tralee, and the *United Ireland* newspapers, was an Irish Parliamentary Party MP for Westmeath and was Lord Mayor three times, from 1901 to 1904. His brother Edward, the editor of the *Sentinel*, whose former offices are now part of the credit union offices on Ashe Street, was elected the Irish Party member for West Kerry in 1885. Thomas Sexton from Waterford was Lord Mayor in 1888 and sat in Westminster as MP for North Kerry from 1892 to 1896 and John O'Connor from Staplestown, County Kildare, was the Lord Mayor of the capital in 1885. He was returned by the electorate of South Kerry for the Irish Party in the same year and ran unopposed in 1886. However, he resigned in 1887 and died in 1891.

* * *

For some reason, people elected from the Kerry constituencies and others from the county were unusually attracted to getting involved in disputes which culminated in fighting duels. George Canning, the Tralee MP mentioned earlier, took on political rival Lord Castlereagh in a duel in 1809. He suffered a wound in the encounter and was passed over by Prime Minister William Pitt the Younger for the position of Chief Secretary for Ireland. The Liberator, Daniel O'Connell, was also involved in a duel in Oughterard in County Kildare, which had fatal consequences for John D'Esterre. It was an experience O'Connell deeply regretted and when the Liberator had a dispute with Lieutenant-Colonel William Arden (2nd Baron Alvanley), his son Morgan – then the MP for Meath – stood in for him and the pair exchanged one set of shots without any harm being done to either man. Morgan almost had another encounter with pistols on his father's behalf in December 1835 when Benjamin Disraeli sent out another challenge to Daniel, but neither of the O'Connells was prepared to take part in any more duels.

Maurice O'Connell, the eldest of the O'Connell boys and also an MP, appended a duel to his *curriculum vitae* following a row with Arthur Blennerhassett of Ballyseedy during the 1832 election campaign for the Tralee seat. They met at dawn on 30 November, but neither suffered any injury. Despite the querulous nature of the O'Connells, the most famous duel involving Kerry politicians featured Sir Barry Denny, who had succeeded his father of the same name as the member for Kerry to the Irish House of Commons. The younger Sir Barry became involved in a dispute over maintaining neutrality in an electoral contest with his cousin John Gustavus Crosbie and they met on 20 October 1794 in an encounter that cost Denny his life. He had married Anne, the daughter of Crosbie Morgell (the MP for Tralee at this time), only the previous January. There was a second tragedy in this instance for the losing duellist's father-in-law then committed suicide by drowning himself. The winner of the duel, John Gustavus Crosbie, subsequently took the seat for Kerry. Sir Barry's widow Anne married again in 1803, to General Sir John Floyd, later to become the father-in-law of Sir Robert Peel, twice prime minister and also Chancellor of the Exchequer and Home Secretary in his career.

Earlier on, there had been another duel involving a Kerry politician, which had resulted in the death of one of the combatants. Dominick Trant, a businessman from Dingle, was elected to the Irish parliament for Kilkenny from 1776 to 1783. On Valentine's Day 1787, he met Sir John Conway Colthurst of Ballyard, Tralee, to settle a matter of honour in a field near Bray, County Wicklow. The pair exchanged six shots. Trant sustained a leg wound, but Colthurst was struck in the chest and died as a result. The Dingle man conducted his own defence and was able to establish that he had acted in self-defence. He died in October 1790.

* * *

Kerry has provided its fair share of political representatives in the United States, perhaps inevitably, given the extent of emigration from the county to North America. There is a dramatic extension to the standard set by the McEllistrim dynasty from Ballymacelligott through Representative Eugene

L. O'Flaherty, a nephew of Marie McEllistrim, wife of the second Tom and mother of the third Tom and councillor Anne. A lawyer in Massachusetts, O'Flaherty entered the state House of Representatives for the Democrats in 1996. In January 2014, he resigned to become the chief legal counsel for Mayor Marty Walsh of Boston. O'Flaherty recalled that knowing Tom McEllistrim Jnr 'was a privilege. Watching him in Ballymacelligott, when he was home from Dublin, leaving his tea to talk at the door or answer the phone call of a constituent will forever be etched in my memory.'[2]

Well before that, Tim D. O'Sullivan – Big Tim – had somewhat confused origins, although it appears that either he or his father came from Glenmore, between Kenmare and Castletownbere. He cut his teeth politically by engaging in some questionable activities, including voting frauds at Tammany Hall. He won a seat in the New York Senate in 1894, again for the Democratic Party. He then won a seat in Congress in 1903. He resigned three years later and returned to the State Senate. In 1912, he returned to Congress. At this point, he was suffering from tertiary syphilis. He died the following year.

From north Kerry to the US, Michael J. Stack was born in Listowel and emigrated to Philadelphia in 1903. He worked in real estate and was twice elected to Congress for the Democrats in the 1930s. Another Kerryman to enter Congress on a Democratic ticket was Denis L. McKenna, born in Farnes, Castlemaine. He travelled to the US with his parents when he was two years old. They left Denis with his uncle to go to Canada, but were refused re-entry by immigration when they endeavoured to return. Denis went into insurance and was elected to the Senate for Somerville, Massachusetts, in 1961. He was described by *The Boston Globe* as 'a pugnacious legislator unafraid to speak his mind on the issues of the day'.[3] In 1961, he came to Ireland to see his mother, then living back in Laharn, Castlemaine. He served in the Senate until 1984. At the time of his retirement, he was Senate chairman of the Legislature's Joint Committee on Government Regulations. He died in 1997.

The Kerry political diaspora wasn't confined to the northern hemisphere. In Australia, Brendan O'Connor is a Labor member of the Australian House of Representatives, initially for Burke in 2001 and Gorton since 2004. He has held several ministries, notably Home Affairs, Immigration and Citizenship, and Employment. Brendan was born in London, but his parents came back to his father's home town, Tralee, where he spent his school days.

In the unlikely location of Pakistan, a most courageous and effective Irish female politician emerged. Bridget (Bridie) Wren was born in Tarmons, Tarbert, in November 1917. She trained as a nurse and began calling herself Jennifer. In 1939, she met Qazi Mohammad Musa – a brother of a Pakistani Movement activist Qazi Muhammad Essa – who was studying in Oxford. When Bridie married him in 1940, she took the name Jehan Musa and they had one son. In 1948, they settled in Balochistan, a particularly impoverished part of Pakistan, and in 1956, after her husband was killed in a motorcycle accident, she moved to his home town. In 1970, she won a seat in the first ever Pakistani parliament and became one of the first people to sign the Pakistani constitution in 1973. She died in January 2008.

✶ ✶ ✶

In more modern times, Austin Stack, Professor John Marcus O'Sullivan, Fionán Lynch, John O'Donoghue, Jimmy Deenihan and Dick Spring have all served as government ministers since the foundation of the state, but a number of other Kerry people have achieved distinction in the governance of the country and have occupied some of the highest offices in the land as representatives of constituencies outside of Kerry. John J. O'Kelly (Seán Ó Raghallaig, 1873–1957), also 'Sceilg' (after Skellig Michael off the south Kerry coast), from Coramore, Valentia, was elected to the First Dáil and served as its first Leas Cheann Comhairle. The Louth and Louth-Meath deputy was then Minister for Irish and Minister for Education (1921–2). He did not take his seat in the Third Dáil and lost out in the 1923 election. The writer of several historical books, he succeeded de Valera as Uachtarán Shinn Féin in 1926 and later became a member of the Save Derrynane Committee.

Batt O'Connor from Brosna (1870–1935) returned from a spell in the US to run a sub-contracting business in Dublin and served in the same company of the Volunteers as Éamon de Valera. He was sent to Kerry prior to the Easter Rising, but returned to Dublin on hearing of Casement's capture and was one of those upon whom a death sentence was passed. He became a close associate of Michael Collins' and was amongst those who advised him not to go to London for the Treaty talks. He was elected to Pembroke Urban District Council in 1920 and was chairman in 1921, but he resigned in 1924 on his election to Dáil Éireann for Cumann na nGaedheal in a by-election in Dublin County. He retained his seat in four subsequent general elections. O'Connor wrote *With Michael Collins in the Fight for Irish Independence*, a memoir of his life and times.

A Listowel native who made his mark on Irish politics – as well as academia and the Catholic Church – was Alfred O'Rahilly, who was born in the town in 1884. A scientist and a prolific writer, he became Professor of Mathematical Physics in UCC in 1917 and was conferred with D.Litt. in 1939. In his academic work, he rejected Einstein's theory of relativity and argued against applying the theory of evolution to human society. He founded the Cork University Press and was registrar and president of UCC for many years. Dr O'Rahilly was elected to Cork City Council as a Sinn Féin and Transport Workers' Union candidate in 1916.

US state senator Denis L. McKenna (left), a native of Castlemaine, pictured in 1961 with his mother, Nora and brother, Maurice (*The Kerryman*).

Along with his fellow Kerry man Fionán Lynch, he was part of the Irish delegation to the negotiations on the Anglo-Irish Treaty in 1921, acting as a constitutional adviser. He strongly supported the accord. He won a Dáil seat for Cumann na nGaedheal in Cork Borough in 1923. He stood down from the Dáil in 1924 and led the Irish delegation to the International Labour Organisation Conference later that year. He rebuffed approaches from Clann na Talmhan, who wanted him to stand as their candidate for the presidency in 1945. Following the death of his wife, Dr O'Rahilly was ordained a priest in 1955, later becoming a monsignor, and was an adviser to the Archbishop of Dublin, John Charles McQuaid. In 1954, Pope Pius XII conferred on him the Pontifical Order of Saint Gregory the Great, the highest distinction awarded by the Pope to Catholic laymen. He died in 1969. His brother, Tomás Prionnsias, and sister, Sisíle, were both UCD-based academics.

One of the few Kerry women to develop a political career outside the county was Dr Ada English, a pioneering medic, as well as a revolutionary firebrand. Born in Cahersiveen in 1875, her family had roots in Mullingar, County Westmeath. They moved to Kerry, where her father took up the role of local pharmacist. Ada, or Adeline, was one of Ireland's first psychiatrists and worked in Dublin and London before becoming Resident Medical Supervisor at the Ballinasloe District Lunatic Asylum. She sought to bring psychiatry out of the dark ages and pioneered occupational therapy, social outings for patients and other initiatives in the early 1900s. Strongly republican in her outlook, she managed to have the image of Queen Victoria replaced by the Galway coat of arms on the buttons of staff uniforms at the asylum.[4] English joined Cumann na mBan and was medical officer with the Irish Volunteers in Athenry at the time of the 1916 Rising. She spent six months in Galway Prison. In 1921, she was elected to the Dáil for the NUI constituency. She spoke out against the Anglo-Irish Treaty, calling it 'a sin against Ireland'.[5] She lost her Dáil seat in 1922, but continued to rail against the Treaty as a member of the Comhairle na dTeachtaí group, which claimed to the be the true government of Ireland. She died in Ballinasloe in 1944.

Also from Cahersiveen, Dr Cormac Breathnach, from Knopogue, made his first bid for national election as a Labour candidate in his native county in 1923, under his name in English, Cormac Walsh. He joined Fianna Fáil in Dublin, was nominated by Killorglin native Denis Guiney, the owner of both Guiney's and Clery's shops, and won a Dáil seat in Dublin North in

1932. He was re-elected in seven subsequent elections (the latter ones for Dublin North-West) before retiring from the Dáil in 1954. He served as Lord Mayor of Dublin from 1945 to 1950 and was also a founding member of the Educational Building Society. He died in May 1956.

Professor John S. Horgan was born to two medical doctors, Joe and Jane Horgan, in Tralee in 1946. A journalist, he became a National University senator for the Labour Party in 1969 and won the contest for a Dáil seat in Dublin South County before losing twice. He was a TD from 1977 to 1981 and replaced Dr John O'Connell in the European parliament in 1981. He resigned in 1983 to return to academia and was appointed Press Ombudsman in 2007.

In recent times, Joe Higgins, from Ballineetig, Lispole, has been one of the more prominent political household names nationally. His brother Liam won All-Ireland football glory with Kerry, whereas Joe entered a seminary initially. He abandoned his plans to become a priest and paid his way through university by working on building sites in the US. He joined the Labour Party in 1974, winning a position on the Administrative Council. But he was expelled from the party along with thirteen other members of the Militant Tendency in 1989. The Milititant Tendency became the Socialist Party in 1996. He won a seat in the Dáil in 1997 for Dublin West, having been narrowly defeated by Brian Lenihan Jnr in the by-election of the previous year. He retained that seat until 2007, when he was beaten

again. However, in 2009, he was elected to the European parliament for the Dublin constituency, but he resigned this position (handing over to Paul Murphy) upon recovering his Dublin West seat in the Dáil in 2011. He did not put his name forward for the 2016 general election. Higgins' turn of phrase and Dáil debates and exchanges with Taoiseach Bertie Ahern made him a well-known figure outside of Kerry and his own constituency.

Pat Carey, born in Castlemaine in 1947, became a school teacher in Dublin and was elected on behalf of

Cormac Breathnach

Fianna Fáil to Dublin North-West in 1997. He was appointed Minister for Community, Rural and Gaeltacht Affairs in 2007 and went on to become Minister of State at the Department of Defence and Minister of State at the Department of An Taoiseach the following year. In 2010, he returned to a full ministerial position at the Department of Community, Equality and Gaeltacht Affairs and in 2011, he was appointed Minister for Transport and the Marine. During the same-sex marriage referendum of 2015, he came out as a gay man and took a prominent role in the yes campaign.

The colourful Máirín Quill was born to parents Danny and Nora Quill, of Gortaloughera, Kilgarvan, in 1936. She became a secondary school teacher in Cork and, following a request by Jack Lynch, put her name forward for election for Fianna Fáil in Cork City in 1977, falling short on that occasion. However, she aligned herself with Desmond O'Malley and became a founding member of the Progressive Democrats and triumphed in Cork North-Central in 1987, retaining her seat in 1989 and 1992, but losing out in 1997 as the party ground towards its termination. She was, however, nominated to the Seanad by Taoiseach Bertie Ahern.

14

'They forget that we exist and that there are such places as Kerry'

A Selection of Quotes about
Kerry Politics over the Last Century

'He is a most successful merchant in that town, and a wave of porter – you can describe it as nothing else – landed him safely on the county council bench.'[1]

The Earl of Mayo tells the House of Lords about the 1908 unseating of county councillor, J.K. O'Connor of Castleisland, following a court petition which heard allegations of bribery, intimidation and plying voters with drink.

'That the members propose that King George V "may be relieved of taking the accession oath in its entirety. We hope that the objectionable clauses may be removed, and that the 12 millions of His Majesty's Catholic subjects may thereby never again have reason to complain about references to their religion which, to say the very least about them, are 'calculated' to perpetuate ill-will in his vast dominions all over the universe."'[2]

Councillor Richard Latchford's motion to Tralee Urban District Council at the May meeting of 1910. He prefaced his proposal by saying that he regretted that there was not another Protestant member in the chamber to second him.

'That we, the members of the Cahersiveen Rural District Council, deeply sympathise with the Boers in their heroic struggle for preserving their liberty; and heartily congratulate them on their successes; and earnestly pray that they will be successful to the end ... "Loyalty springs from a people's consent and the knee that is forced had been better unbent.'"[3]

Motion passed by Cahersiveen Rural District Council, 31 January 1900.

'Sit down, my old dodger, and give me a chance.'[4]

County councillor James T. O'Connor to M.J. Nolan during a fractious debate about superannuation for the county surveyor in May 1919. The chairman, T.T. Foley, asked him to withdraw the remark and he complied.

'Thank God, we have seen the day that such a body of men should be assembled together under the Irish Republican Standard.'[5]

Councillor Tom Slattery in declaring Pádraig Ó Siochfhradha ('An Seabhac') the first chairman of Kerry County Council elected since the foundation of Dáil Éireann, on 25 June 1920.

'We are going to render it not alone impossible for England to keep these men in prison but to keep any kind of control over this country.'[6]

Piaras Béaslaí speaking in Castleisland before he travelled to the meeting of the First Dáil in January 1919 as the TD for East Kerry.

'Belfast Gaol, 5th Dec. 1918 ... The result of West Kerry's choice – and those of the other Kerry constituencies – means that the "Kingdom" stands for the entire Sinn Féin policy. Four-fifths of Ireland will to-morrow follow the good lead given by the 26 constituencies in which Parliamentarianism feared to show its head. I am proud to be one of those selected to sign Ireland's Declaration of Independence.'[7]

Austin Stack, newly elected MP for West Kerry, in a letter from prison to John Conroy, honorary secretary, West Kerry Sinn Féin Executive.

'P.S. – I am sorry if I have been guilty of any deception in this matter, but it was necessary for the success of the scheme. A. S.'[8]

Austin Stack TD in a letter to Governor J.J. Fitzclarence of Strangeways Prison, Manchester, following his escape from the prison in October 1919.

'I only wanted to get the British out of Ireland, and the country in our hands. But my thoughts went further than that. I hoped to see a Gaelic Ireland, the home of strong and happy men and women in which a thousand splendid things could be done. The dreams of Davis, of William Rooney, of Pearse – men who saw Ireland with a prophetic vision and imagination – could be realised in a Gaelic State unchecked by foreign influence ... As the Minister of Finance has said: "Is Ireland ever to get a chance? The nation, do you ever think of the poor Irish nation that is trying to be born?" I appeal to you – give it a chance.'[9]

Piaras Béaslaí, TD for Kerry–Limerick West, speaking in favour of the Anglo-Irish Treaty in the Dáil in January 1922.

'Now I am alive, and I took my chance of being killed as well as any white man in this assembly, and I challenge any man to deny that. Now I am here to interpret myself, and I stand for this Treaty; if I were dead, and if I were to be interpreted, I should ask to be interpreted by the men who soldiered with me, and by the men who worked with me in the national movement.'[10]

Fionán Lynch, TD for Kerry–Limerick West, speaking in support of the Anglo-Irish Treaty of 1921.

'I credit the supporters of the Treaty with being as honest as I am, but I have a sound objection to it. I think it is wrong; I have various reasons for objecting to it, but the main one is that, in my opinion, it was wrong against Ireland, and a sin against Ireland ... We are now asked not only to acknowledge the King of England's claim to be King of Ireland, but we are asked to swear allegiance and fidelity in virtue of that claim ... Ireland has been fighting England and, as I understood it, the grounds of this fight always were that we denied the right of England's King to this country.'[11]

Cahersiveen native, Dr Ada English TD, representing the NUI constituency, speaks against the Treaty in 1922.

'I was nurtured in the traditions of Fenianism. My father wore England's uniform as a comrade of Charles Kickham and O'Donovan Rossa when as a '67 man he was sentenced to ten years for being a rebel, but he wore it minus the oath of allegiance. If I, as I hope I will, try to continue to fight for Ireland's liberty, even if this rotten document be accepted, I will fight minus the oath of allegiance and to wipe out the oath of allegiance if I can do it. Now I ask you has any man here the idea in his head, has any man here the hardihood to stand up and say that it was for this our fathers have suffered, that it was for this our comrades have died on the field and in the barrack yard. If you really believe in your hearts that it was, vote for it. If you don't believe it in your hearts vote against it.'[12]

Austin Stack, the only Kerry TD to vote against the Anglo-Irish Treaty.

'He gave us a cigarette and he said "That's the last cigarette ye'll ever again smoke." He said "We're going to blow ye up with a mine." We were marched out and made to lie down flat in a lorry and taken out to Ballyseedy. The language was abusive language; it wasn't too good. One fella called us Irish bastards and he was an Irishman himself. One of our lads asked to be left say his prayers. He said "No prayers, our fellas didn't get any time for prayers" … They tied us then, our hands behind our back … and they tied us in a circle around the mine and they tied our legs then and our knees with a rope and they threw off our caps and said we could be praying away now as long as we like … "Goodbye lads" and up it went … and I went up with it …'[13]

Stephen Fuller, Fianna Fáil TD for Kerry North (1937–43), recounts the Ballyseedy Massacre during the Civil War in 1923, of which he was the only survivor.

'There are complaints, some of them exaggerated, some of them quite justified, about the condition of schools in the country. There are complaints even about the general type of schools that we are setting up. I do not think, with the economic resources of this country, that we shall ever, at least in our time, be able to provide the type of school that is to be found in many other countries.'[14]

Minister for Education and Kerry TD, John Marcus O'Sullivan, on school facilities in the 1920s.

'every action taken by this officer [Garda Commissioner Eoin O'Duffy] before this Government took power, and since this Government took power, so far as we know, has been action of a kind to strengthen the confidence that the head of the Government ought to have in him, and for that reason he is thrown to the wolves. What are the Guards to do? How can the Guards feel that they have any backing behind them in doing their duty when they see the highest officer in the Gárda Síochána being dismissed for doing his duty?'[15]

John Marcus O'Sullivan, Cumann na nGaedheal TD for Kerry, condemns the Fianna Fáil government's decision to sack General Eoin O'Duffy as garda commissioner in 1933.

'There are some places in this country where the duty of compiling the Parliamentary Register devolves on the Civic Guards. Kerry is one of these places. My experience is that they work in a very partial manner. They disfranchised hundreds of Fianna Fáil voters in Kerry at the last election and they went so far as to tear down Fianna Fáil posters from the gates at some of the polling booths. I can only come to the conclusion that they are a semi-political body, and I leave it at that.'[16]

Kerry South Fianna Fáil TD Thomas O'Reilly in the Dáil in 1928.

'The Tralee people want a most expensive institution; anything up to £20,000 has been suggested. It would be an outrage to ask the people of Kerry to subscribe £20,000 towards the erection of a hospital which, call it what you will, will not serve the needs of the county. Everyone knows that serious surgical and medical cases have to be treated by team work, and they have to go where there are medical schools ... it would be unfair to saddle the ratepayers with a big sum of money for building a most expensive institution. I think we ought to improve the existing institution and carry on for a while until we reach better times.'

Senator Dr William O'Sullivan from Killarney on the cost of a new hospital for Tralee in 1929.

Dan Spring and Dick Spring TD pictured in the 1980s. (*The Kerryman*)

Dan Spring TD addresses supporters in 1977. To his right are Labour leader Brendan Corish TD and Cllr Michael O'Regan. (*The Kerryman*)

Members and staff of Kerry County Council pictured in 1976, front row, l–r: Cllr John Joe O'Sullivan (Lab), Cllr Mick Long (FF), Cllr Kit Ahern (Senator) (FF). Second row, l–r: Noel Dillon (Deputy County Engineer), Tim Murphy (Law Agent), Cllr Tom Fleming (FF), Cllr Tom McEllistrim TD (FF), Cllr Tommy Cahill (FF), Cllr Mary O'Donoghue (FF), Cllr Jack Lawlor (FF), Cllr Dan Barry (FG). Third row, l–r: Peter Malone (County Engineer), Cllr Michael Connor-Scarteen (FG), Cllr Eamon Walsh (FF), Cllr Noel Brassil (FF), Cllr John O'Leary TD (FF), Cllr John Blennerhassett (Senator) (FG). Fourth row, l–r: John O'Connor, Teddy Healy, Cllr Jack Larkin (Ind), Cllr Christy McSweeney (FG), Christy Neilan, Tom Collins (County Manager), John Ronayne (County Accountant), Cllr Danny Kissane (FG). Back row, l–r: Cllr Michael Moynihan (Senator) (Lab), Seamus Hayes (Assistant County Manager), Cllr James Courtney (Ind), Cllr Redmond O'Sullivan (SF), Cllr Gerard Lynch TD (FG), Cllr Jackie Healy-Rae (FF), Cllr Tom Fitzgerald (FF), Blaise Treacy (County Secretary), Cllr Timothy 'Chub' O'Connor TD (FF), Cllr Dan Spring TD (Lab), Cllr Michael Begley TD (FG).

Dan Spring TD and Labour members pictured in Tralee during the 1977 general election. (*The Kerryman*)

Clare TD Sylvester Barrett (left) discusses strategy before the 1977 general election with Kerry North candidates and activists, l-r: Denis Foley, Cllr Maurice Lawlor, Cllr Kit Ahern, Cllr Mick Long and Tom McEllistrim TD. (*The Kerryman*)

Fianna Fáil candidates in Kerry North at the November 1982 general election, l-r: Senator Dan Kiely, Tom McEllistrim TD and Denis Foley TD. (*The Kerryman*)

Minister for Energy George Colley (centre) campaigns with Tom McEllistrim TD (left) in Kerry North during the 1981 general election. (*The Kerryman*)

Tom McEllistrim TD addresses a Fianna Fáil rally in Tralee during the 1981 general election. Pictured to his right are Taoiseach Charles Haughey, Kit Ahern TD, Cllr Noel Brassil, Cllr Ted Fitzgerald and Cllr Paudie Fuller. (*Kerry's Eye*)

Kit Ahern, Fianna Fáil TD for Kerry North from 1977 to 1981, pictured with Taoiseach Charles Haughey during the 1981 general election campaign. (*The Kerryman*)

Fine Gael leader Garret FitzGerald leads his supporters through Killorglin during the February 1982 election campaign. (*The Kerryman*/Kevin Coleman)

Labour TD for Kerry South Michael Moynihan and his daughter, Breeda Moynihan-Cronin, who succeeded him in the Dáil, pictured in 1982. (*The Kerryman*)

Fine Gael TD for Kerry North Gerard Lynch (left) pictured in 1977 with, l–r, his mother, Kit Lynch, Taoiseach Liam Cosgrave, Julia Mary Stack and Paddy Walsh (front). (Lynch family)

Jimmy Deenihan TD and his running mate, Bernie Gannon, speaking in Tralee during the November 1982 general election campaign. On the left is Fine Gael deputy leader Peter Barry TD. (*The Kerryman*/Kevin Coleman)

Fianna Fáil leader Charlie Haughey and candidate John O'Donoghue greet Kerry football team manager Mick O'Dwyer – whom Haughey mooted as a party candidate – during the November 1982 election. (Michelle Cooper-Galvin)

Fianna Fáil candidates submitting their nomination papers to returning officer Louise McDonagh at the 1987 general election, l–r: Paul O'Donoghue, Cllr John O'Donoghue, Cllr Jackie Healy-Rae, Cllr Brendán Mac Gearailt, Liam Crowley. Seated is John O'Leary TD. (*The Kerryman*/Kevin Coleman)

Members of Kerry County Council elected in 1991. Front row, l–r: Senator Denis Foley (FF), Pat Finnegan (FF), Dick Spring TD (Lab), John O'Donoghue TD (FF), Tom McEllistrim TD (FF), Breeda Moynihan-Cronin (Lab), Maeve Spring (Lab), Bobby O'Connell (FG), Pat Leahy (Lab). Second row, l–r: Ted Fitzgerald (FF), John O'Leary TD (FF), Noel Brassil (FF), Jackie Healy-Rae (FF), Dan Kiely (FF), Dan Barry (FG), Paul Coghlan (FG), Jimmy Deenihan TD (FG), Tom Fleming (FF), Tommy Foley (Ind). Back row, l–r: Ned O'Sullivan (FF), James Courtney (Ind), Tim Buckley (FG), Michael Connor-Scarteen (FG), Michael Cahill (FF), Danny Kissane (FG).

'I think that the House should know that there is under £40,000 of [land] annuities outstanding in Kerry – that some £11,000 is outstanding in the richest district in the county, and that the very great majority of the whole is owed by men with a valuation of over £20. I can safely say that very few mountainy men owe a penny, and the reason is that they work and do not read the newspapers or debates in this House. If they can live, surely the others can, too.'[17]

The McGillycuddy of the Reeks, senator from Beaufort, on outstanding land annuity payments to the British government in Kerry in 1930.

'I am precluded by the judicial position which I occupy from expressing in public any political views and I have never done so, but I am entitled to say that I cannot countenance the policy of hunger striking with a view to forcing the hand of the government elected by the people. I regard such a course of action as being destructive of the very foundations of democratic government; but [Johnny] O'Connor is a young man, I believe of character and of ideals, and I believe that in pursuit of these ideals he would persist in the course he has adopted to the last extreme. All questions of political and of morals aside, I cannot find myself a party – a willing party – to the loss of a young life which under altered conditions may be of value to the state. I would regard it as criminal folly if any government elected by popular franchise should yield to this weapon of hunger-strike as it would render the enforcement of law impossible. Yet on this occasion, in view of the fact that O'Connor has been in custody on remand for three months, I would not have imposed on him a greater sentence had he been convicted. I propose to ask respectfully that Governor-General to remit the unexpired portion of the sentence I have passed upon him and release him pending his trial.'[18]

Judge E.J. McElligott, from Listowel, speaking of Johnny O'Connor (later TD) at Tralee Circuit Court, on 30 April 1933. O'Connor had been charged with possession of a shotgun and eight cartridges without a certificate. The judge had already sent Dan Keating of Castlemaine to jail for contempt of court (three months). O'Connor had been on remand for three months and went on hunger strike immediately after sentence and was released five days later. At the court on 30 June 1933, the state asked that a nolle prosequi be entered. The judge asked the governor of Cork Jail to release both men and they returned home the following Tuesday.

'Go around the roads and hillsides of Kerry and see the crosses put up by the people in memory of those who were killed in 1922, not by the Black and Tans nor by the British. A man who can say that they have no guilty past of which to be ashamed, has he not a face of brass to make a statement of that kind to the people of Kerry?'[19]

President Seán T. O'Kelly addressing the Killarney Aeridheacht in August 1933.

'Kerry's entire record in the Black and Tan struggle consisted in shooting an unfortunate soldier the day of the Truce.'[20]

General Eoin O'Duffy, the leader of the Army Comrades' Association, speaking at a meeting in Bandon on 16 October 1933, shortly after he had been organising meetings which met with vigorous opposition in Kerry. O'Duffy was attacked and suffered an injury to his head at Bridge Street, Tralee, and alleged that he had been hit with a hammer. His car was also burned out and shots were fired at the garda station.

'The obvious way for the President [Éamon de Valera] to consult the Irish people is to look into his own heart, and when he knows what is there he knows what the Irish people want. Then he retires to his study. I do not know that he even consults the Cabinet – he may have ... The President retires to his study, looks into his own heart and produces this. Then the Irish people are to say whether they will have it or not, "take it or leave it." They have to take it or leave it, but if they do take it, the shackles that are in this Constitution will be bound on them for a long time.'[21]

Fine Gael's John Marcus O'Sullivan criticises the draft constitution of 1937.

'I think that censorship is definitely necessary. Those who do not think so have only to look to Buenos Aires in one direction and Port Said in another where there is no censorship. The result in both places is that practically everybody is inoculated with depravity through their bodies. I feel that we do not want that, so that censorship must definitely continue. But no censorship will turn what I call a Dirty Dick into a clean one. He will find something obscene and depraving in almost every sentence that he reads, but those Dirty Dicks are few and far between. I believe that of the many books that I have read, coarse and vulgar as they were, the average young man and young woman would pass that sort of writing by.'[22]

Senator The McGillycuddy of the Reeks speaks on censorship in the Seanad in 1942.

'It is most unfair to ask [IRA leader] Seán McCaughey and his comrades to wear prison garments, to deny them political treatment, and to compel them to exist under such conditions for the last four years. The Minister, if he owned a dog, would not keep him tied up for four years in a box. He certainly would take him out for a walk once or twice a day. Are the Minister and the Government going to be inhuman and allow men to die because they are fighting for political treatment?'[23]

Dan Spring TD, then a member of National Labour, urges the release of IRA prisoner, Seán McCaughey, who was on hunger strike in Portlaoise Prison in 1946.

'all drinks at dances should be abolished. When I say that, you can call me a pussyfoot, if you like, but I am very emphatic about the abuses that have taken place at dances.'[24]

Fianna Fáil TD for Kerry South Fred Crowley on the demon drink.

'the better a public house is – in its appointments – the better will be the conduct in it … In this country a licence is issued to a respectable man, quite regardless of the condition of his premises. I feel it is time that legislation was introduced to try to bring about an improvement in the condition of the licensed houses in which our citizens take their refreshments. In England and in France, the premises in which refreshments are taken are conducted in a most orderly way. I hope the Minister will consider in what way pressure could be brought to bear to bring about an improvement in the licensed premises in this country.'[25]

Senator The McGillycuddy of the Reeks shares his proposals for improvements to public houses.

'The Fianna Fáil Party stated that they never accepted the Treaty. If that is so, why was it that in 1927 they entered the Dáil and accepted all the implications of that Treaty? In 1937 they passed the Constitution which they stated made this country a republic. Why was it that in after years Deputy de Valera on various occasions in this House and elsewhere was continually called upon to describe the status of this State and even had to refer to and, I suppose, carry about with him those weighty dictionaries in order that he might be able to convince his questioners of the status of the nation?'[26]

Kerry South Fine Gael deputy Patrick Palmer on the Republic of Ireland Bill in 1948.

'this measure is just as big a thing in my life as Pádraig Pearse's declaration was to him. I should like to see it passed into law, because it certainly removes from our midst the dissipation of our national energies which we have witnessed for many a year ... I should like to see all our energies devoted to and concentrated on following our star and backing up that moral compelling force which must find its answer in the application *de facto* of this measure to all Ireland.'[27]

Castleisland native and Clann na Talmhan senator Patrick Woulfe on the Republic of Ireland Bill in 1948.

'As far as I can see, Government Ministers resident in Dublin consider Dublin as Ireland. They forget that we exist and that there are such places as Kerry.'[28]

Jack Flynn, Kerry South Independent TD, speaks on the nomination of Taoiseach in 1948.

'I would like to hear Deputy John Flynn in whose constituency one of the candidates was almost torn to bits. I would like to know if Deputy John Flynn told the people of South Kerry, who pulled the headlights off Deputy de Valera's car, that Deputy Éamon de Valera was going to be his choice of Taoiseach in this country ...'[29]

Oliver J. Flanagan, Independent and later Fine Gael TD for Laois–Offaly, challenges Kerry South Independent Jack Flynn during the election of the Taoiseach in the Dáil in 1951.

'When we were in opposition, we expressed the belief that, as a community, we were living beyond our means; that we were consuming more than we produced; that we were eating in on our reserve capital and that government expenditure exceeded revenue.'[30]

Taoiseach Éamon de Valera speaking in Tralee in January 1952, echoing one of his successors.

'Are you following the de Valera who fought in Easter Week or the de Valera who put the Special Powers Act into operation one day after the British Ambassador in Dublin cracked his whip? ... Repression only intensifies resistance and so surely as one republican is interned there will be five others to take his place.'[31]

Kerry South Sinn Féin TD John Joe Rice speaks in Firies in 1957 in opposition to the Special Powers Act, which was used to intern suspected IRA members in the 1950s.

'The question of the appointment of an auxiliary postman at Knocknagoshel, County Kerry, has been raised ... I am satisfied that the man who was appointed is suitable in every respect ... He is a man with a good national record and for his services in Fianna Éireann he holds a national service medal. I am surprised to find Deputy Palmer (Fine Gael TD for Kerry South) ... raising this matter in the Dáil. Presumably it is due to the fact that another candidate who happens to be the secretary of the local Fine Gael club, was not successful.'[32]

Fianna Fáil's Thomas McEllistrim supports the appointment of an auxiliary postman by the Minister for Posts and Telegraphs, Erskine Childers (FF), in 1952.

'I must say that while I have a certain amount of sympathy with the point of view put forward by Senator Mrs Connolly O'Brien as to a stigma being attached to young girls who are sent to St Mary Magdalen's Asylum, I am afraid the Senator overlooks the fact that no young girl can be sent there without her consent so I think the position is not as the Senator represents it to be. After all, there must be some place of detention for such young girls who are remanded in custody for whatever time is thought to be necessary.'

Kerry senator and former junior minister Eamonn Kissane discusses the Magdalen Laundries with Senator Nora Connolly O'Brien, daughter of James Connolly, during a debate on the Criminal Justice Bill, 1960.

'I got approximately 12,880 votes from the people of south Kerry and I thank them for it but I did not deserve to have missiles, cigarette boxes and butts thrown at me. I conducted a clean campaign and I did not deserve the jeering parade that came into Dingle on Friday night last.'[33]

Michael Begley, Fine Gael candidate in the Kerry South by-election of 1966, referring to the antics of his opponents following the election in which Fianna Fáil's John O'Leary won a seat.

'Without me in the Senate, the people would be like sheep without a shepherd.'[34]

Fianna Fáil's Kit Ahern speaking during the 1969 general election campaign.

'My constituents in South Kerry want Fianna Fáil to remain in office because, they, too, know that Fianna Fáil is the only party capable of running the country. Fianna Fáil is synonymous with Ireland.'[35]

Fianna Fáil Kerry South TD John O'Leary speaking in the Dáil debate on the Arms Crisis in 1970.

'Far too many women are entering married life without realising the responsibility of marriage and too many are unprepared in the household management area ... Some women regard housework as having such a low status, as is stated in the report, that many of them boast they cannot boil an egg. I have been advocating for a long while that there should be courses on home-making, such as proper cooking, care and management of children and proper balancing of the household budget ... A diploma in household management is as important as a diploma in creamery management or in rural science.'[36]

Senator Kit Ahern on the report of the Commission on the Status of Women in 1973.

'I have very decided ideas of women's role in life and in my own county the women are doing a great job of work in keeping their homes going and directing and bringing up their families. This I think is what almighty God intended them to do ...'[37]

Kerry South Fianna Fáil TD, Timothy Chub O'Connor, responds to a questionnaire from the Women's Political Association in 1977.

'I would go along with George Colley who said we have too many low standards in high places in this country.'[38]

Kit Ahern, former Fianna Fáil TD and senator, speaking in 1985, just before she joined the PDs.

'Vote number 1 Tom McEllistrim and number 2 Kit Ahern in the order of your choice.'[39]

The reported words of an agent for Fianna Fáil TD Tom McEllistrim in Abbeydorney during the 1973 general election campaign, in which there was a dispute between the candidates over being given equal billing in election material.

'Furthermore, if Fianna Fáil are re-elected to office, this will be followed by the dissolution of many local authority bodies which in the past have opposed the government policy.'[40]

Labour deputy Dan Spring issues a warning before the 1973 general election.

'They should have more charm, wit and style about them. I would prefer if they were not so dull on TV; they are always so menacing.'[41]

Cahersiveen publican and playwright Pauline Maguire when asked her opinion of politicians in February 1973.

'He was a man of action and I found him very forceful and determined to have free speech at any cost. Of course, it did not go down with what I would call the rightist side of Fine Gael.'[42]

The retired county and Listowel Urban District councillor Louis O'Connell, chairman of the county council from 1954 to 1955 and Listowel UDC from 1955 to 1965, speaking about Eoin O'Duffy, leader of the Blueshirts.

'I would be grateful if you could please request the relevant member of your staff to send some Fianna Fáil balloons to Peggy Murphy, Dooks, Glenbeigh, Co. Kerry as she wants to put them up for the Fianna Fail social in Glenbeigh on January 8, 1988. I have no doubt that these balloons will be the only hot air in evidence on the night!'[43]

John O'Donoghue TD to Fianna Fáil general secretary, Frank Wall.

'If Ronald Reagan, at seventy-four, can run America, I think, at seventy-two, I can represent the people of south Kerry.'[44]

Labour TD for Kerry South Michael Moynihan on seeking re-election to the Dáil at the 1989 general election.

'I remember there was a fear that he [Dick Spring] might not survive. I visited him in hospital and he was on this rotating bed or this upside-down bed and he was black and blue, broken up and bandaged. And I really remember the time that Charlie Haughey made him come from the hospital in to cast a vote and I remember my grandmother being so upset and my grandfather and my dad. I think if he could have caught a hold of Charlie Haughey at that time, he would have been two inches smaller than the 5'4" that he was.'[45]

Former Labour TD, Arthur Spring, recounts the occasion on which his uncle, Dick Spring, was stretchered through the division lobbies in January 1982 following a car accident in December 1981. Haughey had denied Spring a 'pair' in the Dáil, which would have allowed him to absent himself from the vote.

'This debate, essentially, is about the evil spirit that controls one political party in this Republic, and it is about the way in which that spirit has begun to corrupt the entire political system in our country. This is a debate about greed for office, about disregard for truth and about contempt for political standards. It is a debate about the way in which a once-great party has been brought to its knees by the grasping acquisitiveness of its leader. It is ultimately a debate about the cancer that is eating away at our body politic and the virus which has caused that cancer, An Taoiseach Charles J Haughey.'[46]

Labour leader Dick Spring speaking in the Dáil in October 1990.

'the one thing that I never ever heard him [Charles Haughey] say was say a bad word against another politician, except one – Dick Spring in the Dáil one day said something like the following: "You sir, are a cancer to Irish politics." And Charlie said to me, "Tom, how could he say that? Do you know what a cancer is, something that eats away and eats away." He said: "The dirty fucker."'[47]

Senator Tom Fitzgerald recounts Haughey's response to Dick Spring's comments from 1990 (above).

'The GAA is the only reason I am a politician.'[48]

Former minister and Fine Gael TD for Kerry North, Jimmy Deenihan.

'Dáil Éireann can be a very artificial place, with its own distinctive culture outside of the chamber, sometimes a culture based on insincerity and flattery.'[49]

Former minister and Fine Gael TD for Kerry North, Jimmy Deenihan.

'No tears. No anger. Just typical sound analysis. As Pádraig Harrington said when he forgot to mark his card, Nobody's dead. Life goes on.'[50]

Former Tánaiste Dick Spring following his defeat to Sinn Féin's Martin Ferris in Kerry North in 2002.

'He [Bertie Ahern] got up. I said one last thing of it. I said "Bertie, don't send me down the road on an Independent Fianna Fáil ticket. I've gone around the bend with ye" … He said "We're having a meeting with [Ray] MacSharry's team on Monday morning at ten o'clock. And you can take my word you will not go down the road on an Independent Fianna Fáil ticket."'[51]

Jackie Healy-Rae on his meeting with Fianna Fáil leader, Bertie Ahern, months before the general election of 1997. He was later elected as an Independent TD for Kerry South.

'You can imagine, a Cheann Comhairle, how perplexed I was when I returned to find my wardrobe almost empty. The Taoiseach [Bertie Ahern] has been busy robbing my clothes ... He said "I am one of the few socialists left in Irish politics." Immediately, Tomás Ó Criomhthain came to mind as he lamented the last of the Blasket Islanders: "Ní bheidh ár leithéidí arís ann." I then thought "Good, Taoiseach. There are two of us in it and we will go down together."'[52]

Joe Higgins to Taoiseach Bertie Ahern in the Dáil in 2004.

'I guarantee the Ceann Comhairle that if there is a bad pothole around Waterville, on Dursey Island in west County Cork or anywhere in Cahersiveen, I will do my very best ... in the Ceann Comhairle's absence, I will do my best to sort them out and I will keep him well informed all the time.'[53]

Independent TD Jackie Healy-Rae congratulates constituency colleague John O'Donoghue on his election as Ceann Comhairle in June 2007.

'I assure the Deputy that I will never be far away.'[54]

O'Donoghue's retort to Healy-Rae (above).

'I'm a failed politician. I tried again and again to get elected and I failed. But it's like being a gambler. You always want to stay in the pot. To have one last go. Once you're in it you're hooked. There's just no getting out of it. It's like the mafia.'[55]

Listowel senator and former Dáil candidate Ned O'Sullivan.

'She was an extraordinary woman because here she was, pregnant with her seventh child, her husband dead, she a widow in her forties, living on the side of the street in Caherciveen, really facing very difficult times and she still did what she was asked. She was greatly admired and loved in the community here – I think much more than I ever could be.'[56]

Former minister John O'Donoghue reflects on how his mother, Mary, became a county councillor on the death of her husband, Dan, in 1964.

'I have rarely been asked by RTÉ on to a major programme. I wouldn't have a sexy enough image for the some of the fellows out in Donnybrook; but if I held different views, you can bet your bottom dollar that I would be on.'[57]

John O'Donoghue TD, speaking in 1994.

'I went down with the ship and I think the ship will bob to the surface again one day … On the graffitied walls of Baghdad during the war with the United States, it was written, "I would rather be a cock for a day than a chicken for a week" … I can only really think of two nasty occasions [during the campaign]. One was in the town of Dingle when a so-called respected businessman started shouting obscenities on the street and I ignored him. But then again, there is no point being respected, is there, if you don't have any self-respect. On another occasion, outside Daly's garage in Killarney when a very beautiful looking lady drove up or had herself driven up in an SUV and did something similar … I won't say obscenities but it was quite nasty, but then there is no point in being beautiful, is there, if you are that ugly underneath.'[58]

John O'Donoghue following his defeat at the 2011 general election.

'On the morning I got married, we were waiting to go to the church, and my father [Michael Moynihan] was always on time for everything and I had said to him this is one time we would have to be ten minutes late. And the doorbell rang and I thought it was the driver and I was going to say to him, "Hold on another five minutes", but it was a client looking for my dad. I was in my wedding dress and all ready to go and he said, "Oh my God, are you getting married?" and I said I was, but he asked to see my father for a minute and I said to him, "Keep him for ten minutes."'[59]

Labour TD for Kerry South Breeda Moynihan-Cronin recalls her wedding-day encounter with one of her father's constituents.

'I was born with politics in my blood. As a child, politics was as much the sustenance at the family dinner table as the food on our plates. My appetite for politics was born out of the determination of my father. That determination was about serving the public good.'[60]

Breeda Moynihan-Cronin on her political upbringing.

'I have nothing against pigeons – I can take or leave pigeons – but I am very much against seagulls. I think something needs to be done to address the seagull problem in this city ... It seems that the seagulls have lost the run of themselves completely ... They are very raucous and are keeping people awake. They are getting so cheeky now that they attack young children and dispossess them of their lollipops and stuff like that. It might be funny to many people but it is a serious issue in the city. They really are vermin.'[61]

Ned O'Sullivan raises the scourge of seagulls in the Seanad in July 2014.

'I go to funerals because I'm friends with an awful lot of people. Maybe the people in Dublin don't go to their friends' funerals because maybe they don't have many friends, I don't know. But I do know that I have friends and I respect people whether they're living or dead.'[62]

Michael Healy-Rae TD on funerals.

'I believe God above is in charge of the weather and that we here cannot do anything about it.'[63]

Danny Healy-Rae TD sets out his views on climate change.

An apology from the BBC

Senator Ross Kinloch, 'The McGillycuddy' of the Reeks

Ross Kinlough, the McGillycuddy of the Reeks.

Seanad Éireann – the Irish parliament's second chamber – has often been home to a diversity of colourful and interesting personalities who, it could be argued, might never have been elected to the Dáil in a general election. In fact, a number of the most effective and sometimes controversial figures in Irish politics were never elected to Leinster House at all – many senators are appointed at the discretion of the Taoiseach without the inconvenience of an election. Until the late 1930s, all senators were appointed by the Executive Council (cabinet) of the day. From its inception, the Seanad was designed to partly address the need for a unionist and Protestant voice in Leinster House and to ensure a diverse array of views were brought to national political debate. One of the most interesting and colourful characters to grace the so-called Upper House was Beaufort's Ross Kinlough McGillycuddy, better known as 'The McGillycuddy' or 'The McGillycuddy of the Reeks'.

'The McGillycuddy of the Reeks' derives from one of the ancient, hereditary titles of the chieftains of Ireland and throughout Ross' Seanad career of thirteen years, he was always referred to formally and informally as 'The McGillycuddy'. The *Daily Telegraph* records that:

> The McGillycuddys were a cadet branch of the O'Sullivans, once the most powerful family in the wild mountainous country in the south-west corner of Ireland. Like other Gaelic families, they fought the invading Normans and English over many centuries. But unlike most Gaelic chieftains, the princely McGillycuddy eschewed exile, and stood his ground as the Gaelic order was finally crushed in the 17th century. Craftily, he sent sons to fight on both sides at the Battle of the Boyne in 1690. A few years later he swore allegiance to the victorious William of Orange and conformed to the Established Church.[1]

Another report claimed that the family could trace their lineage to the kings of Munster and Milesius, as well as Robert the Bruce and Alfred the Great.[2] The

Reeks was the name of the large estate at Churchtown near Beaufort – once part of a 15,000-acre holding – which came into the family's ownership in the nineteenth century and which The McGillycuddy inherited from his father in the early 1920s.

Born on 26 October 1882, the son of Denis Charles McGillycuddy and Gertrude Laura Miller, The McGillycuddy was educated in Edinburgh and the Royal Artillery College in Woolwich before serving with the armed forces in India between 1903 and 1905. He was decorated several times for his military service. He fought in France, alongside Lawrence of Arabia, during the First World War, for which he won the Légion d'honneur. His family records that at his home in Beaufort, he installed upstairs and downstairs lavatory bowls that tilt backwards to facilitate squatting, to which he had grown accustomed in the desert.[3] The McGillycuddy was among those who advocated that Irishmen join the First World War effort; along with Thomas O'Donnell, MP for West Kerry, he called in 1914 for all able-bodied men to 'join the British Army and any man who was unfit or too old for active service should volunteer for Home Defence.'[4]

The McGillycuddy inherited The Reeks home and estate at Churchtown from his father in 1921, at the beginning of the War of Independence. Over 15,000 acres of The Reeks estate were handed over to tenants following the passage of the 1923 Irish Land Act. He pursued his interest in political affairs by serving on Kerry County Council in the Killorglin Electoral Area as an Independent from 1926. He was first nominated to the Free State Senate on 1 March 1928 to fill the vacancy created by the death of the Earl of Mayo. He was proposed for the seat by another Kerry senator, the Marquess of Lansdowne. He was a supporter of W.T. Cosgrave's Cumann na nGaedheal government. In his proposition papers on the official Senate record, The McGillycuddy's qualifications for the seat were set out as:

> Chairman Agricultural Committee, Kerry County Council: member of Consultative Council under Live Stock Breeding Act, 1925: past President of the Kerry Cattle Society: Area Counsellor British Legion, Kerry area: actively interested in Local Government reforms: lives continuously in Ireland and concerns himself with all movements, local and otherwise, for social betterment: farms a considerable area on most modern lines and breeds pedigree cattle.[5]

A very frequent contributor to debates in the Seanad, he was known for his colourful turn of phrase, as this 1942 contribution on the subject of censorship illustrates:

I think that censorship is definitely necessary. Those who do not think so have only to look to Buenos Aires in one direction and Port Said in another where there is no censorship. The result in both places is that practically everybody is inoculated with depravity through their bodies. I feel that we do not want that, so that censorship must definitely continue. But no censorship will turn what I call a Dirty Dick into a clean one. He will find something obscene and depraving in almost every sentence that he reads, but those Dirty Dicks are few and far between. I believe that of the many books that I have read, coarse and vulgar as they were, the average young man and young woman would pass that sort of writing by.[6]

In March 1930, The McGillycuddy instructed his solicitor to write to the BBC to seek an apology for the broadcast of a programme to which he took offence. A well-known radio comedian, Leonard Henry, remarked on air that he had come across a mountain range called the McGillycuddy Reeks. He went on,

> for this song, I have engaged the services of Mr McGillycuddy, the owner of the famous Irish Reeks, and the more famous Scottish Breeks, who brings his bagpipes, or strange amalgam of mystery into the studio tonight. Then the bagpipes made somewhat weird noises, exploded and were subsequently, as listeners were told, mended with a puncture outfit.[7]

At his home in Beaufort, The McGillycuddy happened to be listening to the programme. He wrote to the broadcaster to demand an apology. He did not receive the desired apology at first. The BBC replied that 'he is taking an unproportionate view of the incident'. The McGillycuddy then instructed his solicitor to repeat the demand and this time the station did tender the requested apology:

> The BBC and Mr Leonard Henry deeply regret the name of The McGillycuddy was mentioned on the occasion referred to and that any representations that were then made in regard to him which may have given offence. They take this opportunity to express their sincere apology for any annoyance caused to him and undertake not knowingly to allow any repetition of the subject matter of complaint.

It is believed that this was the first time the BBC issued an apology.

In later years, The McGillycuddy sought to re-enter military service with the British army during the Second World War, but his offer was declined due to his age. As a colonel, however, he was given responsibility for a transport training depot in County Down. He frequently wrote letters to local newspapers in which he shared his opinions on a wide range of topics. He died in May 1950. His obituary in *The Kerryman* records that his funeral cortege had to take a circuitous route from his home to Churchtown cemetery because the nearby bridge over the Gaddagh River had recently collapsed following flooding.[8] His grandson, Richard, who died in 1959 as a result of wounds sustained during the Second World War and who was married to Lord Astor's daughter, Virginia, was the last of the family to live at the Reeks, which was sold in 1985.[9] The current holder of the McGillycuddy name is Dermot Patrick Donough McGillycuddy, a grandson of the senator, who lives in South Africa.[10]

APPENDICES

Appendix 1: Kerry TDs since 1919

Ahern, Catherine Ita (Kit) (1915–2007)

Party: Fianna Fáil. Constituency: Kerry North.
Years of service: 1977–81

A native of Athea in County Limerick, Catherine (Kit) Ahern (née Liston) holds the distinction of having been the only woman ever to serve as a Fianna Fáil TD in the constituency of Kerry North. Born in 1915, she studied at the National College of Art and Design and qualified as an art teacher. She married Dan Ahern from Athea in 1941 and joined the Women's Home Guard and the Irish Countrywomen's Association. Ahern was first elected to Kerry County Council when she topped the poll in the Listowel Electoral Area in 1967. She became the first female chairperson of the council in 1977 and is one of four women to have held the post.[1] She was nominated to Seanad Éireann by Taoiseach Seán Lemass on 25 November 1964 to replace the late Senator Pádraig Ó Siochfhradha ('An Seabhac') from Dingle. Her first general election outing came in 1965 when she was a running mate to Thomas McEllistrim Snr. She failed to win a seat, but secured a nomination from Fianna Fáil again in 1969 and 1973, with her percentage of the vote increasing on each occasion. She retained her Seanad seat in 1969 and was elected to the Cultural and Educational Panel. Again, following defeat at the general election of 1973, she was re-elected to the Seanad. She was defeated for the position of Leas Cathaoirleach in June 1973 by Fine Gael's Evelyn Owens.

The Jack Lynch-led Fianna Fáil landslide of 1977 helped to propel Ahern into the Dáil with a vote (20.29 per cent) almost as high as that of her running mate, Thomas McEllistrim Jnr (20.98 per cent). Her time in the Dáil was short, however. She was defeated at the 1981 general election. Ahern later moved to Ballybunion and did not contest another general election. In 1985, she left Fianna Fáil to join the Progressive Democrats. An Irish-language enthusiast, she was active in the Irish Countrywomen's Association, serving as its national president from 1961 to 1964. She also served for a time on Bord Fáilte. On her death on 27 December 2007, aged ninety-two years old, Ahern was the oldest surviving former member of the Oireachtas.

Béaslaí, Piaras (1881–1965)

Party: Sinn Féin. Constituency: East Kerry/
Kerry–Limerick West. Years of service: 1919–23

One of the four MPs returned for Kerry at the 1918 general election, Percy Frederick Beasley, or Piaras Béaslaí as he was better known, was born in Liverpool on 15 February 1881. His father, Patrick Langford Beasley, was a native of Aghadoe and was the editor of the *Catholic Times* newspaper in England. The family moved to Dublin in 1906 and Piaras worked as a journalist for newspapers including the *Irish Independent* and the *Freeman's Journal*. He joined the Irish Volunteers in Dublin in 1913 and fought in the Easter Rising in Dublin city centre in 1916. He was jailed in prisons in England and released in 1917. He was active in the Gaelic League and the Irish Republican Brotherhood and he is credited by some sources as having given the name 'Óglaigh na hÉireann' to the IRB.[2]

Béaslaí was elected Sinn Féin MP for East Kerry at the general election in 1918 and, like his fellow party members, refused to take up his seat at Westminster, instead joining the First Dáil in January 1919. He was the only one of the four Kerry TDs elected to the First Dáil that was present at its first sitting. The other three – Austin Stack, James Crowley and Fionán Lynch – were all in prison at the time. The East Kerry TD read the Democratic Programme of the Dáil at its first meeting. He was re-elected in 1921 for the newly formed constituency of Kerry–Limerick West and again in 1922 as a pro-Treaty candidate. He did not contest the 1923 election. He became a major general in the Free State Army and was Head of Press Censorship, but he left the army in 1924.

Béaslaí was a prolific poet, playwright, novelist and author. Among his publications was a two-volume biography of Michael Collins. After his death, the National Archives acquired his papers, which total some 17,000 different documents. Béaslaí contributed columns to a number of national newspapers in the 1950s and was a regular contributor to programmes on Raidió Éireann. He died in June 1965 and is buried in Glasnevin Cemetery.

Begley, Michael (1932–2012)

Party: Fine Gael. Constituency: Kerry South. Years of service: 1969–89

Michael Begley, born in Dingle in 1932, was a minister of State for three periods in the 1970s and 1980s. A carpenter, he was active in local community groups before entering politics. He is said to have been encouraged to enter politics because he felt that 'Fianna Fáil had blackguarded the [Dingle] peninsula.'[3] He was elected to Kerry County Council for the Tralee Electoral Area in 1960 and contested his first general election in 1965, but did not win a seat.

Begley was the party's candidate at a by-election in Kerry South in December 1966 following the death of the Fianna Fáil TD, Honor Mary Crowley, a ballot that was won by the Fianna Fáil candidate, John O'Leary. In 1969, Begley secured 4,564 votes, enough to secure a seat, though he displaced his party colleague Patrick Connor from Kenmare, who had been elected for the first time in 1961. When Fine Gael and Labour came to power in 1973, Begley was appointed by Taoiseach Liam Cosgrave as parliamentary secretary to the Minister for Local Government. Two years later, he took up the junior ministry position at the departments of Finance and Defence. He served briefly in the Department of Trade, Commerce and Tourism in the short-lived 1981–2 government.

In the 1980s, Begley was at odds with the leadership of Garret FitzGerald and was considered to have been part of the more conservative Cosgrave wing of the party. He lost his seat at the 1989 general election and failed to get elected to the Seanad that year. It was to be eighteen years before Fine Gael regained a seat in the Kerry South constituency. He served for thirty-one years on Kerry County Council (as chairman in 1967–8) and died in 2012.

Brassil, John (1963–)

Party: Fianna Fáil. Constituency: Kerry. Years of service: 2016–

A pharmacist and engineer from Ballyheigue, John Brassil was born in 1963. He was first elected to the Dáil for the Kerry constituency in 2016; it was his first time contesting a general election. His father, Noel Brassil, was a long-serving county councillor. Upon his father's retirement in 1999, John was elected to the council on his first attempt, representing the Listowel Electoral Area. Brassil was Mayor of Kerry from 2014 to 2015 and is a former chairman of Shannon Development. On his election to the Dáil in 2016, he became Fianna Fáil spokesperson on primary care and community health services. He was replaced on the county council by John Lucid from Ballyheigue.

Cahill, Patrick J. (1883–1946)

Party: Republican/Sinn Féin. Constituency: Kerry–Limerick West/Kerry. Years of service: 1921–7

Patrick J. (Paddy) Cahill from Tralee was born at Caherina, Tralee, in 1883. He attended Tralee CBS and was a contemporary of Éamon de Valera as a student at Blackrock College. Cahill won an All-Ireland senior football medal with Kerry in 1904 alongside Austin Stack (the final was played in 1906) and played with Kerry for several years. He worked at John Donovan & Sons in the Square, Tralee. Cahill joined and rose up through the ranks of the Irish Volunteers and he was involved in plans to land arms at Fenit for the Easter Rising. He took over the leadership of the Kerry Volunteers when Austin Stack was arrested, but he was almost immediately interned himself at Richmond, then Wakefield and Frongoch, until the general release of December 1916.

Cahill left his employers in protest because it was supplying to British troops in the First World War. He led the Lispole Ambush and other engagements during the War of Independence. The cinema he ran with others at County Hall on Staughton's Row in Tralee was burned down by the Black and Tans in November 1920. He was elected to the Second and Third Dáils as a Sinn Féin TD for the then constituency of Kerry–Limerick West and was on the anti-Treaty side in the Civil War. He sat in the Fourth Dáil as a republican deputy for the seven-seat Kerry constituency. During the Civil War, Cahill was imprisoned and again went on hunger strike, becoming seriously ill at one stage. He was released at Christmas in 1923. Cahill turned to journalism and went on to found *The Kerry Champion* newspaper with Thomas Lynch from Armagh, who would later serve as a chairman of Tralee Urban District Council. The newspaper was published between 1928 and 1958 and Cahill was editor and managing director for many years. A lifelong public advocate of abstinence from alcohol, he died on 12 November 1946. Cahill's Park in Tralee is named after him.

Collins, Con (1881–1937)

Party: Sinn Féin. Constituency: Kerry–Limerick West. Years of service: 1921–3

Con (Cornelius) Collins was born at Arranagh, Newcastle West, County Limerick, in 1881. He was a member of the Dáil for two years. A postal worker, he was active in the Irish Volunteers and the Gaelic League, through which he came to know Cathal Brugha. Along with Austin Stack, he was involved in attempting to ensure that the ill-fated shipment of arms for the 1916 Rising was landed in Kerry. He was jailed in Frongoch in Wales and was on hunger strike for a period.

Collins was initially elected a Sinn Féin MP for Limerick West in December 1918 and took his seat the following month in the newly established Dáil Éireann. A vehement opponent of the Anglo-Irish Treaty of 1921, he was returned as one of seven TDs for Kerry–Limerick West in both the 1921 and 1922 general elections. He did not contest the 1923 election and retired from politics. He later worked as superintendent of Limerick General Post Office. He died following an operation in the Mater Hospital in Dublin on 26 November 1937 and was interred in Limerick.

Connor, John (1901–1955)

Party: Clann na Poblachta. Constituency: Kerry North. Years of service: 1954–5

John (Johnny) Connor, originally O'Connor, was the first Clann na Poblachta TD ever elected in Kerry and he and his daughter, Kathleen, are the only Dáil representatives the party ever had in Kerry. He dropped the 'O' from O'Connor to ensure a higher placement on the alphabetical ballot paper. Born at Poulawaddra, Farmer's Bridge, near Tralee, in 1901, Connor was active in the IRA and played a prominent role in the

War of Independence. He was involved in attacks on police barracks in Gortatlea, Brosna and Scartaglin and he took the anti-Treaty side in the Civil War. In 1923, he was captured in a dug-out near his home and went on hunger strike when jailed.

A farmer and an auctioneer, Connor emigrated to Chicago and returned home in 1930 to became a clerk of works for the Board of Health. He was jailed with other IRA activists during the Second World War. He joined Clann na Poblachta and was elected to Kerry County Council in October 1948, one of four councillors elected in what was the new party's first local authority outing. Connor had contested the general election in Kerry North in February 1948, the year his party helped form the first inter-party government under Taoiseach John A. Costello, but he did not win a seat.

Connor also stood in 1951, but he didn't make it to the Dáil until 1954, when he took the fourth and final seat in Kerry North with 5,003 votes. After just over a year in the Dáil, Connor was killed in a car accident on 11 December 1955 as he was returning to Tralee from Dublin, having attended a meeting of the Clann na Poblachta national executive. The accident occurred at Ballyduff on the Castleisland to Abbeyfeale road, where a memorial stands. His death prompted the only by-election held in the constituency of Kerry North, at which he was succeeded by his 21-year-old daughter, Kathleen O'Connor (Fitzgerald).

Connor-Scarteen, Patrick (1906–1989)

Party: Fine Gael. Constituency: Kerry South. Years of service: 1961–9

Patrick Connor-Scarteen (sometimes Connor or O'Connor-Scarteen) from Kenmare was born in 1906. He was active in the IRA during the War of Independence and was pro-Treaty during the Civil War. His brothers, Timothy and John, were soldiers in the Free State Army when they were killed in their home in Kenmare in September 1922. Connor-Scarteen spent time in the United States before returning home to work in the family grocery and bakery. He won a seat on Kerry County Council in 1948, a position he held until 1961. He was elected to the Seanad on the Administrative Panel in 1957 and went on to win a Dáil seat in Kerry South in the general election of 1961. He lost his seat in 1969 when one of his running mates, Michael Begley from Dingle, won the Fine Gael seat in the constituency. He was succeeded on Kerry County Council in 1973 by his son, Michael Connor-Scarteen, who was in turn succeeded on the local authority by his son, Patrick Connor-Scarteen, in 2009, Leas Cathaoirleach of the body in 2017–18. Patrick Snr's brother, Timothy, represented the Killorglin Electoral Area on Kerry County Council from 1960 to 1967. Connor-Scarteen died in 1989.

Crowley, Frederick (1880–1945)

Party: Fianna Fáil. Constituency: Kerry South.
Years of service: 1927–45

Frederick (Fred) Hugh Crowley was born in Gurteen, near Banteer, County Cork, in 1880 and later lived and farmed at Rathmore. His father, Michael, operated the Rathmore Mills and was one of the founder members of the Land and Labour Association with Michael Davitt. Fred received a diploma in textile manufacturing from the University of Leeds. He joined the Irish Volunteers in Rathmore before the Easter Rising and was involved in key IRA attacks during the War of Independence, such as the Headford Junction Ambush in 1921.

Later residing at Listymuragh, Killarney; Shinnagh, Rathmore; and Danesfort in Killarney, Crowley was elected to Kerry County Council in 1917 and was first elected to the Dáil at the September 1927 general election. This was the beginning of an unbroken electoral track record, which lasted until his death in 1945. He had stood unsuccessfully as a candidate at the June 1927 general election, polling 3,370 votes. In 1939, he married Honor Mary Boland, a daughter of John Pius Boland, Member of Parliament for South Kerry from 1900 to 1918.

Crowley was president of the Irish National Ploughing Championships, which took place on Lord Kenmare's estate in Killarney in February 1939. He was also a director of the Irish Tourist Association and a member of the Governing Body of University College Cork. When he died on 5 May 1945, a by-election was held. His wife, Honor Mary, was the Fianna Fáil candidate and she successfully retained the party seat.

Crowley, Honor Mary (1903–1966)

Party: Fianna Fáil. Constituency: Kerry South.
Years of service: 1945–66

Honor Mary Crowley (née Boland) holds the distinction of being the first ever woman elected to the Dáil as a representative for the constituency of Kerry South. Born in Dublin on 19 October 1903, she was a daughter of John Pius Boland, the Irish Parliamentary Party MP for the South Kerry constituency between 1900 and 1918. A social worker, she married Fred Hugh Crowley, Fianna Fáil TD for Kerry South, in 1939. When Fred died in 1945, she was nominated to contest the by-election. Crowley succeeded in retaining the seat for Fianna Fáil and fended off the challenge of the only other candidate, Edmund Horan of Clann na Talmhan. By holding the seat, she helped Fianna Fáil to retain all three seats in Kerry South, which they had held since a by-election the previous year.

In winning the seat, Crowley made history by becoming the first woman from Kerry to enter the Dáil. She also became the first woman ever to have been elected at a by-election to succeed her husband in Dáil Éireann. In addition, she took over Fred's county council seat, retaining it at each local authority election until her death and topping the poll in the Killarney Electoral Area at each election. Crowley also holds the distinction of being the first woman to represent Ireland on a delegation to the Council of Europe in Strasbourg – from 1954 to 1957. Such was her popularity in her constituency that she was known to many as 'Mrs Fred'. She later lived at Dromhall, Killarney, where she died in October 1966. Her death prompted the holding of a by-election in Kerry South on 4 December 1966. This was won by Fianna Fáil's John O'Leary.

Crowley, James (1880–1946)

Party: Sinn Féin/Cumann na nGaedheal. Constituency: Kerry North. Years of service: 1919–32

James Crowley was born in 1880 in Listowel. He studied at Trinity College Dublin and became a veterinary surgeon based in Listowel, covering north Kerry and west Limerick. He married Clementine Burson and they lived on Upper Church Street. Crowley joined the Irish Volunteers in 1914 and was immersed in Sinn Féin. He became an intelligence officer for the organisation. In August 1918, he was arrested for reading the Proclamation of the Irish Republic at a public meeting in Listowel. Along with fellow Kerry prisoners – and future fellow Kerry TDs – Austin Stack, Piaras Béaslaí and Fionán Lynch, Crowley took part in the Belfast Prison riot of December 1918.

At the 1918 general election, Crowley was elected MP for North Kerry, but, like other Sinn Féin MPs, did not take his seat in Westminster. He was in prison when the First Dáil sat in 1919 but on his return to Kerry became a prominent IRA leader during the War of Independence and was involved in instigating the Listowel Mutiny of 1920, in which RIC members refused to obey orders to shoot IRA prisoners. Crowley was interned again following his arrest on Grafton Street in February 1921. He supported the Anglo-Irish Treaty. Crowley held his seat in the Dáil – later for Cumann na nGaedheal – until 1932, when he lost his seat and retired from politics. Clementine Crowley was active in the Blueblouses, the women's wing of the Blueshirts and James was vice-president of the organisation locally. He died aged sixty-six in 1946.

Daly, Denis (1886–1965)

Party: Fianna Fáil. Constituency: Kerry. Years of service: 1933–7

Denis 'Dinny' Daly was born on Main Street, Cahersiveen, in 1886. At the age of nineteen, he travelled to London, where he studied for and joined the civil service. In

London, he became active in Irish cultural and political organisations and joined the Irish Republican Brotherhood. As a clerical worker in the London GPO in 1912, he made the acquaintance of Michael Collins. He returned to Dublin ahead of the Easter Rising in 1916 and joined the IRB.

On Good Friday 1916, Daly was one of a party of five IRB members (along with Colm Ó Lochlainn, Con Keating, Dan Sheehan and Charles Monahan) who were travelling in two cars from Killarney to Cahersiveen to seize radio equipment to assist in the landing of arms on the Kerry coast for use in the Easter Rising. One of the cars, containing Keating, Monahan, Sheehan and their driver, Tommy McInerney, took a wrong turn in Killorglin, however, and drove off the end of Ballykissane Pier near the town. Only McInerney survived drowning.

Daly returned to Dublin on Easter Saturday and fought in the General Post Office in Dublin during the Easter Rising. He was subsequently interned in Frongoch Prison in Wales and Stafford Jail in England. Following his release, he was vice-commandant of the Kerry No. 3 Brigade during the War of Independence and later opposed the Anglo-Irish Treaty. Following a spell in prison, he returned to the family bakery business in Cahersiveen in 1923.

Daly served one term in the Dáil as a TD for the seven-seat Kerry constituency between 1933 and 1937, when the county was divided into two constituencies. He was one of five Fianna Fáil TDs returned at the 1933 election. Not keen on political life, he once told Piaras Béaslaí that he had told his party he disliked speaking on public platforms. Daly was a chairman of the South Kerry GAA Board for many years. He died in 1965.

Deenihan, Jimmy (1952–)

Party: Fine Gael. Constituency: Kerry North/ Kerry North-West Limerick. Years of service: 1987–2016

One of the many Kerry politicians to have had a successful career in Gaelic games, Jimmy Deenihan was part of the Kerry senior football side that won several All-Ireland titles in the 1970s and 1980s. A native of Finuge, near Listowel, where he was born in 1952, he captained Kerry in 1981 and holds five All-Ireland senior football medals. A former secondary school teacher at Tarbert Comprehensive School, Deenihan was first nominated to Seanad Éireann by Taoiseach Garret FitzGerald after the November 1982 general election, in which he had been a candidate. He has credited the Listowel playwright and writer, John B. Keane, with convincing him to enter politics. Deenihan won a seat for Fine Gael in Kerry at the 1987 general election, heading the poll with 10,087 votes and displacing the long-serving Fianna Fáil TD, Thomas McEllistrim Jnr, in the process. Fine Gael had been without a seat in Kerry North for the previous ten years.

In December 1994, Deenihan was appointed Minister of State at the Department of Agriculture, Food and Forestry, a position he held until 1997. In opposition, he held a number of portfolios for Fine Gael. He became Minister for Arts, Heritage and the Gaeltacht in March 2011 and moved to a junior ministry in the Department of An Taoiseach in July 2014, becoming the minister with responsibility for the Irish diaspora. He lost his Dáil seat at the 2016 general election and announced his retirement from politics. Deenihan published his footballing memoir, *My Sporting Life*, in 2011.

Ferris, Martin (1952–)

Party: Sinn Féin. Constituency: Kerry North/ Kerry North-West Limerick/Kerry. Years of service: 2002–

Martin Ferris was the first ever Sinn Féin TD elected in the Kerry North constituency. Born in Tralee in 1952, he served on Kerry County Council and Tralee Town Council for a number of years prior to his election to the Dáil. He played football at club and county level in his youth. Active in the IRA from a young age, Ferris joined the organisation in the early 1970s and was imprisoned for his paramilitary activities a number of times, most notably serving a ten-year prison sentence for attempting to import arms for the IRA at Fenit in Kerry in September 1984.

Contesting his first general election in 1997, Ferris received almost 5,700 votes. Five years later, he ousted the former Labour Party leader, Dick Spring, to take a seat in Kerry North. He had also contested the European elections in Munster in 1999. He has been spokesperson on agriculture and fisheries for Sinn Féin. Ferris, who lives in Ardfert, was the subject of a biography by J.J. Barrett in 2005. Ferris was a member of Kerry County Council (1999–2003) and Tralee UDC/Town Council (1999–2003). His daughter, Toiréasa Ferris, replaced him on Kerry County Council in 2002, following his election to the Dáil. She is a former Mayor of Kerry and a former member of Tralee Town Council and was selected as a Dáil candidate for Sinn Féin in Kerry in December 2017.

Finucane, Patrick (1899–1984)

Party: Clann na Talmhan/Independent. Constituency: Kerry North. Years of service: 1943–69

Born in Clounprohus, Moyvane, in 1899 and later residing in Lisselton and Listowel, Patrick (Paddy) Finucane was one of the longest-serving TDs for Kerry North. He joined

the Irish Volunteers at the age of seventeen and fought in the War of Independence. He took the anti-Treaty side in the Civil War. From a farming background, Finucane was always seen as a champion of the farming community and was attracted to the short-lived, but quite successful agrarian party, Clann na Talmhan, which was formed in 1939. He topped the poll in the Listowel Electoral Area at his first county council election in 1942 and was elected to the Dáil the following year, representing Clann na Talmhan. It was the beginning of twenty-six years of unbroken service in Leinster House.

Clann na Talmhan formed part of the first inter-party government between 1948 and 1951, but Finucane became increasingly disillusioned with the coalition's treatment of the farming community. On 18 April 1951, he resigned from the party, expressing his concern for dairy farmers in a letter to one of the party's ministers, Joseph Blowick. Finucane was re-elected to the Dáil as an Independent at the general election a month later, but rejoined the party only to resign again ahead of the 1957 election in a dispute over milk prices and the failure to deliver a factory for Listowel, as promised during the 1956 by-election in Kerry North.[4] Despite the reduction from four seats to three in Kerry North in 1961, he retained his seat as an Independent. One of his significant achievements was securing of a number of drainage schemes in north Kerry, which had been promised for many years.

In an accident at his home shortly after the 1965 general election, Finucane was severely injured and was in poor health for many years. He stood down at the 1969 election and his son, Michael, contested the poll as an Independent, but failed to win a seat. Finucane acted as election agent to Sinn Féin's Robert Beasley at the 1974 local elections, but took no other major role in politics. He died aged eighty-four in 1984. He was the only Independent TD ever to sit for the Kerry North constituency.

Fleming, Tom (1951–)

Party: Independent. Constituency: Kerry South. Years of service: 2011–16

Born in 1951, Tom Fleming from Scartaglin was first elected to the Dáil in Kerry South as an Independent member in 2011. He was the fourth generation of his family to have served on Kerry County Council, following his father, his grandfather and his great-grandfather Michael J. Fleming, who had won a seat on Kerry County Council in 1902. Tom Fleming was first co-opted to the council in 1984 following the death of his father, Thomas. Fleming had been a life-long member of Fianna

Fáil and had contested the general elections of 2002 and 2007 as a running mate to John O'Donoghue in Kerry South. He narrowly lost out on a seat on both occasions.

At the 2011 general election, Fianna Fáil decided to nominate just one candidate in Kerry South – John O'Donoghue – and Fleming withdrew from the contest. Within days of the selection convention, Fleming, along with county councillor Michael Cahill, resigned from Fianna Fáil and Fleming declared his intention to stand as an Independent. He won the third and final seat in Kerry South in 2011 and joined the Dáil's Technical Group of non-party TDs. Despite initially indicating his intention to contest the 2016 general election in the new Kerry constituency, Fleming withdrew from the race just weeks before polling day and retired from the Dáil. In August 2018, he signalled a return to local politics.

Flynn, John (1894–1968)

Party: Fianna Fáil/Independent. Constituency: Kerry/Kerry South. Years of service: 1932–43, 1948–57

A native of Brackhill, Castlemaine, John (Jack) Flynn was born in 1894. He was active in the IRB and the 6th Battalion of the Kerry No. 1 and No. 2 Brigades during the War of Independence. The family home was repeatedly raided by police. Flynn was a central player in many incidents during the War of Independence, including an ambush of Black and Tans at Ballymacandy near his home on 1 June 1921. Flynn was first elected to the Dáil for Fianna Fáil in 1932, initially representing the Kerry constituency, and was a county councillor from 1934. He retained his seat in the Dáil without a breach until 1943, when he did not contest the election, having failed to receive a nomination for Fianna Fáil. It was rumoured that Flynn had been involved in a relationship with a young woman and that he had fathered a child out of wedlock. Fianna Fáil chose not to nominate Flynn and instead selected Cahersiveen solicitor John B. Healy, who won a seat in 1943 alongside party colleague, Fred Crowley.

Flynn did not contest the 1944 general election, but returned to the Dáil in 1948, this time as an Independent TD. He retained his seat in 1951, again as an Independent, but had reconciled with Fianna Fáil before the 1954 general election, when he was returned as a TD for the party. He had voted for Éamon de Valera as Taoiseach in 1951. Flynn's career in the Dáil ended in 1957, however, when he was unseated by John Joe Rice of Sinn Féin.

During a debate on the Order of Business in the Dáil in 1952, Flynn was the subject of a throwaway remark from Independent TD, Oliver J. Flanagan. Dr Noël Browne TD had raised the issue of the Adoption of Children Bill, and Flanagan had suggested that 'Deputy Flynn would be more qualified' to comment on the matter – a perceived reference to Flynn's alleged extra-marital relationship. Flynn later assaulted Flanagan in the Dáil restaurant and both deputies were censured by the Committee of Procedures and Privileges for their behaviour. Flynn farmed at Castlemaine in his retirement and he and his wife,

Mary (née Ryle), later moved to Killarney, where the couple ran the East Avenue House guesthouse. Following the sale of that business, the couple retired to Tralee. Flynn died in 1968 in Dublin.

Foley, Denis (1934–2013)

Party: Fianna Fáil. Constituency: Kerry North.
Years of service: 1981–9, 1992–2002

Denis Foley, born in 1934 and from Staughton's Row, Tralee, served as a Fianna Fáil TD for Kerry North between 1981 and 2002, except for a three-year period between 1989 and 1992. Formerly a rates collector and businessman, he was elected to Kerry County Council in 1979 for the Tralee Electoral Area. He held a number of senior roles in the constituency organisation and contested the 1977 general election alongside Kit Ahern and outgoing TD Thomas McEllistrim, but he was not elected. Four years later, however, he displaced Ahern to take a seat in the Dáil alongside his great constituency rival, McEllistrim.

Despite losing his seat at the 1989 general election and not being a close supporter of Taoiseach Charles Haughey, Foley succeeded in winning a Seanad seat on the Industrial and Commercial Panel. He returned to the Dáil in 1992 and was the only Fianna Fáil TD in the Kerry North constituency for the following ten years. He resigned from Fianna Fáil in 2000, following revelations that he held an offshore account with Ansbacher Bank to avoid tax. He told the Moriarty Tribunal that year that he had known, since the early 1980s, that he held tens of thousands of pounds in the offshore account. He had been a member of a Dáil committee that had been investigating deposit interest retention tax (DIRT) and was suspended from the Dáil for fourteen days under the Ethics in Public Office Act of 1995.

Foley retired at the 2002 general election. He was succeeded on Kerry County Council by his daughter, Norma Foley, also a member of Tralee Town Council. Norma Foley contested the 2007 general election, but did not win a seat. She was Mayor of Tralee in 2017–18 and County Cathaoirleach in 2018–19. Denis Foley died in October 2013.

Fuller, Stephen (1900–1984)

Party: Fianna Fáil. Constituency: Kerry North.
Years of service: 1937–43

A farmer from Fahavane, Kilflynn, Stephen Fuller was active in the IRA during the War of Independence and took the anti-Treaty side in the Civil War. He was the sole survivor of one of the worst atrocities of the Irish Civil War when at Ballyseedy, near Tralee, on 7 March 1923, he survived an explosion following the detonation of a mine by Free State soldiers. Fuller was one of eight republican prisoners taken from prison in Tralee and tied to the mine as a reprisal for the IRA bomb in Knocknagoshel that caused the deaths of five soldiers. Fuller escaped with minor injuries. He joined Fianna Fáil and won a seat for the party in Kerry North at the 1937 and 1938 general elections. Despite his background, it is noted that he never mentioned Ballyseedy on an election platform.[5] Stephen Fuller was also a county councillor between 1934 and 1938. He lost his Dáil seat in 1943 and retired from politics. He died in 1984. His son, Paudie Fuller, was a member of Kerry County Council from 1972 to 1974 and 1980 to 1985.

Griffin, Brendan (1982–)

Party: Fine Gael. Constituency: Kerry South/ Kerry. Years of service: 2011–

Brendan Griffin became the first TD from the Castlemaine area in over fifty years when he was first elected to the Dáil at the 2011 general election. A native of Keel and a representative of Fine Gael, Griffin had been a member of Kerry County Council since 2009, having previously contested the 2004 local elections in the Dingle Electoral Area. He topped the poll and displaced his running mate and sitting Fine Gael TD Tom Sheahan to win a Kerry South Dáil seat at the 2011 election. At twenty-eight, he became the youngest ever TD elected for the constituency. On his election, Griffin announced that he would accept only half of his salary as a Dáil deputy, with the other half set aside to cover the salary of a teacher in a local school. His cousin Matt Griffin replaced him on Kerry County Council in 2011 and held his seat until 2014. Griffin retained his seat in the new Kerry constituency in 2016 and was the sole Fine Gael candidate elected. He was an outspoken critic of Enda Kenny's leadership of the party. On the election of Leo Varadkar as Taoiseach in June 2017, Griffin became Minister of State at the Department of Transport, Tourism and Sport.

Healy, John B. (1903–1995)

Party: Fianna Fáil. Constituency: Kerry South. Years of service: 1943–8

From Valentia Road, Cahersiveen, John B. Healy was the fourth son of M.J. Healy, a member of Kerry County Council from 1928. He studied at Blackrock College and Dublin University and received an Honours BA and LLB. He was admitted to the roll of solicitors in 1931. Healy was approached by the Fianna Fáil leadership prior to the 1943 general election and asked to stand in place of the sitting deputy, John Flynn from Castlemaine, who had become embroiled in a personal controversy which was made known to party headquarters and party leader, Éamon de Valera. He succeeded in winning a seat alongside party colleague Fred Hugh Crowley. Healy retained his seat at the 1944 general election, but lost out in 1948 when Flynn was re-elected as an independent republican deputy. Healy did not contest another election. In later years, he remained active in the Fianna Fáil organisation in Kerry South, serving as chairman of the Comhairle Dáil Ceantair for several years. He died aged ninety-two in 1995.

Healy-Rae, Jackie (1931–2014)

Party: Independent. Constituency: Kerry South. Years of service: 1997–2011

Born in 1931 near Kilgarvan in Reacaisleach (from which the 'Rae' part of his surname derives), John Patrick Healy set up a plant-hire business on his return after a period in the US. He won county hurling medals with Kilgarvan in 1956 and 1958. Healy-Rae was a long-serving county councillor for Fianna Fáil. He was co-opted to Kerry County Council in 1973, replacing Michael Doherty. He held the council seat until 2003, when his son Danny Healy-Rae replaced him, following the abolition of the dual mandate. Renowned for his colourful campaigns and his co-ordination of many Fianna Fáil by-election campaigns over the years, he failed to secure the nomination for the Dáil in Kerry South in 1997, prompting him to leave the party and contest the election as an 'Independent Fianna Fáil' candidate.

Healy-Rae topped the poll in Kerry South, denying Fianna Fáil two seats. The failure of Fianna Fáil and the Progressive Democrats to command a majority in the new Dáil meant that Healy-Rae, along with fellow Independents Tom Gildea, Mildred Fox and Harry Blaney, were needed to provide the new Taoiseach, Bertie Ahern, with a working majority. In return for his support for the new government, Healy-Rae secured a commitment of funding for many projects in his constituency. A similar deal was negotiated with Ahern following the 2002 general election and again in 2007, when Fianna Fáil, the Progressive Democrats and the Green Party formed a coalition government. The voting agreements with three governments often attracted controversy and led to a strong rivalry with his constituency counterpart and former party colleague, John O'Donoghue.

Jackie Healy-Rae stood down at the 2011 general election and was replaced in the Dáil by his son, Michael Healy-Rae. The latter was replaced on Kerry County Council by his nephew and Jackie's grandson, Johnny Healy-Rae in 2011. Jackie's other son, Danny Healy-Rae, was also elected to the Dáil in 2016 alongside his brother, Michael, and in 2016, Jackie's granddaughter, Maura, joined the council, replacing Danny Healy-Rae when he was elected to the Dáil. Jackie Healy-Rae died in December 2014.

Healy-Rae, Danny (1954–)

Party: Independent. Constituency: Kerry. Years of service: 2016–

From a well-established political dynasty, Danny Healy-Rae was born in Kilgarvan in 1954 and operates a pub and plant-hire business. He first entered politics ahead of the 2004 local elections, when he was co-opted to a seat in the Killarney Electoral Area as an Independent. At the time, his father, Jackie Healy-Rae, was an Independent deputy for Kerry South and his brother, Michael, was a councillor in the Killorglin Electoral Area. When Michael was elected to the Dáil in 2011, Danny's son, Johnny, took a seat beside his father on Kerry County Council, having replaced Michael as a councillor for the Killorglin district.

Danny Healy-Rae submitted nomination papers to contest the 2016 general election just minutes before the close of nominations to join his brother on the ballot paper. Between them, the brothers polled 38 per cent of first-preference votes and became the first pair of brothers to represent the same Dáil constituency. Danny was replaced on the county council by his daughter, Maura, a teacher. Healy-Rae has provoked controversy for his views on drink-driving restrictions in rural Ireland and the causes of climate change.

Healy-Rae, Michael (1967–)

Party: Independent. Constituency: Kerry South/Kerry. Years of service: 2011–

Born in 1967, Michael Healy-Rae, from Kilgarvan, succeeded his father, Jackie Healy-Rae, in the Dáil at the 2011 general election, following a career on Kerry County Council. First elected to the local authority in 1999, he was joined on the county council by his brother Danny Healy-Rae in 2004, making them the fourth set of brothers ever to serve simultaneously on the authority. He resigned from Fianna Fáil with his father in 1997, when Jackie Healy-Rae contested his first general election as an Independent candidate.

On his election to the Dáil, Michael Healy-Rae opted not to join the Dáil's Technical Group of Independent TDs, unlike his constituency colleague, Tom Fleming, also an Independent. Following his election to the Dáil, Healy-Rae was succeeded on Kerry County Council by his nephew, Johnny Healy-Rae, who sits for the South and West Kerry Municipal District. Following a dispute with Minister for Social Protection Joan Burton in 2012, Deputy Healy-Rae stood down as a director of the Citizens' Information Board, to which he had been appointed by a previous government. In 2016, in the reformed Kerry constituency, Michael Healy-Rae secured the highest first-preference vote in the country, with 20,378 first-preference votes, and was elected alongside his brother, Danny Healy-Rae – the first occasion on which two brothers were returned for the same constituency. Michael runs a shop and post office in his native village. His niece, Maura, is a member of Kerry County Council.

Kissane, Eamonn (1899–1979)

Party: Fianna Fáil. Constituency: Kerry/Kerry North. Years of service: 1932–51

Born in 1899 in Newtownsandes (later Moyvane) to a family of twelve, Eamonn Kissane was first elected as a Fianna Fáil TD for the then constituency of Kerry in 1932. He continued to hold his seat until 1951, representing Kerry North from 1937 onwards. A teacher and a barrister, Kissane was active in the Irish Volunteers, Sinn Féin and the Gaelic League and was co-opted to Kerry County Council in 1920. He opposed the Anglo-Irish Treaty and was jailed during the Civil War in the Curragh and Mountjoy. A fluent Irish speaker, he became an organiser for the Gaelic League and toured Kilkenny and Wexford, arranging Irish language classes. He married the then medical officer of New Ross, Dr Anne Kehoe, in 1935.

Kissane pursued a degree in law. He was called to the Bar in 1938 and practised on the Eastern Circuit. He was appointed parliamentary secretary to the Minister for Lands with responsibility for the Gaeltacht areas for a brief period in 1943 and subsequently held junior ministerial posts in the Department of the Taoiseach and Department of Defence between 1944 and 1948. He was also Government Chief Whip from 1943 to 1948. Kissane was defeated at the general election of 1951, but was appointed to the Seanad on the nomination of Taoiseach John A. Costello. He was re-elected to the Seanad on the Cultural and Educational Panel in 1954, 1957 and 1961. He retired from politics in 1965 and died in May 1979 at his home in New Ross, County Wexford.

Lynch, Fionán (1889–1966)

Party: Sinn Féin/Cumann na nGaedheal/Fine Gael. Constituency: Kerry South/Kerry. Years of service: 1919–44

Fionán (also Finian) Lynch TD was born at Kilmackerin in Waterville on St Patrick's Day, 1889. He was educated at St Brendan's College, Killarney, and later Rockwell College, Blackrock College and St Patrick's Teacher Training College. He taught at St Michan's national school on Halston Street in Dublin between 1912 and 1916. Lynch was captain of a company of the Dublin Brigade of the Irish Volunteers which fought in the area of the Four Courts during the Easter Rising. He was sentenced to death for his part in the rebellion. This was commuted to ten years' penal servitude. He went on hunger strike in May and again in November 1917. He was jailed again in 1918, serving time variously in Mountjoy, Portland, Strangeways and Belfast.

Lynch was elected as the Sinn Féin MP for South Kerry in 1918 and was in jail when the First Dáil met in January 1919. On his release from jail, he took part in the operation that saw fellow Kerry TDs, Piaras Béaslaí and Austin Stack, escape from Strangeways Prison in Manchester on 25 October 1919. A supporter of the Anglo-Irish Treaty, he was re-elected to the Dáil for the Kerry constituency in 1921 and 1922 and travelled to London as joint secretary to the Irish delegation during the Anglo-Irish Treaty negotiations in 1921. He was one of three Cumann na nGaedheal TDs elected for Kerry in 1923. He retained this seat for twenty-one years, as a Fine Gael TD for Kerry South from 1937. During a varied ministerial career, Lynch was Minister for Education (1922), minister without portfolio (1922), Minister for Fisheries (1922–7) and Minister for Lands, Fisheries and the Gaeltacht (1928–32). He was Leas Ceann Comhairle of the Dáil from 5 July 1938 to 12 May 1939.

Lynch became deputy leader of Fine Gael for a short period in February 1944. He resigned as a TD on 10 October 1944, following his appointment by the Fianna Fáil government as a Circuit Court judge on the Sligo–Donegal circuit. The vacancy created prompted the holding of the first ever Dáil by-election in Kerry South, at which Donal O'Donoghue won a seat for Fianna Fáil. Lynch retired from the judiciary in 1959 and died in 1966.

Lynch, Gerard (1931–)
Party: Fine Gael. Constituency: Kerry North.
Years of service: 1969–77

Gerard M. Lynch, from Listowel, served as a Fine Gael TD for Kerry North from 1969 to 1977. He was born in Listowel in 1931. His father John (Jack) Lynch, an ex-Free State Army officer, had been a TD for the constituency between 1951 and 1954. A baker and grocer, Lynch was elected to Kerry County Council in 1967 for the Listowel Electoral Area and also sat on Listowel Urban District Council, of which he was chairman in 1980–1. Following success at the 1969 general election, he was re-elected in 1973. Lynch lost his seat in 1977, but he was elected to the Seanad that year on the Agricultural Panel. He failed to regain his Dáil seat in 1981 and retired from national politics. His daughter, Mary Horgan, later served on Listowel UDC from 1994 to 1999. Apart from Gerard Lynch and his father, John, just two other Fine Gael TDs – John Marcus O'Sullivan and Jimmy Deenihan – have represented Kerry North in the Dáil.

Lynch, John (1888–1957)

Party: Fine Gael. Constituency: Kerry North. Years of service: 1951–4

Listowel baker and merchant John (Jack) Lynch was first elected to Dáil Éireann in 1951, becoming the first Fine Gael TD in Kerry North since Professor John Marcus O'Sullivan. He was born at Stack's Mountains, Kilflynn, in 1888. He was active during the War of Independence and was on the pro-Treaty side in the Civil War, later becoming a captain in the Free State Army. Lynch was elected in 1951, but failed to retain his seat at the 1954 general election. However, he was elected to the Seanad on the Industrial and Commercial Panel that year. He contested the general election of March 1957, but was unsuccessful. He died suddenly just three months later.

Lynch's son, Gerard Lynch, followed him into the Dáil, but not until 1969. His granddaughter, Mary, also served for a number of years on Listowel Urban District Council.

Lynch had an interesting experience on his first day in the Dáil in 1951, when the new government convened. In the mailroom at Leinster House, he was handed a letter addressed to 'Jack Lynch' and opened it. It was a letter from Éamon De Valera inviting him to take up the post of parliamentary secretary (junior minister) to the government. The Listowel man handed it to the other Jack Lynch from Cork. 'This news should please you, Jack,' he said.

McEllistrim, Thomas (Snr) (1894–1973)

Party: Fianna Fáil. Constituency: Kerry/ Kerry North. Years of service: 1923–69

Born at Ahane, Ballymacelligott, in 1894, Thomas McEllistrim's father, also Thomas, had been a member of the local Rural District Council and the Tralee Board of Guardians. Thomas worked on the family farm. He was one of the first members of the Irish Volunteers following their foundation in 1913 and, during Easter 1916, helped Captain Robert Monteith – who had landed at Banna Strand on Good Friday as part of a failed attempt to import arms for a rebellion – to evade capture by police.

McEllistrim was arrested and served time in a number of prisons in Britain. During the War of Independence, he was a leading figure in the IRA in Kerry, featuring in numerous engagements with British forces, such as the Headford Junction Ambush of 1921.

Opposed to the Anglo-Irish Treaty, he was elected to the Dáil for Kerry in 1923 and was a founder member of Fianna Fáil three years later. He was amongst those who proposed Jack

Lynch for the leadership of the party when Seán Lemass stood down in 1966. McEllistrim remained a TD until 1969 without ever losing an election, making him the longest-serving TD for Kerry North. He was succeeded in the Dáil by his son, Thomas (1969–87 and 1989–92), and his grandson, Thomas (2002–11). His granddaughter, Anne, was also a member of Kerry County Council from 2004 to 2014. They are the only family in Irish politics to send three generations of the same name to Leinster House. McEllistrim died in December 1973 and Fianna Fáil established a memorial fund for student scholarships in his name.

McEllistrim, Thomas (Jnr) (1926–2000)

Party: Fianna Fáil. Constituency: Kerry North.
Years of service: 1969–87, 1989–92

Thomas McEllistrim (Junior) was born on the family farm at Ahane, Ballymacelligott, in 1926, three years after his father, Thomas, had been elected a TD for Kerry. When Thomas Snr stood down from the Dáil in 1969, Thomas Jnr succeeded him. He had been elected to Kerry County Council in 1967 (and was chairman in 1991–2). McEllistrim was a strong supporter of Charles Haughey and he was one of the so-called Fianna Fáil 'Gang of Five', a group of party backbenchers who pressurised Jack Lynch into standing down as party leader in 1979. He also publicly questioned why British aircraft were allowed to fly over Irish airspace as the Troubles in Northern Ireland continued, telling his parliamentary party that his father, who had 'started guerrilla warfare in Ireland after 1916', would 'turn in his grave' if he knew that British military aircraft were crossing the border.[6]

On Haughey's election as Taoiseach, McEllistrim became Minister of State at the Department of Finance and was briefly the junior minister in Fisheries and Forestry during the short-lived Fianna Fáil government of 1982. His announcement of many projects for his native Kerry North resulted in him being dubbed 'Mac Millions' by one local newspaper.[7] At the 1987 general election, McEllistrim lost his seat to Fine Gael's Jimmy Deenihan, losing out to Labour leader Dick Spring on the final count by a margin of just four votes.

After two years in the Seanad, he returned to the Dáil before being defeated again at the 1992 general election. Ten years later, his son, Thomas, was elected to represent Kerry North. His daughter, Anne, was a county councillor. McEllistrim died in February 2000.

McEllistrim, Thomas (III) (1968–)

Party: Fianna Fáil. Constituency: Kerry North.
Years of service: 2002–11

The fourth generation of his family in local politics, Thomas McEllistrim's grandfather was first elected to the Dáil in 1923 and his father was elected in 1969. Thomas McEllistrim, a teacher, was born in 1968 and was immersed in politics from a young age. Thomas' father lost his Dáil seat in 1992 and Thomas contested his first general election in 1997, but Fianna Fáil won just one seat, through Denis Foley on that occasion. McEllistrim increased his vote significantly in 2002, taking the first seat in Kerry North. In the newly created constituency of Kerry North–Limerick West in 2011, however, McEllistrim lost out to Labour's Arthur Spring.

McEllistrim's sister, Anne, had been elected to Kerry County Council in 2004 following the abolition of the dual mandate. She retained her seat in the Tralee Electoral Area in 2009. At the 2014 local elections, she transferred to the Killarney Electoral Area, but failed to win a seat. Thomas McEllistrim regained his former council seat in Tralee and was mayor of the town in 2015–16. He failed to win the Fianna Fáil nomination at their conventions in 2016 and 2018. His first cousin, Eugene L. O'Flaherty, was a member of the Massachusetts House of Representatives for seventeen years.

Moloney, Daniel (1909–1963)

Party: Fianna Fáil. Constituency: Kerry North. Years of service: 1957–61

Born in Carrigcannon, Lyreacrompane, in 1909, Daniel (Danny Jim) Moloney was an insurance agent and a motor trader who bought a garage in 1946 in Listowel, where he lived thereafter. He was involved in the establishment of the Kerry Motorists' Association, which lobbied for improvements to the county's roads. A member of Listowel UDC – of which he was chairman for one year – and Kerry County Council from 1955, his first Dáil contest came at a by-election on 29 February 1956 following the death of the Clann na Poblachta TD, Johnny Connor. Moloney was the only candidate at the poll other than Connor's daughter, Kathleen, who won. He stood as one of the two Fianna Fáil candidates (with Tom McEllistrim) at the 1957 general election and topped the poll in the then four-seat constituency.

Moloney was defeated at the 1961 election, however, when the number of seats in Kerry North dropped from four to three. He was subsequently elected to the Seanad on the Cultural and Educational Panel. In June 1963, on the first day of President John F. Kennedy's visit to Ireland, Moloney took ill and died suddenly. His place in the Seanad was taken by John Costelloe from Ballyduff. Moloney's daughter Kay Caball was a member of Tralee UDC for many years and his grandson, Jimmy Moloney, was a member of Listowel Town Council and was elected to Kerry County Council for the Listowel Electoral Area in 2014.

Moynihan, Michael (1917–2001)

Party: Labour. Constituency: Kerry South.
Years of service: 1981–7, 1989–92

Michael Moynihan from Headford, near Killarney, was born in 1917. A psychiatric nurse at St Finan's Hospital in Killarney and a trade union official, he became the first ever Labour TD elected in Kerry South. He was a prominent labour activist, serving on the national executive of the Irish Transport and General Workers' Union from 1950 to 1973. Despite contesting six general elections between 1954 and 1977 – and the 1966 by-election – Moynihan was not elected until 1981, when he topped the poll with 8,221 votes to take a seat in the three-member constituency. He displaced the Fianna Fáil deputy, Timothy 'Chub' O'Connor, in the process. Moynihan had been a senator between 1973 and 1977.

Moynihan was appointed Minister of State at the Department of Trade, Commerce and Tourism in December 1982 and resigned, along with other Labour ministers, from government on 20 January 1987, precipitating a general election. He lost his Dáil seat to Fianna Fáil's John O'Donoghue at that election, but regained the seat in 1989 at the age of seventy-four. He retired at the 1992 general election when he was replaced in the Dáil by his daughter, Breeda Moynihan-Cronin. He was a member of Kerry County Council (1974–82) and Killarney UDC from 1955 to 1995; he was chairperson of the urban council on three occasions. Charges in the 1980s relating to his alleged involvement in supplying forged P60 forms to constituents to secure headage grants were dismissed in court. He died in June 2001.

Moynihan-Cronin, Breeda (1953–)

Party: Labour. Constituency: Kerry South.
Years of service: 1992–2007

Born in Ballydowney, Killarney, in 1953, Breeda Moynihan-Cronin is the only woman ever to have represented Kerry South in the Dáil as a Labour deputy. A former bank official, she was first elected in 1992, succeeding her father, Michael Moynihan, who retired from the Dáil at the November general election that year. Moynihan-Cronin had taken a seat on Kerry County Council in 1991 in the Killarney Electoral Area, but her selection as a candidate on that occasion prompted the departure from Labour of a sitting councillor, Michael Gleeson, who failed to win the nomination. Gleeson and a number of other party members left Labour to form a new organisation, the South Kerry Independent Alliance.

Moynihan-Cronin retained her seat at the 1997 and 2002 general elections and was party spokesperson on tourism and disability issues, as well as being chairperson of Labour's national executive. At the 2007 election, she lost out to Fine Gael's Tom Sheahan. She had signalled prior to the election that she was retiring, but later decided to contest the election. She was co-opted to Kerry County Council in 2011 to replace Marie Moloney in the Killarney Electoral Area following her election to the Seanad. She, in turn, stood down from the council and retired from public life in February 2013 and was replaced on the county council by Killarney town councillor Seán Counihan.

O'Connor, Kathleen (Fitzgerald) (1934–2017)

Party: Clann na Poblachta. Constituency: Kerry North. Years of service: 1956–7

Kathleen O'Connor (later Fitzgerald) became the youngest TD in the Dáil in 1956 when, at the age of twenty-one, she succeeded her late father Johnny Connor at the first and only by-election ever held in Kerry North. Born in 1934 at Farmer's Bridge, near Tralee, she studied at Coláiste Íde in Dingle and Carysfort College in Dublin before qualifying as a teacher. She became a teacher at Meen national school in Knocknagoshel. Her father, Johnny Connor, was elected a Clann na Poblachta TD for Kerry North in 1954 and Kathleen occasionally assisted with his constituency work in Leinster House and at home. In December 1955, Johnny Connor was killed in a road accident between Castleisland and Abbeyfeale. Kathleen was asked to stand at the by-election by the leader of Clann na Poblachta, Seán MacBride. Her candidacy was actively supported by Clann na Poblachta's coalition partners in the early 1950s, Fine Gael, Labour and Clann na Talmhan, each of which decided not to field a candidate.

O'Connor's only opponent at the by-election was Fianna Fáil's Dan Moloney from Listowel. Despite being too young to have been included on the electoral register, O'Connor was elected on 29 February 1956. Apart from being the youngest TD in the Fifteenth Dáil, Kathleen O'Connor was one of just seven female deputies at the time – one of whom was Honor Mary Crowley of Kerry South – and was one of only three Clann na Poblachta TDs. She decided not to contest the 1957 general election and Clann na Poblachta did not field a candidate. She left politics and returned to teaching. She died, aged eighty-three, in December 2017.

O'Connor, Timothy (1906–1986)

Party: Fianna Fáil. Constituency: Kerry South. Years of service: 1961–81

Timothy 'Chub' O'Connor from Killorglin was a Fianna Fáil TD for Kerry South for twenty years between the 1961 and 1981 general elections. Born in 1906 in London, where his family lived at the time, he moved to Meanus, Killorglin, as a child. Both his parents died when he was young and his only brother died of TB in 1911. He played rugby and football

and trained greyhounds, securing national success with several dogs, including 'Spanish Battleship', which won three Irish derbys. O'Connor served with the No. 2 Brigade of the IRA during War of Independence. He founded T. O'Connor & Sons builders' providers in Killorglin and worked as a general merchant and contractor. During the Second World War, he secured contracts for the supply of turf from Kerry bogs to the government for use in the major cities.

A member of Kerry County Council for the Killorglin Electoral Area from 1948, O'Connor served as its chairman in 1974–5. He was first elected to the Dáil in 1961 alongside party colleague, Honor Mary Crowley. He continued to hold his seat at all subsequent elections until he lost his seat in 1981 to Labour's Michael Moynihan. He was also a member of the Council of Europe; the French newspaper *France Soir* referred to him as the 'suave, soft spoken Irishman who can explode into fanatical fury when the national aspirations of his country are at stake'.[8] At the age of seventy-two, O'Connor was a candidate at the European elections in 1979, but he failed to win a seat. He died in 1986. His son, Teddy O'Connor, served one term on Kerry County Council and his granddaughter, Susan, married Fianna Fáil councillor Michael O'Shea from Milltown.

O'Donoghue, Donal (1894–1971)

***Party: Fianna Fáil. Constituency: Kerry South.
Years of service: 1944–8***

Donal J. O'Donoghue (Domhnall Ó Donnchú) was a national school teacher who was first elected to the Dáil at a by-election in Kerry South in 1944. Born at Rusheenbeg, Glenflesk, in 1894, he was commandant of the 2nd Battalion of the 1st Brigade of the IRA during the War of Independence and also served with the Kerry No. 2 Brigade. He taught for many years in Cork before becoming principal of Barraduff national school in 1933, a post he held until his retirement. He played football in both Cork and Kerry and won three Sigerson Cup medals with UCC, as well as a Munster senior medal with Cork in 1928.

In November 1944, O'Donoghue was the Fianna Fáil candidate at a by-election in Kerry South, which followed the appointment of the long-serving Fine Gael TD and former minister, Fionán Lynch, as a Circuit Court judge. O'Donoghue polled almost half of all votes cast, defeating Eoin O'Connell of Fine Gael and Edmund Horan of Clann na Talmhan. His election in 1944 meant that for four years, up until the 1948 general election, Fianna Fáil held all three seats in Kerry South. In 1948, O'Donoghue lost his seat and he retired from politics. He later lived at Wilton Road, Cork city, where he died in July 1971.

O'Donoghue, John (1956–)

Party: Fianna Fáil. Constituency: Kerry South.
Years of service: 1987–2011

Born in 1956, John O'Donoghue came from a Cahersiveen family steeped in Fianna Fáil politics. His father, Daniel, and mother, Mary, were members of Kerry County Council. John O'Donoghue, a solicitor, contested the general election in 1981 and both polls in 1982, increasing his vote on each occasion. He succeeded his mother on Kerry County Council in 1985 and was chairman in 1990-1. He won a Dáil seat at the 1987 general election, helping Fianna Fáil to regain two seats in Kerry South, the other being held by John O'Leary from Killarney. In 1991, O'Donoghue was made a junior minister at the Department of Finance by Taoiseach Charles Haughey but lost that ministry when Albert Reynolds became Taoiseach in 1992. Between 1994 and 1997, he was party spokesperson on justice. He published a large amount of legislation and became known for his policy proposal of 'zero tolerance' of crime. O'Donoghue was appointed Minister for Justice, Equality and Law Reform when Fianna Fáil came to power in 1997. His one-time colleague, Jackie Healy-Rae, won a seat at that year's general election after failing to win the nomination to become O'Donoghue's running mate.

As justice minister, O'Donoghue was a prolific legislator and worked closely with Bertie Ahern on the negotiations on the Good Friday Agreement in 1998. He moved to the Department of Arts, Sport and Tourism following the 2002 general election, a position he retained until 2007. Following the establishment of the Fianna Fáil/Progressive Democrat/Green government in 2007, he was appointed Ceann Comhairle. During the summer of 2009, media reports about his expenses as Minister for Arts, Sport and Tourism led to demands for his resignation from the position. Despite claiming that he had done nothing wrong, O'Donoghue was forced to resign on 13 October 2009, becoming the first ever Ceann Comhairle to be forced to leave office. O'Donoghue returned to the Fianna Fáil backbenches and lost his Dáil seat at the 2011 general election. His former running mate, Tom Fleming, who stood as an Independent, secured a seat in Kerry South at that election. Following his retirement from politics, he qualified as a barrister in July 2014. O'Donoghue's wife,

Kate Ann, is the daughter of the late Labour TD for Cork South West, Michael Pat Murphy, a deputy from 1951 to 1981. His brother, Paul was also a member and former chairman of Kerry County Council.

O'Donoghue, Thomas (1889–1963)

Party: Sinn Féin/Republican. Constituency:
Kerry–Limerick West. Years of service: 1921–7

Thomas O'Donoghue (Tomás Ó Donnchú) came from Reenard, near Cahersiveen, where he was born in 1889.

He went to London to work as a civil servant in the post office. There he joined Conradh na Gaeilge, the IRB and the Irish Volunteers. He returned to Ireland before the Easter Rising in 1916 and fought at the GPO during Easter Week alongside his brother, Patrick.[9] Following his arrest, O'Donoghue was interned in Wandsworth, Wakefield and Frongoch. He was released from custody in July 1916. On refusing to enlist in the British army, he was sentenced to fifty days' hard labour and was transferred to the Tower of London on 1 January 1917. Sentenced to a further period in prison, he was moved to Pentonville Prison and released in March 1917.

O'Donoghue was active in Kerry during the War of Independence. He was elected to the Second Dáil in 1921 for the Kerry–Limerick West constituency, at which time he resided at Church Street, Listowel. He took the anti-Treaty side in the Civil War, unlike his brother, Patrick, and was imprisoned in 1923 in Newbridge, County Kildare, going on hunger strike for forty-three days before being released. He was re-elected as a TD for Kerry–Limerick West in 1922 and for Kerry in 1923. O'Donoghue retired at the general election of June 1927. He taught Irish in Kerry and Limerick in the years that followed. He lived in Limerick and later in Dublin, where he died in 1963.

O'Leary, John (1933–2015)

Party: Fianna Fáil. Constituency: Kerry South. Years of service: 1966–97

A former senior Kerry County Council official, John O'Leary from Killarney was first elected to the Dáil at a by-election in Kerry South in 1966, which was caused by the death of the incumbent Fianna Fáil TD, Honor Mary Crowley. He was born at Dunrine, Kilcummin, in 1933 and attended St Brendan's College. A competent footballer and athlete, O'Leary joined the health department of Kerry County Council in 1952, becoming a staff officer and later worked in the planning department. He was director of elections for Fianna Fáil in Kerry South for the presidential election campaigns of 1959 and 1966. He was chosen as the party's candidate for the 4 December 1966 by-election in Kerry South, in which he defeated Fine Gael's Michael Begley and Labour's Michael Moynihan. He was re-elected at the 1969 general election and went on to hold his seat continuously until his retirement in 1997. In 1977, Taoiseach Jack Lynch appointed him Minister of State at the Department of the Environment, a post he held until 1979, when Charles Haughey became party leader.

O'Leary stood down from Kerry County Council in 1996 and his son, Brian, a Killarney auctioneer, was co-opted in his place. Brian O'Leary was selected by Fianna Fáil as a candidate for the 1997 general election, but he failed to retain his father's Dáil seat. Instead, Fianna Fáil ceded a seat to the Independent candidate, Jackie Healy-Rae. John O'Leary polled the highest ever percentage of first-preference votes at any general election in Kerry South, winning 30.6 per cent of votes cast in 1969. He published his memoirs, *On the Doorsteps: Memoirs of a Long-Serving TD*, in April 2015 and he died in October 2015.

O'Leary, William (1894–1955)

Party: Fianna Fáil. Constituency: Kerry. Years of service: 1927–32

A native of Ardfert, William O'Leary was born in 1894. A farmer and publican who later lived at Irrebeg, Lixnaw, he was a member of the IRA during the War of Independence with the Kerry No. 1 Brigade. He took the anti-Treaty side in the Civil War and was jailed in Limerick Prison for a period. A founder member of Fianna Fáil in 1926, he was elected a councillor for the Listowel Electoral Area in 1926. O'Leary was elected to the Dáil, representing Kerry, at the June 1927 general election and held the seat at the September election of that year. He stood down at the 1932 election and moved to Dublin, where he later became the founding chairman of the Agricultural Wages Board in 1937. He lived on Haddon Road, Clontarf, and died in November 1955. O'Leary's brother, Florence, was chairman of the Irish Pigs and Bacon Commission.

O'Reilly, Thomas (1876–1944)

Party: Fianna Fáil. Constituency: Kerry South. Years of service: 1927–33

A native of Scarriff in Waterville and later residing at Mastergeeha, Thomas J. O'Reilly was a farmer and school teacher and immediately prior to his election to the Dáil at the June 1927 general election was principal of Emlagh national school in Ballinskelligs. O'Reilly built and owned his own creamery at Scarriff, one of the first in the county, which became operational in 1905. It sold butter from local farmers to the Cork butter markets via the train service from Cahersiveen. O'Reilly, who frequently contributed to Dáil debates on rural matters, remained a Fianna Fáil TD until the general election of 1933, when he retired from politics. His nephew, Robert O'Reilly, also from Waterville, was elected to Kerry County Council in 1942, serving one term. His sister, Elizabeth (Lizzie), was a founder member of Fianna Fáil. O'Reilly was sub-postmaster in Waterville for many years. He died suddenly on 22 October 1944, having attended Sunday Mass earlier in the day.

O'Sullivan, John Marcus (1881–1948)

Party: Cumann na nGaedheal/Fine Gael. Constituency: Kerry/Kerry North. Years of service: 1923–43

Born in Killarney in 1881, John Marcus O'Sullivan was an academic, historian, writer and scholar. He studied at UCD from 1898 and, along with his professor, William Magennis,

founded the Academy of St Thomas Aquinas. In 1904, O'Sullivan won a scholarship to study in Germany and was awarded a doctorate in philosophy at Heidelberg University in 1906. On his return to Dublin, he was appointed Professor of History at UCD, a position he held until his death. He became a prolific writer and published a number of works on history and philosophy.

O'Sullivan won a seat in Kerry for Cumann na nGaedheal at the 1923 general election. A year later, he became parliamentary secretary to the Minister for Finance with responsibility for the Office of Public Works. W.T. Cosgrave appointed him Eoin MacNeill's successor as Minister for Education in 1926. He set up the Commission on Technical Education and its recommendations led to what is regarded as O'Sullivan's most significant ministerial contribution: the passage of the Vocational Education Act in 1930, which introduced a vocational educational infrastructure in Ireland for the first time. Cosgrave appointed him as a delegate to the League of Nations in 1924 and in 1928–30. In debates in the Dáil, he made lengthy and articulate speeches, regularly clashing with Fianna Fáil on the differences between the two Civil War parties. O'Sullivan lost his seat at the 1943 general election and died in 1948 at his home in Rathgar, Dublin. His uncle, Charlie O'Sullivan, was Bishop of Kerry from 1917 to 1927. His brother, Timothy, was MP for East Kerry from 1910 to 1918. A summer school in his name is hosted annually by the Irish Vocational Education Association.

Palmer, Patrick W. (1899–1971)

Party: Fine Gael. Constituency: Kerry South. Years of service: 1948–61

Patrick W. Palmer was born in Templenoe in 1899 and was a national school teacher. He was active in the Irish Volunteers and became chairman of Sinn Féin in the Kenmare area. He supported the Anglo-Irish Treaty of 1921 and was a close acquaintance of the O'Connor-Scarteen brothers from Kenmare, who were killed during the Civil War. Palmer settled in Kilgarvan and later Glenlough and took up a teaching post in Direendaragh national school. Active in Cumann na nGaedheal and later Fine Gael, he was initially nominated to contest the Kerry South by-election of 1945, but was withdrawn when the party opted not to take part. At the 1948 general election, he took the third seat with 19 per cent of the vote and retained his seat at the 1951, 1954 and 1957 elections. He became chairman of Kerry County Council on his election to the local authority in 1955. He was chairman of the Irish National Teachers' Organisation in Kerry. Palmer retired to Dublin, where he died in 1971.

Rice, John Joe (1893–1970)

Party: Sinn Féin. Constituency Kerry South.
Years of service: 1957–61

John Joe Rice was the first and only Sinn Féin TD ever elected for the constituency of Kerry South. A native of Kilmurry, Kenmare, where he was born in 1893, he worked as a clerk with the Great Southern and Western Railways in Killarney, Killorglin and Kenmare. Rice joined the Irish Volunteers in 1913; his sister Rosalie Rice was instrumental in the sending of a message to the Clan na Gael leader in the United States, John Devoy, during Easter 1916 to inform him that a rebellion had begun in Dublin. Rice became Officer Commanding of the 5th Battalion of the Kerry No. 2 Brigade and commanded the same brigade during the Civil War. He opposed the Anglo-Irish Treaty and led a group which tried to prevent Michael Collins speaking in its favour in Killarney in April 1922. He continued to be a member of the IRA and Sinn Féin after the Civil War. In the 1930s, he worked for Nash's mineral water company in Tralee and became a key figure in the GAA in Kerry.

Rice was elected to the Dáil in 1957, but did not take his seat, in compliance with Sinn Féin's policy of abstentionism from Dáil Éireann. He campaigned against the Special Powers Act, which provided for the internment of IRA suspects. He was expelled from Sinn Féin in 1966, along with, among others, veteran Kerry republican and former footballer, John Joe Sheehy. He supported Provisional Sinn Féin on its establishment in 1970. He died in July 1970.

Roche, Edmond (–1952)

Party: Sinn Féin. Constituency: Kerry–West
Limerick. Years of service: 1921–3

Edmond (also Edmund and Eamonn) Roche was a native of Bansha, County Tipperary, and later lived at Knockfenora, Bruree, County Limerick, and Mitchelstown, County Cork. He was active in the Irish Volunteers, becoming head of the Bruree Company in 1917, and later joined the IRA. Following an ambush near Bruree in July 1920, he was jailed for two years. Roche was nominated to contest the 1921 general election on behalf of Sinn Féin in the Kerry–Limerick West constituency, though he was in prison at the time. Among his nominators for the election was Albinia Brodrick, a prominent republican and the first female county councillor in Kerry.

The seven Sinn Féin candidates for the constituency were elected unopposed. The *Kerry People* newspaper recorded at the time that it was 'well known the new members in this and other Southern constituencies will not sit, so that the proposed "Parliament" will be strangled at birth'.[10] Roche took the anti-Treaty side in the Civil War and retained his seat in 1922. He did not contest the 1923 election, when Kerry reverted to a single seven-seat constituency. Towards the end of the Civil War, he was jailed in Gormanstown. He was released in November 1923. Renowned for his knowledge of cheese-making, he was the first manager of Bruree Co-Operative Creamery and he became manager of Mitchelstown Creamery in County Cork in 1925, overseeing its expansion and becoming a champion for the rights of workers in the sector.[11] He died suddenly in Dublin in 1952.

Sheahan, Tom (1968–)

Party: Fine Gael. Constituency: Kerry South. Years of service: 2007–11

Born in 1968, Thomas (Tom) Sheahan from Rathmore won a Dáil seat for Fine Gael in Kerry South at the 2007 general election. Kerry South hadn't had a Fine Gael representative in the Dáil since Michael Begley, who was a Kerry South TD until 1989. Sheahan had been elected to Kerry County Council in the Killarney Electoral Area in 2004. He displaced Labour's Breeda Moynihan-Cronin at the Dáil election three years later and served as Fine Gael's junior agriculture spokesperson in opposition. Sheahan lost his seat at the 2011 general election to his running mate, Brendan Griffin, who topped the poll in Kerry South. He was subsequently elected to the Seanad on the Administrative Panel, but lost the seat at the 2016 Seanad election. Tom Sheahan's brother, John Sheahan, became a member of Kerry County Council in 2007 and his brother, Denis, was a candidate for Fine Gael at the 1987 general election in Kerry South.

Spring, Arthur John (1976–)

Party: Labour. Constituency: Kerry North-West Limerick. Years of service: 2011–16

Arthur John Spring, who was born in 1976, worked in banking and ran his own juice drinks business before entering politics. He was first elected to the Dáil in 2011, having won a seat on Kerry County Council and Tralee Town Council two years previously. A former mayor of Tralee, Spring is a nephew of the former Tánaiste, Dick Spring, and a grandson of the former TD for Kerry North, Dan Spring. His election in 2011 regained a seat for Labour, which had last been represented by Dick Spring in 2002. His aunt, Maeve, and brother, Graham, have also been county councillors. Spring lost his seat in 2016 in the newly revised Kerry constituency.

Spring, Dan (1910–1988)

Party: Labour. Constituency: Kerry North.
Years of service: 1943–81

Dan (Daniel) Spring was the first ever Labour TD elected in Kerry, winning a seat in Kerry North at the general election of 1943. Born at Spa Road, Tralee, in 1910 to a family of fourteen, Spring came to prominence as a footballer and won two All-Ireland medals with his native county, captaining Kerry to victory in 1940. He was elected for Labour to Kerry County Council – of which he was chairman in 1968–9 – and Tralee Urban District Council in 1942. He worked as a mill worker with Latchford's and Kelliher's in Tralee. He became an organiser for the Irish Transport and General Workers'

Union across Munster. First elected to the Dáil in 1943 – a position he retained until 1981 – Spring was among a group of six Labour deputies who broke away from the party in 1944 to form what was known as National Labour under William O'Brien. The split was caused partly by a dispute within the Irish Transport and General Workers' Union (ITGWU), of which Spring was a member. The breakaway faction rejoined Labour in 1950.

Spring was suspended from the Labour Party for seeking clemency for a neighbour and IRA activist Charlie Kerins, who was executed for murdering a garda sergeant in 1942. In 1946, he raised the situation of IRA leader, Seán McCaughey, who was on hunger strike in prison, demanding that he be released.[12] Spring was appointed parliamentary secretary to the Minister for Local Government in 1956, a position he held until the 1957 general election. He remained a backbencher for the remainder of his career. He served on Kerry County Council until 1979. Following his retirement, he was succeeded by his son, Dick Spring, at the 1981 general election. His grandson, Arthur John Spring, became a TD for

Kerry North in 2011. Another grandson, Graham, was co-opted to his brother's seat on Kerry County Council in 2011. Dan Spring's daughter, Maeve, was also a member of Kerry County Council and Tralee UDC. He died in September 1988.

Spring, Dick (1950–)

Party: Labour. Constituency: Kerry North.
Years of service: 1981–2002

Richard (Dick) Spring from Tralee succeeded his father, Dan Spring, in the Dáil in 1981, when he won a seat at his first general election. He had been elected to

Kerry County Council in 1979. A former footballer and hurler with Kerry, Spring won three international rugby caps with Ireland in 1979. A barrister by profession, Spring became a Minister of State for Law Reform on his first day in the Dáil. Following the resignation of Michael O'Leary as Labour leader in 1982, Spring was elected to the position, despite his youth and despite his having spent just one year in the Dáil. He became Tánaiste in 1982, when Labour formed a coalition government with Fine Gael. During that administration, he served also as Minister for the Environment between 1982 and 1983 and Minister for Energy from 1983 to 1987. Much of Spring's early time as party leader was taken up with internal disputes in the party, particularly attempts to rid the organisation of the so-called Militant Tendency and senior figures like Michael D. Higgins and Joe Higgins, who were opposed to Labour's participation in coalition government. In 1985, Spring was closely involved with Taoiseach Garret FitzGerald in the negotiations which led to the Anglo-Irish Agreement. Two years later, he narrowly held his Dáil seat when he defeated Fianna Fáil's Thomas McEllistrim by just four votes for the final seat in Kerry North.

In 1990, Spring was instrumental in securing the candidacy of Mary Robinson for the presidential election and two years later led the party to its second best ever electoral success, when Labour won thirty-three Dáil seats in the so-called 'Spring Tide' at the November 1992 general election. The party entered coalition with Fianna Fáil under Albert Reynolds as Taoiseach, but the government collapsed in 1994, following a controversy involving the appointment of the President of the High Court and the extradition of two priests wanted in relation to sexual abuse offences. Spring led Labour into a new government with Fine Gael and Democrat Left under John Bruton, a coalition which was formed without a general election. He continued to serve as Minister for Foreign Affairs, as he had since 1992. Labour suffered heavy losses at the 1997 general election and Spring stood down as party leader soon after. He was succeeded by Ruairi Quinn. Spring remained a backbench TD, but lost his seat at the 2002 general election to Sinn Féin's Martin Ferris. His nephew, Arthur John Spring, regained the Labour seat in the constituency in 2011. Dick Spring's sister, Maeve, who died in 2010, was an urban and county councillor for many years and also served as his constituency secretary. In later years, Spring held a number of corporate directorates and was a public interest director of Allied Irish Bank for six years.

Stack, Austin (1879–1929)

Party: Sinn Féin. Constituency: Kerry/Kerry–Limerick West. Years of service: 1919–27

Born in Ballymullen, Tralee, in 1879, Austin (Augustine Mary Moore) Stack came to prominence on the playing field when he captained Kerry to the All-Ireland senior football title of (this is because the 1904 final wasn't played until 1906!!) 1904. He was a founder, along with Maurice McCarthy, of the John Mitchels GAA Club and was its first captain and committee secretary. He was secretary and chairman of the GAA County Board. Stack was active in the Irish Republican Brotherhood and was head of the Kerry Brigade of the Irish Volunteers, which was involved in plans to land arms in Kerry in 1916. Stack was arrested and sentenced to death. The sentence was later commuted to penal servitude, but he was released from prison in 1917. He spent time on hunger strike with Thomas Ashe, who died on 25 September 1917.

Stack was elected as the MP for Kerry West at the 1918 general election, becoming a member of the First Dáil in January 1919, though he was in prison in Manchester when the Dáil met. He was elected for Sinn Féin for Kerry–Limerick West in 1921 and served as Minister for Home Affairs from 1919 to 1922, making him the first Kerry TD to hold a cabinet post. Returned unopposed to the Third Dáil as an anti-Treaty TD, he sided with Éamon de Valera in opposing the Anglo-Irish Treaty. He fought during the Civil War before being captured by Free State forces in County Tipperary in April 1923. At the 1923 general election, he received 10,333 first-preference votes and remained a deputy until the election of June 1927, losing his seat in September that year, when he was a Sinn Féin candidate – he had chosen not to join Fianna Fáil. Stack had gone on hunger strike after being interned during the Civil War. The toll of a forty-one-day hunger strike before his release in 1924 was considerable and contributed to his premature death in April 1929.

Appendix 2: Kerry Senators since 1922

Note: The Free State Seanad existed from 1922 and 1936 and members were appointed for three-year terms. Following its abolition in 1936, the Seanad was restored in 1938, after the enactment of the Constitution of Ireland, and senators were elected on vocational panels, with some nominated by the Taoiseach of the day. While senators have never represented constituencies like TDs, this list comprises senators from Kerry or who were born in Kerry. Where senators were also TDs, they are listed here, but their biographical notes are found in Appendix 1, 'Kerry TDs since 1919'.

Ahern, Catherine Ita (Kit) (1915–2007)

Party: Fianna Fáil. Panel: Taoiseach's nominee. Years of service: 1964–77.

See list of Kerry TDs.

Blennerhassett, John (1930–2013)

Party: Fine Gael. Panel: Taoiseach's nominee/ Labour. Years of service: 1973–82

John Blennerhassett was a descendant of the Blennerhassett family from Tralee, which sent several generations to parliament in Dublin and London. A native of Ballymacelligott, he was born in 1930. He was elected to Kerry County Council for Fine Gael in 1974, having contested the general elections of 1969 and 1973 in Kerry North. In both contests, he was the running mate for Deputy Gerard Lynch from Listowel. Blennerhassett was nominated by Liam Cosgrave to the Seanad following the 1973 general election. Unsuccessful in the Dáil election four years later, he was elected to the Seanad on the Labour Panel and retained the seat until 1982. He remained on Kerry County Council until 1991 and lost his Tralee Urban District Council seat by just two votes in 1994. He contested the UDC election five years later as an Independent candidate without success. He died in 2013.

Brosnan, Seán (1916–1979)

Party: Fianna Fáil. Panel: Administrative. Years of service: 1973–4

Seán Brosnan was born in Dingle in 1916. He won three All-Ireland medals with Kerry and in 1939 was team captain, but was unable to play in the final due to influenza. He taught in Dublin for several years before becoming a barrister. He moved to Youghal in County Cork and worked on the Cork Circuit. He was elected to the Dáil in 1969 to represent Cork North-East as a Fianna Fáil deputy. Losing his seat at the 1973 general election, he was elected to the Seanad on the Administrative Panel. It was a short-lived period in the Seanad as he regained his Dáil seat at a by-election in November 1974, following the death of Liam Ahern TD. Brosnan retained his seat in 1977 and died in 1979.

Coghlan, Paul (1944–)

Party: Fine Gael. Panel: Industrial & Commercial. Years of service: 1997–

Killarney auctioneer Paul Coghlan was born in 1944. He was a candidate for Fine Gael at the 1992 general election in Kerry South, alongside Michael O'Connor-Scarteen, but neither secured a seat. Coghlan stood as a candidate for the Seanad at the election which followed, contesting the Agricultural Panel, but was unsuccessful. He prevailed in 1997, however, this time winning a seat on the Industrial and Commercial Panel. In 2011, Taoiseach Enda Kenny appointed him Government Chief Whip in the Seanad. He became Leas Cathaoirleach of the Seanad in June 2016. Later a resident of Ballydowney, Coghlan was a founding director of Radio Kerry and is a trustee of Muckross House. He is a former member of Kerry County Council (1991–9) and Killarney Urban District Council (1985–99).

Costelloe, John (1900–1983)

Party: Fianna Fáil. Panel: Industrial & Commercial. Years of service: 1963–5

Born in 1900 and from Knopogue, Ballyduff, John Costelloe was a shopkeeper and farmer who was active during the War of Independence with the Ballyduff Volunteers and fought on the anti-Treaty side during the Civil War. He was jailed and sentenced to death in 1923. He considered himself lucky not to have been selected as one of the prisoners tied to the mine which was detonated by Free State soldiers at Ballyseedy. A close associate of Austin Stack, he later joined Fianna Fáil and was elected to Kerry County Council for the Listowel Electoral Area in 1948. Costelloe was nominated to the Seanad in November 1963 to replace the late Daniel Moloney, the former Fianna Fáil TD for Kerry North and then a senator. He was not re-elected at the 1965 Seanad election. He was a trustee of the Thomas McEllistrim Memorial Fund. He died in 1983.

Counihan, John Joseph (1879–1953)

Party: Independent/Cumann na nGaedheal/ Fine Gael. Panel: Agriculture. Years of service: 1922–36, 1938–51

John Joseph Counihan was born at Madam's Hill in Killarney in 1879. His family later lived in the Town Hall in the town. Counihan, a farmer, was nominated as a member of the first Seanad of 1922 and he remained a member of the House until its dissolution in 1936. He moved to Ballybough in Dublin, where he farmed. He was elected on the Agricultural Panel in 1938, successfully retaining his seat until 1951, when he lost his seat. He was the author and a proponent of the Land Bill of 1946 and was chairman of the National Executive of the Irish Livestock Exporters and Traders' Association. He died in October 1953.

Daly, John (1915–1988)

Party: Fine Gael. Panel: Industrial and Commercial. Years of service: 1975–7, 1982–7

John (Jackie) Daly was born in Castleisland in 1915, a son of Dr William Daly. He established a garage at High Street, Killarney, and in 1970 opened Daly's Autos Ltd on Park Road, later the location of Daly's supermarket and filling station. He was a member of the council of the Society of the Irish Motor Industry. A member of Fine Gael, he was first elected to the Seanad in a by-election on 23 April 1975, which was caused by the death of Senator Denis Farrelly (FG). He lost his seat in 1977, but was re-elected five years later. He was appointed Fine Gael Chief Whip in the Seanad in 1987 and was a member of the Fine Gael national executive. Daly took ill in Leinster House on 5 May 1988 and died, having attended the Seanad earlier in the day. The by-election which followed was won by Tony Bromell of Fianna Fáil.

Daly, Mark (1973–)

Party: Fianna Fáil. Panel: Administrative. Years of service: 2007–

Mark Daly from Kenmare became the youngest member of the twenty-third Seanad in 2007, when he won a seat on the Administrative Panel on his first attempt. Born in 1973, Daly came to national prominence when he appeared on an RTÉ reality show, *Treasure Island*, in 2002. He held many portfolios for Fianna Fáil in the Seanad, including Communications, Energy and Natural Resources. In the past, he worked on election campaigns for Fianna Fáil MEP, Brian Crowley. In 2013, he succeeded in having the House recalled from its summer recess to discuss an EU directive on organ donation. He is a relative of the former general election candidate May Daly and her brother Charlie Daly, from Firies, who were both active in the republican movement. He is deputy leader of the Fianna Fáil group in the Seanad and spokesperson on Foreign Affairs and the Irish Diaspora.

Deenihan, Jimmy (1952–)

Party: Fine Gael. Panel: Taoiseach's nominee. Years of service: 1983–7.

See list of Kerry TDs.

Dorgan, Seán (1968–)

Party: Fianna Fáil. Panel: Taoiseach's nominee. Years of service: 2007

From Coolroe, Castlegregory, Seán Dorgan was educated at Meanscoil an Leith Trúigh in Cloghane, the IT Tralee and the Michael Smurfit Graduate Business School at UCD, where he later lectured. He became general secretary of Fianna Fáil in 2007. The same year, he was nominated as an interim senator by Taoiseach Bertie Ahern to fill one of four vacancies that arose due to the election of four senators to the Dáil in the 2007 election.

Fitzgerald, Tom (1939–2013)

Party: Fianna Fáil. Panel: Agricultural/ Taoiseach's nominee. Years of service: 1981–2, 1987–2002

Born in 1939 in Lispole, Tom Fitzgerald was one of the longest-serving Kerry senators. He first contested a Seanad election in 1977, but it was to be 1981 before he succeeded and was elected to the Agricultural Panel. A fisherman and guesthouse owner in Dingle, Fitzgerald lost his Seanad seat in 1983, but regained it in 1987. He remained on the Agricultural Panel until 1997, when he was appointed to the Seanad as one of Taoiseach Bertie Ahern's nominees. A close ally and associate of the former Taoiseach Charles Haughey, he was an unofficial caretaker of Haughey's Blasket island, Inishvickillane. Fitzgerald remained in the Seanad until 2002, when he resigned due to ill health, shortly before that year's general election. He was a member of Kerry County Council between 1974 and 1985. His son, Breandán, was a candidate at the Kerry County Council elections of 2009 in the Dingle Electoral Area and in 2014 in the South and West Kerry Municipal District.

Foley, Denis (1934–2013)

Party: Fianna Fáil. Panel: Industrial & Commercial. Years of service: 1989–92.

See list of Kerry TDs.

Hartnett, Noel (1909–1960)

Party: Clann na Poblachta/Independent.
Panel: Labour (Independent senator). Years of service: 1951–4

A native of Kenmare, where he was born in 1909, Noel Hartnett was a barrister, writer and broadcaster who was instrumental in the establishment of the political party, Clann na Poblachta. Prior to entering politics, Hartnett worked as a barrister in Dublin, representing, along with Seán MacBride, many republicans who were tried for paramilitary activities in the 1940s. Hartnett was a member of the Fianna Fáil national executive in the early 1940s and was sacked from Raidio Eireann, where he worked as a broadcaster, following pressure from Taoiseach Éamon de Valera, who considered him a risk to RTÉ due to his involvement in defending republicans. A founder member of Clann na Poblachta in 1946, he handled public relations for the party. He was its director of elections in 1948, following which the party helped form the first inter-party coalition under John A. Costello. Hartnett unsuccessfully contested the Dun Laoghaire–Rathdown constituency. He resigned from Clann na Poblachta in February 1951, partly because of the Baltinglass Affair, in which the Minister for Posts and Telegraphs, Jim Everett, appointed a supporter as a postmistress in his Wicklow constituency. He succeeded in winning a seat in the Seanad on the Labour Panel as an Independent in August 1951. He later joined the National Progressive Democrats, which was founded in 1958 by disgruntled Clann na Poblachta members, standing unsuccessfully for the new party in a by-election in Dublin South Central in June 1958. Hartnett died suddenly in October 1960 at his home in Stillorgan, County Dublin.

Healy, Denis (1870–1946)

Party: Fianna Fáil. Panel: Administrative. Years of service: 1934–6, 1938–48

Denis D. Healy (Donnchadha Ó hEaluighthe) was born at Churchground in Kilgarvan in 1870 and worked in his youth as a saddler and harness maker in Macroom, County

Cork, and in his native village with Edward McCarthy of Church Street. He moved to Dublin in 1897 and established his own saddlery at Merchant's Quay. An Irish language and culture enthusiast, Healy joined the GAA, Sinn Féin and the Gaelic League. He was in attendance at the league's inaugural meeting in Dublin in 1898. He was a member of the committee for the first ever Irish Language Feis, held in March 1901. Healy was elected to Dublin Corporation for Sinn Féin in 1908. He later joined Fianna Fáil and was elected to the Seanad in 1934, serving until its abolition in 1936. He was elected to the Administrative Panel in 1938, a seat he retained until his death in November 1946. Healy, who later lived at Usher's Quay in Dublin, also served as president of the Association of Municipal Authorities of Ireland.

Horan, Edmund (1891–1987)

Party: Independent/Clann na Talmhan. Panel: Agricultural. Years of service: 1944–8

Edmund (Ned) Horan was born in Lissivane, Milltown, in 1891, but grew up and lived in Rathmore, Firies. He was educated at Rockwell College. He was active during the War of the Independence and the Civil War, opposing the Anglo-Irish Treaty. A high-profile advocate for the farming community in Kerry, he was a founder member of the Kerry Farmers' Association in 1939 and served as chairman for a period. He stood as an Independent Farmers' candidate in Kerry North at the 1943 general election, but was not elected. Switching to Kerry South for the 1944 general election, he polled in fourth place, just ninety-eight votes shy of Fine Gael's Fionán Lynch, winning 23 per cent of the poll. He was subsequently elected on the Agricultural Panel of the Fifth Seanad. He joined Clann na Talmhan, a party which won several local authority seats in Kerry in the 1940s, and became its first national vice-chairman in 1943. Horan was the only other candidate in the Kerry South by-election of 1945, which followed the death of Fianna Fáil's Fred Crowley and in which his widow, Honor Crowley, was elected. Horan remained in the Seanad until 1948. He was a member of the County Committee of Agriculture for many years and was active in the Irish Creamery Milk Suppliers' Association. He died in 1987. A *Kerryman* tribute read: 'Your were to Kerry, What Davitt was to Sweet Mayo: An inspiration for the future, That Ireland's land might grow.'[1]

Kiely, Daniel (Dan) (1943–)

Party: Fianna Fáil. Panel: Labour. Years of service: 1981–2, 1987–2002

Born in 1943 in Tarbert, Dan Kiely was one of seventeen children. He worked in the US, where he owned a nightclub in New York for several years. On returning to Ireland, he became involved in the dancehall and hotel business in the south-west. Kiely was elected to Kerry County Council in 1979 and the Seanad in 1981. He came close to winning a Dáil seat at the February 1982 general election and also contested the November election that year. Following a failed attempt to win a Dáil seat in Kerry North in 1987, he was re-elected to the Labour Panel in the Seanad, a seat he retained until the Seanad election of 2002, when he lost his seat. Kiely again contested a general election, his fourth, in 2002, running alongside Thomas McEllistrim (III). Following the election of Ned O'Sullivan to the Seanad in 2007, Kiely was co-opted by Fianna Fáil to Kerry County Council as a representative for the Listowel Electoral Area. He lost that seat at the 2009 local elections.

An Independent candidate in the Listowel Electoral Area in 2014, Kiely petitioned the Circuit Court to overturn the result when he lost out on a seat by just two votes on the grounds that some ballots beginning with a preference other than number 1 had been admitted to the count. His case was rejected in the Circuit Court and he appealed to the Supreme Court. The Supreme Court upheld the claim that there was a 'mistake' in the conduct of the local election according to the relevant provision of the Local Elections (Petitions and Disqualifications) Act 1974, which rendered it unlawful. A full recount of all votes cast in the Listowel Electoral Area was ordered and held on 10 February 2016, but the same seven candidates were deemed elected without any material change to the result (see Chapter 10).

Kissane, Eamonn (1899–1979)

Party: Fianna Fáil. Panel: Taoiseach's nominee, Cultural & Educational Panel. Years of service: 1951–65.

See list of Kerry TDs.

Lee, Joe (1942–)

Party: Independent. Panel: National University of Ireland. Years of service: 1993–7

John Joseph (Joe) Lee was born in Tralee in 1942 and grew up in Castlegregory in west Kerry. He graduated from UCD in 1962 and became a historian and accomplished author. In 1973, he published *The Modernisation of Irish Society, 1848–1918*. He become Professor of Modern History at University College Cork in 1974. His seminal *Ireland 1912–1985 – Politics and Society* (1989) remains a landmark history of the period. In 1993, Professor Lee was elected to the Seanad as one of three representatives on the National University of Ireland Panel and he retired from the House in 1997. A member of the Royal Irish Academy, he became Glucksman Chair of Irish Studies at Glucksman Ireland House at New York University in 2002, a post from which he retired in 2017.

Lynch, Gerard (1931–)

Party: Fine Gael. Panel: Agricultural. Years of service: 1977–81.

See list of Kerry TDs.

Lynch, John (1888–1957)

Party: Fine Gael. Panel: Industrial & Commercial. Years of service: 1954–7.

See list of Kerry TDs.

McEllistrim, Thomas (Jnr) (1926–2000)

Party: Fianna Fáil. Panel: Taoiseach's nominee. Years of service: 1987–9.

See list of Kerry TDs.

McGillycuddy, Ross Kinloch (The McGillycuddy of the Reeks) (1882–1950)

Party: Independent. Panel: Agricultural. Years of service: 1928–36, 1938–43

Born in 1882, Ross Kinloch McGillycuddy, better known by the hereditary title the McGillycuddy of the Reeks, inherited the ancient Irish chieftain's title from his father, Denis Charles. He was educated in Edinburgh and Woolwich and served with the British army in India. He had an illustrious career in the First World War, winning the Distinguished Service Order (DSO) and the Légion d'honneur. The McGillycuddy inherited The Reeks home and estate at Churchtown, Beaufort, from his father in 1921. Much of the 15,000-acre estate was transferred to tenants under the 1923 Land Act. He was first appointed to the Free State Senate in 1928 for a three-year term, having been proposed by the Marquess of Lansdowne, another Kerry senator. Following the abolition of the Seanad in 1936 and its re-instatement in 1938, he succeeded in winning a seat on the newly formed Agricultural Panel in both the second and third Seanads, serving up until 1943. He was a regular contributor to debates. Elected to Kerry County Council in 1926, he was chairman of its agricultural committee and was president of the Kerry Cattle Society. During the Second World War, he assisted the war effort at an army training depot in County Down. His son Patrick died of wounds sustained while fighting in the Second World War. The McGillycuddy died in 1950.

Moloney, Daniel (1909–1963)

Party: Fianna Fáil. Panel: Industrial & Commercial. Years of service: 1961–3.

See list of Kerry TDs.

Moloney, Marie (1958–)

Party: Labour. Panel: Labour. Years of service: 2011–16

Marie Moloney from Kilcummin, who was born in 1958, contested her first Seanad election in 2011 and won a seat on the Labour Panel. She had stood at the general election in Kerry in February of that year along with party colleague Arthur Spring. It was her first general election and she received 4,926 first-preference votes. She had previously been an employee of the Services Industrial Professional and Technical Union and a constituency secretary to Breeda Moynihan-Cronin TD from 1992 to 2007. Moloney was a member of Kerry County Council between 2009 and 2011, representing the Killarney Electoral Area. She was replaced on the county council by the co-option of Moynihan-Cronin in 2011.

Moynihan, Michael (1917–2001)

Party: Labour. Panel: Industrial & Commercial. Years of service: 1973–81.

See list of Kerry TDs.

O'Connor, Aidan (1972–)

Party: Fine Gael. Panel: Taoiseach's nominee. Years of service: 1997

From Rathmore, Aidan O'Connor contested the 1997 general election in Kerry South as one of two Fine Gael candidates, along with Jim Kelly. In that election, he polled 3,041 first-preference votes, but did not win a seat. Following the general election, he was appointed to the outgoing Seanad in July 1997 by the then Taoiseach John Bruton for the brief period before the new House met – there were a number of vacancies created by senators elected to the Dáil. He was a candidate in the subsequent Seanad election on the Administrative Panel, but was not elected. O'Connor had worked as an adviser to the former Minister of State and Cork TD, Hugh Coveney. He later worked as a journalist with Radio Kerry, the *Irish Independent, The Kerryman* and *Kerry's Eye*. He has published a biography of Fr Neil

Horan and wrote a play focusing on the life of Patrick O'Connor from Rathmore, who died during the 1916 Rising.

Ó Siochfhradha, Pádraig (1883–1964)

Party: Independent. Panel: Taoiseach's nominee. Years of service: 1946–8, 1951–4, 1957–64

Pádraig Ó Siochfhradha ('An Seabhac') was born in Burnham, Dingle, in 1883 and was best known as an Irish-language writer, folklorist and teacher. He worked as a *timire*, or travelling Irish teacher, in counties including Kerry, Cork and Waterford. Active in Conradh na Gaeilge, he published numerous Irish-language texts, school textbooks and dictionaries and contributed to journals and other publications under the pen name 'An Seabhac' (The Hawk). In 1913, Ó Siochfhradha joined the Irish Volunteers and was a member of the Dingle Battalion. He was instrumental in the foundation of the Volunteers in Killarney, convening their first meeting. A confidant of Austin Stack, he was sent to Dublin on Good Friday 1916 to find out the final arrangements for the Easter Rising. On his arrest after the Rising, he was interned in Durham Jail in England. Ó Siochfhradha served several jail terms between 1916 and 1922, but he played no role in the Civil War.

A member of Kerry County Council representing the Tralee Electoral Division, he was council chairman from 1920 to 1923. For the remainder of the 1920s, he worked for the Health Board in the midlands and then moved to the Department of Education in Dublin. He left the civil service in 1936 to work full-time as a writer and publisher. Éamon de Valera appointed Ó Siochfhradha to the Seanad in February 1946, but he did not contest the 1948 Seanad election. He was re-appointed in 1951, 1957 and 1961. Ó Siochfhradha lived for most of his life in Donnybrook in Dublin and was involved in cultural organisations such as the Oireachtas and Foras Muirí na hÉireann. He worked with the Irish Manuscripts Commission for four years. He died in 1964 and was replaced in the Seanad by Kit Ahern from Ballybunion.

O'Sullivan, Ned (1950–)

Party: Fianna Fáil. Panel: Labour. Years of service: 2007–

A draper and teacher by profession, Ned O'Sullivan from Listowel contested two general elections for Fianna Fáil in Kerry North, without success, before his election to Seanad Éireann in 2007. He stood at the Dáil elections of 1989 and 1992 alongside Thomas McEllistrim and Denis Foley. O'Sullivan was elected on the Labour Panel in 2007, a seat he retained at the 2011 and 2016 Seanad elections. A former Mayor of

Kerry (2004–5) and member of Kerry County Council, he was replaced on Listowel Town Council by his wife, Madeleine, on his election to the Seanad. He chaired the urban council on three occasions in the 1990s. His Kerry County Council seat was taken up by Dan Kiely from Tarbert. In 2012, O'Sullivan closed his drapery business on William Street, Listowel. He was a member of the Oireachtas committee which considered the Eighth Amendment to the Constitution in 2017.

O'Sullivan, Dr William (1873–1953)

Party: Independent. Panel: Taoiseach's nominee. Years of service: 1922–36

Born in Batterfield, Firies, in 1873, William O'Sullivan attended St Brendan's College and Queen's College in Cork and qualified as a doctor. He won an Irish rugby cap against Scotland in 1895 and was captain of the Queen's College team which won the Munster Senior Rugby Cup in 1895. Also a footballer, he played for Dr Croke's in the Kerry County Senior Football Final of 1900. He was the doctor for the Dr Croke's team that won the Kerry county senior title in 1903. He left Ireland during the War of Independence and worked for periods as a doctor in Newcastle and Edinburgh. O'Sullivan was medical officer for the Killarney No. 2 District for sixty years and was also the coroner for East Kerry. He was a strong proponent of the Anglo-Irish Treaty and in 1922, he was appointed to the Free State Senate by W.T. Cosgrave. A home he owned at Dooks, Glenbeigh, was burned during the Civil War. He remained in the Seanad until its abolition in 1936. He died in 1953 at his home at Inch House, New Street, Killarney.

O'Toole, Joe (1947–)

Party: Independent. Panel: National University of Ireland. Years of service: 1987–2011

Born in Dingle in 1947, Joe O'Toole was an Independent senator who represented the National University of Ireland from 1987 to 2011. A teacher and former school principal, he was general secretary of the Irish National Teachers' Organisation (INTO) between 2000 and 2003. He is also a former president of the Irish Congress of Trade Unions (ICTU). He retired from the Seanad in 2011. In 2012, he was among a group of political figures who published a series of potential reforms for the Seanad.

O'Toole published a book about his childhood in Dingle in 2003 entitled *Looking Under Stones*.

Petty-Fitzmaurice, Henry William Edmund (Earl of Kerry) (1872–1936)

Party: Independent. Panel: Nominated by Executive Council. Years of service: 1922–9

The Earl of Kerry and later the 6th Marquess of Lansdowne, Petty-Fitzmaurice served in the Free State Senate between 1922 and 1929 as an appointee of the Executive Council. The Earl of Kerry was a hereditary title of the British peerage. A descendant of the Petty-Fitzmaurice family with roots in Lixnaw in north Kerry, the earl was the great-great-grandson of William Petty, 2nd Earl of Shelburne, who was British prime minister in 1782–3. Petty-Fitzmaurice had a decorated army career and was awarded the Distinguished Service Order (DSO) in 1900 for his service in the Boer War. He returned to the army during the First World War, reaching the rank of Lieutenant-Colonel and was the Liberal Unionist MP for West Derbyshire from 1908 to 1918. He succeeded his father as Marquess of Lansdowne in 1927, which entitled him to sit in the House of Lords. He therefore has the rare distinction of having served in two national parliaments in two different countries simultaneously – the House of Lords at Westminster and Seanad Éireann in Dublin. He remained a senator until his resignation on 5 June 1929. He died six years later. His great-grandson, Charles Maurice Petty-Fitzmaurice, the 9th Marquess of Lansdowne currently holds the title and is a member of the House of Lords.

Sheahan, Tom (1968–)

Party: Fine Gael. Panel: Administrative. Years of service: 2011–16.

See list of Kerry TDs.

Vincent, Arthur Rose (1876–1956)

Party: Independent. Panel: Nominee of Executive Council. Years of service: 1928–34

Arthur Rose Vincent of Muckross House, Killarney, was a nominee to the Free State Senate of the Executive Council and served from 1928 to 1934. He was born in India in 1876, where his father, Colonel Arthur Hare Vincent served in the army. The family had roots in Clonlara, County Clare. He was called to the Bar in 1901 and emigrated soon after, serving as an assistant judge in Zanzibar and a judge of the Appeal Court for East Africa, as well as in judicial roles in Siam, China and Korea. Vincent was made a Commander of the British Empire (CBE) and he acquired Muckross House and Gardens in Killarney through his marriage to Maud Bourn of California in 1909. Her father, William Bowers Bourn, made a wedding gift of the house to his daughter and son-in-law.

Vincent was nominated to the Free State Senate on 28 May 1931 to fill the vacancy caused by the death of Senator Patrick W. Kenny. He was appointed for a nine-year term, but he resigned on 21 February 1934 due to poor health. In 1932, the vast, 11,000-acre Muckross Estate was donated to the State by Senator Vincent and his parents-in-law, the Bourns, as they considered it too difficult and expensive to administer. The estate now forms part of Killarney National Park. Vincent, who was pre-deceased by Maud in 1929, lived for much of the remainder of his life in Monaco. He died in March 1956 and is interred at Killegy graveyard near Muckross House.

Wall, Frank (1949–)

Party: Fianna Fáil. Panel: Taoiseach's nominee. Years of service: 1982–3

A native of Tarbert, where he was born in 1949, Frank Wall was general secretary of Fianna Fáil from 1981 to 1991. His father, also Frank, was the first chairman of Kerry Co-Op and a director of Bord Bainne. Wall was nominated to the Seanad by the Taoiseach Charles Haughey, on 13 December 1982, to fill a vacancy following the November 1982 general election. He did not contest the 1983 Seanad election however. A solicitor, he was a member of the European Movement. In April 1991, he was appointed director at the Secretariat of the Council of Ministers in Brussels. He lives in Saggart, County Dublin.

Woulfe, Patrick (1914–1977)

Party: Clann na Talmhan. Panel: Taoiseach's nominee. Years of service: 1948–51

Patrick Woulfe, a native of Knockeen, Castleisland, was a solicitor with an office at Ashe Street, Tralee. A member of Clann na Talmhan, he was nominated to the Seanad in April 1948 by Taoiseach John A. Costello. Clann na Talmhan had formed an inter-party government with Fine Gael, Labour and Clann na Poblachta. A member of the County Committee of Agriculture, he was elected to Kerry County Council for the Tralee Electoral Area in October 1948. In July, 1952, he was struck off the roll of solicitors by the Statutory Committee of the Incorporated Law Society of Ireland for professional misconduct. He was found guilty of misappropriating sums of £335 and £779 received from clients. He resigned from the County Council at the August meeting. He died in London in 1977.

Appendix 3: General Election Results since 1918

1st Dáil – 21 January 1919
East Kerry – Piaras Béaslaí (Sinn Féin)
North Kerry – James Crowley (Sinn Féin)
South Kerry – Fionán Lynch (Sinn Féin)
West Kerry – Austin Stack (Sinn Féin)

2nd Dáil – Elected 16 August 1921
Kerry/Limerick West
Piaras Béaslaí (Sinn Féin)
Patrick J. Cahill (Sinn Féin)
Con Collins (Sinn Féin)
James Crowley (Sinn Féin)
Fionán Lynch (Sinn Féin)
Thomas O'Donoghue (Sinn Féin)
Edmond Roche (Sinn Féin)
Austin Stack (Sinn Féin)

3rd Dáil – Elected 9 September 1922
Kerry / Limerick West
Piaras Béaslaí (Sinn Féin)
Patrick J. Cahill (Sinn Féin)
Con Collins (Sinn Féin)
James Crowley (Sinn Féin)
Fionán Lynch (Sinn Féin)
Thomas O'Donoghue (Sinn Féin)
Edmund Roche (Sinn Féin)
Austin Stack (Sinn Féin)

4th Dáil – Elected 27 August 1923
Kerry
Patrick J. Cahill (Republican)
James Crowley (Cumann na nGaedheal)
Fionán Lynch (Cumann na nGaedheal)
Thomas McEllistrim Snr (Republican)
Thomas O'Donoghue (Republican)
John Marcus O'Sullivan (Cumann na nGaedheal)
Austin Stack (Sinn Féin)

5th Dáil – Elected 9 June 1927
Kerry
James Crowley (Cumann na nGaedheal)
Fionán Lynch (Cumann na nGaedheal)
Thomas McEllistrim Snr (Fianna Fáil)
William O'Leary (Fianna Fáil)
Thomas O'Reilly (Fianna Fáil)
John Marcus O'Sullivan (Cumann na nGaedheal)
Austin Stack (Sinn Féin).

6th Dáil – Elected 15 September 1927
Kerry
James Crowley (Cumann na nGaedheal)
Frederick Hugh Crowley (Fianna Fáil)
Fionán Lynch (Cumann na nGaedheal)
Thomas McEllistrim Snr (Fianna Fáil)
William O'Leary (Fianna Fáil)
Thomas O'Reilly (Fianna Fáil)
John Marcus O'Sullivan (Cumann na nGaedheal)

7th Dáil – Elected 16 February 1932
Kerry
Frederick Hugh Crowley (Fianna Fáil)
John Flynn (Fianna Fáil)
Eamonn Kissane (Fianna Fáil)
Fionán Lynch (Cumann na nGaedheal)

Thomas McEllistrim Snr (Fianna Fáil)
Thomas O'Reilly (Fianna Fáil)

John Marcus O'Sullivan (Cumann na nGaedheal)

8th Dáil – Elected 24 January 1933
Kerry
Frederick Hugh Crowley (Fianna Fáil)
Denis Daly (Fianna Fáil)
John Flynn (Fianna Fáil)
Eamonn Kissane (Fianna Fáil)

Fionán Lynch (Cumann na nGaedheal)
Thomas McEllistrim Snr (Fianna Fáil)
John Marcus O'Sullivan (Cumann na nGaedheal)

9th Dáil – Elected 1 July 1937
Kerry North
Stephen Fuller (Fianna Fáil)
Eamonn Kissane (Fianna Fáil)
Thomas McEllistrim Snr (Fianna Fáil)
John Marcus O'Sullivan (Fine Gael)

Kerry South
Frederick Hugh Crowley (Fianna Fáil)
John Flynn (Fianna Fáil)
Fionán Lynch (Fine Gael)

10th Dáil – Elected 17 June 1938
Kerry North
Stephen Fuller (Fianna Fáil)
Eamonn Kissane (Fianna Fáil)
Thomas McEllistrim Snr (Fianna Fáil)
John Marcus O'Sullivan (Fine Gael)

Kerry South
Frederick Hugh Crowley (Fianna Fáil)
John Flynn (Fianna Fáil)
Fionán Lynch (Fine Gael)

11th Dáil – Elected 23 June 1943
Kerry North
Patrick Finucane (Clann na Talmhan)
Eamonn Kissane (Fianna Fáil)
Thomas McEllistrim Snr (Fianna Fáil)
Daniel Spring (Labour)

Kerry South
Frederick Hugh Crowley (Fianna Fáil)
John B. Healy (Fianna Fáil)
Fionán Lynch (Fine Gael)

12th Dáil – Elected 30 May 1944
Kerry North
Patrick Finucane (Clann na Talmhan)
Eamonn Kissane (Fianna Fáil)
Thomas McEllistrim Snr (Fianna Fáil)
Daniel Spring (Labour)

Kerry South
Frederick Hugh Crowley (Fianna Fáil)[1]
John B. Healy (Fianna Fáil)
Fionán Lynch (Fine Gael)[2]

13th Dáil – Elected 4 February 1948
Kerry North
Patrick Finucane (Clann na Talmhan)
Eamonn Kissane (Fianna Fáil)
Thomas McEllistrim Snr (Fianna Fáil)
Daniel Spring (Labour)

Kerry South
Honor Mary Crowley (Fianna Fáil)
John Flynn (Independent)
Patrick W. Palmer (Fine Gael)

14th Dáil – Elected 30 May 1951

Kerry North
Patrick Finucane (Independent)
John Lynch (Fine Gael)
Thomas McEllistrim Snr (Fianna Fáil)
Daniel Spring (Labour)

Kerry South
Honor Mary Crowley (Fianna Fáil)
John Flynn (Independent)
Patrick W. Palmer (Fine Gael)

15th Dáil – Elected 18 May 1954

Kerry North
Johnny Connor (Clann na Poblachta)[3]
Patrick Finucane (Clann na Talmhan)
Thomas McEllistrim Snr (Fianna Fáil)
Daniel Spring (Labour)

Kerry South
Honor Mary Crowley (Fianna Fáil)
John Flynn (Fianna Fáil)
Patrick W. Palmer (Fine Gael)

16th Dáil – Elected 5 March 1957

Kerry North
Patrick Finucane (Independent)
Thomas McEllistrim Snr (Fianna Fáil)
Daniel J. Moloney (Fianna Fáil)
Daniel Spring (Labour)

Kerry South
Honor Mary Crowley (Fianna Fáil)
Patrick W. Palmer (Fine Gael)
John Joe Rice (Sinn Féin)

17th Dáil – Elected 4 October 1961

Kerry North (becomes three-seat constituency)
Patrick Finucane (Independent)
Thomas McEllistrim Snr (Fianna Fáil)
Daniel Spring (Labour)

Kerry South
Patrick Connor (Fine Gael)
Honor Mary Crowley (Fianna Fáil)
Timothy 'Chub' O'Connor (Fianna Fáil)

18th Dáil – Elected 7 April 1965

Kerry North
Patrick Finucane (Independent)
Thomas McEllistrim Snr (Fianna Fáil)
Daniel Spring (Labour)

Kerry South
Patrick Connor (Fine Gael)
Honor Mary Crowley (Fianna Fáil)[4]
Timothy 'Chub' O'Connor (Fianna Fáil)

19th Dáil – Elected 18 June 1969

Kerry North
Gerard Lynch (Fine Gael)
Thomas McEllistrim Jnr (Fianna Fáil)
Daniel Spring (Labour)

Kerry South
Michael Begley (Fine Gael)
Timothy 'Chub' O'Connor (Fianna Fáil)
John O'Leary (Fianna Fáil)

20th Dáil – Elected 28 February 1973

Kerry North
Gerard Lynch (Fine Gael)
Thomas McEllistrim Jnr (Fianna Fáil)
Daniel Spring (Labour)

Kerry South
Michael Begley (Fine Gael)
Timothy 'Chub' O'Connor (Fianna Fáil)
John O'Leary (Fianna Fáil)

21st Dáil – Elected 16 June 1977

Kerry North
Kit Ahern (Fianna Fáil)
Thomas McEllistrim Jnr (Fianna Fáil)
Daniel Spring (Labour)

Kerry South
Michael Begley (Fine Gael)
Timothy 'Chub' O'Connor (Fianna Fáil)
John O'Leary (Fianna Fáil)

22nd Dáil – Elected 11 June 1981

Kerry North
Denis Foley (Fianna Fáil)
Thomas McEllistrim Jnr (Fianna Fáil)
Dick Spring (Labour)

Kerry South
Michael Begley (Fine Gael)
Michael Moynihan (Labour)
John O'Leary (Fianna Fáil)

23rd Dáil – Elected 18 February 1982

Kerry North
Denis Foley (Fianna Fáil)
Thomas McEllistrim Jnr (Fianna Fáil)
Dick Spring (Labour)

Kerry South
Michael Begley (Fine Gael)
Michael Moynihan (Labour)
John O'Leary (Fianna Fáil)

24th Dáil – Elected 24 November 1982

Kerry North
Denis Foley (Fianna Fáil)
Thomas McEllistrim Jnr (Fianna Fáil)
Dick Spring (Labour)

Kerry South
Michael Begley (Fine Gael)
Michael Moynihan (Labour)
John O'Leary (Fianna Fáil)

25th Dáil – Elected 17 February 1987

Kerry North
Jimmy Deenihan (Fine Gael)
Denis Foley (Fianna Fáil)
Dick Spring (Labour)

Kerry South
Michael Begley (Fine Gael)
John O'Donoghue (Fianna Fáil)
John O'Leary (Fianna Fáil)

26th Dáil – Elected 15 June 1989

Kerry North
Jimmy Deenihan (Fine Gael)
Thomas McEllistrim Jnr (Fianna Fáil)
Dick Spring (Labour)

Kerry South
John O'Donoghue (Fianna Fáil)
John O'Leary (Fianna Fáil)
Michael Moynihan (Labour)

27th Dáil – Elected 25 November 1992

Kerry North
Jimmy Deenihan (Fine Gael)
Denis Foley (Fianna Fáil)
Dick Spring (Labour)

Kerry South
John O'Leary (Fianna Fáil)
John O'Donoghue (Fianna Fáil)
Breeda Moynihan-Cronin (Labour)

28th Dáil – Elected 6 June 1997

Kerry North
Jimmy Deenihan (Fine Gael)

Denis Foley (Fianna Fáil)
Dick Spring (Labour)

Kerry South
Jackie Healy-Rae (Independent)

Breeda Moynihan-Cronin (Labour)
John O'Donoghue (Fianna Fáil)

29th Dáil – Elected 17 May 2002
Kerry North
Jimmy Deenihan (Fine Gael)
Martin Ferris (Sinn Féin)
Thomas McEllistrim III (Fianna Fáil)

Kerry South
Jackie Healy-Rae (Independent)
Breeda Moynihan-Cronin (Labour)
John O'Donoghue (Fianna Fáil)

30th Dáil – Elected 24 May 2007
Kerry North
Jimmy Deenihan (Fine Gael)
Martin Ferris (Sinn Féin)
Thomas McEllistrim III (Fianna Fáil)

Kerry South
Jackie Healy-Rae (Independent)
John O'Donoghue (Fianna Fáil)
Tom Sheahan (Fine Gael)

31st Dáil – Elected 25 February 2011
Kerry North–West Limerick
Jimmy Deenihan (Fine Gael)
Martin Ferris (Sinn Féin)
Arthur Spring (Labour)

Kerry South
Tom Fleming (Independent)
Brendan Griffin (Fine Gael)
Michael Healy-Rae (Independent)

32nd Dáil – Elected 26 February 2016
Kerry (single constituency)
Michael Healy-Rae (Independent)
Danny Healy-Rae (Independent)
John Brassil (Fianna Fáil)
Brendan Griffin (Fine Gael)
Martin Ferris (Sinn Féin)

Glossary and Abbreviations

Ceann Comhairle – chairperson of Dáil Éireann

Comhairle Dáil Ceantair – constituency executive of Fianna Fáil

Cumann – local unit of Fianna Fáil party (sometimes used in Fine Gael)

IPP – Irish Parliamentary Party

IRA – Irish Republican Army

IRB – Irish Republican Brotherhood

JP – Justice of the Peace

MD – Municipal District

MP – Member of Parliament

RDC – Rural District Council

RIC – Royal Irish Constabulary

TD – Teachta Dála (Member of Dáil Éireann)

UDC – Urban District Council

Endnotes

INTRODUCTION

1   *The Kerryman*, 24 February 1973.
2   Hannon, Katie, *The Naked Politician* (Gill & Macmillan, 2004), p. 11.
3   Dáil Debates, 18 February 1948.
4   Dáil Debates, 3 January 1922.
5   *The Kerryman*, 18 February 2000, from Breda Joy, *The Wit and Wisdom of Kerry* (Mercier Press, 2015), p. 71.

CHAPTER 1

1   Dáil Debates, 21 January 1919.
2   The new Dáil used the existing parliamentary constituencies of South Kerry, North Kerry, West Kerry and East Kerry only until the 1921 general election, when a new constituency of Kerry–Limerick West was formed.
3   Dáil Debates, 21 January 1919.
4   Dáil Debates, 21 January 1919.
5   *The Kerryman*, 7 December 1918.
6   *The Kerryman*, 9 February 1957.
7   *Kerry News*, 8 January 1919.
8   *Kerry News*, 13 January 1919.
9   *The Kerryman*, 1 November 1919.
10 Dáil Debates, 3 January 1922.
11 *Irish Independent*, 30 June 1965.
12 *The Kerryman*, 24 August 1918.
13 *The Kerryman*, 21 September 1918.
14 *Kerry News*, 2 December 1918.
15 *Kerry News*, 29 January 1919.
16 *The Kerryman*, 7 December 1918.
17 *The Kerryman*, 28 December 1918.
18 *Kerry News*, 25 April 1919.
19 *Kerry People*, 19 February 1921.
20 McAuliffe, Bridget, Mary McAuliffe and Owen O'Shea, *Kerry 1916: Histories and Legacies of the Easter Rising – A Centenary Record* (Irish Historical Publications, 2016), p. 158.
21 Ibid., p. 159.
22 *Kerry News*, 27 November 1918.

23   Dáil Debates, 20 December 1921.

24   John J. O'Kelly from Valentia, a TD for Louth, was Leas Ceann Comhairle from 1919
     to 1921.

25   De Valera speaking during a meeting in Tralee in 1922, *The Kerryman*, 25 March
     1922.

26   McMorrow, Conor, *Dáil Stars: From Croke Park to Leinster House* (Mentor Books,
     2010) p. 81.

27   *Kerry News*, 25 November 1918.

28   *The Kerryman*, 7 December 1918.

29   McAuliffe et al., *Kerry 1916*, p. 96.

30   Ferriter, Diarmaid, *The Transformation of Ireland: 1900–2000* (Profile Books, 2005) p.
     186.

31   Dáil Debates, 19 December 1921.

32   Ibid.

33   Dáil Debates, 9 January 1922.

34   McMorrow, *Dáil Stars*, p. 88.

CHAPTER 2

1   *Kerry Sentinel*, 4 February 1905.

2   *Kerry Weekly Reporter*, 27 January 1906.

3   *Kerry People*, 18 December 1909.

4   *The Killarney Echo and South Kerry Chronicle*, 24 January 1914.

5   Bureau of Military History, Witness Statement 132 (Michael O'Sullivan and Michael
    Spillane).

6   *Kerry People*, 29 January 1917.

7   *The Kerryman*, 12 June 1915.

8   *Cork Examiner*, 21 September 1927.

FROM BUCKINGHAM PALACE TO CAHERDANIEL

1   Wickham, Ann, 'The Nursing Radicalism of the Honourable Albinia Brodrick, 1861–
    1955', in *Nursing History Review* 15 (2007), p. 51.

2   *The Kerryman*, 2 January 1965.

3   Ibid., p. 52.

4   Ibid., p. 52.

5   Ibid., p. 53.

6   Clarke, Frances, *Dictionary of Irish Biography* (Cambridge University Press, 2009), p.
    855.

7   *The Irish Times*, 17 February 2017.

8   *The Kerryman*, 8 May 1920.

9   Clarke, *Dictionary of Irish Biography*, p. 855.

10 *The Kerry People*, 14 May 1921.

11   Dáil Debates, 20 December 1921.
12   Wickham, 'The Nursing Radicalism of the Honourable Albinia Brodrick, 1861–1955', p. 56.
13   *The Kerryman*, 2 January 1965.
14   Clarke, *Dictionary of Irish Biography*, p. 856.

CHAPTER 3

1   *Kerry People*, 29 August 1908.
2   *Kerry Evening Post*, 10 March 1906.
3   *Kerry Sentinel*, 12 April 1899.
4   *Kerry Weekly Reporter*, 29 August 1908.
5   *Kerry Weekly Reporter*, 12 August 1911.
6   *Kerry People*, 5 September 1908.
7   Ibid.
8   A tierce measured approximately 160 litres, the contents of a barrel.
9   Ibid.
10   Ibid.
11   Ibid.
12   *Kerry People*, 12 September 1908.
13   Ibid.
14   *Kerry Evening Star*, 26 November 1908.
15   House of Lords debates, 14 March 1912.

CHAPTER 4

1   Dáil Debates, 31 January 1952.
2   Report of the Committee on Procedure and Privileges, 28 February 1952.
3   Dáil Debates, 5 March 1953.
4   O'Leary, John, *On the Doorsteps: Memoirs of a long-serving* TD (Irish Political Memoirs), pp. 43–4.
5   *Irish Press*, 27 May 1943.
6   O'Leary, *On the Doorsteps*, p. 44.
7   *The Kerryman*, 26 June 1943.
8   *The Kerryman*, 24 January 1948.
9   O'Leary, *On the Doorsteps*, p. 45.
10   Dáil Debates, 18 February 1948.
11   Correspondence between Tom Mullins and Fr Myles Allman, Fianna Fáil Constituency Files (IE UDDA P176), UCD Archives.
12   *The Kerryman*, 19 May 1951.
13   Dáil Debates, 13 June 1951.
14   Ibid.
15   Comhairle Dáil Ceantair Minutes, Fianna Fáil Constituency Files (IE UDDA P176).

16 O'Shea, Owen, *Heirs to the Kingdom: Kerry's Political Dynasties* (O'Brien Press, 2011), pp. 217–18.

17 Report of a Killorglin Comhairle Dáil Cheantair meeting, May 1955, Fianna Fáil Constituency Files (IE UDDA P176), UCD Archives.

18 *The Kerryman*, 19 October 1957.

THE QUEEN OF BALOCHISTAN

1 Kemp, Danny, 'The Queen of Baluchistan', <http://www.thingsasian.com> (retrieved 15 April 2018).

2 *Daily Telegraph*, 18 January 2008.

3 Ibid.

4 Ibid.

5 Ibid.

CHAPTER 5

1   Boland, Bridget, *At My Mother's Knee* (The Bodley Head, 1978) p. 30.

2   Gillmeister, Heiner, *From Bonn to Athens: The Diary of John Pius Boland, Olympic Champion, Athens, 1896* (Academia Verlag, Sankt Augustin, 2008), p. 32.

3   Boland, *At My Mother's Knee*, p. 38 and 40.

4   Ibid., p. 40.

5   *Irish Independent*, 16 June 1951.

6   Boland, *At My Mother's Knee*, pp. 50–1.

7   Ibid., p. 51.

8   *Cork Examiner*, 27 May 1938.

9   Dáil Debates, 15 October 1942.

10 Dáil Debates, 15 October 1942.

11 *Irish Press*, 14 January 1938.

12 O'Shea, *Heirs to the Kingdom:* p. 104.

13 *The Kerryman*, 8 December 1945.

14 O'Leary, *On the Doorsteps:* p. 46.

15 Boland, *At My Mother's Knee*, p. 73.

16 Dáil Debates, 26 July 1961.

17 Dáil Debates, 2 July 1954.

18 Dáil Debates, 22 May 1958.

19 Dáil Debates, 7 July 1948 and 17 June 1953.

20 Dáil Debates, 6 December 1951.

21 Dáil Debates, 1 June 1950.

22 *Irish Independent*, 16 October 1954.

23 O'Leary, *On the Doorsteps*, p. 50.

24 Letter from Seán Lemass, Fianna Fáil Constituency Archives, (P176/295/26) UCD Archives.

25   Boland, *At My Mother's Knee*, p. 51.
26   Dáil Debates, 18 October 1966.

CHAPTER 6

1   *Kerry Weekly Reporter*, 3 January 1920.
2   *The Kerryman*, 14 June 1969.
3   O'Shea, *Heirs to the Kingdom*, p. 221.
4   Interview with Paul O'Donoghue, 23 June 2010.
5   Ibid.

'WHY ARE ALL THE PEOPLE TALKING ABOUT DICK SPRING, MAMMY?'

1   *The Kerryman*, 20 February 1987.
2   *The Kerryman*, 13 February 1987.
3   Collins, Stephen, *Spring and the Labour Story* (O'Brien Press, 1993), p. 155.
4   Woulfe, Jimmy, *Voices of Kerry* (Blackwater Press, 1994), p. 113.
5   Ibid., p. 114.
6   *The Kerryman*, 20 February 1987.
7   *The Kerryman*, 27 February 1987.
8   RTÉ News Archives, 18 February 1987.
9   Kavanagh, Ray, *Spring, Summer and Fall – The Rise and Fall of the Labour Party, 1986–1999* (Blackwater Press, 2001), p. 29.
10 Collins, *Spring*, p. 153.
11 Woulfe, *Voices of Kerry*, p. 115.
12 Collins, *Spring*, p. 156.

CHAPTER 7

1   *The Kerryman*, 17 December 1955.
2   Ibid.
3   *The Kerryman*, 17 December 1955.
4   Dáil Debates, 14 December 1955.
5   *The Kerryman*, 17 December 1955.
6   Bureau of Military History, Witness Statement 1181 (Johnny Connor).
7   Horgan, Tim, *Dying for the Cause* (Mercier Press, 2014,) p. 71.
8   Clann na Poblachta ran a total of eleven candidates at the 1948 local elections in Kerry, three of whom won seats alongside Johnny Connor: J.J. O'Leary in the Killarney Electoral Area, William Langford in the Killorglin area and Louis O'Connell in Listowel.
9   Rafter, Kevin, *The Clann – The Story of Clann na Poblachta* (Mercier Press, 1996), p. 163.

10   Ibid., p. 163.

11   *The Kerryman*, 22 May 1954.

12   O'Shea, *Heirs to the Kingdom,* p. 110.

13   From an interview with Kathleen O'Connor-Fitzgerald in 2010.

14   O'Shea, *Heirs to the Kingdom*, p. 110.

15   From an interview with Kathleen O'Connor-Fitzgerald in 2010.

16   Ibid.

17   O'Shea, *Heirs to the Kingdom*, p. 112.

18   Ibid., p. 112.

19   From an interview with Kathleen O'Connor-Fitzgerald in 2010.

20   Ibid.

21   *Cork Examiner*, 25 February 1956.

22   *The Kerryman*, 18 February 1956.

23   *The Kerryman*, 25 February 1956.

24   *The Kerryman*, 11 February 1956.

25   Kathleen O'Connor was just three months short of her twenty-second birthday when she was elected, making her the third youngest TD elected by 1956 and the fourth youngest person ever elected to Dáil Éireann, after William Murphy (Cork West, 1949), Joseph Sweeney (Donegal, 1921) and Lorcan Allen (Wexford, 1961).

26   *The Kerryman*, 3 March 1956.

27   *Cork Examiner*, 2 March 1956.

28   *Cork Examiner*, 8 March 1956.

29   *Daily Express*, 2 March 1956.

30   *Evening Mail*, 2 March 1956.

31   *Cork Examiner*, 15 February 1957.

32   *Irish Independent*, 3 September 1956.

33   Rafter, *The Clann*, p. 175.

34   *The Kerryman*, 10 December 2008.

CHAPTER 8

1   *The Kerryman*, 10 June 1911.

'SINGLE-MINDED PURSUIT OF HIS OBJECTIVES'

1   Laffan, Michael, *Judging W.T. Cosgrave* (Royal Irish Academy, 2014), p. 8.

2   Lee, Joseph, *Ireland: 1912–1985* (Cambridge University Press, 1989), p. 130.

3   McManus, Antonia, *Irish Education: The Minister Legacy 1919–99* (The History Press, 2014), p. 46.

4   Dáil Debates, 4 June 1926.

5   McManus, *Irish Education*, p. 50.

6   Laffan, *Judging W.T. Cosgrave*, p. 258.

7   Lee, *Ireland 1912–85*, p. 132.

8   McManus, *Irish Education*, p. 49.
9   Ibid., p. 132.
10 Speech in Dingle, 27 November 1936, John Marcus O'Sullivan Papers, (LA60/135) UCD Archives.
11 John Marcus O'Sullivan: obit. 9 February 1948, Mary M. Macken, *Studies: An Irish Quarterly Review*, vol. 37, no. 145 (March 1948).
12 McManus, *Irish Education*, p. 58.

CHAPTER 9

1   *Kerry Champion*, 4 November 1944.
2   Ibid.
3   Ibid.
4   Correspondence between J.B. Healy TD and Fianna Fáil Head Office, 27 October 1944, Fianna Fáil Constituency Files, (IE UDDA P176) UCD Archives.
5   Letter from Richard Godsil to Fianna Fáil Head Office, 16 July 1945, Fianna Fáil Constituency Files, (IE UDDA P176) UCD Archives.
6   List of ministers assigned to church gate collections, Fianna Fáil Constituency Files, (IE UDDA P176) UCD Archives.
7   *The Kerryman*, 11 November 1944.
8   The authors have not found an equivalent situation during their research.
9   Letter from Jack O'Dwyer to Fianna Fáil Head Office during 1945 by-election campaign, Fianna Fáil Constituency Files, (IE UDDA P176) UCD.
10 There were four other by-elections to take place on the same day as the one in Kerry South in December 1945: Clare, Dublin North-West, Mayo South and Wexford.
11 Letter to Denis O'Brien from Tom Mullins, Fianna Fáil Head Office, Fianna Fáil Constituency Files, (IE UDDA P176) UCD Archives.
12 Letter from Jimmy Cronin, Milltown to Fianna Fáil Head Office, 9 March 1945, Fianna Fáil Constituency Files, (IE UDDA P176) UCD Archives.
13 Letter from Dermot Horan to Éamon de Valera, 26 June 1945, Fianna Fáil Constituency Files, (IE UDDA P176) UCD Archives.
14 *The Kerryman*, 17 November 1945.
15 Ibid.
16 Dáil Debates, 14 November 1945.
17 Apart from Kerry South, by-elections were to be held in Clare to replace Patrick Burke (FG), in Dublin North-West to replace Seán T. Ó Ceallaigh, in Mayo South to fill the seat of Michael Cleary (FF) and in Wexford following the death of Labour TD, Richard Corish.
18 O'Leary, *On the Doorsteps*, p. 45.
19 *The Kerryman*, 25 February 1956.
20 Ibid.
21 Report from Oliver J. Flanagan to Colonel P.F. Dineen, Fine Gael Head Office, 3 December 1954, Fine Gael Constituency Archives, (IE UCDA P39/C), UCD Archives.

22 Colonel P.F. Dineen to John Lynch TD, 7 June 1956, Fine Gael Archives, (IE UCDA P39/C), UCD Archives.
23 From an interview with Tom Fitzgerald, 3 May 2013.
24 O'Leary, *On the Doorsteps*, p. 84.
25 Ibid., p. 85.
26 Ibid., p. 99.
27 Devine, Francie, *An Eccentric Chemistry: Michael Moynihan and Labour in Kerry 1917–2001* (SIPTU, 2004), p. 38.
28 Note, undated from 1966 by-election campaign, Fine Gael Archives, (IE UCDA P39/C), UCD Archives.
29 *Irish Independent*, 5 December 1966.
30 *Irish Independent*, 3 December 1966.
31 *Irish Independent*, 9 December 1966.
32 *The Kerryman*, 10 December 1966.
33 *Irish Press*, 9 December 1966.
34 *Cork Examiner*, 9 December 1966.

CHAPTER 10

1 O'Shea, *Heirs to the Kingdom,* pp. 163 and 165.
2 *The Kerryman*, 26 February 2014.
3 Interview with Dan Kiely, 24 January 2018.
4 Interview with Paul O'Donoghue, 31 January 2018.
5 Interview with Paul O'Donoghue, 31 January 2018.
6 The Circuit Court, South Western Circuit, County of Kerry, In the matter of the Local Elections (Petitions and Disqualifications) Act, 1974 between Dan Kiely (Petitioner/Plaintiff) and Kerry County Council (Respondent/Defendant), Judgement of His Honour Judge Carroll Moran delivered the 18 July 2014.
7 *Irish Examiner*, 11 August 2014.
8 Interview with Dan Kiely, 24 January 2018.
9 Supreme Court Judgements – Kiely v Kerry County Council (17 December 2015), <http://www.supremecourt.ie>.
10 *The Irish Times*, 19 December 2015.
11 Radio Kerry News, 11 February 2016.
12 Interview with Dan Kiely, 24 January 2018.
13 Interview with Dan Kiely, 24 January 2018.
14 Interview with Paul O'Donoghue, 31 January 2018.

'PACK YOUR BAGS AND GET OUT'

1 *The Kerryman*, 18 April 1986.
2 *The Kerryman*, 7 June 1985.
3 *The Kerryman*, 10 January 1986.

4   The only other candidate to stand for the PDs at a general election was John Kelly
     from Killarney, who polled 1,458 votes in Kerry South in 1989. Marie O'Sullivan
     stood in the Killorglin Electoral Area at the council elections of 1991 and Gerard
     Burke contested the Listowel Electoral Area in 2004.
5   *The Kerryman*, 19 June 1987.
6   Ibid.
7   *The Kerryman*, 22 January 1988.

CHAPTER 11

1   Interview on the *Late Late Show*, RTÉ, 4 March 2016.
2   Ibid.
3   Interview with Jerry O'Sullivan, Radio Kerry, November 2017.
4   *Irish Times*, 11 February 2016.
5   RTÉ One, 26 February 2016.
6   Mike Johnny and Jamsie Fleming from Scartaglin were members of the council in
     1919 and Fine Gael TD Patrick Connor (Scarteen) and his brother, Timothy, were
     both elected to Kerry County Council in June 1955, Patrick in the Killarney Electoral
     Area and Timothy in the Killorglin Electoral Area.
7   Dwyer, T. Ryle, *Tans, Terrors and Troubles: Kerry's Real Fighting Story, 1913–1921*
     (Mercier Press, 2001), p. 10.
8   Ibid., p. 11.
9   *The Kerryman*, 31 May 1969.
10   *Kerry's Eye*, 4 January 2018.
11   *The Kerryman*, 12 January 2011.
12   Interview with John O'Donoghue, 30 April 2010.
13   O'Shea, *Heirs to the Kingdom*, p. 217.
14   Note from Killorglin Comhairle Dáil Cheantair meeting, May 1955, Fianna Fáil
     Constituency Files (P176/295), UCD Archives.
15   Letter from Daniel O'Donoghue, Draper, West Main Street, Cahersiveen, dated 15
     May 1955, to Fianna Fáil Head Office, Fianna Fáil Constituency Files (P176/295),
     UCD Archives.
16   Ibid.
17   O'Shea, *Heirs to the Kingdom*, p. 219.
18   Interview with John O'Donoghue, 30 April 2010.
19   Ibid.
20   Meeting of Fianna Fáil Constituencies Committee, 19 February 1986, Fianna Fáil
     Constituency Files (P176/295), UCD Archives.
21   *The Economist*, 12 February 1998.
22   *Irish Independent*, 3 October 2009.
23   *The Sunday Tribune*, 2 August 2009.
24   Letter from John O'Donoghue to fellow TDs, 11 September 2009 (<http://www.
     oireachtas.ie>).

25 Dáil Debates, 14 October 2009.
26 Ibid.
27 *Kerry's Eye*, 22 February 2012.

CHAPTER 12

1 *The Kerryman*, 17 June 1977.
2 Interview with John O'Leary, 24 July 2014.
3 *Cork Examiner*, 30 April 1952.
4 *Kerry Reporter*, 20 February 1932.
5 *The Kerryman*, 30 January 1987.
6 *Kerry Champion*, 31 January 1948.
7 *The Kerryman*, 22 March 1985.
8 Letter dated 1 July 1952, Fianna Fáil Constituency Archives, (P176/105), UCD Archives.
9 *The Kerryman*, 9 August 1985.
10 Letter from Patrick O'Sullivan, Church Street, Ballybunion (secretary, Ballybunion Cumann), 28 May 1952, Fianna Fáil Constituency Archives, (P176/105), UCD Archives.
11 *The Kerryman*, 28 May 1927.
12 Letter from Fr Seán Cunningham, Holy Cross Priory, Tralee, to Séamus Brennan, Fianna Fáil general secretary, 23 January 1975, Fianna Fáil Constituency Archives, (P176/105), UCD Archives.
13 *The Kerryman*, 10 March 1973.
14 *The Kerryman*, 10 March 1973.
15 *The Kerryman*, 10 March 1973.
16 Letter from Con O'Riordan to Séamus Brennan, Fianna Fáil general secretary, 25 August 1974, Fianna Fáil Constituency Archives, (P176/105), UCD Archives.
17 *The Kerryman*, 28 January 1977.
18 Letter from Kit Ahern to Fianna Fáil headquarters, 2 February 1977, Fianna Fáil Constituency Archives, (P176/105), UCD Archives.
19 Letter from Councillor Michael Long to Fianna Fáil headquarters, 21 July 1977, Fianna Fáil Constituency Archives, (P176/105), UCD Archives.
20 Letter from Michael Murphy to Fianna Fáil headquarters, 10 November 1977, Fianna Fáil Constituency Archives, (P176/105), UCD Archives.
21 Letter from Denis Foley to Séamus Brennan, Fianna Fáil general secretary, 18 April 1978, Fianna Fáil Constituency Archives, (P176/105), UCD Archives.

'YOU ARE VERY BADLY IN NEED OF A REST'

1 Browne, Noël, *Against the Tide* (Gill & Macmillan, 1986), p. 89.
2 Ibid., p. 91.
3 Rafter, *The Clann*: p. 40.
4 Ibid., p. 90.
5 Rafter, *The Clann*, pp. 39–40.

6   *The Irish Times*, 23 May 1997.
7   Keane, Elizabeth, *Seán MacBride: A Life* (Gill & MacMillan, 2007), p. 86.
8   *Kerry Champion*, 24 January 1948.
9   MacDermott, Eithne, *Clann na Poblachta* (Cork University Press, 1998), p. 56, and Trinity College Dublin, Irish film and TV Research Online, <http://www.tcd.ie/irishfilm/showfilm.php?fid=36205> (retrieved 8 November 2017).
10 Keogh, Dermot, *Twentieth Century Ireland* (New Gill History of Ireland, 2004), p. 176.
11 McCullagh, David, *The Reluctant Taoiseach: A Biography of John A Costello* (Gill & Macmillan, 2010), p. 237.
12 Minute taken by Seán MacBride, 19 November 1950, Clann na Poblachta Papers, (P125/4) UCD Archives.
13 MacBride, Sean, *That day's struggle: A memoir 1904-1951* (Currach Press, 2005) p. 224.
14 Letter from Seán MacBride to Noel Hartnett, 2 March 1951, Clann na Poblachta Papers, (P12/33) UCD Archives.
15 Letter from Seán MacBride to Noel Hartnett, 21 February 1951, Clann na Poblachta Papers, (P12/33) UCD Archives.
16 Browne, *Against the Tide*, p. 92.

CHAPTER 13

1   Lyne, Gerard J., *The Lansdowne Estate in Kerry under WS Trench 1849-72* (Geography Publications, 2001), pp. Xxxiv-xxxxv.
2   O'Shea, *Heirs to the Kingdom*, p. 207-8.
3   *The Boston Globe*, 3 September 1997.
4   *The Irish Times*, 13 October 2014.
5   Dáil Debates, 4 January 1922.

CHAPTER 14

1   House of Lords, 14 March 1912.
2   *Kerry Sentinel*, 4 June 1910.
3   Motion passed by Cahersiveen Rural District Council, 31 January 1900.
4   *The Kerryman*, 10 May 1919.
5   *The Kerryman*, 26 June 1920.
6   *Kerry News*, 13 January 1919.
7   *The Kerryman*, 14 December 1918.
8   *Kerry Weekly Reporter*, 22 November 1919.
9   Dáil Debates, 3 January 1922.
10 Dáil Debates, 20 December 1921.
11 Dáil Debates, 4 January 1922.
12 Dáil Debates, 19 December 1921.

13 Speaking to TV series, *Ireland: A Television History* by Robert Kee in 1980 and featured in *Ballyseedy*, which was broadcast by RTÉ in 1997, <https://www.youtube.com/watch?v=4819v-lH_OQ&t=201s> (retrieved 28 March 2018).
14 Dáil Debates, 4 June 1926.
15 Dáil Debates, 14 March 1933.
16 Dáil Debates, 1 November 1928.
17 Seanad Debates, 10 December 1930.
18 *Cork Examiner*, 2 May 1933.
19 *The Kerryman*, 19 August 1933.
20 *Kerry Reporter*, 21 October 1933.
21 Dáil Debates, 12 May 1937.
22 Seanad Debates, 3 December 1942.
23 Dáil Debates, 8 May 1946.
24 Dáil Debates, 15 October 1942.
25 Seanad Debates, 17 February 1943.
26 Dáil Debates, 26 November 1948.
27 Seanad Debates, 10 December 1948.
28 Dáil Debates, 18 February 1948.
29 Dáil Debates, 13 June 1951.
30 *The Kerryman*, 26 January 1952.
31 *The Kerryman*, 24 August 1957.
32 Dáil Debates, 5 November 1952.
33 *The Kerryman*, 17 December 1966.
34 *The Kerryman*, 14 June 1969.
35 O'Leary, *On the Doorsteps*, p. 145.
36 Seanad Debates, 25 July 1973.
37 Letter from Timothy O'Connor TD, Fianna Fáil deputy for Kerry South, to Audrey Conlon, secretary, WPA, 9 March 1977, remarking that he will not fill out the questionnaire and describing it as a 'directive'. Gemma Hussey Papers, (P179/38), UCD Archives.
38 *The Kerryman*, 7 June 1985.
39 *The Kerryman*, 10 March 1973.
40 *The Kerryman*, 17 February 1973.
41 *The Kerryman*, 24 February 1973.
42 *The Kerryman*, 4 April 1986.
43 John O'Donoghue TD to Frank Wall of Fianna Fáil Head Office, 22 December 1987, Fianna Fáil Constituency Files (IE UDDA P176), UCD Archives.
44 Devine, *An Eccentric Chemistry*, p. 49.
45 O'Shea, *Heirs to the Kingdom:* p. 201.
46 Dáil Debates, 31 October 1990.
47 Interview with Tom Fitzgerald, 3 May 2013.
48 McMorrow, *Dáil Stars*, p. 61.
49 Woulfe, Jimmy, *Voices of Kerry* (Blackwater Press, 1994), p. 201.
50 *The Kerryman*, 23 May 2002.

51 Hannon, *The Naked Politician*, p. 123.
52 Dáil Debates, 17 November 2004.
53 Dáil Debates, 14 June 2007.
54 Dáil Debates, 14 June 2007.
55 Hannon, *The Naked Politician*, p. 6.
56 O'Shea, *Heirs to the Kingdom*, p. 220.
57 Woulfe, *Voices of Kerry*, p. 202.
58 Radio Kerry, 22 April 2011.
59 O'Shea, *Heirs to the Kingdom*, p. 82.
60 Dáil Debates, 30 June 2000.
61 Seanad Debates, 17 July 2014.
62 *The Irish Times*, 11 February 2016 (video interview with Harry McGee).
63 Dáil Debates, 4 May 2016.

AN APOLOGY FROM THE BBC

1 *Daily Telegraph*, 15 January 2005.
2 *Kerry Reporter*, 8 March 1930.
3 Information from his grandson, Donough McGillycuddy.
4 McAuliffe *et al.*, *Kerry 1916*, p. 59.
5 Seanad Debates, 1 March 1928.
6 Seanad Debates, 3 December 1942.
7 *Irish Independent*, 26 March 1930.
8 *The Kerryman*, 6 May 1950.
9 *Daily Telegraph*, 15 January 2005.
10 *The Times*, 22 January 2011.

APPENDIX 1

1 The others were Mary O'Donoghue (FF, 1982–3), Toiréasa Ferris (SF, 2005–6) and Norma Foley (2018–19).
2 National Library of Ireland, Collection List No. 44, Piaras Béaslaí Papers, Biographical Note, p. 5.
3 *The Irish Times*, 31 March 2012.
4 McCullagh, *A Reluctant Taoiseach*, p. 366.
5 *Ballyseedy* documentary on RTÉ, <https://www.youtube.com/watch?v=pC8-CcUJDNY> (retrieved on 10 December 2017).
6 Dwyer, T. Ryle, *Nice Fellow – A Biography of Jack Lynch* (Mercier Press, 2001), pp. 369–70.
7 *Kerry's Eye*, 22 May 1981.
8 *The Kerryman*, 14 June 1969.
9 McAuliffe *et al.*, *Kerry 1916*, p. 261.
10 *Kerry People*, 14 May 1921.

11   *Limerick Leader*, 8 September 1952.
12   Dáil Debates, 8 May 1946.

APPENDIX 2

1   *The Kerryman*, 13 November 1987.

APPENDIX 3

1   Died 5 May 1945. Replaced by his wife, Honor Mary Crowley (FF), at a by-election on 4 December 1945.
2   Resigned 3 October 1944 to become Circuit Court judge. Replaced by Donal J. O'Donoghue (FF) at a by-election on 10 November 1944.
3   Died 11 December 1955. Replaced by his daughter, Kathleen O'Connor, at a by-election on 29 February 1956.
4   Died 18 October 1966. Replaced by John O'Leary (FF) at a by-election on 7 December 1966.

Index

Illustrations are indicated by page numbers in bold.

Abbeydorney, 182–3
Adacemy of St Thomas Aquinas, 122
Adoption of Children Bill, 51, 56
Aghadoe, 8, 30, 113, 114
agriculture *see* farming
Ahern, Bertie, 200, 201, 215–16
Ahern, Kit, 84–5, 117, 141, 155, 182–5, 212–13
Ahern, Michael, **154**, 155–7
Ahern, William, 28
Aiken, Frank, 128, 163
All-For-Ireland League, 26
Allman, Dan, 95, 181
Allman, Fr Myles, 58–9, 181
American War of Independence, 192
Anglo-Irish Agreement, 2
Anglo-Irish Treaty, 2, 9–10, 12, 13–14, 17–18, 35, 197, 199, 204–5, 209–10
Arden, William, 194–5
Ardfert, 13, 39, 80, 113, 114
Ashe, Thomas, 10, 13, 116
Association of the Old Dublin Brigade, 10
Asylum Committee, 38
At My Mother's Knee (Boland), 67
Athenry, 199
Aud, 110
Austin Stack Park, Tralee, 18
Australia, 196

Baily, James, 109, 111
Baily, John, 111
Baker, Thomas J., 112, 115
Ballinasloe, 199
Ballincoona hospital, Caherdaniel, 34, 83
Ballinskelligs, 81
Ballybunion, 80, 141, 181
Ballyduff, 133
Ballyferriter, 105–6

Ballyheigue, 114, 133
Ballykissane Pier, 110
Ballylongford, 11
Ballymacandy Ambush, 54–5, 57, 95
Ballymacelligott, 55, 162–3, 195–6
Ballyseedy Massacre, 2, 101, 205
Balochistan, 62–4, 197
Baltinglass Affair, 189
Baring, Edward Charles, 79
Barrett, Jacqueline, 89
Barrett, William, 114
Barry, Tom, 120
Bateman, Frederick R., 108
Bealtaine 1916 (Béaslaí), 10
Béaslaí, Piaras, 2, 6–10, 11, 12, 13, **16**, 35, 203, 204
Beasley, Fr John, 181
Beasley, Patrick Langford, 8
Beasley, Robert, 144
Beazley, Fr James, 8
Begley, Michael, 75, 119, 136, 138, 155, 157, 212
Behan, Bernie, 119
Belfast Prison, 11, 13, 15–16, 203
Black and Tans, 55, 208
Blaney, Neil, 135–7, 138, 163, 181
Blayney, John, 156–7
Blennerhassett, Arthur, 195
Blennerhassett, John, 119, 156, 173
Blennerhassett, Rowland, 110
Blowick, Joseph, 102, 133
Blueblouses, 12
Blueshirts, 12, 214
Blythe, Ernest, 115, 122
Boland, Bridget, 66, 67, 68, 77
Boland, Eileen (née Moloney), 65, 67
Boland, J.P., 13, 65–7, 68–9, 129
Boland, Jack, 114

Boland, Kevin, 137
Boland, Maureen, 68, 77
Boland's Mills, Dublin, 65
Boston Globe, 196
Bourke, Dermot, 7th Earl of Mayo,
    48–50, 202, 220
Brassil, John, 141, 144, 159, 162
Breathnach, Cormac, 199–200, **200**
Breen, Dan, 99
Breen, Fr Francis, 83
Breen, John, 83, 84
Breen, Fr Joseph, 83
Breen, Kate, 55, 83–4, 88, 116
Brennan, Joseph, 189
Brennan, Séamus, 182, 183, 185
Breslin, Cormac, 51, 104
Brewster, Francis, 194
Briscoe, Robert, 53
British Broadcasting Corporation (BBC),
    3, 221
British Journal of Nursing, 34
Brodrick, Albinia (GobnaitNíBhruadair),
    33, 33–6, 82–3, 115
Brodrick, Augusta (née Freemantle), 33
Brodrick, St John, 1st Earl of Midleton,
    33, 34–5, 82
Brodrick, William, 8th Viscount
    Midleton, 33, 82
Brosna, 42, 44, 45, 95, 197
Brosnan, Michael, 41
Brown Fergus (greyhound), 176
Browne, Daniel J., 11, 17
Browne, Donal, **90**, 91
Browne, George R., 108
Browne, Noël, 51, 96, 98, 188, 189
Browne, Patrick 'Fad', 138
Browne, Valentine, 4th Earl of Kenmare,
    20
Browne, Valentine, 5th Earl of Kenmare,
    22, 69, 79, 109, 111
Brugha, Cathal, 5–6, 8, 12
Buckingham Palace, 3, 33
Buckley, Vaughan, 175
Burke, Liam, 127
Burke, Pádraig, 158
Burke, Patrick, 53
Butcher, John, 194
Butler, James E., 108, 109

Butt, Isaac, 5
by-elections: 1872, 110; 1944, 14, 57, 70,
    125–8; 1945, 57, 71, 116, 128–31;
    1956, 85, 100–4, 132–5; 1966, 75–6,
    135–8

Caball, Kay, 87
Caherdaniel, 33–4, 36, 83
Cahersiveen, 61, 71, 81, 85, 131, 167–8,
    199, 216
Cahersiveen Board of Guardians, 107
Cahersiveen Rural District Council, 81,
    202–3
Cahill, Jackie, 180
Cahill, Michael, 120, 164
Cahill, Paddy, 15
Cahill, Tommy, 156
Callaghan, Margaret, 43
Callinan, Frank, 149
Canning, George, 192, 193, 194
Carey, Pat, 200–1
Casement, Roger, 13, 15, 39, 197
Casement's Fort, Ardfert, 13
Casey, Sheila, 88
Castlegregory, 84, 88, 113, 114–15, 116
Castleisland, 9, 25, 37–50, 113, 119–20,
    159, 176–7, 202
Castlemaine, 54–5, 61, 177, 196, 200–1
Castlerosse, Elizabeth, Lady, 79
Catholic church, 122, 123, 181–2, 199
Catholic Times, 8
Catholic Total Abstinence Federation,
    181–2
Catholic Truth Society, 67
Causeway, 133
censorship, 208–9, 220–1
Central GAA Council, 20
Charleton, Peter, 150
Childers, Erskine, 180, 211
Church of Ireland, 22, 36, 83
Chute, Francis, 71
Civil War, 2, 14, 35, 55, 83, 95–6, 115,
    163, 167, 187, 205
ClaidheamhSoluis, An, 8, 9, 112
Clan na Gael, 8
Clancy, George, **121**
Clandillon, Seumas, **121**
Clann Éireann, 32

ClannnaPoblachta, 2, 94–106, 117, 132–5,
    187, 188–90
ClannnaTalmhan, 2, 71, 101–3, 105, 117,
    127–8, 131, 132, 199
Clarke, Frank, 148
Clifford, John B., 169
Coghlan, Paul, 178
Colley, George, 155, 213
Collins, Cornelius, 26
Collins, Donal F., 126–7
Collins, Michael, 8, 10, 12, 197
Collins, Niall, 142
Collins, Stephen, 92
Collins, Tom, 156
Collis-Sandes, Faulkiner, 108
Colthurst, Sir John Conway, 195
Comerford, Jim, 81
Comerford, Mary Etta (née O'Shea), 81
Comerford, Thomas, 81
ComhairlenadTeachtaí, 199
Commane, John, 119
Commission on Technical Education,
    122–3
Congested Districts Board, 34
Connolly O'Brien, Nora, 211–12
Connor, Johnny, 68, 85, 94–100, 96, 102,
    117, 132, 162, 189, 207
Connor, Patrick, 75, 162
Conroy, John, 203
Constitution of Ireland (1937), 208, 210
Cooper, Tom, 26
Corish, Brendan, 102, 132
Cork, 198, 201
Cork City Council, 198
Cork Constitution, 27
Cork Examiner, 69, 104, 138
Cork University Press, 198
Cosgrave, Liam, 51, 173–4
Cosgrave, W.T., 14, 122, 123, 126, 220
Costello, John A., 52–3, 60, 95, 96, 98,
    101–2, 132, 188
Costello, Nuala, 152
Council of Europe, 73–4
Counihan, Cornelius, 26, 28
Courtney, Con, 177
Courtney, Denis J., 28
Courtney, James, 117
Cousins, Liam, 136

Cowan, Peadar, 96
Craig, Charles, 27
Creally, Mary, 156
Cronin, Brendan, 179
Cronin, Jimmy, 129–30
Cronin, P.J., 155, 178–9
Cronin, Rosemary, 151–2
Crosbie, James D., 108, 109, 112
Crosbie, John Gustavus, 195
Crowley, Clementine (née Burson), 10,
    12, 16
Crowley, Fred Hugh, 55, 57, 65, 67–71,
    75, 77, 84, 100, 115, 116, 126, 128–9,
    162, 209
Crowley, Honor (née Cronin), 67
Crowley, Honor Mary (née Boland),
    57–8, 65, 67–9, 71–7, 75, 84, 100,
    104, 116, 129–31, 135, 162
Crowley, James, 6, 9, 10–12, 16
Crowley, Jeremiah, 25
Crowley, Michael, 68–9
Cuffe, Hamilton, Earl of Desart, 50
Cuffe, James, 192
Culloty, Michael, 40
CumannnamBan, 34, 36, 83, 199
CumannnanGaedheal, 12, 14, 19–20, 31,
    122, 123, 125–6, 154, 181, 197–8,
    199, 220
Cunningham, Fr Seán, 182
Curragh Camp, 96
Curranes, 41, 42
Currow, 37, 174
Curtin, Antohny, 89
Curtin, John O'Connell, 24
Cusack, M.F., 193
Cussen, Richard Stack, 113

Dáil Committee on Procedure and
    Privileges, 52, 53–4
Dáil Courts, 2, 17
Dáil Éireann, 5–18, 51–61, 69–75, 84–6,
    95, 98–106, 112, 116, 117, 121–38,
    139, 158–72, 183–5, 197–201
Daily Express, 104
Daily Telegraph, 63, 219
Daly, Edward, 8
Daly, Mark, 159
Daly, Patrick, 25, 26

Danar, An (Béaslaí), 10
dancehalls, 70, 209
Davin, Seamus, 128
Davitt, Michael, 68
Dawn, The (film), 26
de Moleyns, Arthur, Lord Ventry, 108, 109
de Valera, Éamon, 2, 13, 14, 17, 18, 55–60, 71, 73, 75–7, **76**, 83, 96, 126, 130, 131, 187–8, 197, 208, 210–11
de Valera, Vivion, 52–3
Dease, J.A., 110
Deasy, Rickard, 136
Declaration of Independence, 6, 203
Deenihan, Jimmy, 2, 91, 93, 119, 121, 156, 197, 215
Defence of the Realm Act (DORA), 11
Democratic Programme, 6–7, 9
Dennehy, Bill, 71
Dennihy, Sir Thomas, 108
Denny, Anne (née Morgell), 195
Denny, Sir Barry, 195
Department of Social Welfare, 84
Derrynane, 67, 197
Desmond, Barry, 92, 136–7
D'Esterre, John, 194
Devane, Edward, 42
Devoy, John, 8
Dickson-O'Shea, Sheila, 88
Dineen, P.F., 133
Dingle, 99, 102, 112, 114, 119, 123, 134, 194, 195, 212, 217
Dingle Board of Guardians, 107
Dingle Light Railway Company, 115
Dingle Rural District Council, 109, 113, 114
Disraeli, Benjamin, 195
Dobson, Bryan, 161
Dr Croke's GAA club, Killarney, 20, 32
Doherty, Michael, 117
Doherty, Tom, 142
Donnelly, Nicholas, 65–6
Donovan, Eileen (née O'Connor), 109
Donovan, Francis Mary Philipa, 78, 79–80, **86**
Donovan, Sir Henry, 79, 109
Donovan, P.J., 119
Donovan, St John, 39, 78, 80, 108, 109, 113, 114

Donovan, Susan, 109
Doran, David, 109, 111
Downing, Eugene, 79
Downing, John, 180
drink, 37–50, 70, 80, 113, 114, 181–2, 202, 209
Drummond, Timothy, 175
Dublin, 8, 12–13, 65–7, 82, 99, 187, 192, 194, 199–201, 210
Dublin City Council, 82
duels, 194–5
Dwyer, T. Ryle, 163

EachtraPheadair Schlemiel (Béaslaí), 8
Easter Rising, 8, 12–13, 15, 34, 65, 68, 83, 101, 110, 126, 163, 197, 199
Edenburn Hospital, 84
education, 2, 63, 66, 121–4, 154, 205–6
Egan, James, 113
election posters, 177, 206
elections *see* by-elections; general elections; local elections
emigration, 34, 96, 112, 140, 188, 195–6
Emmet, Robert, 193
English, Ada, 199, 204
Esmonde, Sir Thomas, 110
European Parliament, 139, 142, 145, 200
Evening Mail, 104–5
Everett, Jim, 189
evictions, 20, 23–4
expenses scandals, 170–3

Fáinne, An, 8
Farmer's Bridge, 95, 96, 99, 132
farming, 31, 34, 83
Farrell, Brian, 92
Fear an MilliúnPúnt(Béaslaí), 10
female candidates, 78–89
Fenian rebellion (1867), 17–18, 205
Fernane, Mairead, 88
Ferris, Martin, 86, 162, 215
Ferris, Toiréasa, 85, 86, 119, 120
Ferriter, Diarmaid, 17
Fianna Fáil, 2, 3, 12, 14, 18, 19, 31–2, 35, 55–61, 70–7, 83–5, 90–3, 98, 101–3, 106, 116–20, 123, 126–31, 133–8, 139–44, 154–7, 163–6, 167–74, 177–88, 199, 201, 209–10, 212–16

Fine Gael, 2, 14, 71, 90–1, 95, 98, 101–3, 116–20, 123, 126–7, 130–3, 136–7, 139, 165, 173–4, 177, 179–80, 181
Finnegan, Pat, 119
Finucane, D.J., 8–9
Finucane, Paddy, 98, 105
Firies, 20, 23–4, 71, 211
First World War, 34, 114, 220
Fitzgerald, Eamon, 106
Fitzgerald, Edward, 30
FitzGerald, Garret, 90, 180
FitzGerald, Joan, 180
Fitzgerald, John, 42
Fitzgerald, Maureen Henry, 87
Fitzgerald, Maurice, 81
Fitzgerald, Teresa, 81
Fitzgerald, Tom, 134, 137, 215
Fitzgerald Memorial Committee, 20
Fitzmaurice, Anne, 191
Fitzpatrick, John, 146
Flanagan, Oliver J., 51–4, 60, 95, 133, 210
Fleming, James 'Jamsie', 112, 117, 166–7
Fleming, John 'Small Jack', 166–7
Fleming, Michael J. 'Mike Johnny', 112, 117, 166
Fleming, Tom (Tom II), 112, 116, 117, 167
Fleming, Tom (Tom III), 112, 118, 159–61, 162, 164–6, 167
Fleming, Tom Michael, 112, 117, 165, 166–7
Floyd, Sir John, 195
Flynn, Edward, 55
Flynn, Jack, 1, 51–61, 55, 74, 116, 131, 167–8, 210
Flynn, Johanna, 55
Flynn, Mary (née Ryle), 61
Foley, Charlie, 22
Foley, Denis, 91, 93, 141, 162, 183–5
Foley, Norma, 85, 86, 87, 120
Foley, T.T., 203
Food Prices Commission, 84
Foran, Bibiana 'O'S', 80–1, 88
Foran, Jeremiah, 80
Four Courts, Dublin, 13
Free State Army, 10, 14, 18
Freeman's Journal, 8
Frongoch internment camp, 13, 34

Fuller, Paudie, 185
Fuller, Stephen, 2, 101, 162, 205

Gaelic Athletic Association (GAA), 15, 18, 20, 32, 140, 141, 170, 215
Gaelic League, 8, 12, 35, 68
Gaelic revival, 33
Galvin, Thomas, 108
Galway Prison, 199
'Gang of Five', 163
Gannon, Seán, 36
Garda Síochána, 72–3, 119, 140, 185–6, 206
Gardiner, Charles, 192
Gardiner, Luke, 192
Gaughan, Fr Anthony, 17
General Council of County Councils, 84, 111
general elections: 1900, 20; 1906, 21–2, 37; 1910, 19, 23–7, 39; 1918, 5–6, 8–9, 11, 13, 15–16, 35, 67; 1921, 9, 35, 199; 1922, 10, 18, 199; 1923, 10, 122, 197; 1927 (June), 18, 31, 69; 1927 (September), 18, 31–2; 1932, 55; 1937, 84; 1938, 126; 1943, 56–7, 126; 1944, 57, 70, 126; 1948, 57–8, 74, 96–8, 131, 168; 1951, 59, 98, 168; 1954, 61, 95, 97, 98–9, 132, 133; 1957, 61, 105–6, 166–7, 189; 1961, 75, 175; 1965, 75, 136; 1969, 155, 174, 212; 1973, 182–3; 1977, 84–5, 173, 183–5, 201; 1982, 141; 1987, 90, 90–3, 141, 155–6, 170, 201; 1997, 149, 161, 200, 201, 215–16; 2002, 165; 2007, 165, 171, 200; 2011, 86, 159, 164–5, 167, 172, 217; 2016, 139, 151, 158–62
Gilmore, Eamon, 171
Gladstone, W.E., 193
Glasnevin Cemetery, Dublin, 10
Gleeson, Michael, 119, 165
Gleeson, Tim, 180
Glenbeigh, 66, 112, 214
Glenmore, 196
Godsil, Richard, 128
Good Friday Agreement, 2
Goodman, T.C., 38
Gorman, Maria, 88

Gormley, John, 149
Gortatlea, 95
Gortroe, 22–3
Griffin, Brendan, 162, 165
Griffin, Daniel, 59
Griffin, Thomas, 41
Groarke, Jim, 186
Grosvenor, Beatrice, 23
Guest, Ivor, Lord Ashby St Ledgers, 50
Guiney, Denis, 188, 199
Guiney, Patrick, 26
Gurteen, Co. Cork, 67–8

Hanafin, Des, 136
Hannon, Katie, 1
Harmon, James, 59
Harrington, Mary, 79
Harrington, Mary E. (née Cremin), 79
Harrington, Ned, 79, 110, 194
Harrington, Tim, 110, 194
Hartnett, Noel, 96, **187**, 187–90
Harty, Edmund, 112, 114
Haughey, Charlie, 85, 134, 136, 155, 163, 170, 214–15
Hawkins, Fred, 128
Headford, 113
Headford Junction Ambush, 68, 95
healthcare, 34, 36, 73, 80, 83–4, 107, 108, 206
Healy, John (Kerry County Council), 30, 114
Healy, John B. (Fianna Fáil TD), 57, 59, 70, 126, 128, 131, 167, 206
Healy, Michael J., 116
Healy, Philip, 112
Healy, Teddy, 139, 185
Healy, Thomas, 39, 80, 113, 114
Healy, Timothy, 39
Healy-Rae, Danny, 86, 117, 119, 120, 158–62, 218
Healy-Rae, Jackie, 1, 117, 119, 157, 161, 162, 165, 178–9, 215–16
Healy-Rae, Johnny, 86, 117, 120, 158–9, 161
Healy-Rae, Maura, 86, 117, 120, 161
Healy-Rae, Michael, 117, 119, 151, 153, 158–62, 165, 218
Healy-Rae, Rosemary, 151

Heidelberg University, 122
Henry, Leonard, 221
Higgins, Joe, 200, 216
Higgins, Liam, 200
Hilliard, John, 22, 28–9
Hogan, Patrick, 52–3, 54
Hogan, Phil, 140, 172
Holly, Denis, 186
Home Rule, 5, 16, 33, 114
Horan, Dermot, 130
Horan, Eamon, 32
Horan, Edmund, 71, 127–8, 131
Horgan, Christy, 178
Horgan, Jane, 200
Horgan, Joe, 200
Horgan, John S., 200
Horgan, Mary, 88–9
Houlihan, Con, 1
Houlihan, Maisie, 88
House of Lords, 48–50, 113
housing, 108
Huggard, Peter, 28
hunger strikes, 13, 15, 18, 35, 83, 85, 96, 187, 207, 209
Hurley, David, 28
Hussey, Gerard, 180
Hussey, John E., 108, 109
Hussey, Sam, 78–9

Ideal Homes Exhibition, 91
Independents, 3, 19, 26, 57–60, 71, 98, 117, 118, 120, 131, 142, 155, 159, 164–5, 168–9, 178–9, 220
infrastructure, 68–9, 107–8, 174
International Labour Organisation Conference, 199
Irish Freedom, 36
Irish Hospital Sweepstakes, 55
Irish Independent, 8, 10, 73–4, 137
Irish Land and Labour Association, 38, 68
Irish language, 6–7, 8, 33, 35, 66, 83, 122, 187
Irish National Foresters, 15
Irish Nurses' Organisation, 88
Irish Parliamentary Party, 5, 8, 13, 16, 20, 21–2, 30, 39, 66–7, 111, 194
Irish Press, 56, 70

Irish Republican Army (IRA), 2, 12, 13,
    35, 54–5, 57, 65, 68, 83, 95–6, 99,
    101, 127, 132, 163, 181, 187, 209, 211
Irish Republican Brotherhood (IRB), 8,
    12, 15, 187
Irish Transport and General Workers'
    Union, 20, 136, 198
Irish Tourist Association, 69, 72
Irish Unionist Alliance, 33, 82
Irish Volunteers, 8, 10, 12–13, 15, 27–8,
    68, 95, 101, 114, 199
Irishman's Day (Boland), 67

Jinnah, Mohammad Ali, 62
John Mitchels GAA club, Tralee, 15, 139,
    142, 151
Johnson, Michael, 59
Johnson, Richard, 156, 175
Johnson, Thomas, 7, 122
Julian, Edward, 110
Julian, J.E.J., 112–13
Julian, Samuel, 112–13

Kavanagh, Liam, 92
Keane, John B., 112, 173
Keane, Simon, 42
Kearney, Peadar, 10
Kearney, Thomas, 20, 111, 166
Keating, Dan, 207
Keating, Denis, 168
Keating Branch, Gaelic League, 8, 12
Kelleher, Niall, 159
Kelliher, Cornelius, 25, 26, 113
Kenmare, 84, 180, 193, 194
Kenmare Board of Guardians, 107, 111
Kenmare Conservatory Board, 84
Kenmare Rural District Council, 111
Kenmare Shamrocks GAA club, 83
Kennedy, Albert, 89
Kennedy-Henchy, Margo, 89
Kennelly, Mike, 143–4, 148, 152–3
Kenny, Enda, 139
Kerry Babies Tribunal, 14
Kerry Champion, 127, 177–8
Kerry County Board of Health, 55, 83–4,
    96, 108
Kerry County Committee of Agriculture,
    35, 112, 220

Kerry County Council, 3, 20, 25, 33, 35,
    37–50, 55, 58, 61, 69, 71, 78, 80,
    82–6, 98, 108–20, 139–53, 156–7,
    161, 166–9, 172, 174, 178–9, 203, 220
Kerry County GAA Board, 15, 20
Kerry County Infirmary Committee, 35
Kerry Evening Post, 81
Kerry Farmers' Association, 116, 117
Kerry Farmers' Union, 31
Kerry Grand Jury, 78, 107, 108, 109
Kerry News, 21
Kerry People, 23, 24, 43, 44, 46, 48, **49**
Kerry Reporter, 177
Kerry Sentinel, 79, 176, 194
Kerry Today (radio programme), 158
Kerry Weekly Reporter, 82, 83
Kerryman, 10, 11, 35, 59, 84, 90, 92–3,
    101–4, **102**, 114, 128, 130, 137–8,
    142, 155, 157, 173–4, 178–9, 180,
    183–6, **184**, 222
Kerry's Eye, 164, 172
Kickham, Charles, 18, 205
Kiely, Dan, 3, 91, 119, 140–53, **152**
Kiely, Dan, Snr, 140
Kilcrohane agricultural cooperative, 34, 83
Kilcummin, 112, 165–6
Kilgarvan, 155, 158, 201
Kilgobbin, 113
Killarney, 8–9, 20–32, 61, 67, 69, 71, 72,
    75–7, 78–9, 88, 115, 117, 119, 121,
    126–7, 131, 142, 155, 161, 177–80,
    194, 217
Killarney Asylum, 21
Killarney Board of Guardians, 78–9, 107,
    166
Killarney Echo and South Kerry Chronicle,
    26–7
Killarney Junior Chamber, 178
Killarney Legion GAA club, 32
Killarney Mineral Waters, 31
Killarney Race Company, 31
Killarney Rural Distric Council, 25, 30,
    111, 166
Killarney Trout Anglers' Association, 69
Killarney Urban District Council, 20, 22,
    26–31, 83–4, 88, 108, 116, 126, 178
Killorglin, 71, 83, 115, 117, 119, 131,
    168–9

Kinlen, Dermot, 134
Kinloch, Ross 'The McGillycuddy of the
    Reeks', 116, 207, 208–9, **219**, 219–22
Kissane, Eamonn, 55, 59, 84, 98, 211–12
Knocknagoshel, 32, 40, 42, 100, 189, 211

Labour Party, 2, 85, 90–3, 98, 101–3, 116,
    119, 133, 136–7, 181, 199, 200
Land League, 15, 24, 110, 111, 166
Land War, 23–4
Latchford, Richard, 108, 109–10, **118**, 202
Late Late Show (RTÉ), 119
Lawlor, Thomas, 114
League of Nations, 123
Leahy, John White, 108
Leane, Thomas, 40
Lee, Joe, 123
Lemass, Seán, 51, 74, 76–7, 103, 135, 187
Lenihan, Arthur, 116
Lenihan, Brian, Jr, 200
Lenihan, Charlie, 117
Lennon, J., **121**
Leonard, Maurice, 20, 28, 78–9, 108
Leonard, Theresa, 78–9
Leslie, R., 108
Lewes Prison, 8
Limerick Prison, 32
Lispole, 200
Lisselton, 114
Listowel, 10–12, 80–1, 86, 88–9, 98, 102,
    112, 115, 119, 120, 133, 140–53,
    173–4, 188, 196, 198
Listowel Board of Guardians, 80, 107
Listowel Mutiny, 12
Listowel Race Committee, 112
Listowel Urban District Council, 80,
    88–9, 108, 214
literacy, 63, 66
Liverpool, 7–8
Lixnaw, 112, 113, 191
Lloyd George, David, 2, 17
local elections: 1899, 38, 78–9, 108–9,
    166; 1902, 38, 111–12, 166; 1905,
    20, 38, 112–13, 166; 1908, 20, 25,
    37–50, 113, 166; 1911, 20, 22, 26,
    39, 81, 114, 166; 1914, 26–8, 80,
    81, 87, 114–15; 1917, 69; 1920, 35,
    83, 115, 166; 1926, 55, 69, 81, 83,

115–16; 1928, 83, 88, 116, 167; 1934,
    84, 88, 116, 167; 1942, 88, 116, 167;
    1945, 88; 1948, 98, 117; 1950, 88;
    1955, 117, 168–9; 1967, 84, 117, 167;
    1974, 87, 117, 141, 167; 1979, 87,
    88, 117–18, 167, 178; 1985, 87, 88,
    118; 1991, 88, 119, 179; 1994, 87, 89;
    1999, 87, 88, 117, 119, 179; 2004, 88,
    119, 141, 163; 2009, 119–20; 2014,
    120, 139–53, 164, 172
Local Government Acts: 1898, 107–8;
    1925, 108, 115
local government reform, 86, 107–8, 115,
    118, 120
London, 33, 65, 67, 69, 199
Long, Jerh, 116
Long, Mick, 157, 184–5
Lynch, Brigid (née Slattery), 13, 14
Lynch, Finian, 12
Lynch, Fionán, 2, 6, 9, 11, 12–14, **17**, 31,
    35, 57, 67, 70, 121, 126–7, 197, 199,
    204
Lynch, Gerard, 162, 173, 184
Lynch, Helen (née McCarthy), 12
Lynch, Jack, 135, 137, 138, 155, 163,
    173–4, 201
Lynch, John, 98, 133, 162
Lynch, Kevin, 14
Lynch, Thaddeus, 135

McAuliffe, Cornelius, 42
McAuliffe, Xavier, 185
MacBride, Seán, 51, 53, 95, 96, 98, 99,
    100, 102, 104, 105, 132–3, 187–90
McCabe, Jerry, 119
McCarthy, Maurice, 15
McCarthy, Michael, 59
McCarthy, Myra, 12
McCartie, Maurice, 29
McCaughey, Seán, 187, 209
McCowen, Robert, 108, 109
McCyntre, R., 108
Mac Diarmada, Seán, 8
McDonagh, Louise, **90**, 91, 93
McDowell, Michael, 149
McElligott, Ned, 39, 45, 207
McElligott-Rusk, Bríd, 87
McEllistrim, Anne, 86, 163–4

McEllistrim, Marie, 196
McEllistrim, Thomas, 55, 68, 84, 85, 95,
    98, 162–3, 211
McEllistrim, Thomas (Tom II), **90**, 91–3,
    117, 141, 156, 157, 162, 163, 182–6,
    184, 196, 213
McEllistrim, Thomas (Tom III), 141, 162,
    163–4
MacGearailt, Breandán, 118
McGillycuddy, Denis Charles, 220
McGillycuddy, Dermot Patrick Donough,
    222
McGillycuddy, Gertrude Laura (née
    Miller), 220
McGillycuddy, John, 108, 109
McGillycuddy, Miriam, 87
McGillycuddy, Thomas, 59
McGillycuddy of the Reeks *see* Kinloch,
    Ross
McKechnie, William, 150
McKenna, Denis L. 196, **198**
McKenna, Jack, 30–1
McMahon, Jeremiah, 40
McMahon, Michael, 142–4, 147–8, 151
McMahon, William, 112
McManus, Antonia, 124
MacMonagle, Paddy, 21
MacNeill, Eoin, 15, 122, 124
McQuaid, John Charles, 199
McSweeney, Jeremiah, 116, **118**
McSweeney, John, 113
MacSwiney, Mary, 36, 104
Magdalene Laundries, 211–12
Magennis, William, 122
Maguire, Pauline, 213
Maher-Loughnan, James, 20
Maher-Loughnan, John, 22–3
Mahony, Thomas McDonagh, 109
Mail on Sunday, 194
Mangan, Joseph, 39
Mason, Jerry, 139
Maxwell, Commissioner, 37–50
Meade, Tony, 185–6
Meredith, R.C., 39
Mernin, Lily, 10
Message to the Free Nations of the World, 6
*Michael Collins and the Making of a New
    Ireland* (Béaslaí), 10

Militant Tendency, 200
Miller, Colin, 119
Milltown, 136
MnánaPoblachta, 36, 83
Moloney, Dan 'Danny Jim', 87, 101–3,
    106, **133**, 133–4, 141, 162
Moloney, Jimmy, 141, 143–4, 148, 152–3
Moloney, Marie, 86
Monahan, Philip, 115
Moonlighters, 23–4
Moore, John, 114–15
'Morality in Relation to the Public Health'
    (Brodrick), 36
Moran, Carroll, 146–8
Moran, Patrick, 168
Morgell, Crosbie, 195
Moriarty, David M., 109, 111, 112
Moriarty, J.F., 39, 40–1, 43
Moriarty, Jonathan, 114
Moriarty, Michael T., 113, 114
Moriarty, Norma, 86, 120, 144, 159
Mother and Child Scheme, 51, 98, 189
Mountjoy Prison, 96
Moylan, Seán, 71
Moynihan, Dermot, 136
Moynihan, Maurice, 38, 39
Moynihan, Michael, 75, 136, 142, 162,
    178, 214, 217
Moynihan, P.J., 30
Moynihan-Cronin, Breeda, 85–6, 119,
    162, 217–18
Moyvane, 185–6
Muckross Abbey, 77
Mulcahy, Richard, 10, 51, 95, 126–7,
    130–1
Mullins, Tom, 58–9, 129, 186
Mulvihill, Dan, 57
Mulvihill, Tom, 59
Munster GAA Council, 20
Murphy, Anne (née McCarthy), **29**
Murphy, Daniel 'Dan Spud', 41, 42–3, 45,
    46
Murphy, Elizabeth, 144–5, 148–9, **152**
Murphy, John, 19–32, **29**, 38, 39, 111
Murphy, Michael, 185
Murphy, Mrs (Castleisland trial witness),
    41–2
Murphy, Paul, 200

Murray, Michael, 29
Musharraf, Pervez, 64

Nash, Leahy, 108
National Archives, 10
National Awami Party (Pakistan), 63
National Farmer's Association, 136
National Council of Nurses, 36
National Ploughing Championships, 31, 69
National Progressive Democrats (NPD), 190
National University of Ireland, 66, 67, 199
Nolan, Dianne, 86, 89, 120, 144
Nolan, Michael J., 29–30, 111, 203
North Dublin Union, 35
Nun of Kenmare (Cusack), 193

Ó Briain, Barra, 175
O'Brien, Denis, 129
O'Brien, Richard, 176
O'Callaghan, Jim, 149
O'Callaghan, Michael, 59
Ó Cinnéide, Caoimhín, 85
O'Connell, Bobby, 119–20, 177
O'Connell, C.G., 112
O'Connell, Daniel, 67, 108, 193, 194–5
O'Connell, Eoin, 127, 128
O'Connell, J.D., 16
O'Connell, John (European Parliament), 200
O'Connell, John (solicitor), 15
O'Connell, Louis, 214
O'Connell, Maurice, 195
O'Connell, Mick, 3
O'Connell, Morgan, 194–5
O'Connor, Batt, 136, 197–8
O'Connor, Brendan (Australia), 196
O'Connor, Brendan (brother of Kathleen), 99, 100
O'Connor, Bryan, 42
O'Connor, Daniel, 42
O'Connor, Dee, 57
O'Connor, Denis, 61
O'Connor, Hanoria, 39–40, 45, 46
O'Connor, J.K., 25, 37–50, 109, 113, 202
O'Connor, James T., 20, 24–5, 26, 29–31, 203

O'Connor, John, 194
O'Connor, Johnny see Connor, Johnny
O'Connor, Kathleen, 3, 85, 99–106, 132–5, 162
O'Connor, Margaret (née Corkery), 96, 100
O'Connor, Pádraig, 100
O'Connor, T.T., 28, 112
O'Connor, Thomas, 59
O'Connor, Timothy 'Chub', 75, 162, 168, 169, 174–6, 213
O'Connor-Scarteen, Patrick, 117
O'Connor-Scarteen, Timothy, 117
Ó Donnchú, Tomás, 35
O'Donnell, Donal, 149–50
O'Donnell, Grace, 88
O'Donnell, John, 110, 112, 113
O'Donnell, John Kerry (GAA), 140
O'Donnell, John P. (nephew of John), 110, 113, 115
O'Donnell, Michael A., 115
O'Donnell, Michael J., 30, 110, 113, 115
O'Donnell, Patrick (doctor), 94
O'Donnell, Patrick (Kerry County Council), 110
O'Donnell, Thomas (Irish Parliamentary Party), 16, 110, 220
O'Donnell, Thomas E. (Circuit Court judge), 151–2
O'Donnell, William, 110
O'Donoghue, Dan, 61, 85, 116, 167–9, 217
O'Donoghue, Donal 'Danny Jim', 14, 57, 127, 128, 131
O'Donoghue, John, 2, 3, 61, 85, 116, 119, 121, 159, 162, 164, 165, 167, 169–72, 197, 214, 216–17
O'Donoghue, Mary (née Healy), 61, 85, 87, 169, 216–17
O'Donoghue, Paul, 85, 116, 119, 144–6, 148–9, 152, 153, 172
O'Donoghue, Thomas, 112
O'Donoghue, Henry Vincent, 101
O'Donovan Rossa, Jeremiah, 18, 205
O'Driscoll, Alexander, 112, 113
O'Duffy, Eoin, 206, 208, 214
O'Dwyer, Jack, 129
O'Dwyer, Mick, 170

O'Farrell, Seán, 115
O'Flaherty, Eugene L., 195–6
O'Flaherty, Timothy, 113
O'Gorman, George, 30, 113, 114
O'Gorman, Michael 'Pixie', 143
O'Hagan, Mary, 193
O'Hagan, Thomas, 193
O'Halloran, Mary, 87
O'Halloran, Tom, **90**, 92, 143
O'Higgins, Joan (née O'Shea), 81
O'Higgins, Niall, 81
O'Higgins, T.F., 130
O'Kelly, J.J. (Sceilg), 18, 24, 197
O'Kelly, Seán T., 7, 208
O'Kelly, Seumas, **121**
Old Criticism and the New Pragmatism
    (O'Sullivan), 122
O'Leary, Brian, 119, 151, 164
O'Leary, John, 55–6, 57, 71–2, 74–5, 76,
    131, 135–8, **138**, 162, 174, 178, 181,
    212
Olympic Games, 66
O'Malley, Des, **154**, 155, 201
O'Malley, Donogh, 134, 136, 137, 154–5
O'Malley, Hilda (née Moriarty), 154–5
O'Neill, Arthur, 84
O'Neill, Michael, 59
O'Neill, Sheila, 84
O'Rahilly, Alfred, 198–9
O'Rahilly, Tomás Prionnsias, 199
O'Rahilly, Sisíle, 199
O'Reilly, Thomas, 55, 206
O'Riordan, Con, 183, 185–6
O'Riordan, Jeremiah, 115
Ó Sé, Páidí, 170
O'Shea, Dan, 20
O'Shea, James, 22, 25, 29–31, 81, 113, 114
O'Shea, John, 81
O'Shea, Mary, 81, **87**, 116
O'Shea, Michael D., 119, 159
O'Shea, Mort, 88
O'Shea, Pat, 88, 168
Ó Siochfradha, Pádraig (AnSeabhac), 28, 203
Ó Suilleabháin, EoghanRua, 24
O'Sullivan, Agnes (née Crotty), 26, 123
O'Sullivan, Billy 'Gogo', 19, 24
O'Sullivan, Charlie (returning officer),
    151–2

O'Sullivan, Charles (Bishop of Kerry),
    111, 121
O'Sullivan, Denis J., 111
O'Sullivan, Eugene, 19–32, **29**, 39,
    115–16, 121
O'Sullivan, Florence, 25, 111
O'Sullivan, Jerry, 158–60
O'Sullivan, John Marcus (Kerry County
    Council), 20, 115–16
O'Sullivan, John Marcus (Minister for
    Education), 2, 19–20, 26, 31, **121**,
    121–4, 162, 197, 205–6, 208
O'Sullivan, John Ulick, 26
O'Sullivan, Luisa (née Crotty), 26
O'Sullivan, Michael (Emporium owner,
    Killarney), 20
O'Sullivan, Michael (Irish Volunteers
    leader, Kilarney), 27–8
O'Sullivan, Ned, 141, 216, 218
O'Sullivan, Tim, 8, 22, 26, 162
O'Sullivan, Tim D. 'Big Tim', 196
O'Sullivan, William, 206
Our Country (film), 188

Pakistan, 3, 62–4, 197
Palmer, Patrick W., 57, 71, 130–1, 210
Parnell, Charles Stewart, 5
Parnell split, 110
Peamount Sanatorium, Dublin, 80
Pearse, Margaret, 104
Pearse, Patrick, 12–13, 15, 112
Peel, Sir Robert, 195
Pembroke Urban District Council, 82,
    197
Petty, John, 191
Petty, Sir William, 191–2
Petty-Fitzmaurice, William, Lord
    Shelburne, 191–2
Pierse, Garret, 114
Pitt, William, the Younger, 194
Pius XI, 123
Pius XII, 199
political dynasties, 158–72
Pontifical Order of Saint Gregory the
    Great, 199
Poor Clare Convent, Kenmare, 193
Poor Laws, 107
Portland Prison, 8, 13

Portlaoise Prison, 209
poverty, 33–4, 63, 66, 83, 99
Powell, Enoch, 170
Prendiville, Maurice, 166
Prime Time (RTÉ), 1
Proclamation of the Irish Republic, 6, 11
Progressive Democrats (PDs), 154–6,
    178–9, 185, 201
proportional representation, 115, 154–7,
    166
Provisional Constitution (1919), 6
psychiatry, 199
Purtill, Liam, 144

Qazi, Ashraf Jehangir, 63, 64
Qazi Mohammad Essa, 62, 197
Qazi Mohammad Musa, 62–3, 197
Question Time (RTÉ), 187–8
Quill, Danny, 201
Quill, Maureen, 155, 201
Quill, Nora, 201
Quilter, Frank, 139
Quinlan, John Laurence, 48, 113
Quinlan, Patrick, 48
Quinlan, William, 48

Radio Kerry, 158
RaidióTeilefís Éireann (RTÉ), 1, 119, 137,
    161, 187–8, 217
Rathmore, 68
Redmond, John, 5, 21, 33
Reidy, Denis J., 37–48, 113
Reidy, John, 176–7
Reilly's Fort, Dublin, 8
Republic of Ireland Bill, 210
Revington, Joe, 92
Rice, John Joe, 61, 83, 166–7, 211
Rice, R.J., 108
roads, 68–9, 107, 174
Robinson, Mary, 156
Roche, Bernard, 39
Roche, Sir Boyle, 193
Roche, David (returning officer), 8
Roche, David (solicitor), 39
Roche, Edmond, 35
Roche, Redmond, 38, 109
Rossdohan Island, 66
Rowan, Annie, 78, 79

Rowan, William, 108
Royal Irish Constabulary (RIC), 11, 12,
    15, 95

St Catherine's Hospital, Tralee, 55, 84
St James Gazette, 33
St Patrick's Day celebrations, 178
St Stephen's magazine, 122
same-sex marriage referendum, 201
sanitation, 107–8
Save Derrynane Committee, 197
Scally, Joe, 178
Scartaglin, 20, 25, 95, 112, 159, 164, 166,
    167
Seanad Éireann, 19, 28, 59, 86, 116, 117,
    127, 141, 189, 201, 218, 219–22
Second Afghan War, 63
Second World War, 96, 128, 129, 222
Selewin, Catherine, 194
Seven Years' War, 191
1798 rebellion, 192
Sexton, Thomas, 194
Shanahan, Richard, 44, 46
Shaw, Ann (née Boland), 77
Sheahan, Tom, 162, 165
Sheehan, Jeremiah D., 111
Sheehan, John J., 30, 115
Sheehy, James, 114
Sheehy, Patrick, 59
Sheridan, Richard Brinsley, 193
Sinn Féin, 2, 5, 8–9, 11, 15–16, 18, 23,
    34–6, 61, 67, 83, 115, 119, 120,
    166–7, 171, 176–7, 182, 197, 198, 203
Sláinte Insurance Society, 80
Slattery, Tom, 203
slavery, 193
Smith, Patrick, 163, 186
Sneem, 35, 36, 83, 180
Socialist Party, 200
Society for the State Registration of
    Trained Nurses, 36
South Kerry Independent Alliance, 119
Spanish Lad (greyhound), 174–6
Special Powers Act, 211
Spectator, 34–5
Spillane, Michael, 27
spoiled votes, 142–53
Spring, Arthur, 86, 91, 162, 214

Spring, Dan, 90, 98, 116, 133, 162 213
Spring, Dick, 2, 3, 85, 90–3, 117, 119, 121,
    162, 178, 197, 209, 214–15
Spring, Donal, **90**, 92
Spring, Kay, 92
Spring, Maeve, 85, 87, 117
Spring, Michael, 85
Stack, Austin, 2, 6, 9, 11, 13, 14–18, **16**,
    35, 121, 197, 203–4, 205
Stack, Michael J., 196
Stack, Nanette (née O'Neill), 14–15
Stack, Una 'Winnie' (née Gordon), 18
Stack, William Moore, 14–15, 17–18
Stephen, James, 193
Stephen, Sarah (née Clark), 193
Stephens, James, 111
Stewart, Robert, Lord Castlereagh, 194
Strangeways Prison, 9, 13, 16, 204
suffragette movement, 79
Sugrue, James, 113
Sullivan, A.M., 39, 43–5
Sunday Tribune, 170
Sutton, David, 149
Swansea, 12

Taca, 136, 137
Taliban, 64
Tarbert, 62, 140, 197
Taxpayer's News, 1
Teahan, Gerald, 57
Teahan, Johnny, 180
television political broadcasts, 137
Thatcher, Margaret, 194
Thornton, Aoife, 86, 120, 144
Tobin, Karen, 87–8
tÓglach, An, 8
Toler, John, Lord Norbury, 192–3
tourism, 69, 72
Tralee, 3, 14–15, 18, 36, 38, 61, 78–82,
    86–8, 90–3, 96, 98, 102, 113–16,
    119, 120, 133, 142, 158–9, 178, 182,
    192–3, 195, 196, 200, 206, 208
Tralee and Fenit Harbour Commissioners,
    38, 109, 110
Tralee Board of Guardians, 23, 25, 38, 78,
    80, 82, 107
Tralee Race Company, 109

Tralee Rural District Council, 23, 78, 79,
    80, 82, 110, 176
Tralee Urban District Council, 48, 80, 81,
    87–8, 107, 109, 110, 202
Trant, Dominick, 195
Traun, Friedrich, 66
Trench, F., 108
Trent Staughton, Harrison, 108
Trinity College Dublin, 10, 187
tuberculosis, 80, 84
Tully, John, 98, 105
Tuohy, Patrick J., 32
Twomey, Maurice, 186

United Ireland, 194
United Irish Party, 21, 24, 117
United States, 8, 10, 17, 18, 34, 83, 140,
    192, 195–6, 200
University College Cork, 69, 198
University College Dublin, 84, 121–2,
    124, 199

Valentia, 18, 68–9, 112, 113, 181, 197
venereal disease, 36
violence, 51–61, 174, 185–6, 194–5
vocational education, 2, 122–3, 124
vote rigging, 25, 39
voter inducements, 25, 37–50, 113, 202
voter intimidation, 25, 39, 113, 114,
    202
voter personation, 25, 39, 46

Wall, Frank, 214
Wall, Johnnie, 142
Walsh, Eamy, 183
Walsh, Harry, 81–2
Walsh, Jack, 136
Walsh, John (ClannnaPoblachta), 98
Walsh, John (Tralee Urban District
    Council), 81
Walsh, Marty, 196
Walsh, Maud, 81–2, 87
Walsh, Tom, 142
War of Independence, 12, 13, 35, 54–5,
    57, 65, 68, 95, 101, 127, 132, 140,
    163, 167
Warren, Timothy, 40

Waterville, 12, 81, 126, 170, 216
Wellesley, Sir Arthur, Duke of Wellington, 192
West Indies, 193
Wharton-Slattery, Gillian, 86, 88
Whelan, Noel, 149
Whiteboys, 24
Wilberforce, William, 193
With Michael Collins in the Fight for Irish Independence (O'Connor), 198
Women's National Health Association, 80

Women's Poor Law Guardian Committee, 79
women's rights, 63, 72–3
workhouses, 35, 107
Woulfe, Patrick, 71, 210
Wren, Jennifer (JehanZeba), **62**, 62–4, 197

Young Ireland Society, 15

Zeba, Jehan *see* Wren, Jennifer